PROSECUTING
THE
POWERFUL

Also by Steve Crawshaw

Goodbye to the USSR: The
Collapse of Soviet Power

Easier Fatherland: Germany and
the Twenty-First Century

Small Acts of Resistance: How Courage,
Tenacity and Ingenuity Can Change
the World (with John Jackson)

Street Spirit: The Power of Protest and Mischief

PROSECUTING THE POWERFUL

War Crimes and the Battle for Justice

STEVE CRAWSHAW

The
Bridge
Street
Press

THE BRIDGE STREET PRESS

First published in Great Britain in 2025 by The Bridge Street Press

1 3 5 7 9 10 8 6 4 2

A CIP catalogue record for this book
is available from the British Library.

Hardback ISBN 978-0-349-12893-1
Trade Paperback ISBN 978-0-349-12894-8

Typeset in Bembo by M Rules
Printed and bound in Great Britain by
Clays Ltd, Elcograf S.p.A.

Papers used by The Bridge Street Press are from well-managed forests
and other responsible sources.

MIX
Paper | Supporting
responsible forestry
FSC® C104740

The Bridge Street Press
An imprint of
Little, Brown Book Group
Carmelite House
50 Victoria Embankment
London EC4Y 0DZ

The authorised representative
in the EEA is
Hachette Ireland
8 Castlecourt Centre
Dublin 15, D15 XTP3, Ireland
(email: info@hbgi.ie)

An Hachette UK Company
www.hachette.co.uk

www.littlebrown.co.uk

For Eva and Ania,
with love

Contents

Introduction

There is of course no reason why places of horror should be easily identifiable as such. There is no appropriate location for mass murder. No sinister lighting or music nudges us into guessing what might have happened here. Pain and tragedy may surround us on all sides, but past atrocities do not announce themselves to the visitor once the bodies have been removed, the blood washed away, the shattered windows replaced. Still, though, I never can get used to the fact that places where the most terrible things have happened – a sun–dappled meadow that once housed a Nazi camp, say, or the soft hills around Srebrenica in Bosnia where cuckoos can be heard calling in the woods – can look and sound so normal.

I had that same unsettling feeling when I first arrived in Bucha in April 2023. Until a year earlier, this commuter town north–west of Kyiv was best known for the quality of the fungi that grow in abundance in the surrounding woods. Every autumn, crowds flocked from the city to search out the tastiest mushrooms. Now, the name of Bucha will be remembered always for reasons its residents could never in their worst nightmares have imagined.

My visit came a year after the Russian full-scale invasion of Ukraine. By the time I arrived in Kyiv, the worst of the missile attacks on the Ukrainian capital were over, for the moment at least. Air raid sirens still sounded frequently. Everybody had an app on their phone which told them when to take shelter. The dangers were real: residents of the capital had lost their lives; the city was dotted with buildings that had been damaged or destroyed; four months before my arrival, a Russian rocket hit a children's playground close to my hotel. But many Ukrainians had begun to ignore the alerts and take their chances. Daily life had to continue, after a fashion. I went to an early-evening ballet performance which was greeted with standing ovations. At the Lesya Ukrainka Theatre, Brian Friel's *Translations*, set in nineteenth-century British-ruled Ireland and addressing themes of colonial erasure of the local language, was playing to packed houses, though performances sometimes started late because of air raids. Kyiv's restaurants and cafés were lively and full, though they shut early to let customers and staff get home before curfew. It was an abnormal kind of normality.

At the beginning, Russian forces were confident they would reach the Ukrainian capital within days. 'Now we will take Kyiv! Kyiv is ours!' soldiers shouted as their tanks rolled through the countryside. They had been instructed to pack parade uniforms for a triumphal march along the broad Khreshchatyk boulevard in central Kyiv and through Maidan Square, heart of pro-democracy protests eight years earlier. It wouldn't take long, President Vladimir Putin thought, for the 'special military operation' – not a war, that word was forbidden in Russia – to be complete. Despite fierce fighting at and around Hostomel airport, Russian forces failed to seize the capital. They did, however, reach towns on the road to Kyiv. One of those was Bucha.

My springtime drive to the town is simple enough. There are desultory checkpoints beside the pink-blossoming apricot trees; tank traps, no longer essential, are clustered in the middle of the carriageway. A layby is piled high with vehicles whose drivers and passengers had been shot at or burned to death – a mixture of dumping ground and memorial. Some of the cars are painted with bright yellow sunflowers and messages like #flowersforhope.

In Bucha itself, some buildings are badly damaged, others have been recently repaired. But much looks like any other commuter town: apartment blocks, shopping malls, advertisements for spas. In reality, nothing is normal here, nor will it be for years to come. On Yablunska Street ('Street of Apple Trees'), properties are advertised for sale – *taunhausi*, in Ukrainian real estate sales-speak. A poster lists the 'advantages of suburban living' – summer terraces, panoramic views. And there, just across the road from the empty *taunhausi*, is an inconspicuous junction which became notorious worldwide.

In February 2022, fifty-two-year-old Iryna Filkina signed up for classes to train as a make-up artist, telling her beautician friend Anastasiia Subacheva, 'I finally understood the most important thing. You need to love yourself and live for yourself.' A few weeks later, she was dead. A Russian armoured vehicle killed Filkina at this junction as she rode her bicycle home on 5 March 2022; she had tried and failed to escape the town that day. It was too dangerous for her neighbours to recover her body and so, like many others, the decomposing corpse lay on the ground for weeks until Ukrainian forces liberated Bucha at the end of March. An image by Reuters photographer Zohra Bensemra of Filkina's hand with her special Valentine's Day manicure – four red nails, and a fifth with a purple heart bordered by silver varnish – was enough to identify her. Subacheva immediately recognised her friend's hand: 'I stopped breathing.'

Iryna Filkina was one of more than four hundred civilians killed in Bucha. Several dozen Ukrainians were killed on Yablunska Street alone. At a four-storey office building at number 144, used by the Russian forces as their headquarters, the windows have been repaired. At the side of the building, photographs of eight men killed with shots to the head are pinned to the wall. Flowers lie on the ground. The men were seized as part of what the Russians called *zachistki*, or 'cleansing operations' – the same word used in Putin's war in Chechnya twenty years earlier – and summarily executed.

Close to the junction where Filkina died, I see a house is being rebuilt. Natasha, the house's owner, who was repeatedly shot at as she fled her home in the first days of the occupation, tells me: 'Our neighbours are gone. They haven't been found, dead or alive. Russia needs to understand what has happened here. They need to see the tears of the people here.'

The crimes in Bucha and elsewhere were horrific. But can the perpetrators of these and other crimes – and their commanders, and their commanders' commanders – ever be held accountable? In earlier years, the answer would have been a clear no. But the possibilities of global justice have changed beyond recognition in recent decades.

In 1992, when I asked Slobodan Milošević, then president of Serbia, whether he might one day stand in the dock charged with war crimes, he seemed startled by the idea. Just nine years later, he was in The Hague, facing charges of crimes against humanity and genocide. The creation of the Yugoslavia and then Rwanda war crimes tribunals in the mid-1990s was soon followed by agreement on an

international criminal court – an idea that a determined few
had been pressing for, but which had for decades seemed
unachievable. The guaranteed impunity of Latin American
dictatorships was dented, too, when former Chilean leader
General Augusto Pinochet was arrested after travelling to
London for back surgery. Politicians responsible for grave
crimes, it became clear, had more reason to be worried than
ever before.

For decades, the Nuremberg trials (and the Tokyo tribunal that followed) had seemed to be a one-off. After 1945,
governments who had prosecuted Nazi crimes were happy
to commit crimes of their own, confident that those crimes
would go unpunished. They turned a blind eye to genocide,
too – the word that Raphael Lemkin, a lawyer from what is
now Ukraine, invented in 1944. Now, as described throughout this book, the prospects for justice have multiplied in
many different ways.

The themes of justice – its elusiveness, and the ways that
dreamers have fought for it against the odds – have interested
me for many years. I came of age at a time when torture-
loving military governments were spreading like a virus
across Latin America and when those who expressed different
views in the Soviet Union and across the Soviet bloc could be
jailed or sent to a labour camp. The need to confront those
twin madnesses, and the apparent impossibility of doing so,
shaped my thinking. I became interested in the long shadows
of history, too: when studying Russian and German, I lived in
St Petersburg (Leningrad, as it was then) and Berlin, and got
to know two societies which in different ways were grappling
with how to confront their own past, forty years after Stalin's
purges and thirty years after the Second World War.

I witnessed historic moments of hope, too, when I was

living in Poland in 1980, and saw millions force unthinkable concessions from the Communist regime even while Leonid Brezhnev, famous for sending tanks into Czechoslovakia and Afghanistan, was still in the Kremlin. Those unprecedented victories – which, despite arrests and killings, were never quite reversed – significantly influenced my thinking in the years to come. They helped me understand the extraordinary things that courage and determination can sometimes achieve, even in seemingly impossible contexts and when dismissed by others.

My experiences in Poland and central-eastern Europe, and a Granada Television documentary that I worked on in Belarus on truth, lies and the Second World War, helped get me hired for what became the dream job of working on the foreign desk of the *Independent*, which I joined when the newspaper launched in 1986. Three years later, I found myself reporting on what would become (to quote the headline to a piece I wrote in April 1989, seven months before the Berlin Wall came down) 'the crumbling of an empire'. The east European revolutions and the fall of the Wall followed on from the extraordinary things I had witnessed in Poland nine years earlier; it was not just the arrival of the reformist Soviet leader Mikhail Gorbachev which paved the way for change in 1989. It was a privilege to report from Warsaw, Leipzig, Prague and Budapest during those days of hope when walls tumbled across the region. I even saw flickers of optimism in Russia, too, after protesters defeated a hardline coup in 1991, leading to the end of the Soviet Union itself.

Western politicians failed to see what was coming and how much had changed. As I wrote in a publisher's pro-posal submitted four months before the coup, for a book that was originally called *Road to Nowhere*, based on my travels around the country from the Baltic states to Siberia, the impending collapse of the Soviet Union was perhaps the most important story of the late twentieth century. A violent clampdown to stop change, I suggested, could provide 'only the most short-term of solutions'. And yet, politicians seemed unwilling or unable to face up to the momentousness of what was already under way. I quoted the Russian writer Yuri Karyakin: 'Hundreds and thousands of bottles have been opened in the last six years, and their genies couldn't be enticed back inside or sealed up any more. How can that be done?' Or, as the headline to one of my pieces had summed it up in February 1991: 'The Kremlin cannot put the lid back on.' In the end, the long-feared crackdown fell apart after just three chaotic days in August. For a brief moment, hope did not feel absurd. 'It was the happiest day of my life,' a friend in Moscow told me after the coup failed, 'happier even than when my child was born.' Such sunny words would soon seem unthinkable.

All the good news was soon followed by bad. My first glimpse of Yugoslavia had been at the end of my student year in the Soviet Union in 1976, when I took an overnight train to Odessa on the Black Sea (Odesa, to use the Ukrainian spelling which most Odessans ignored until Russia's invasion changed the politics of language for ever) and then a tourist boat up the Danube to Budapest, stopping off in Belgrade. I was charmed by the relaxed atmosphere in the nominally Communist Yugoslav federation, so different from the suffocating pressures in the Soviet Union, where I and my Russian friends alike (who were courting trouble, even by talking to me and other foreigners) were always aware of the ubiquitous lurking presence of the Committee for State Security, the KGB. When I returned to Belgrade in 1982, two years after the death of Marshal Tito, the Second World War hero who had led the country for forty years, multi-ethnic Yugoslavia still felt more tolerant than its central and east European neighbours with their secret-police regimes. From 1989 onwards, however, political leaders who felt threatened by the multi-party democracy breaking out across the region grasped nationalism as a way to hold on to power.

Full-scale war began in the Yugoslav republics of Croatia and Bosnia in 1991 and 1992. Like other journalists covering the Balkans, one of my abiding memories is the impossibility of getting politicians to focus on the unfolding horror at that time. This was 'the hour of Europe', a leading European politician declared in June 1991, suggesting things would soon be sorted out. Two weeks after that complacent summary, I was in Osijek in eastern Croatia, sheltering with an elderly couple who had invited me into their home (and shared a glass of calming plum brandy) as a gun battle raged outside for hours; I don't know which of us was more frightened. Through her tears, my host said, 'They'll kill us all one day. I'm so afraid.' The doctor who certified the deaths on that day told me: 'It's terrible. I think it will be worse. I am losing all hope.'

This was the beginning of four long years of war in the collapsing Yugoslav federation. It seemed that the many crimes, committed by Serb and Croat forces especially, would never see punishment. Gradually, though, the possibilities of accountability grew, including the creation in 1993 of the first new war crimes tribunal since 1945. In 2001, a few months after standing amid vast crowds who forced the resignation of Milošević after a bloody decade in power, I spent time at the Yugoslav war crimes tribunal talking to the people who hoped to put him behind bars. My magazine story, 'Unfinished Business: Behind the scenes at the new Nuremberg', was published shortly before a new government in Belgrade delivered Milošević to The Hague.

*

In the meantime, a new permanent war crimes court, un-limited by geography, was on its way, too. Human rights organisations played a key role in making it happen. I became the UK director of Human Rights Watch in 2002, just before the International Criminal Court was born. Until then, I had been reporting on human rights and other themes; my job was above all to describe what I had seen and heard. I would still in some ways continue to be a re-porter, sharing stories of human rights abuses in the hope of making change. From now on, however, a core part of my work – together with remarkable colleagues around the world – would also be to play a part in seeking to make the possibilities of justice and accountability real. My experi-ences and the people I met on the front lines of justice in the next twenty years through my work at Human Rights Watch, Amnesty International and Freedom from Torture are central to this book.

I first sketched out thoughts on the themes of international justice in 2005. If I had found the time to write *Crimes and Punishment* (as I called those early jottings), it would have been a different and too-optimistic book. The world looked simpler then. In the two decades since, there have been many new reasons for despair. There have also, however, been new reasons for hope. That Faustian tussle between despair and hope is at the heart of *Prosecuting the Powerful*.

This book tells stories from the changing landscape of global justice, how those changes happened, and the obstacles to change. Powerful figures have been prosecuted and jailed in ways that once seemed unthinkable. Survivors of conflict make their voices heard as never before. For many years, it seemed that justice could never be evenly spread. The pattern that was visible during the Cold War continued to repeat itself: those who had been happy to prosecute the crimes of others wanted a free pass for themselves and their friends.

That confident sense of impunity has, however, been dented – including during the writing of this book. First came the indictment in 2023 of the Russian president. The arrest warrant for Vladimir Putin, whose country is a veto-wielding member of the UN Security Council, was extraordinary by any measure. Then, even more remarkably, we saw arrest warrants issued in 2024 for the prime minister and defence minister of one of America's closest allies, a government which assumed it would always be protected from accountability, no matter what it chose to do. US president Joe Biden described the initial request for an indictment by the International Criminal Court of Israeli prime minister Benjamin Netanyahu and defence minister Yoav Gallant as 'outrageous'. British prime minister Rishi Sunak said it was 'deeply unhelpful'.

When I meet the court's chief prosecutor, Karim Khan, in his offices in The Hague a few days after the arrest warrants, he is in no mood to back down. On the contrary, he emphasises that this is what his job is for. 'The problem is existential in that if we do apply the law vigorously in some cases and we close our eyes in others, that brings the law into disrepute. It goes back to Shakespeare.' Khan closes his eyes for a moment to find the exact words, then quotes *King Lear*:

> Robes and furr'd gowns hide all. Plate sin with gold,
> And the strong lance of justice hurtless breaks:
> Arm it in rags, a pygmy's straw does pierce it.

Khan argues that Shakespeare's description of the inequalities of justice is recognisable today. In his paraphrase, 'If you're poor, if you're weak, the law will come down on

you – but plate that with gold, somehow you get a free pass.'
He believes his job is to help that change.

At the time of the requested indictments, Khan talked
of a 'senior figure' who warned him off arrest warrants for
Israelis, telling him the court was 'built for Africa and thugs
like Putin'. When we see each other, Khan does not mince
his words on that perception of the court's role: 'That racist,
colonial approach unfortunately still afflicts some people's
mindset.'

Politicians who condemned Khan's requested indictments
of Israeli leaders did not seriously challenge the allegations
or facts that the prosecutor put on the table. Khan had
consulted a panel of six respected lawyers, including an
Israeli-American former ambassador and former president
of the Yugoslav war crimes tribunal and a former judge of
the International Criminal Court. The panel emphasised its
unanimity in supporting the prosecutor's request for an arrest
warrant. Instead, Washington and others argued it was wrong
as *a matter of principle* to accuse a democratically elected leader
of committing grave crimes. This – as should be self-evident,
even for the most deliberately obtuse politicians – turns
things upside down. We hope democratically elected leaders
will not usually choose to commit serious crimes. If they do
commit crimes, however – especially if they appear to believe
they are entitled by circumstances (including the behaviour
of their enemy) to do so – that needs to be confronted, not
ignored. To argue otherwise is dishonest and dangerous.

Khan's indictments were not just in connection with the
alleged crimes of Israeli leaders but also what he called the
'unconscionable' crimes of Hamas. A year after my visit
to Bucha, I was at the site of the Supernova music festival
near Re'im kibbutz in the south of Israel, advertised as an

embracing of 'friends, love and infinite freedom'. Video shows crowds dancing into the sunrise on 7 October 2023. And then, just before six-thirty in the morning, the horror. Kidnap, rape and murder followed. Twelve hundred men, women and children, including eight hundred civilians, were killed when attackers from Hamas and other armed groups breached the fences round Gaza with motorcycles, paragliders and pick-up trucks, at the festival and at Re'im and other kibbutzim. Two hundred and forty were taken hostage, including soldiers, civilians, Thai farm workers, thirty children and a nine-month-old baby.

Another place of horror lies just three miles from Re'im. Israeli television viewers barely see even a sanitised version of the catastrophe that the Israel Defense Forces have unleashed behind the high barriers which keep two million Gazans penned in; foreign journalists, despite protests from media organisations worldwide, are forbidden to enter. The once-popular viewpoint near the southern town of Sderot where, during earlier assaults on Gaza, Israeli picnickers celebrated and reporters delivered their pieces to camera against a televisual backdrop of destruction – the 'hill of shame', as it came to be known – is sealed off with rolls of barbed wire when I visit. The immediate border area is closed. But, for anybody who wants to know, the suffering of those trapped, starved, orphaned, maimed and killed inside the Gaza Strip is no secret.

In 2022, governments overwhelmingly condemned Russia's destruction of lives, homes and infrastructure in Ukraine. Twenty months later, when the Israeli government repeated many of Russia's actions, some of those who had condemned Putin's crimes responded differently. The scales and blindfold of Lady Justice were cast aside. *Who* committed the crimes (do we support them, do we oppose them?) became as important, for some politicians, as *what* those crimes were.

Putin's war on Ukraine and Israel's assault on Gaza came in different contexts. Putin's excuse for the invasion – the need to defeat Ukrainian 'fascism' and prevent 'genocide' of Russian-speakers – was absurdly false. Ukraine's real crime, from the Kremlin's perspective, was that it wanted to make its own choices and did not wish to remain under Moscow's thumb. The immediate trigger for Israel's offensive against Gaza, by contrast, was an attack of lawless brutality. In that respect, the two cases could hardly be more different.

In terms of how those wars were conducted, however, there were obvious parallels, even if Israeli politicians were enraged when such comparisons were made.

In different ways, two courts in The Hague both address questions related to the worst war crimes. The International Criminal Court can prosecute individuals, including presidents and prime ministers. The inter-governmental International Court of Justice, the UN's highest court, plays an important role in a different way, calling out the crimes not of individuals but of states. Four months before the requested indictments of Netanyahu and Gallant at the ICC, I was sitting in the Peace Palace in The Hague to hear the president of the International Court of Justice pronounce an almost unanimous judges' ruling that there was a 'real and imminent risk' that 'irreparable prejudice will be caused' to the Palestinians' plausible right to be protected from genocide in Gaza, in a case brought by South Africa. The court warned against incitement to genocide, too – a central part of the genocide convention.

As with the International Criminal Court, some governments seemed eager to shoot the messenger. The International Court of Justice has enjoyed global respect since its creation as the 'world court' at the same time as the founding of the

United Nations in 1945. Putin's Russia might scorn the court; generally, democratic governments did not. In 2024, that changed. Western governments condemned South Africa for bringing the case against Israel – and implied, without evidence, that the judges (including the respected American president of the court) had somehow themselves become biased.

Nobody could miss the brutal irony that the country whose leaders were now facing potential indictment for crimes against humanity and which the International Court of Justice now criticised in connection with allegations of genocide came into existence, eight decades earlier, partly because of the crimes, including genocide, committed against its own people. Those crimes, via the example of Nuremberg, indirectly paved the way for the International Criminal Court itself. Israel's leaders sometimes behaved as though the crimes of the Holocaust meant Israel's own army could and should never be a subject for prosecution. Netanyahu complained of 'blood libels'. He accused prosecutor Karim Khan of 'callously pouring gasoline on the fires of antisemitism' and compared him to the 'infamous German judges' whose decisions helped enable the Holocaust. Khan saw it differently, saying as he requested the arrest warrants, 'If we do not demonstrate our willingness to apply the law equally, if we apply the law selectively, we will be creating the conditions for its collapse.'

The indictments of Putin and then Netanyahu – two men who just a few years earlier had enjoyed a tough-guy bromance – are part of a broader pattern of change. For most of the twentieth century, impunity for war crimes was a given. Nuremberg was a lonely exception to the rule. Now, the slogan 'Send him to The Hague!' is heard worldwide from those who believe powerful leaders should be held accountable. In recent years, that destination can be metaphorical as much as literal, with multiplying war crimes prosecutions closer to home. Nor is it just political leaders who have gone on trial: there have been attempts to hold companies to account, too, for alleged complicity in atrocity crimes.

In 1985, the Nobel Prize-winning author Czesław Miłosz wrote a foreword to *Letters from Prison* by the Polish opposition thinker Adam Michnik. Miłosz talked of our tendency to place the possible in the past, leading us to overlook those who are acting in the present, who 'defy the presumably immovable order of things' and 'achieve what at first sight has seemed impossible or improbable'. The Berlin Wall came down four years after Miłosz wrote those words – in significant measure because of people like Michnik and others across the region who defied the 'presumably immovable' order of things.

Raphael Lemkin was another who defied immovable realities by identifying the unnamed crime of genocide and then, against significant opposition, pressing for a convention which called for genocide to be prevented and punished. Lemkin died in 1959, believing his work had been in vain. In the past quarter of a century, however, we have seen genocide convictions in international and domestic courts for everything from Rwanda and Bosnia to the rape and killings of thousands of Yazidis in Iraq and Syria by Islamic State. More trials are on the way, not least because of the determination of the survivors of those crimes.

Even after the ICC indictments, there is no immediate prospect of seeing Putin or Netanyahu in handcuffs, though their travel plans will be limited. But the arrest warrants, confirmed by judges after three weeks and seven months respectively, send a powerful signal: justice applies to all.

Shakespeare's lance of justice need no longer break, even when confronted with gold-plated sins. As a result of what has been achieved in recent decades, we now have the tools that can, as US chief prosecutor Robert Jackson put it at Nuremberg, 'stay the hand of vengeance', thus allowing for a less dangerous world. We cannot afford to put those tools to one side.

Chapter One

'This is Most Inconsistent'

Geneva, Lwów, Nuremberg, Paris (1863–1948)

When Henry Dunant arrived in Castiglione, thirty miles west of Verona, on the evening of 24 June 1859, changing the world was not on his mind. His main goal was to obtain an audience with Napoleon III. Dunant, a thirty-one-year-old Swiss businessman, owned an agricultural enterprise in French-ruled Algeria which had run into difficulties because of lack of access to water. The authorities in Paris had refused to engage with him so Dunant decided to go to the top.

Dunant – born Henri, but he swapped the i for a y to give his name an English twist – hoped to find the French emperor in the area of Lombardy where Franco-Piedmontese-Sardinian forces had been battling with the Austrians for the previous two months. To pave the way for a meeting, the white-suited Dunant – 'the gentleman in white', as he became known in Castiglione over the next few days – had brought with him a self-published homage to the emperor entitled *The Empire of Charlemagne Restored*. But nothing played out as Dunant expected.

On the day he arrived, three hundred thousand troops met in battle at Solferino, a few miles from Castiglione. Thirty thousand now lay dead amid the tangle of mulberries and vines, with another thirty thousand wounded. Stumbling into the aftermath of the carnage, Dunant was horrified. 'Heartrending voices kept calling for help,' he recalled in *Memory of Solferino*. 'Bodies of men and horses covered the battlefield; corpses were strewn over roads, ditches, ravines, thickets and fields.' He was appalled not just by the stench of the dead but also by the suffering of the living. 'With faces black with the flies that swarmed around their wounds, men gazed around them, wild-eyed and helpless. Others were no more than a worm-ridden, inextricable compound of coal and shirt and flesh and blood.' Dunant pulled together a team of volunteers to care for the wounded: his helpers included English tourists, a French journalist and the Swiss chocolate-maker Philippe Suchard, who bandaged wounds and wrote letters of farewell for the dying.

Dunant's meeting with Napoleon III didn't happen; his request to dedicate his book to the emperor was rejected; his business in Algeria collapsed. Instead, Dunant found a different focus for his life – one that has played a key role in shaping the rules of war and protecting civilians in conflict to this day. Dunant proposed a new set of international principles, according to which national societies should 'help the wounded in different countries of Europe'. Monarchs and emperors praised him; the Goncourt brothers said his battlefield descriptions in *Memory of Solferino* were 'a thousand times better than Homer'.

In 1863, delegates from sixteen countries came together

in Geneva for a meeting organised by a small group including Dunant and a lawyer and philanthropist called Gustave Moynier. They agreed on the creation of a neutral medical corps to help the wounded. The emblem to identify medical personnel and facilities on the battlefield would be an inversion of the Swiss flag: instead of a white cross on a red background, a red cross on a white background. The organisation that would come to be known as the International Committee of the Red Cross was born. The first Geneva Convention was agreed in 1864. Dunant (to Moynier's annoyance) became the first recipient of Alfred Nobel's new peace prize in 1901. 'Geneva Conventions' today is a global shorthand for the laws of war – all because Geneva happened to be the native city of a determined entrepreneur who was moved to action by the suffering in a bloody battle in which, as he put it, 'all false pride, all human regard were set aside'.

The idea that even the most violent conflict should be constrained by basic rules was, in theory at least, not new: there were precepts dating back to Ancient Greece and earlier. The Athenian slaughter of all men of military age on the island of Melos during the Peloponnesian War was notorious even at the time. In the seventh century, the first caliph of Islam, Abu Bakr, told his commanders: 'Neither kill a child, nor a woman, nor an aged man ... Slay not the enemies' flock, save for your food.' In 1410, Christine de Pizan, daughter of an astrologer-physicist from Bologna, published *Book of Deeds of Arms and of Chivalry*, with injunctions on the treatment of prisoners of war and on the protection of non-combatants: 'Those who engage in warfare may be hurt, but the humble and peaceful should be shielded from their force.' Ahead of the Battle of Agincourt in 1415, King Henry V issued instructions which included prohibitions on the burning of property 'without special command of the king' and on 'affray which might endanger woman and her child'. He published orders so that commanders 'may have plain knowledge and inform their men of these foresaid ordnances and articles' and to ensure that 'no subject shall be able to pretend ignorance'. In truth, Shakespeare's description in *Henry V* of soldiers with 'conscience wide as hell' and the 'filthy and contagious clouds / Of heady murder, spoil and villainy' was, perhaps, a more accurate reflection of the prevailing reality. There were, however, some early attempts at accountability. In 1474, in a case that would be quoted at the Nuremberg trials five centuries later, twenty-eight judges convicted Peter von Hagenbach in Breisach, south of Strasbourg, for 'trampling underfoot the laws of God and man'. Von Hagenbach was charged with rape and murder committed by those under his command; he was deemed to have a duty to prevent those crimes.

Gradually, the rules were codified. In 1625, the Dutch jurist Hugo Grotius, who came to be known as the 'grandfather of international law', published *On the Law of War and Peace*. He wrote: 'When arms have once been taken up there is no longer any respect for law, divine or human; it is as if, in accordance with a general decree, frenzy had openly been let loose for the committing of all crimes.' Grotius wanted to change that, with injunctions on everything from 'moderation in despoiling an enemy's country' to the treatment of prisoners of war.

Today, a statue of Grotius stands on the main square in his home town of Delft. During his lifetime, though, the Dutch authorities were not so keen on the independent-minded lawyer: Grotius fled the Netherlands after his wife and maid helped him escape his castle prison hidden in a book chest. *On the Law of War and Peace* quickly became influential. While fighting the Thirty Years' War in which millions died,

King Gustavus Adolphus of Sweden reputedly slept with the book under his pillow; a copy was found in his tent after his death. This was not just for show: in a war notorious for its cruelty, Gustavus Adolphus exhorted his troops to avoid abuse. Grotius's work remained popular long after his death: a fine-looking leather-bound English edition published in 1715 (available at the time of writing for a mere $1,250) is dedicated to 'His Royal Highness the Prince of Wales', the future King George II, who had arrived in Britain with his father from Hanover via the port of The Hague the previous year. And yet, despite all the interest in Grotius and his pronouncements, it was not until two centuries after his death that the need for enforcement of the laws of war began to be taken seriously.

In 1863, the same year as the creation of the Red Cross in Geneva, President Abraham Lincoln asked a Berlin-born law professor, Francis Lieber, to prepare a set of rules for Union forces in the already raging American Civil War. For Lieber, these were no legal abstractions. At sixteen, he himself had been severely wounded and left for dead at Waterloo; his geologist son Oscar, fighting on the Confederate side, was killed at the Battle of Williamsburg in 1862; his younger son, Hamilton, with the Union forces, lost an arm. The *Instructions for the Armies of the United States in the Field, General Orders No. 100*, or Lieber Code, quickly became influential. In Lieber's own words, 'short and pregnant and weighty, like some stumpy Dutch woman when in the family way with coming twins', the code was translated and endorsed by France, Prussia, Britain and others.

The need for basic rules began to be recognised at the highest level. In 1898, Tsar Nicholas II proposed a conference 'in the best interests of humanity' on restricting or prohibiting dangerous new weapons ('terrible engines of de-struction') and to codify 'the laws and customs of war'. The Russian emperor suggested the conference, which was to be a 'happy presage for the century which is about to open', should take place not in St Petersburg, Berlin, Paris or London but in the less contested setting of the Netherlands. And so it was that top-hatted delegates gathered in 1899 in the Huis ten Bosch ('House in the Wood'), the Dutch royals' summer residence in The Hague. On 4 July, at the tomb of Grotius in nearby Delft, US ambassador Andrew White laid a silver wreath and spoke of the need for 'strengthening peace and humanising war'; White's wreath is still in place in Delft's sixteenth-century New Church. The ambassador praised Grotius's role: 'In the domain of international law, Grotius said, "Let there be light" – and there was light.' The Hague conference could, White suggested, give the world 'at least the beginning of an effective, practical scheme of arbitration', building on Grotius's legacy.

From then on, as a result of the conference and Russia's proposals – and in homage to Grotius – The Hague would become the go-to venue for international law, describing itself as the world's 'city of peace and justice' today. At the sugges-tion of Russia's delegate to the 1899 conference, Ambassador White persuaded steel magnate and philanthropist Andrew Carnegie to fund a 'temple of peace', which opened in 1913 and contained the Permanent Court of Arbitration. The Peace Palace on Carnegieplein is today home to the International Court of Justice, which in recent years has issued rulings on Ukraine, Gaza and more.

There were attempts to build in accountability from the start. As early as 1872, Gustave Moynier, now president of the Red Cross, proposed an institution that would 'prevent and repress infringements' of the Geneva Convention agreed eight years earlier. In the wake of the Franco-Prussian War, Moynier concluded that a 'purely moral sanction' was inadequate to 'check unbridled passions' on the battlefield. But his idea of an independent tribunal went nowhere. Then as now, governments were happy to sign up for obligations but less eager to see them enforced. The Hague Conventions of 1899 and 1907 forbade the use of 'asphyxiating or deleterious gases' and prohibited the targeting of civilian buildings. But the 'effective, practical' enforcement that Ambassador White hoped for remained non-existent – as the First World War, which began eleven months after the opening of the Peace Palace, made clear.

After 1918, there was a series of attempts to close the gap between noble statements and bleak reality, which included the frequent use of poison gas in the First World War. As required under the terms of the Versailles treaty, war crimes trials of German soldiers took place in Leipzig. The trials were, however, notable because of the vanishingly small number of convictions – six out of 1,700 cases.

There were attempts to prosecute Kaiser Wilhelm II, too. The Versailles Treaty accused the German emperor of 'a supreme offence against international morality and the sanctity of treaties' and proposed the creation of a tribunal with judges from Britain, France, Italy, Japan and the United States. France argued, on the principle of what would come to be known as 'command responsibility', that 'all the cruelty, the iniquities, and the horrors ... have been countenanced and in no way discouraged by him'. In Britain, 'Hang the Kaiser!' was a popular slogan; prime minister David Lloyd George announced that the tribunal would take place in London. King George V was surprised and indignant at the idea that his own cousin, Queen Victoria's eldest grandson (who had been at her deathbed), might go on trial just down the road from Buckingham Palace. But all these proposals came to nothing. Another cousin, Queen Wilhelmina of the Netherlands, reluctantly offered Wilhelm II asylum after he was forced to wait for twelve hours on a railway platform at Eijsden on the Dutch-Belgian border while the Dutch made up their minds. 'You surely recognise me! I am the German emperor,' Wilhelm told a border guard as he waited. 'I see you are the Kaiser,' came the reply. 'But my orders are to allow none to pass.'

France and its allies wanted the Netherlands to hand over the Kaiser, citing 'unassailable reasons', but that came to nothing. A bizarre kidnap attempt ended in chaos, too. 'I was thinking of motoring up to Holland and kidnapping the Kaiser,' Luke Lea, newspaper owner and former US senator, told a friend at Christmas 1918. Dutch police interrupted the bungled venture and the American visitors got away with nothing more than an imperial ashtray. Kaiser Wilhelm went to live in the comfort of Huis Doorn, the country house where Audrey Hepburn's Dutch aristocrat mother spent much of her childhood, for the next twenty years. He died in exile in 1941, a year after the German invasion of the Netherlands (Queen Wilhelmina had in the meantime escaped to London). A German military band played at the Kaiser's funeral; Hitler sent a huge wreath. As Geoffrey Robertson notes in his imagine-if book, *The Trial of Vladimir Putin*, 'It remains one of history's most intriguing hypotheticals, whether [the Kaiser's] trial for aggression would have given pause to Hitler.'

There were other failed attempts at prosecutions. Western newspapers prominently reported the Ottoman massacres of Armenians during the First World War. In 1915, under the headline 'Extinction menaces Armenia', the *New York Times* talked of claims that hundreds of thousands had been killed and – using language that would gain resonance in years to come – reported the suggestion that the Ottoman Turkish authorities sought to achieve 'nothing more or less than the annihilation of an entire people'. The US ambassador, Henry Morgenthau, protested to Turkish interior minister Mehmet Talaat. Talaat replied: 'Why are you so interested in these Armenians anyway? You are a Jew, these people are Christians ... Why can't you let us do with these Christians as we please?'

Britain, France and Russia denounced the killings. A draft protest note complained that Ottoman forces had committed 'crimes against Christianity and civilisation'. On reflection, 'crimes against Christianity' was replaced with the less loaded 'crimes against humanity'; a legal phrase was born. In 1919, the Ottoman Courts-Martial conducted a series of trials in Constantinople for 'crimes of enormous magnitude', including deportations and massacres. But the trials unravelled in what diplomats described as dead failure and farce. None of those most responsible for massacres of Armenians was jailed. The Constantinople trials became, as historian Gary Bass put it in *Stay the Hand of Vengeance*, 'the Nuremberg that failed'.

The broader lesson that emerged from all these confused initiatives seemed to be that – despite all the conventions and rules that had been agreed in the past half-century – impunity remained baked into the system.

In 1939, Hitler himself identified the connection between impunity past and present. Ahead of the invasion of Poland, he encouraged his generals to ignore all rules because there would be no consequences, asking 'Who, after all, speaks today of the annihilation of the Armenians?' Unspeakable crimes had quickly been forgotten after 1918. The same pattern, it seemed, could now be repeated. Hitler's cold logic — 'They got away with it, why wouldn't I?' — can still be heard from over-confident war criminals in conflict zones around the world today.

Despite what Hitler believed, the fate of the Armenians had not been entirely forgotten. A Polish-Jewish lawyer from Lwów (now the Ukrainian city of Lviv) had for years been reflecting on the failure to address the horror of those killings and how to ensure such crimes would see punishment. Raphael Lemkin's stubborn determination paved the way for new mechanisms for punishing the worst atrocities in ways that would have their greatest impact long after his death.

Lemkin's interest in what happened to the Armenians — and, above all, what *didn't* happen to those responsible for planning and committing mass murder — had begun in 1921. He read newspaper reports on the trial of Soghomon Tehlirian, charged with shooting Mehmet Talaat, known as Talaat Pasha, outside his home in Charlottenburg in Berlin. The assassination was in revenge for Talaat's role as chief architect of the Armenian massacres a few years earlier. Tehlirian himself lost dozens of relatives. Ever since, he told the court, 'I have lived only to avenge the deaths not only of my own mother and father but also the persecution and massacres of the Armenian people, of whom Talaat Pasha is the wholesale murderer.' The jury acquitted Tehlirian on the grounds of temporary insanity, accepting his argument: 'I killed a man. But I am not a murderer.'

As a student in Lwów, Lemkin was struck by the paradox: how could it be a crime to kill one man, 'but not a crime for his oppressor to kill more than a million men?' Or, as the German satirist Kurt Tucholsky summarised it at around the same time: 'One man's death: that is a catastrophe. A hundred thousand dead: that is a statistic.' A law professor explained

to Lemkin that state sovereignty – the 'Westphalian principles', enshrined since the end of the Thirty Years' War three
centuries earlier – meant governments could do what they
liked within their own borders. The professor compared the
fate of the Armenians to a farmer slaughtering his chickens.
'He kills them. Why not? It is not your business. If you interfere, it is trespass.' For Lemkin, the disconnect between
the individual crime and the non-prosecutable mass crime
was unacceptable. Or, as he put it: 'This is most inconsistent.'
Sovereignty, he argued, 'cannot be conceived as the right to
kill millions of innocent people'.

That sense that things were 'most inconsistent' would
remain a driving force for Lemkin in years to come. The
growth of fascism across Europe gave new urgency to his
concerns. Nine months after Hitler took power in 1933,
Lemkin – now deputy public prosecutor in the district court
in Warsaw – prepared proposals for presentation at an international law conference in Madrid, which argued for the
creation of two new international crimes, 'barbarity' and
'vandalism'. Lemkin described barbarity as the destruction
of a national or religious group; he defined vandalism as destroying works of culture, 'which represent the specific genius
of these national and religious groups'.

Moscow hated Lemkin's ideas. Stalin's legal attack dog,
Andrei Vyshinsky, described Lemkin as a criminal inter-
ventionist and a representative of the 'counter-revolutionary
bourgeoisie' for suggesting the world should respond if a
country committed crimes within its own borders. The
Kremlin was right to be wary of Lemkin's logic, given its
own actions: in the same year as the Madrid meeting, millions
of Ukrainians died in a state-created famine now known as
the Holodomor – 'death by hunger'. As Stalin wrote to the
novelist Mikhail Sholokhov, who expressed concerns about

the mass starvation: 'These people deliberately tried to undermine the Soviet state. It is a fight to the death!' In *Red Famine:
Stalin's War on Ukraine*, Anne Applebaum quotes a survivor's
description of that terrible time: 'The air was filled with the
ubiquitous odor of decomposing bodies. The wind carried
this odor far and wide, all across Ukraine.' After the Second
World War, in a speech marking the twentieth anniversary of
the Holodomor, Lemkin would describe Moscow's treatment
of Ukraine as 'perhaps the classic example of Soviet genocide . . . the destruction of the Ukrainian nation'.

In 1933, however, Lemkin was worried above all by the
growth of fascism in Europe and what it might mean. As he
put it later: 'Hitler had already promulgated his blueprint for
destruction . . . The world was behaving as if it were ready
to acquiesce in his plans.' Six years after the Madrid conference, the deadly blueprint became real. Lemkin escaped from
Warsaw when Hitler's armies invaded, his path to the railway
station lit by houses 'burning like candles'. In a description
that viewers of television news reports from Lviv and other
Ukrainian cities would recognise eighty years later, he was
confronted at the station by 'an ocean of human heads − it
was impossible to see people's bodies, they were pressed so
tightly together'. Lemkin was eventually 'carried on top of a
storming crowd' and 'fell like a heavy bundle amid the other
passengers' on a train that was later bombed. After weeks on
the road, he reached his family in eastern Poland. His parents
insisted he must leave while they would stay. It was, Lemkin
said, 'like going to their funeral while they were still alive'.

Lemkin reached Lithuania and then Sweden. In 1941, after
receiving the offer of a teaching post at Duke University
in North Carolina, he arrived in the United States after a
fifteen-thousand-mile voyage by train and ship via Moscow,
Vladivostok, Yokohama and Vancouver. His mother wrote to

him: 'We are all healthy and have what we need for our existence. Be calm about us!' Not long afterwards, the Germans
burned the family home to the ground. Both his parents were
killed in the Nazi death camp at Treblinka.

Lemkin, though he did not yet know of his parents' fate,
understood better than anyone the scale of the unfolding
apocalypse. He had started collecting decrees issued throughout Nazi-occupied Europe while he was in Stockholm and
brought them with him to America. For those who wanted
to know, there was no shortage of information. In 1942, the
Polish diplomat Jan Karski risked his life to be smuggled into
and out of both the Warsaw Ghetto and a transit camp near
Bełżec death camp ('like forcing my way through a mass of
sheer death and decomposition') in order to bring first-hand
testimony of the Holocaust to political leaders in London and
Washington. Karski was ignored. 'Maybe they did not believe,' he said later, 'maybe they thought I was exaggerating.'
Lemkin, too, found it hard to interest people in Nazi crimes.
The issues, he said, 'seemed too theoretical and even fantastic'.
In Lemkin's words, 'The silence of murder started the day the
first reports of mass executions reached London from Warsaw
late in 1942 [in other words, following Karski's dangerous
mission]. It lasted until December 1944, almost two years.'

In theory at least, politicians agreed the crimes were
without precedent. Given the scale of the Nazis' 'methodical, merciless butchery', Winston Churchill concluded as
early as 1941: 'We are in the presence of a crime without a
name.' (In practice, the Allies had other priorities. Even as
US planes bombed industrial targets near Auschwitz in 1944,
it was decided – despite pleas from Jewish organisations and
others – not to bomb the railway line to Auschwitz nor the
gas chambers in the camp itself because of the need to focus
on 'decisive operations elsewhere'.)

Lemkin would give a name to the unthinkable crime. The Carnegie Endowment for International Peace agreed to publish the hundreds of Nazi decrees and other documents that he had assembled, together with his analysis and recommendations. *Axis Rule in Occupied Europe* appeared in 1944. Lemkin was keen to ensure his book was widely distributed: the copy I am looking at, borrowed from the London Library and originally belonging to the US embassy on Grosvenor Square, is inscribed 'with the compliments of the author'.

At the heart of the 670-page volume is its ninth chapter, 'Genocide: A New Term and New Conception for Destruction of Nations'. Lemkin noted that tyrannicide, homicide and infanticide were existing words. He proposed a new word combining *genos*, the Greek word for race or tribe, and *cidium*, the Latin word for killing. Building on his Madrid proposals from eleven years earlier, he defined 'genocide' as: 'A coordinated plan of different actions aiming at the destruction of essential foundations of the life of national groups, with the aim of annihilating the groups themselves.'

Lemkin was not alone in reflecting on how Nazi criminals might one day be brought to justice. From a modern perspective, Hitler's defeat can seem inevitable. We take for granted the arc of history that runs from the never-ending German victories between 1939 and 1942 through defeat at Stalingrad in 1943 to the retreats and eventual collapse after just twelve years of the 'thousand-year Reich'. Seen from the perspective of early 1942, however, Allied victory was far from a given. Almost all of mainland Europe was Nazi-occupied or allied with Hitler. To quote the headline of a German paper I found in a Lviv flea market eighty years later, trumpeting Hitler's seemingly unstoppable advance: 'Tsar's palaces near Leningrad are in German hands.'

Germany was so confident of victory that Hans Frank, head of Nazi-occupied Poland or the 'General Government' – the 'Butcher of Poland' who would later be hanged at Nuremberg – encouraged publisher Karl Baedeker to produce a guidebook detailing the art and architecture that German travellers could admire across the conquered territories. The immaculately presented 250-page *Baedekers Generalgouvernement* which sits on the desk in front of me was published in 1943 and is focused mostly on items of tourist interest. The industrial town of Auschwitz is included in Rail Route 2a Vienna–Kraków as 'former capital of the Piast duchies of Auschwitz and Zator'. Bełżec, site of the death camp where half a million Jews had been delivered to be killed in the previous year, is mentioned as a destination on Rail Route 18a from Lublin to Lwów. Items of interest in a nearby 'beautiful forested region' include a seventeenth-century Dominican monastery, 'rebuilt after a fire in the Baroque style'. In addition to its touristic descriptions, Baedeker also finds room to boast about the consequences of expulsion and murder. The guide refers in a casual parenthesis to Kazimierz, Kraków's historically Jewish district for the past four hundred years, as '(*jetzt judenfrei*)' – '(now free of Jews)'.

And yet: it was in this bleakest of contexts, when Nazis ruled triumphant and Allied victory seemed so distant, that the exiled governments of Poland, Czechoslovakia and seven other occupied countries agreed a statement at St James's Palace in London (historically the royal residence, until Queen Victoria moved into Buckingham Palace) on 13 January 1942. The statement was entitled *Punishment for War Crimes*. What came to be known as the St James's Declaration noted that the German occupiers had 'set aside the restraining influence of the laws of war and the laws of nations'. One of the principal war aims would be 'the punishment, through the channel of organised justice, of those guilty of or responsible for these crimes, whether they have ordered them, perpetrated them or participated in them'. Those responsible would be 'sought out, handed over to justice, and judged'.

The chair of the meeting, Polish prime minister and commander-in-chief General Władysław Sikorski, said the full value of the declaration would not be clear 'until the day of final victory'. But, he insisted, it had immediate significance: 'It serves as a warning to all those who oppress our civil populations, by making them clearly understand that there can be no crime without punishment.' Sikorski's message – accountability as a form of 'never again!' education – would be central to the message of Nuremberg three years later and in other conflicts in the years to come.

None of the signatories could have guessed at that time quite how far the Nazis had already tossed aside any 'restraining influence'. Reinhard Heydrich, head of the Nazi security service, had sent out invitations for a meeting to be held a few days later in a grand villa beside Lake Wannsee in southwest Berlin. Adolf Eichmann, bureaucratic architect of the Holocaust, remembered the two-hour meeting passed in an atmosphere of 'much friendliness – politely and nicely'. Fine wines and cognac were served as the participants discussed how they could best and most efficiently organise 'the final solution to the Jewish question'. The existence and agenda of the conference would only become known much later; today, the villa is a museum documenting the decisions of that day. Even without knowledge of the Wannsee decisions, however, it was clear from the outside that the Nazis were committing unspeakable crimes. The St James's signatories called for future accountability which would 'satisfy the sense of justice to the civilised world'.

*

In the next two years, the prospects gradually brightened. A UN War Crimes Commission was tasked with gathering evidence (although, as Nuremberg prosecutor Telford Taylor later noted, the Commission was 'in for a very thin time – it had no investigatory staff or, for that matter, a staff for any substantial undertaking'). One initiative for a war crimes tribunal even came from inside Germany. Helmuth von Moltke, namesake and great-grandnephew of Bismarck's chief military commander and an opponent of Hitler from the start, asked: 'What will I say in the future, when someone asks me: and what did you do during this time?' In March 1943, von Moltke wrote via neutral Sweden to his friend Lionel Curtis, a fellow at All Souls College, Oxford and co-founder of the Royal Institute of International Affairs at Chatham House; in his letter, he talked of the need for future war crimes prosecutions. In the months to come, von Moltke and others met secretly at his home in Kreisau in what is now Poland and drew up proposals for a 'universal international court' where those who 'contemptuously disregarded' international law would be held accountable by 'the community of nations' in The Hague after the war. Von Moltke quoted the Victorian historian Lord Macaulay on the importance of holding senior leaders to account: in his *History of England*, Macaulay argued that 'the ringleaders, the men of rank' are 'the proper objects of severity'.

Von Moltke's approaches to Britain through Curtis were ignored. He was arrested by the Nazis in 1944 and later hanged; his wife Freya hid documents in her beehives on the Kreisau family estate. But, just a few months after the Kreisau meetings, the Allies moved forward with plans of their own. In October 1943, Roosevelt, Churchill and Stalin agreed a joint declaration, 'Concerning Responsibility of Hitlerites for Committed Atrocities', warning that Nazi leaders would be pursued 'to the uttermost ends of the earth . . . in order that justice may be done'. The Moscow Declaration said the 'atrocities, massacres and cold-blooded mass executions' would be judged and prosecuted by 'the peoples whom they have outraged'. Churchill said he hoped the statement might make 'some of these villains reluctant to be mixed up in butcheries'.

The Russians were the first to turn those ambitious words into action. On 15 December 1943, six weeks after the Moscow Conference and two years before Nuremberg, a Nazi war crimes trial opened in the opera house in the Ukrainian city of Kharkiv. Charges included the starvation and shooting of civilians, bombing of hospitals and 'burning down and destroying entire towns'. The prosecutor compared these crimes to the actions of 'medieval barbarians or the hordes of Attila the Hun'. The soldiers 'cannot but know', the prosecutor concluded, that such actions 'constitute a travesty of international law and the laws of all civilised countries'. The author Ilya Ehrenburg reported on the trial: 'I waited a long time for this hour . . . On this day we stopped speaking about a future trial for the criminals. We began to judge them.'

In one of the dark ironies of history, eighty years after the Kharkiv trial, Moscow's forces murdered civilians and shelled hospitals in the region and across Ukraine. When I was in Kharkiv in 2023, I visited the theatre where the trial had taken place. Spattered with shrapnel damage, it was closed due to Russian attacks. For modern Ukrainians, it was now the Russians who conducted themselves like 'medieval barbarians'. In 2022, the Ukrainian novelist Andrey Kurkov echoed Ehrenburg's words about the importance of account-ability – this time, for Moscow's own crimes. A few weeks after the full-scale invasion, Kurkov wrote: 'Ukrainians are looking forward to the verdict on the murderers and war criminals. But for now, they must survive under the constant shelling of the Russian army . . . They are waiting for the end of the war and the beginning of the trial.'

Even as Allied victory approached in the Second World War, there was still no consensus about what justice should or shouldn't look like. Anthony Eden, Britain's foreign secretary, pointed early on to the 'ill-starred enterprise' of war crimes trials after 1918 and concluded: 'I am convinced that we should avoid commitments to "try the war criminals" and to "hang the Kaiser" (*alias* Hitler).'

Simpler versions were proposed instead. A month after the Moscow declaration, Roosevelt, Stalin and Churchill met in Moscow's embassy in Tehran (whose previous claim to fame was that a mob murdered and beheaded one of Russia's most famous playwrights there, as commemorated by a statue in the garden today). Stalin proposed a toast suggesting fifty thousand Germans should be shot. Churchill retorted that he would 'rather be taken out into the garden here and now and be shot myself than sully my own and my country's honour by such infamy'. Stalin's suggestion was clearly unsavoury. Churchill's indignation was, however, partly disingenuous. He, too, was at this point in favour of summary executions – just not on the scale that Stalin was talking about. Partly echoing Eden's earlier concerns, Churchill liked the idea of a few dozen top leaders being 'shot to death within six hours' in order to 'avoid all the tangles of legal procedure', as he put it in November 1943.

American thinking was initially closer to Stalin than Churchill. In July 1944, General Dwight Eisenhower, Supreme Allied Commander, wanted to 'exterminate all of the General Staff', which he reckoned to be three and a half thousand. Treasury Secretary Henry Morgenthau Jr (whose father, as US ambassador to Turkey, had spoken out about the Armenian killings in 1915) said that those whose 'obvious guilt has been generally recognised' should be 'put to death forthwith' by firing squad. War Secretary Henry Stimson noted in September 1944 that his civilian colleagues seemed 'anxious to chop everybody's head off without trial or hearing'.

At the next Big Powers summit, hosted by Stalin at the tsars' summer retreat near the resort of Yalta in the Crimea in February 1945, Churchill remained keen on 'bumping off' key Nazis. But the winds were changing. Roosevelt, influenced by Stimson (and by Stalin himself), was now in favour of war crimes trials. Stalin insisted he had been 'joking' when he suggested that fifty thousand should be shot. He had become an enthusiastic advocate of high-profile trials, of which he had significant experience. His own show trials had ended with pre-ordained executions. Guy Liddell, Britain's head of counterespionage, wrote in his diary: 'Winston had put [the idea of summary executions] forward at Yalta, but Roosevelt felt that the Americans would want a trial. Joe supported Roosevelt on the perfectly frank grounds that Russians liked public trials for propaganda purposes.'

As late as April 1945, Churchill was still arguing that any trial would be 'a farce'. By the time the war ended, however, the principle of holding war crimes trials was more or less agreed, even if the framework was not. Some on the ground remained sceptical that anything useful would come of it. A twenty-six-year-old Transylvanian-born Jewish Harvard law graduate and US army sergeant called Benjamin Ferencz wrote to his college sweetheart (and future wife of seventy-three years) Gertrude Fried, back home in the Bronx: 'There will be war crimes work over here for a long time to come, but I'm not anxious to take part in it. The whole thing is really a joke from the legal point of view ... Not one person has been tried yet. I think we don't want to hurt their feelings.' Not least because of Ferencz's own groundbreaking work in the years to come, his pessimistic assessment would be proved wrong.

Prosecutors from Washington, Paris and Moscow travelled to Britain for the London Conference that began on 26 June 1945. The four Allied powers met daily in Church House beside Westminster Abbey to thrash out what the proposed International Military Tribunal should look like. It was complicated. Moscow insisted defendants should be treated as guilty from the start – 'verdict first, trial afterwards', as the Queen of Hearts might have put it. Iona Nikitchenko, who had been a judge in Stalin's show trials, argued too much weighing up of the evidence would only be an annoyance: 'If such procedure is adopted that the judge is supposed to be impartial, it would only lead to unnecessary delays.'

The Russians eventually conceded that defence lawyers would be entitled to challenge evidence in court before judges determined questions of innocence or guilt. Still, however, there was little clarity on what the charges should be. That wasn't the only problem. As Robert Jackson, the US Supreme Court justice who led the American team, wrote to a colleague, 'Even after words are agreed upon, we find them to mean different things.' The poor quality of the interpreting didn't help: one participant noted that talking to the Russians could be like having a 'conversation through a double mattress'. As delegates attempted to find common ground, social encounters helped smooth the way. The Americans toasted Stalin's health at a black-tie dinner at Claridge's Hotel in Mayfair (the Russians were unimpressed by a drink that 'claimed to be vodka'). The Soviet delegation returned the compliment with a lunch at the equally grand Savoy Hotel on the Strand.

*

Three lawyers, each linked by family ties to what the historian Timothy Snyder has described as the 'bloodlands' of central and eastern Europe, played key roles in the London discussions as the indictments took shape.

The Soviets' lead adviser, Aron Trainin, was born into a Jewish merchant family in Vitebsk in present-day Belarus. (His contemporary was Moishe Shagal, better known as Marc Chagall, who was briefly the city's art commissar after 1917.) As early as 1937, Trainin argued for the creation of 'crimes against peace' as a new category of international crime. Where Lemkin had been unhappy with his professor's reference to farmers having the right to kill their chickens, Trainin made a different comparison. 'Unlawfully hunting rabbits,' he complained, 'is punished more severely than organising the military destruction of people.'

Trainin returned to the theme a few years later, calling in 1944 for a new international convention prohibiting acts of aggression, propaganda of aggression, and more. His *Criminal Responsibility of the Hitlerites* was translated into English and became influential. A report for President Roosevelt suggested that, as a result of Trainin's arguments, the idea of prosecuting crimes against peace would 'rest on solid grounds' and would take on the power of 'valid international law'. Crimes against peace were listed as one of the indictments when the Charter of the International Military Tribunal was published on 8 August 1945. The final Nuremberg judgment found crimes against peace to be the 'supreme international crime, differing only from other war crimes in that it contains within itself the accumulated evil of the whole'. The emphasis on the crime of aggression was a victory for the Russians. It would return to haunt them in the twenty-first century.

A second lawyer who played a key role was Hersch Lauterpacht, who studied in Lemberg in the Austro-Hungarian empire (Lwów after the restoration of Polish independence in 1918, and today's Lviv in Ukraine) and then in Vienna. In 1923, Lauterpacht moved with his pianist wife Rachel to London, where she studied at the Royal College of Music. He taught at the London School of Economics and in 1938 became professor and chair of international law at Cambridge. By the time the Second World War began, he enjoyed world renown. But, unknown to his colleagues with whom he maintained tranquil dealings everywhere from Cambridge to Washington, the distinguished Lauterpacht would from now on suffer from the agony of divided lives. With his parents living under Nazi occupation in Lwów, Lauterpacht wrote to Rachel in 1941: 'The thing is constantly with me like a nightmare. It is astonishing how a human being can split his personality.'

In 1942, Lauterpacht gave a speech at the Grotius Society in London on the need for the 'revolutionary immensity' of a new international bill of human rights; it received (he told Rachel) 'embarrassing praise'. Soon afterwards, he again wrote to Rachel about his fears: 'I do not know whether [the family] are alive. And the situation is so terrible that it is quite conceivable that they may prefer death to life.' Four months earlier, unknown to Lauterpacht, his father had indeed been dragged from his hiding place in a bathroom cupboard in the family apartment in Lwów and killed; his mother, sister and brother had all been taken or would be murdered in the next three years. As regards preferring death to life: his twelve-year-old niece Inka tried to poison herself and was disappointed that she failed to do so.

Lauterpacht learned these details only later but, like Lemkin, he knew enough to guess at the worst. Meanwhile, he helped shape the international law that frames our world today. Even as he worried about the fate of his family in 1942, he drafted a memorandum with carefully composed proposals for future war crimes prosecutions. In 1945, as discussions about trials got under way, Robert Jackson and his British counterpart, Hartley Shawcross, both sought him out for advice. That included, as Lauterpacht and Jackson strolled through Cambridge in the July sunshine, the suggestion that prosecutors might usefully revive the phrase 'crimes against humanity' that had been used in response to the Ottoman massacres of Armenians thirty years earlier. Jackson liked the idea and the Russians, after some hesitation, agreed.

And then, last but not least, there was Raphael Lemkin. Lemkin and Lauterpacht never met. But Lemkin's influence was everywhere, even when he was not; Jackson carried a copy of Lemkin's *Axis Rule*, borrowed from the US Library of Congress, when he travelled to Nuremberg. The indictments did not formally include Lemkin's word, which came under 'war crimes'. His neologism was, however, woven through the proceedings: prosecutors talked of 'deliberate and systematic genocide', explained as '*viz.*, extermination of racial and national groups'.

Even after reaching agreement on what defendants should be charged with, the Allies still had to choose a venue. The Russians wanted the trial to take place in Berlin, in the heart of the Soviet zone of eastern Germany. The razing of the German capital made that impractical; it was eventually agreed the prosecutions would be in the medieval city of Nuremberg, site of Hitler's biggest pre-war rallies, in the American zone in the south. (To mollify Moscow, Berlin became the 'seat' of the tribunal – in practice that meant an opening ceremony before everybody decamped to Nuremberg.) Nuremberg was, in truth, nearly as destroyed as Berlin. Remarkably, however, the city's vast Palace of

Justice, inaugurated by Bavaria's last king in 1916, was almost undamaged.

The trial opened in Courtroom 600 of the Palace of Justice on 20 November 1945. There was a smell of fresh paint; German prisoners of war had been busy redecorating until the previous day. Novelist John Dos Passos set the scene for *LIFE* magazine:

> A GI is smoothing out the folds of the four flags that stand behind the judges' dais ... The guards stand still against the wall with the serious faces of a high-school basketball team waiting to be photographed. Under them, crumpled and torn by defeat, are the faces that glared for years from the front pages of the world.

The twenty-one defendants in the dock included Hitler's deputy, Hermann Göring, his foreign minister, Joachim von Ribbentrop, and his nominated successor, Admiral Karl Dönitz. The courtroom had been remodelled and rebuilt to accommodate press, simultaneous interpreters in four languages and movie-camera lighting – so bright that some defendants wore dark glasses. (Courtroom 600 today offers visitors a powerful re-imagining which blends recordings and reality as you sit in the space where history was made.)

In his opening speech, Robert Jackson called the trial 'one of the most significant tributes that power has ever paid to reason' and emphasised the uniqueness of the moment: 'The wrongs which we seek to condemn and punish have been so calculated, so malignant, and so devastating, that civilisation cannot tolerate their being ignored – because it cannot survive their being repeated.'

Jackson's words remain resonant to this day. But the omissions from the charge sheet were significant, too. One issue that was missing was Germany's destructive bombing. In 1942, the Soviet-Jewish author Vasily Grossman had warned, with reference to German aerial bombing, of the day of reckoning when 'a man with fat, sagging cheeks, the boss of the Fascist air force' would squirm 'on the bench of shame'. Grossman's prediction seemed to be fulfilled three years later when Göring, head of the Luftwaffe, indeed found himself 'on the bench of shame' at Nuremberg. (In the *New Yorker*, Rebecca West described Göring as having the 'preternaturally deep wrinkles of the drug addict . . . sometimes, particularly when his humor is good, he recalls the madam of a brothel'; Dos Passos said Göring's face wore 'the naughty-boy expression of a repentant drunkard'.)

At the time he was writing, Grossman's focus on the horror of German air raids seemed logical. Thousands had died in the flames and ruins of Warsaw, Rotterdam, Coventry, Belgrade and cities across Europe, many more than in the 1937 bombing of Guernica in the Spanish Civil War that itself became so notorious around the world. Hitler would have killed more, if he could have managed it. As he boasted to his dinner guests in 1940, 'We can do it with incendiaries; we can destroy London completely. What will their firemen be able to do once it's really burning?' Hersch Lauterpacht, like Grossman, proposed in 1942 that a future tribunal should include the crime of aerial bombing if used to terrorise the civilian population, 'as in the case of the bombardment at Rotterdam' (where German air raids in 1940 killed more than a thousand and made tens of thousands homeless).

There was one obvious reason, however, why German bombing would not be included in the Nuremberg indictments. If it became a focus, that drew obvious comparisons. Six hundred thousand civilians had died in Allied bombing raids on Germany – ten times more than in all of Germany's raids put together. In Hamburg in July 1943, tens of thousands died when the Allies put Hitler's incendiary fantasies from three years earlier into practice. German author W. G. Sebald later described the aftermath: 'Bluish little phosphorus flames still flickered around many of [the corpses]; others had been roasted brown or purple and reduced to a third of their normal size. They lay doubled up in pools of their own melted fat, which had sometimes already congealed.'

Most famously of all, thirty thousand died in Dresden, 'Florence on the Elbe', on 13 and 14 February 1945. Nobody who lived through it would ever forget: first the 'Christmas tree' flares that lit up the sky, then the high–explosive bombs, then the incendiaries. Gertraude Hedler, a child at the time, remembered her house exploding. 'It was like a giant had come under the cellar and picked it up,' she told me when, during my time in Germany for the *Independent*, I met her in Dresden half a century later. 'Women were lying there, all charred. Dead babies. When I found my father, he didn't recognise us.' Or, as Kurt Vonnegut, another survivor of that night, described it in *Slaughterhouse-Five*: 'Dresden was like the moon now, nothing but minerals. The stones were hot. Everybody else in the neighbourhood was dead.'

Even at the time, the destruction of Dresden and other German cities was controversial. Churchill expressed concerns, leading Arthur Harris, head of Bomber Command, to retort: 'I do not personally regard the whole of the remaining cities of Germany as worth the bones of one British Grenadier.' Harris had learned his trade as a squadron leader twenty years earlier in British–ruled Iraq, where he complained of 'the appalling climate, the filthy food, and the ghastly lack of any sort of amenity', and bombed villages to bring to heel what the air minister described as 'recalcitrant chiefs'. As historian A. J. P. Taylor put it: 'He genuinely believed that the German people could be cowed from the air as he had once cowed the tribesmen of Iraq.'

The killing of almost 1 per cent of Germany's civilian population meant the *tu quoque* defence — 'you, too, committed these same crimes' — would be overwhelming if the Allies decided to make an example of the German bombing of European cities. The solution: the theme was set aside, becoming what US prosecutor Telford Taylor would later call 'the silence of Nuremberg'. (Nobody at the trial went so far as to *defend* the scale of the civilian deaths, although — remarkably — a senior Israeli ambassador would, in the context of Gaza eighty years later, where 2 per cent of the population were killed, praise the Allied bombing as an example to be admired and imitated.)

Grave crimes committed by the Russians were airbrushed out, too. The Soviet forces committed rape on an unprecedented scale as they wreaked revenge on a defeated Germany. As Soviet war correspondent Natalya Gesse later remembered: 'The Russian soldiers were raping every German female from eight to eighty. It was an army of rapists.' More than a million were raped, often many times over. The outline of all this was known, and ignored. (The subject remains taboo in Russia. In 2002, when historian Antony Beevor described the mass rapes in *Berlin: The Downfall 1945*, including evidence from Russian archives, Moscow described his book as 'an act of blasphemy'. In 2015, Beevor's books were banned.)

In some ways, most remarkable of all was a set of crimes that *was* included in the indictments at Nuremberg but should not have been. The Russians accused the Germans of murdering twenty thousand Polish prisoners at Katyn near Smolensk in western Russia in 1941. The crimes were unspeakable. But they were not the responsibility of the Germans, however loudly the Russians said differently. When the Germans discovered the mass graves in the woods in 1943, they knew their own accusations would be disbelieved, so they invited the Red Cross and other independent experts to visit the site and examine the corpses.

The Red Cross concluded the killings had taken place in 1940 – in other words, when Russia was still in control after the Hitler–Stalin carve-up of Poland a few months earlier. In September 1939, Nazi and Soviet troops had shaken hands and even staged a joint parade to mark the dividing line of their respective invasions. Stalin's foreign minister, Vyacheslav Molotov, boasted: 'One swift blow, by the German Army and then the Red Army, and nothing was left of this ugly offspring of the Versailles treaty.' A document dated March 1940, released by Moscow fifty years after the events, shows Stalin himself approved the mass executions. The document describes the Polish officers and other prisoners as 'persistent enemies of Soviet power' who must receive 'the ultimate measure of punishment – shooting'. (In 2023, apparently in punishment for Poland's support for Ukraine, Moscow again began to suggest – despite the documents that the Kremlin itself had already released – that Russia might not be responsible, and that the circumstances of the killings were 'unclear'.)

Asked to choose between two known liars, it is unsurprising that the rest of the world was unsure who to believe. Moscow broke off relations with Poland's government in exile ('Hitler's Polish collaborators', as the Kremlin put it) to punish the Poles for concluding that, on this occasion at least, the Germans were telling the truth. The Polish authorities had already tried without success to establish the whereabouts of the missing men after their capture by Russian forces, so the discovery of bodies merely confirmed what the Poles already suspected from three long years of silence.

Once the Russians had decided to blame the Germans,

they seemed to feel their only option was to double down. It was, as historian Francine Hirsch put it in *Soviet Judgment at Nuremberg*, 'a bold and potentially risky move'. American, British and French prosecutors tried without success to persuade their Russian colleagues to withdraw the Katyn charges. They feared the accusations, if exposed as false, would call other indictments into question and damage the credibility of the entire trial. In the end, the Allies got lucky: the German defence team challenged the accusations but failed to score a palpable hit against the Kremlin's lies. In the final Nuremberg judgment, the false claims went discreetly unmentioned.

In short: there were plenty of wrinkles at Nuremberg. The Allies left unprosecuted things which they ought to have prosecuted. They prosecuted things which they ought not to have prosecuted. In concept and in execution, the trials were messy and uneven. Going in, nobody knew quite what they wanted. Coming out, nobody knew quite what the result would be. But US chief prosecutor Robert Jackson was justified in looking back with pride on a trial that was achieved, as he put it, 'in the face of obstacles so formidable that many well-wishers thought it a quixotic undertaking beyond our power to accomplish'.

Eden's fears of an 'ill-starred enterprise' had proved unjustified. The defence was robust, and prosecutors had to work hard to succeed. The main Nuremberg trial ended on 1 October 1946, with nineteen guilty verdicts and three acquittals. For many, the acquittals came as a surprise – proof this wasn't pure victors' justice after all. Martha Gellhorn, who reported on the trial, was cautiously hopeful, not least because it had happened at all:

After it was over, there was an empty, stunned feeling in the courtroom, the judges filed out, the room was quiet, the trial was over, justice had been done. Justice seemed very small suddenly; an anticlimax . . . The hope is that this body of law will serve as a barrier against the collective wickedness, greed and folly of any nation. In these dark times it is only a hope. But without hope we cannot live.

There would be twelve more trials at Nuremberg in the next two years – including one led by the young Ben Ferencz, who had complained that prospects for war crimes justice were 'really a joke' but who went on to put leaders of SS *Einsatzgruppen* killer squads behind bars. Jackson's successor as chief prosecutor, General Telford Taylor, appointed the diminutive and determined Ferencz, five foot two at the prosecutor's rostrum, to the role. Taylor told him: 'I've been checking up on your record, but I'm concerned because you're occasionally insubordinate.' Ferencz set him right: 'That's not correct. I'm not occasionally insubordinate. I'm usually insubordinate. I never obey an order which I think is stupid or illegal . . . I've been checking up on you, too. I don't think you'll give me that kind of order.' Taylor concluded: 'You'll go with me.'

At Nuremberg, Lemkin ('a lost and bedraggled fellow', in Ferencz's description) thrust a copy of *Axis Rule* into Ferencz's hands. In tribute to the importance of Lemkin's work, and to the fact that 'one determined individual, in persistent pursuit of a just cause, can make a difference', Ferencz talked of genocide in his opening speech at the *Einsatzgruppen* trial which began in 1947. The trial, in connection with a million deaths in what is now known as the 'Holocaust by bullets', was described at the time as the largest murder trial in history. Ferencz's dedication to justice would continue for three-quarters of a century, up to his death in 2023 at the age of 103. A few weeks before I visited the court in Nuremberg in 2024, there was a ceremony to pay tribute to the man who did so much for justice worldwide. Visitors now reach Courtroom 600 and the museum in the Palace of Justice through a newly renamed Ben-Ferencz-Platz.

Nuremberg helped create a new language around human rights and would become a shorthand for those seeking accountability in conflict zones around the world. Alfred Döblin, author of the classic Weimar-era novel *Berlin Alexanderplatz*, concluded: 'It cannot be said often enough, loudly enough (or joyfully enough): the re-establishment of law in Nuremberg is the rebirth of humanity to which we all belong.' Even critics were grudgingly appreciative. Jean-Paul Sartre wrote that Nuremberg was 'an ambiguous body . . . no doubt born of the right of the strongest', but, partly echoing Gellhorn, he believed it opened perspectives for the future 'by setting a precedent, the embryo of a tradition'. That 'embryo of a tradition' would develop in the decades to come. Germany would organise its own war crimes trials – stumblingly at first, then with ever-increasing confidence. Those, in turn, would help Germany find change of its own, and then to share lessons about the importance of justice with the rest of the world.

On the other side of the world, the US-led trials in Tokyo were closer to Eden's fears of an 'ill-starred enterprise'. The man who did most to shape the Japanese trials that began in April 1946 was General Douglas MacArthur, Allied commander in the Pacific and post-war administrator of occupied Japan. MacArthur was no Robert Jackson. He was more interested in politics than justice. The Americans were determined to hold trials of those most responsible for war crimes. But MacArthur also wanted Emperor Hirohito to remain in power. After the emperor, MacArthur feared the Communist deluge. On his insistence, the indictments at the International Military Tribunal for the Far East were shaped to give the impression that Hirohito had never had any real power to permit or order crimes.

On one occasion, former prime minister General Hideki Tojo went off-script by noting in court that there was 'no Japanese subject who would go against the will of His Majesty'. The American prosecutor had to wrench the narrative back into line a few days later by working with Tojo – who was himself charged with war crimes and would later be hanged – on what Gary Bass in *Judgement at Tokyo* describes as 'an elaborately choreographed effort to undo the shambles'. According to this massaged version, Tojo declared that the emperor had 'consented, though reluctantly' to the war and his 'love for and desire for peace' remained the only constant.

The devastation caused by the firebombing of Tokyo in March 1945 which killed a hundred thousand people, and the atomic bombs dropped on Hiroshima and Nagasaki in August, killing two hundred thousand, went unaddressed. Radhabinod Pal, an Indian judge at the tribunal – whose own country gained its independence halfway through the two-year trial – complained of 'sham employment of legal process for the satisfaction of a thirst for revenge'. Charles Willoughby, MacArthur's intelligence chief, thought the trials were 'the worst hypocrisy in recorded history'.

All of this had consequences. Even today, nationalists resist acknowledging the crimes committed. Ian Buruma noted in *The Wages of Guilt: Memories of War in Germany and Japan*: 'No Japanese politician has ever gone down on his knees, as Willy Brandt did in the former Warsaw ghetto, to apologize for historical crimes.' Despite a strong vein of post-war pacifism and the historic 'Murayama apology' of 1995, some politicians still visit the Yasukuni Shrine in Tokyo where Japanese war dead, including executed war criminals, are revered.

The Nuremberg and Tokyo trials marked the end of one chapter and the beginning of another. Lemkin was disappointed that genocide had not been included as a separate indictment at Nuremberg, alongside crimes against peace, war crimes and crimes against humanity. But his thinking made its mark. *The Times* wrote that the tribunal would be remembered for its examination of genocide, 'the new conception in law of which Nuremberg will remain the fount'. A *New York Times* editorial concluded: 'It now remains to incorporate the term in international law, which is what Professor Lemkin has already half accomplished.'

'Half accomplished' was right. Agreeing on the word genocide was easy in comparison with ensuring that the word could have real-world consequences. Lemkin noted a contradiction that would be conspicuous in the years to come – the eagerness to put crimes always into the past, thus failing to prevent or respond to similar crimes in the present or future. In Lemkin's words: 'The Allies decided their case against a past Hitler but refused to envisage future Hitlers. They did not want to, or could not, establish a rule of international law that would prevent and punish future crimes of the same type.'

Russia, Britain and the United States all worked hard (though not always at the same time) to block the genocide convention that Lemkin was so determined to achieve, apparently fearing that they might themselves one day be held accountable. Shawcross, the British attorney-general who himself used the word genocide at Nuremberg, insisted: 'Nuremberg is enough! A genocide convention cannot be adopted.' Smaller countries became Lemkin's best allies in highlighting the need to prevent and punish genocide.

The Lebanese delegate declared: 'The Attorney-General of England did everything he could to confuse us, but we refuse to be confused. The convention is essential for the protection of small countries. Big countries can protect themselves, but our only protection is international law.'

Lemkin eventually won by being, as he put it, the 'pest Lemkin' who refused to give up. Or, as a more generous John Hohenberg of the *New York Post* wrote, he was 'a lonely crusader ... tilting his lance in solitary grandeur against the ramparts' of UN member states. On 9 December 1948, in the Palais de Chaîllot in Paris, the Convention on the Prevention and Punishment of the Crime of Genocide was finally agreed. The UN General Assembly called for the possibility of an 'international judicial organ' to be looked into, which could punish genocide in the way that the convention called for. But that idea would soon be buried, not to be revived for many years.

The Universal Declaration of Human Rights followed a day later, on 10 December. The Declaration, which Eleanor Roosevelt helped shape, built on the emphasis on individual rights that Hersch Lauterpacht highlighted in his Grotius Society speech in 1942 and developed in book form in 1945. Lauterpacht was the obvious choice to be British representative on the UN Human Rights Commission which would lead on drafting the Declaration. But British antisemitism put paid to that. Eric Beckett, legal adviser at the Foreign Office, wrote that Lauterpacht would be a 'very bad candidate' because, 'though a distinguished and industrious international lawyer', he was 'when all is said and done, a Jew recently come from Vienna'. Lauterpacht had lived in Britain for most of his adult life; he was Britain's most distinguished figure in international law. But Beckett insisted a 'very English Englishman' was needed for the role.

Lemkin felt excluded in a different way. After the genocide convention was agreed, he became ill. His own self-diagnosis: 'Genociditis: exhaustion from work on the Genocide Convention.' In the years to come, Lemkin would feel his work was wasted and that his beloved Convention had proved meaningless. 'The fact is,' he wrote, 'that the rain of my work fell on a fallow plain.' A former student encouraged him to see his achievements in a broader context. 'It is true that you cannot see the results of your work,' she wrote to Lemkin in 1951. 'But your work is great, far greater than this generation. The results can only be known with the passage of time. You yourself will in all likelihood never see the concrete result you wish to see. But generations to come will enjoy and know the ideals you strive to realise.'

Lemkin died in New York in 1959 a forgotten man. Seven people attended his funeral. There seemed to be little possibility that the accountability he dreamed of would ever be achieved. As with Tehlirian and Talaat Pasha in 1921, the only way to punish somebody responsible for mass atrocities was still, it seemed, to gun them down in the street. Governments remained free to slaughter their own citizens 'like chickens'. All thoughts of an international tribunal seemed abandoned. But Lemkin's student was right to take the longer view. The struggles had only just begun.

Sixty years after Lemkin's death, the power and impact of his legacy is everywhere. In 2001, I sat in a court in The Hague to see a Bosnian Serb commander prosecuted for the crime that Lemkin had named. In 2023, when I first met Ukraine's head of war crimes investigations in Kyiv, he had been re-reading arguments that Lemkin made eighty years earlier, with a view to applying them to the war now being waged against his own country. In 2024, I was in a different court in The Hague to hear judges issue an almost unanimous rebuke against Israel – a country whose very identity is bound up with the crime that Lemkin identified – in connection with an alleged risk of genocide in Gaza. The court called for Israel to 'take all measures within its power' to prevent the incitement or commission of genocide.

Later generations are familiar with the ideals that Lemkin 'strove to realise', even if those ideals are far from being fulfilled. In the past twenty years, there have been accusations and prosecutions of genocide across the world. There are different ways to hold those who commit genocide to account, in international and domestic courts alike. With the right political will, Robert Jackson's 'hand of vengeance' can be stayed.

Chapter Two

'We Must Sin Quietly'

*Kenya, Algeria, Vietnam, Frankfurt (1952–75).
Cambodia, Chile, Halabja (1973–90)*

Nuremberg was supposed to send the message that war crimes and atrocities would no longer be ignored. In place of 'what might have been mere acts of vengeance', Jackson was proud that he and his colleagues had created 'a civilised legal precedent that will prevail when the world becomes sufficiently civilised'. The Nuremberg Principles agreed in 1950 – including crimes against peace, war crimes and crimes against humanity – created a notional framework for the future. But the flurry of interest in a tribunal that might punish such crimes quickly died away. Governments were troubled rather than inspired by the aspiration of Jackson and others that Nuremberg might set a legal precedent. They wanted to ensure that the justice they were happy to mete out to others should not be applied to themselves. The four countries that collaborated to prosecute Nazi crimes and were then divided by the Cold War continued to share one thing in common in the years to come: a belief that they were entitled to commit grave crimes of their own, confident in the knowledge they would remain unpunished.

It was unsurprising that the Soviet Union would continue its lawlessness in the years after Nuremberg. In 1940, Stalin had annexed Estonia, Latvia and Lithuania under his secret deal with Hitler. (Or, as my Soviet-era guidebook describes the trampling of an independent state, 'the red flag of freedom fluttered' over the Estonian capital, Tallinn.) After 1945, Moscow deported hundreds of thousands of Balts to Siberia in an attempt to crush their national identity for ever. In Moscow, the deportations and killings went unacknowledged and unpunished. The Balts, however, did not forget those crimes.

On my wall is a taboo-breaking poster I bought in 1989 in a still-Soviet bookshop in Tallinn, ahead of the fiftieth anniversary of the Hitler–Stalin pact. 'A lie has short legs,' the poster says, quoting a popular European proverb. 'But how short?' The image shows the lower half of a figure walking: the back boot has a swastika on it, the front boot a Soviet hammer and sickle. The timeline is '1939 . . . 1989 . . . ' – and then a provocative question mark for the future. Not long after that poster was published, Moscow admitted for the first time the secret deal Stalin had celebrated with vodka and champagne with Hitler's foreign minister Joachim von Ribbentrop in the Kremlin on 23 August 1939, agreeing the carve-up of Poland and the Baltic states; Stalin proposed a toast to the Führer, declaring him to be *molodets*, a 'fine fellow'. (Putin now again defends the swallowing-up of the Baltic nations, saying 'Their accession to the USSR was implemented on a contractual basis . . . in line with international and state law';

the annexations were needed at the time, Putin says, because of Moscow's 'strategic military and defensive goals'.)

It was, however, not just Stalin's totalitarian regime which behaved as though rules were irrelevant. The other three prosecuting powers at Nuremberg all treated their legal and moral obligations as optional extras when they felt it was desirable to retain power and achieve 'security'.

In British-ruled Kenya, for example, atrocities were widespread. Kikuyu, Kenya's largest single ethnic group, were seen as sympathetic to the Mau Mau rebels who demanded the return of their land. Hundreds of thousands of Kenyans were held without trial in British camps and 'screening centres' around the country under a state of emergency declared in 1952. Detainees were castrated, tortured, raped; broken bottles were inserted into detainees' vaginas. Hussein Onyango Obama, grandfather of the future US president, was one of those detained. According to his widow Sarah, 'He said they would sometimes squeeze his testicles with parallel metallic rods. They also pierced his nails and buttocks with a sharp pin, with his hands and legs tied together with his head facing down.' All this happened in the name of better security.

As described by Caroline Elkins in her Pulitzer-winning *Britain's Gulag*, camps displayed slogans like 'He who helps himself will also be helped' and 'Labour and freedom'. Deliberately or otherwise, the echoes were hard to miss: Buchenwald and Auschwitz, liberated less than a decade earlier, notoriously had almost identical slogans over the camp gates, declaring 'To each what he deserves' and 'Work makes you free'. During the eight-year emergency, tens of thousands of Kenyans were killed, accused of being Mau Mau rebels or in league with the rebels. During the same period, thirty-two white settlers were killed.

There were attempts to highlight the abuses at the time. Labour MP Barbara Castle raised concerns after a whistleblower told her conditions were 'worse than he himself had experienced in the Japanese prisoner of war camps'. The *Observer* called for 'No More Whitewash' and said: 'If we tolerate such practices in British territories, on what grounds do we criticise Russian prison camps?' Still, though, little changed. The colony's attorney-general decreed it was fine for the violence to continue, as long as nobody knew. 'If we are going to sin,' Eric Griffith-Jones wrote to governor Sir Evelyn Baring (in a letter that remained secret for more than half a century), 'we must sin quietly.'

The ferocity of Britain's counterinsurgency campaign accelerated the pressure for independence, which came in 1963. Jomo Kenyatta, the country's new leader, called for erasing 'all the hatreds and the difficulties of those years which now belong to history'. That suited the former rulers well. For decades, there would be silence about the crimes, in Britain at least. It would take fifty years, and the determination of survivors, for that to change.

In 2011, a group of Kenyans brought a case in the High Court in London. The British government initially claimed legal liability had transferred to Kenya. Then it cited 'irredeemable difficulties' because so much time had passed. Finally, though, the UK agreed to pay compensation to thousands of elderly Kenyans for the torture and abuse they had suffered. In 2013, foreign secretary William Hague expressed 'sincere regret' for the 'abhorrent violations of human dignity'; claimants celebrated and wept. The government paid compensation and agreed to construct a memorial in Nairobi to the victims; thousands attended the unveiling of the monument in 2015.

*

France, like Britain, believed rules were for their enemies to obey, but not for them. France liked to proclaim its *mission civilisatrice* in the territories it ruled. That included impunity for their own crimes in the fight against Algerian rebels who wanted to end 120 years of colonial rule. The Geneva Conventions had been updated in 1949, with strengthened emphasis on the protection of civilians and a prohibition on collective punishment and reprisals. But that was all ignored. France's war in Algeria had torture at its heart. As one French paratrooper described it, 'All day, through the floorboards, we heard their hoarse cries, like those of animals being slowly put to death.' Robert Lacoste, who became Algeria's French governor-general in 1956, said it was 'nothing serious – just connecting little electrodes'. The paratroopers were, he explained, '*des garçons très sportifs*'.

A minority spoke out. General Jacques Pâris de Bollardière, decorated for his courage in the Second World War, warned of the 'terrible danger if we were to lose sight ... of moral values'. He was jailed for insubordination. Paul Teitgen, secretary-general at the Algiers prefecture and hero of the French Resistance, compared what the French were doing to 'the cruelties and tortures that I personally suffered fourteen years ago in the Gestapo cellars'. It changed nothing.

French lawlessness did not come in a vacuum. In June 1955, Algeria's FLN rebels announced all Europeans were now fair game: 'To colonialism's policy of collective repression we must reply with collective reprisals against the Europeans, military and civilian ... No pity, no quarter!' Two months later, they followed through on that threat. On 20 August 1955, the FLN slaughtered more than a hundred Europeans in and around the port city of Philippeville. In one household alone, a grandmother and her twelve-year-old granddaughter were killed; a father was killed and had his arms and legs hacked off;

a mother was disembowelled and her five-day-old baby placed in her slashed womb. In response, French soldiers were ordered to 'shoot down every Arab we met ... there were so many of them that they had to be buried with bulldozers', in the words of a paratrooper quoted in Alistair Horne's classic account, *A Savage War of Peace*. More than a thousand Algerians were killed – twelve thousand, according to the rebels – in revenge for the hundred French deaths. Philippeville had previously been a 'happy, sweet-smelling town'. Now, as governor-general Jacques Soustelle described it, 'There had been well and truly dug an abyss through which flowed a river of blood.'

Hundreds of thousands of Algerians were killed in the next seven years, before independence came in 1962. Algerians remember the scars. The university in Skikda (as Philippeville is now called) is the University of 20 August 1955, named after that 'river of blood'. The violence was not just in Algeria itself. At the opening ceremony of the Paris Olympics in 2024, the Algerian team dropped red roses into the Seine in memory of more than a hundred Algerian pro-independence protesters who in 1961 were killed by French police, with many bodies thrown into the river; the scale of the 17 October massacre, under Paris police chief and former Nazi collaborator Maurice Papon, was covered up for decades. Nor did the violence end with independence. In January 1998, I visited the town of Sidi-Hamed, south of Algiers, where more than a hundred people had been slaughtered in a Philippeville-style Islamist massacre a few days earlier. In the burnt-out ruins, shocked survivors sat or stood hopelessly in what were once their homes. I met a man whose three children had their throats cut in the room where we were standing; his wood-chopping axe that the killers had used as an additional murder weapon was still stained with his children's blood. Tens of thousands died between 1992 and 2002.

The former colonial power took years to find honesty about its own civil war. Italian director Gillo Pontecorvo's award-winning 1966 film *The Battle of Algiers*, with its graphic depictions of torture, was not shown in France for five years after its release. It would take another forty years before the French parliament acknowledged this had even been a war.

Maurice Audin, a twenty-five-year-old mathematics lecturer at Algiers University, was arrested by French paratroopers in 1957 and never seen again. His widow Josette spent sixty years unsuccessfully appealing to eight successive presidents for the truth to be told. Finally, President Emmanuel Macron acknowledged in 2018: Audin died under torture. Torture developed, Macron said, 'because it was unpunished'. He asked Josette Audin for forgiveness. In 2021, Macron received the grandchildren of an Algerian lawyer, Ali Boumendjel, who had 'fallen out of a window' during French interrogation. In reality, Macron told the family who had campaigned for so long, Boumendjel 'was tortured and then murdered'. He concluded: 'France established human rights in Algeria. It simply forgot to abide by them.'

The last of the four prosecuting powers, the United States, had played a key role in ensuring due process at Nuremberg. Robert Jackson said, 'We are not prepared to lay down a rule of criminal conduct against others which we would not be willing to have invoked against us.' In 1961, Stanley Kramer's Oscar-winning *Judgment at Nuremberg*, starring Spencer Tracy, Marlene Dietrich and Burt Lancaster, was a box office hit. The film, based on the 'judges' trial' of 1947, is a powerful exploration of personal responsibility and accountability for crimes committed – 'a fine dramatic statement of moral probity', in the words of the *New York Times*. Audiences were happy that America had stood up for its principles.

Four years later, however, those noble principles were nowhere to be seen when US combat troops arrived in Vietnam with the proclaimed mission of preventing Communist dominoes from falling, there and across the region. In 1966, philosopher and activist Bertrand Russell convened a 'citizens' tribunal', together with Sartre, James Baldwin and others, to investigate US war crimes. The tribunal, which quoted Jackson's words, condemned the 'massive, systematic and deliberate' bombing of civilian targets and the free-fire zones in Vietnam 'where everything that moves is considered hostile'. The tribunal's conclusions, including a finding of genocide, gained headlines and perhaps influenced world opinion. But its existence was in some respects an admission of failure – a recognition that there was and would be no Nuremberg-style trial where such crimes might be punished.

The most notorious single set of war crimes in the entire Vietnam war came three months *after* the Russell Tribunal announced its verdict in December 1967. My Lai and the hamlet of Son My were in an area known as 'Pinkville', so called because it was coloured pink on American maps. At the pre-operation briefing before a planned US attack, a soldier asked, 'Are we supposed to kill women and children?' Captain Ernest Medina replied, 'Kill everything that moves.' And so they did. Five hundred villagers were killed in a few hours on 16 March 1968. Women and girls were raped. Houses were burned. Water supplies were fouled. A participant later described the operation:

Do you realize what it was like killing five hundred people in a matter of four or five hours? It's just like the gas chambers – what Hitler did. You line up fifty people, women, old men, children, and just mow 'em down ... We just

rounded 'em up, me and a couple of guys, just put the M-
16 on automatic, and just mowed 'em down.

Army photographer Ron Haeberle was taking a photograph of a small boy who had been shot in the foot:

I didn't notice a GI kneeling down beside me with his
M–16 rifle pointed at the child. Then I suddenly heard
the crack and through the viewfinder I saw this child flip
over on top of the pile of bodies. The GI stood up and just
walked away. No remorse. Nothing. The other soldiers
had a cold reaction – they were staring off into space like
it was an everyday thing, they felt they had to do it and
they did it.

Dozens participated or witnessed what was happening, on
the ground and from helicopters circling above. A twenty-
four-year-old helicopter pilot, Hugh Thompson, tried to
stop the killing, but with little success. Afterwards, a con-
gratulatory message from General William Westmoreland,
commander of US forces in Vietnam, praised the 'heavy
blows' US forces delivered to the enemy at My Lai that day.
'US troops surround Reds, kill 128' was the headline in the
army newspaper, the *Stars and Stripes*.

All these atrocities would have remained unknown if not
for the civil courage of a twenty-two-year-old helicopter
gunner, Ron Ridenhour. Ridenhour heard stories of what
had happened and spent months gathering testimonies and
writing to congressmen. When Junior Lieutenant William
Calley was charged eighteen months later with the killings
of 'Oriental human beings', the story went almost unreported
and was ignored. Only after the Washington-based Dispatch
News Service published a Pulitzer-winning series of articles

by Seymour Hersh, a thirty-two-year-old freelance reporter, followed by the publication in the *Cleveland Plain Dealer* of Ron Haeberle's photographs, did the names of My Lai and of Lieutenant Calley become notorious around the world. (*LIFE* and *Look* magazines had both turned Hersh down when he first offered them the story.) Calley was convicted in 1971; on the order of President Richard Nixon, he was released into house arrest three days later. In 1974, Calley was freed.

The focus on My Lai, then and afterwards, could make it seem that those crimes were a terrible exception to the law-abiding rule. They weren't. As Ridenhour noted later, the killings were part of a pattern. 'If you ask people what happened at My Lai, they would say: "Oh yeah, isn't that where Lieutenant Calley went crazy and killed all those people?" No, that was not what happened.' In Ridenhour's summary, 'This was an operation, not an aberration.'

Former Nuremberg prosecutor Telford Taylor noted the contradiction between America's stance in 1945 and its behaviour a quarter of a century later:

How could it ever have been thought that air strikes, free-fire zones and a mass uprooting of the rural population were a way to win 'the allegiance of the South Vietnamese'? . . . We have smashed the country to bits, and will not even take the trouble to clean up the blood and rubble . . . Somehow we failed ourselves to learn the lessons we undertook to teach at Nuremberg, and that failure is today's tragedy.

Taylor pointed to the disturbing implications: 'We had better acknowledge at once that we are prepared to do what we hanged and imprisoned Japanese and German generals for doing.'

Hundreds of thousands of civilians died in the ten years of America's ground war in Vietnam – more than a million, according to some estimates. But there has never been a proper reckoning. The reluctance to confront painful truths can have damaging consequences for victims and perpetrators alike. 'The crimes committed in America's name in Vietnam ... have never been adequately faced,' Nick Turse argues in his award-winning account, *Kill Anything That Moves*. 'As a result, they continue to haunt our society in profound and complex ways ... Americans are still in the thrall of a conflict that refuses to pass quietly into the night.'

All four prosecuting powers felt able to commit crimes with impunity after 1945 – the 'sheerest hypocrisy', in Taylor's words. None had any interest in accountability or justice for their own crimes or those of their allies. One country, however, gradually became more interested in justice, rather than less.

At the time of Nuremberg, most Germans were focused on clearing the rubble, rebuilding the economy and getting on with their lives rather than addressing the crimes the country had committed in the past six years. As W. G. Sebald later wrote in *On the Natural History of Destruction*: 'People's ability to forget what they do not want to know, to overlook what is before their eyes, was seldom put to the test better than in Germany at that time. The population decided – out of sheer panic at first – to carry on as if nothing had happened.' Denial was everywhere. Martha Gellhorn, reporting from a defeated Germany, was brutal in her summary: 'No one is a Nazi. No one ever was ... Obviously not a man, woman or child in Germany ever approved of the war, according to them.'

Nor did it initially seem that the Nuremberg trials had much of their intended educational impact. As one of the US prosecutors wrote in 1946, 'There is little indication so far that the Nuremberg trial had a salutary effect on the thinking of the German people ... When some Germans blame Hitler and his regime, they do not blame them so much for having started the war as for having lost it.' In 1950, almost two in three Germans thought the Nuremberg trials had been unfair. So-called 'Persil certificates' – affidavits which proclaimed the bearer to be politically clean – helped millions turn their backs on the past.

Silence was all-enveloping, as is reflected in accounts of the Third Reich in German schoolbooks of the 1950s. Prescribed history books, reflecting social attitudes, agree in concluding that nobody knew anything; and, if they had known, they could have done nothing. Thirty years ago, when I was based in Germany for the *Independent* and first looked through a pile of history books in the huge national schoolbook collection in Braunschweig in north-west Germany, I sometimes found it hard to believe what I was reading. When I look back through my old pile of photocopied pages today, I again feel that sense of disbelief.

One book published in 1952 lists endless military engagements and battlefield casualties for page after page before finding room for a single sentence: 'In addition came ... the concentration camps, the labour camps, the death chambers etc.' The organised murder of millions has become a literal postscript. Another book, published in 1956, talks at length of 'terrible suffering, such as the world in the twentieth century would no longer have believed to be possible'. The reference is not to what Germans had done to others, but what Germans themselves had endured. In the same book, just two lines are devoted to 'the fate of the Polish Jews', bundled in a single paragraph with Poles who were sent to 'German or Russian' concentration camps. The author finds room to emphasise that Hitler 'could not ask the German army and its officer corps' to commit crimes and therefore had to create special forces to carry out such 'degrading' work. (In 1995, an exhibition called 'Crimes of the Wehrmacht' exploded that enduring myth; a million people in thirty German cities visited the exhibition which documented what their fathers and grandfathers had seen or done on the Eastern Front.)

The determination to look away was everywhere – hardly surprisingly, since the German establishment, including the judiciary, was riddled with former Nazis. One of Chancellor Konrad Adenauer's closest advisers, Hans Globke, had been closely involved with the 1935 Nuremberg laws that paved the way for the Holocaust. In West Germany, there were few effective war crimes prosecutions. Communist East Germany held many more trials, though often with little due process: in one instance, more than three thousand were convicted in a single swoop.

Thirteen years after Nuremberg, that silence began to end. In 1958, members of an SS *Einsatzgruppen* squad went on trial in the south-western town of Ulm, charged with murdering thousands of Jews as part of the 'Holocaust by bullets' – a million individual killings across eastern Europe. The prosecutors drew on the documentation that Ben Ferencz and his colleagues had assembled for the *Einsatzgruppen* trial at Nuremberg eleven years earlier. Casually shocking details – the killers had gone for a celebratory drink after committing one set of murders, using money stolen from the pockets of their victims – helped this become a wake-up call for Germany. The author Ralph Giordano, reporting on the trial, said it 'pierced a storm cloud over the country'.

For years, Germans had shown little interest in prosecuting war criminals. Now, that began to change. The creation as a result of the Ulm trial of a central war crimes unit was followed by the historic Auschwitz trial that began in Frankfurt in 1963. The camp's longest-serving commandant, Rudolf Höss, had been prosecuted and executed in Poland in 1947. (Surreally, Höss appeared at Nuremberg not as a defendant but as a witness for the defence; Höss was happy to explain that Auschwitz, where more than a million people were murdered, was chosen 'because of its easy access by rail'.) But Höss's successor, Richard Baer, went on trial with two dozen others in Frankfurt. The chief prosecutor of the Auschwitz trial, Fritz Bauer (Jewish himself, though he rarely mentioned that fact), had in 1960 quietly persuaded the initially reluctant Israelis to move against Adolf Eichmann, bureaucratic architect of the Holocaust, living in almost plain sight in Buenos Aires (his son was even using the name Eichmann). After Israeli agents captured him in Argentina, Eichmann went on trial in Jerusalem, where he became the bland embodiment of what Hannah Arendt termed the 'banality of evil'. In a description that remains relevant in many contexts around the world today, Arendt observed that Eichmann was 'terribly and terrifyingly normal'. The Eichmann trial was a further wake-up call, including the belated purging of West Germany's chief prosecutor and 140 judges and prosecutors who had what Arendt drily described as a 'more than ordinarily' compromising past.

Bauer believed the Auschwitz trial, which ran from 1963 to 1965, was important not just for establishing the guilt of individuals but for German society to understand the significance of what had happened: 'It is the be-all and end-all of this trial to say: "You should have said no." ... If something is to be learned from this trial, then it is the meaning of the fight for equality, which must be taken seriously, the meaning of tolerance, care and recognition, and the understanding that hate ... leads to such things as Auschwitz.'

The Frankfurt trial was widely reported, though some believed the focus on the most sadistic details was unhelpful. Novelist Martin Walser argued: 'The more horrible the Auschwitz quotations, the more pronounced our distance from Auschwitz becomes. We have nothing to do with these events, with these atrocities, we know this for certain. The similarities [with the defendants] aren't shared here. This trial is not about us.' Peter Weiss's play *The Investigation*, based on transcripts of the trial and composed in the form of eleven cantos with names like 'The Song of the Ramp' and 'The Song of the Black Wall', made a similar argument. *The Investigation* was performed simultaneously in fifteen theatres in West and East Germany, as well as in a production directed by Peter Brook at the Aldwych Theatre in London. One of the witnesses in the trial argues:

> We must get rid of our exalted attitude
> that this camp world
> is beyond our comprehension
> We all knew the society
> which had produced the regime
> that could bring about such a camp
> We were familiar with this order
> from its very beginnings

That 'exalted attitude' would gradually be abandoned. Bauer's lessons about the importance of justice and 'the understanding that hate ... leads to such things as Auschwitz' were absorbed in the fabric of German society, especially after the rebellions of a new generation in 1968 and after. My ancient student copy of Weiss's play includes on its cover a message from the German publishers of *The Investigation* that gives a sense of the more reflective country that was now on its way: '[The play] becomes an investigation into us: into a society which permitted these things to happen.'

There were thousands of German war crimes trials in the following years. Sentences were often absurdly lenient, not least because of a problem with the German definition of criminal responsibility, which continued to reward obedience. As historian Mary Fulbrook summed it up in *Reckonings*, an analysis of post-war German justice: 'In effect, if not in intention, West German law condoned obedience to a deadly regime and condemned only those who had individually stepped beyond Nazism's already murderous limits.' But, though sentences were mild, the impact on society was strong. Support for the principle of justice grew steadily. Beginning with the moment when Chancellor Willy Brandt fell to his knees on the site of the Warsaw Ghetto in 1970 and other smaller milestones in the decades that followed, Germany gained global respect for its honesty about past, present and future. After 1990 a newly united Germany – mindful of its history and the lessons for the world of its own powerful journey from criminality to truth – would become a leading voice in pressing for the establishment of a new institution which could help prevent and punish war crimes worldwide.

On one theme alone Germany found it harder to be honest: its colonial past. Germany's early twentieth-century empire was never on the scale of France or Britain, which between them claimed the right to rule almost the entire African continent. But its crimes more than matched the inhumanity of what Britain and France did in Kenya, Algeria and elsewhere. In 1885, Heinrich Göring (father of the man who would later be tried at Nuremberg) became the first colonial governor of German South-West Africa, now Namibia. In 1904, the killing in the territory of a hundred thousand Herero and Nama people prefigured the Armenian massacres eleven years later. The German commanding officer, General Lothar von Trotha, promised to 'destroy the rebellious tribes by shedding rivers of blood'. He declared: 'The Herero are no longer German subjects . . . Within the German borders every Herero, with or without a gun, will be shot. I will no longer accept women and children. I will drive them back to their people or I will let them be shot at.' Wells were poisoned. Thousands were driven into the desert to die.

Some have drawn parallels between the motivation for those killings and what is happening in Gaza today. Eyal Weizman is the British-Israeli director of Forensic Architecture, which uses digital technologies to investigate state violence and other human rights violations around the world. Weizman, who has worked on and in Namibia for many years, compares the killings in German South-West Africa with Israel's assault on Gaza: 'In both cases, the mass killing, destruction, and displacements followed humiliating military defeats by people they thought to be inferior.' Amos Goldberg, professor of Holocaust history at the Hebrew University of Jerusalem, wrote in 2011 (and re-quoted his own words in 2024): 'From the Herero and Nama genocide we can learn how colonial domination, based on a sense of cultural and racial superiority, can spill over, in the face of local rebellion, into horrific crimes like mass deportation, ethnic cleansing and genocide.' Goldberg's conclusion: 'The case of the Herero rebellion should serve as a horrifying warning sign for us here in Israel.'

By the end of the twentieth century, in sharp contrast to earlier years, the Holocaust was widely discussed in Germany from every possible angle – on television, in books, in class-rooms. But the killings in South-West Africa remained smothered in silence. As with Britain's and France's belated admissions of their crimes against humanity, that has finally begun to change. In 2021, Germany apologised to Namibians for 'abominable atrocities' culminating in what 'today would be called genocide'.

Last but not least among governments with connections to Nuremberg and justice, there was the Netherlands. Although the Dutch were not involved with the tribunal that prosecuted German war crimes, The Hague was now at the heart of international justice. And yet, in parallel to the Dutch self-image as a symbol of justice worldwide, the Hague government committed its own crimes against humanity in what had been the Dutch East Indies as colonial rule came to an end and Indonesia claimed its independence in the years after 1945.

Former soldier Joop Hueting told historian David Van Reybrouck of the pattern of My Lai-style massacres that Dutch forces carried out at that time:

We had machine guns. 'We'll show them who's the most powerful here.' From a distance of 100 or 200 metres, we riddle kampongs [villages] with bullets. Court-martial? What are you talking about! I wasn't stupid. Of course I didn't dare report it. That would have been treason.

Hueting first talked about the crimes in a television interview in 1969; his revelations briefly made headlines. At that time, however, the former colonial power was still in denial. Hueting received death threats; nothing changed. After a brief inquiry, prime minister Piet de Jong told parliament that the army had 'acted correctly' and there had been 'no such thing as systematic cruelty'. A law passed in 1971 made it impossible to prosecute the crimes committed twenty-five years earlier. But, as Van Reybrouck makes clear in *Revolusi*, which tells the story of that time:

> Unlawful violence was anything but a marginal phenomenon during the decolonization war. On the Dutch side, it was not limited to a few excesses at the bottom of the military ladder, but ordered and caused by officers in charge of platoons, companies and battalions. In Jakarta the high command tolerated and tacitly allowed it, the highest levels of the civil administration were aware of it, and the supreme judicial authorities did not prosecute it . . . Ultimate responsibility lay with the government and parliament in The Hague.

Half a century after Hueting first spoke out and seventy-five years after the crimes were committed, *Revolusi* became a bestseller when it was published in the Netherlands in 2020. In 2022, the decades of lies were finally discarded. Prime minister Mark Rutte apologised for 'systematic and widespread extreme violence from the Dutch side' and the 'consistent looking the other way' in past years.

———

America felt entitled to kill civilians in the name of fighting Communism in Vietnam. Washington also turned a blind eye to mass atrocities committed by others where that seemed expedient. 'They were careless people, Tom and Daisy,' F. Scott Fitzgerald wrote in *The Great Gatsby*. 'They smashed up things and creatures and then retreated back into their money or their vast carelessness.' That was a reasonable description of the way President Nixon and his Secretary of State, Henry Kissinger, treated Cambodia.

The last helicopter took off from the roof of the US embassy in the South Vietnamese capital, Saigon, in April 1975. But that did not mark the end of the regional apocalypse. In the previous few years, Nixon and Kissinger had authorised an initially secret carpet-bombing campaign in Cambodia that devastated the country and helped the rise of the Maoist Khmer Rouge rebels. Kissinger's Operation MENU, as the B-52 bombing raids were called, was broken down into Operations BREAKFAST, LUNCH, DINNER, SNACK and DESSERT. More than a hundred thousand civilians died as part of those military 'meals'. Even as the Americans made their final withdrawal from Vietnam, the Khmer Rouge seized power in the Cambodian capital, Phnom Penh.

As part of what came to be known as 'Year Zero', the Khmer Rouge emptied towns, created vast labour camps and carried out mass executions. In the next four years, almost two million – one in four of the population – were killed or died of starvation and disease in what is often described as genocide. Political mass murder as opposed to the targeting of an ethnic group is in fact excluded from the genocide convention, mostly because of pressure from Moscow (with an eye on its own crimes) in 1948. But Vietnamese and other minorities were also targeted in Cambodia; the Khmer Rouge liked to describe their victims as 'Khmer bodies with Vietnamese minds'.

Whatever the scale of the crimes, Western governments were not eager to confront the Khmer Rouge. The regime was opposed by Vietnam, which in turn was backed by Moscow. Vietnam's alignment with the Soviet Union became a reason to let the Khmer Rouge get away with mass murder. As Kissinger put it: 'They are murderous thugs, but we won't let that stand in our way.' President Jimmy Carter's National

Security Adviser Zbigniew Brzezinski took a similar line, describing Khmer Rouge leader Pol Pot as 'an abomination' who America could 'never support' – but adding, with an unsubtle wink: 'China could.'

Even after the Vietnamese forced the Khmer Rouge out in 1979, the regime was allowed to keep Cambodia's seat at the United Nations. Elizabeth Becker summed it up in *When the War was Over*: 'Central to the war – how the sides were drawn, who was punished, who was rewarded – was the international decision to ignore all allegations of genocide and massive human rights violations against the Khmer Rouge.' Early proposals for a war crimes tribunal were, in Becker's words, 'dismissed out of hand'. The United States only reversed its position fifteen years later.

In other contexts, too, geopolitics trumped human rights. On 11 September 1973 – 'the other 9/11', as it came to be known – Salvador Allende, Chile's elected president, was overthrown in a coup. Even as the presidential palace was being bombed, the socialist Allende proclaimed his belief in a different future. 'Much sooner than later,' he declared in a last live broadcast before his death, 'the great avenues will again be opened through which will pass free men to construct a better society.' Allende's optimism would eventually be justified, though it would take many years.

Chile's military rulers, led by General Augusto Pinochet, tortured and killed their opponents. Washington played a key role from the start. On a Sunday morning six days after the coup, Kissinger took a call from Nixon before heading out to watch his beloved Washington Redskins play. Their conversation makes short work of the official version that America was not involved in the coup:

NIXON: Nothing new of any importance, or is there?
KISSINGER: Nothing of very great consequence. The
        Chilean thing is getting consolidated and of
        course the newspapers are bleeding because
        a pro–Communist government has been
        overthrown.
NIXON: Isn't that something. Isn't that something.
KISSINGER: I mean, instead of celebrating – in the
        Eisenhower period we would be heroes.
NIXON: Well we didn't . . . as you know . . . Our hand
        doesn't show on this one, though.

Kissinger was impatient with aides who suggested the
regime's murderous policies might be worth raising in a
meeting with Pinochet's foreign minister, Admiral Patricio
Carvajal. 'I read the briefing for this meeting,' he complained
to Carvajal. 'And it was nothing but human rights.' Kissinger
assured Pinochet: 'We want to help, not undermine you. You
did a great service to the West in overthrowing Allende.'
Even after Chile's return to civilian rule in 1990, there
seemed to be little prospect that any of the crimes committed in the past seventeen years would be punished, not least
because of an amnesty law the junta had put in place before
giving up power. Those who had committed abuses showed
no regret. Manuel Contreras, former director of Dina,
Pinochet's secret police, declared: 'Those who still think war
is a sightly affair with pretty gentlemanly uniforms and white
gloves, with a declaration of war from the last century, are out
of date.' The playwright Ariel Dorfman described the painful
silence he found on return from exile.

Everywhere I turned, I saw victims and tormentors living
side by side, drinking at the same bars, eating at the same

restaurants, jostling each other on buses and streets – never acknowledging the pain and the guilt, not to themselves, not to anybody.

A similar silence existed across Latin America even as dictatorships began to crumble. The standard narrative was that the military had helped bring 'peace'. I still have one of the flyers handed out at military checkpoints in the Guatemalan highlands in 1985. A smiling soldier announces 'peace and progress with security', and apologises to travellers for inconvenience caused by the '*delincuentes subversivos*'. A regional guidebook included descriptions which hinted at the fate of those seen as 'subversive criminals': 'All houses have been burned between Nebaj, Chajul and Cotzal, no one lives in this area ... Although the weather is not very good at this altitude, the views of the Cuchumatanes mountains are spectacular.'

Equally spectacular was the scale of the crimes that had been committed against the indigenous Maya population. Armed soldiers rounded up villagers and burned houses. *Time* magazine photographer Robert Nickelsberg was invited to join the head of the armed forces, the French-trained General Benedicto Lucas García, on a helicopter trip in the region. He described the tactics:

They targeted the enemy with simple, deadly logic: Anyone running from our white Bell helicopter was either a guerrilla or a sympathizer ... [Lucas García] spotted a group of women running away from the approaching helicopter. He ordered the pilot to circle the farm below and bank the helicopter hard so the door gunners could have a better view. Then he yelled out the command to open fire, '*Dale! Dale!*' – 'Give it to them! Give it to them!'

The gunners blasted away in a hail of smoke and spent cartridges, the pilot turned and banked again, noisily circling above as civilians were cut down with the American-supplied M60 machine guns. Gen. Lucas García explained to us that since the *campesinos* (peasant farmers) had run away from the helicopter, they had to have been guilty.

Two hundred thousand were killed or disappeared in what became known as Guatemala's 'silent Holocaust'. The US ambassador praised Efraín Ríos Montt, the military leader who took power in a coup in 1982 and launched a scorched-earth operation against the insurgency, for bringing Guatemala 'out of the darkness and into the light'. Accountability for those crimes would take decades to achieve.

In Guatemala and most countries across the region, the prospects of accountability for the crimes committed seemed slim at this time. There was, however, one early exception. After a coup in Argentina in 1976 – officially, the 'Process of National Reorganisation' – anybody who criticised the military junta was labelled a 'terrorist' or 'terrorist sympathiser'. Tens of thousands were kidnapped, tortured and killed. Hundreds were thrown out of planes into the River Plate or the South Atlantic ('dropped like little ants', as one pilot later described it). The notorious death flights were not a South American invention: twenty years earlier, the French threw Algerians into the Mediterranean after dipping their feet in basins of wet cement: they liked to call their victims *crevettes Bigeard*, or Bigeard shrimps, named after a French commander. Now, *los desaparecidos*, 'the disappeared', became a deadly new noun in the dictionary.

The Mothers of the Plaza de Mayo, unable to find out anything about their missing children, enraged the generals by gathering week after week in the centre of Buenos Aires wearing kerchiefs embroidered with the names of their sons and daughters. Every Thursday at five in the afternoon, beginning in April 1977, the Mothers would meet on the square in front of the pink-painted presidential palace, the Casa Rosada. It was forbidden to meet in groups of more than three, so they walked silently round two by two. The women were harassed and arrested; some were murdered. Eventually, however, they and other opponents of the regime won.

As the military gave way to civilian rule in 1983, the generals gave themselves immunity, noting that all operations 'were executed in accordance with the plans approved and supervised by the appropriate superior commands of the armed forces', and therefore could not be prosecuted. That first amnesty law was struck down, partly as a result of the powerful *Nunca más* ('Never Again') report of 1984. The chair of the truth commission, novelist Ernesto Sabato, said the seven years of military rule had been the 'greatest and most savage tragedy in the history of Argentina'. Argentina's historic 'trial of the juntas' began in Buenos Aires in 1985. The eighty-five-year-old Jorge Luis Borges, who attended the trial, wrote: 'I do not believe in hell or heaven ... However, not to judge and not to condemn this crime would be to foster impunity and to become, in some sense, an accomplice.'

These remained dangerous times: prosecutors and judges alike faced bomb threats. The trial ended with life sentences for junta leader Jorge Videla and his key associates. For the moment, at least, it seemed to be a triumph for justice and for the victims of military rule, but those who opposed accountability still had the upper hand. There were renewed amnesties for General Videla and other military leaders which seemed to shut off the possibilities of justice for all time with what became known as the final full stop, the *punto final*. In fact, as

Videla and others would discover, this, too, was not the end. Justice was delayed, not cancelled. Their time would come.

In a range of different contexts, the old saying 'he's a son of a bitch, but at least he's our son of a bitch' was the implied motto as governments chose which crimes they would condemn or ignore. In the 1980s, the Iraqi leader Saddam Hussein was at war with Ayatollah Khomeini's Iran. He was the enemy of the West's enemy. That meant the US and others were ready to turn a blind eye to Saddam's crimes.

The Iraqi leader and his henchmen were not shy about their tactics. In 1987, Ali Hassan al-Majid, cousin of Saddam and secretary-general of the Northern Bureau of the ruling Ba'ath Party, detailed his plans for dealing with rebellious Kurds in the north. 'I will kill them all with chemical weapons!' al-Majid declared. 'Who is going to say anything? The international community? Fuck them!' Al-Majid, who would come to be known as Chemical Ali, carried out those threats. In the next year, Iraq would commit genocide.

Saddam was not the first to advocate using chemical weapons against the Kurds. In 1919, twenty years after the first Hague Convention which banned 'asphyxiating or deleterious gases', Britain's then war and air minister Winston Churchill declared himself 'strongly in favour' of using poison gas against 'uncivilised tribes' – including Kurds who rebelled in British-ruled Iraq. (Churchill said the 'most deadly' gases need not necessarily be used, only those which 'spread a lively terror'.)

Seventy years on, Churchill's threat was turned into reality. In 1988, as the Iran–Iraq war approached its end after eight years and half a million deaths, Saddam unleashed his Anfal ('spoils of war') campaign against the Kurds, with bombings, deportations, executions – and chemical weapons. The single worst attack at this time came on 16 March 1988 – twenty years to the day after America's acts of slaughter at My Lai – with a mustard gas and sarin attack on the town of Halabja, known as the 'city of poets', near the border with Iran. 'The gas had killed all natural life,' Kurdish cameraman Abbas Akbar later told Joost Hiltermann, author of *A Poisonous Affair*. 'I couldn't hear anything. No birds. There was absolutely no sound. Everything had died.' David Hirst of the *Guardian* reported: 'The skin of the bodies is strangely discoloured, with their eyes open and staring where they have not disappeared into their sockets . . . Here a mother seems to clasp her children in a last embrace, there an old man shields an infant from he cannot have known what.' Five thousand were killed. 'It was like the day of judgment,' a survivor said of that day. 'You stand before God.'

Iraq was a party to the Geneva Protocol of 1925, which bans the use of poison gas in warfare. Targeting civilians is in any case prohibited under international law. But America was willing to let Saddam off the hook. Five years earlier, Donald Rumsfeld, Reagan's special envoy for the Middle East, had brought to Baghdad a presidential gift of golden cowboy spurs for the Iraqi leader. Even after Halabja, Washington did not want to spoil what Saddam had described as 'the beautiful atmosphere between us'. Instead, US statements sought to muddy the waters by talking of chemical weapons 'on both sides', even suggesting that Iran might be responsible for most of the deaths at Halabja. From Washington's perspective, the aim was not to reveal but to conceal the truth. As Rick Francona, a US Defense Intelligence Agency analyst in Baghdad in 1988, later remembered: 'The Iraqis never told us that they intended to use nerve gas. They didn't have to. We already knew.'

Only after Saddam's invasion of Kuwait in 1990 and the Gulf War of 1991 did things begin to change. Kurds seized millions of documents from secret police and other buildings across northern Iraq. Fourteen tonnes of documents were transferred to the United States, where they formed part of a huge investigation conducted by Joost Hiltermann and colleagues at Human Rights Watch. Based on the documents, forensic on-the-ground research and hundreds of interviews, their *Genocide in Iraq* report concluded that between fifty and a hundred thousand people had been killed in the Anfal campaign and at Halabja.

Human Rights Watch and others tried to persuade governments to bring a case against Iraq at the International Court of Justice, arguing this would breathe life into the 'moribund' genocide convention and 'give pause to tyrannical regimes around the world'. Such a case would have been similar to those which Gambia and South Africa brought thirty years later against Myanmar and Israel respectively. Those early attempts were unsuccessful.

Fifteen years after the killings, everything would change. Washington became focused on the crimes that it had once been determined to ignore. In the lead-up to the Iraq war, Rumsfeld, who had once feted Saddam with golden spurs, was US Defense Secretary and keen to warn against the danger of Saddam 'using weapons of mass destruction against his own people and blaming it on us'. That, he said, would 'fit a pattern'. Rumsfeld's description of Saddam's cynical lies was accurate enough, as far as it went. The Iraqi leader had indeed been happy for his own atrocities to be blamed on others, most obviously at Halabja. But Rumsfeld's statement relied on people being unaware of what had come before: he omitted to mention that it was the United States which had facilitated or invented those lies.

I had my own brief encounter with the contradictions that such flexible ethics can create. In December 2002, as the drumbeats for an approaching war with Iraq grew more insistent, the British government published a dossier on the 'human cost of Saddam's policies'. It included the 1988 gassings at Halabja and quoted the *Genocide in Iraq* report in support of the case for invasion. I was UK director of Human Rights Watch at the time, so Rupert Murdoch's Fox News invited me into the London studio to comment.

The item began with images from Halabja. The presenter in New York encouraged me to agree that the horror of what we were looking at meant the prospective invasion of Iraq was a no-brainer. I agreed that the images were disturbing, and began to make the follow-up point that it was regrettable that the United States and others had been so eager to make sure Saddam didn't take the blame at the time of the genocide, when diplomatic, economic and legal pressures might all have been effective. I had been speaking for perhaps half a minute when the interviewer interrupted: 'I'm sorry, we've run into the satellite window, we'll have to end it there.' I asked the studio engineer afterwards if there was indeed an issue with the booked satellite time. 'No, no,' he said. 'They use that line when they don't like what they hear.'

The changed attitude to Saddam's crimes was obviously inconsistent and hypocritical. As one survivor put it: 'In 1988 they closed their eyes to Halabja because Saddam was the enemy of Iran. But now he's the enemy, and they are using my town as an excuse. We feel bitter, used, sickened.' It was also short-sighted. Two decades after Halabja, Saddam Hussein and Chemical Ali would be convicted in a US-led tribunal in Baghdad of crimes against humanity and genocide. But it was America which had first been so determined to ignore those same crimes.

*

From Chile to Cambodia, it seemed impunity was destined to remain the default. Nuremberg had become nothing but a distant memory. But the Halabja killings and the Anfal genocide were in some ways the last gasp for unchallenged impunity. New 'pests' were already working to ensure that the aspirations of Lauterpacht and Lemkin for the prosecution of those who committed crimes against humanity and genocide might at last become real. Terrible crimes would continue. From now on, though, there might also be consequences.

Chapter Three

'Everything is Going to Plan'

Yugoslavia, Rwanda (1991–2001)

Slobodan Milošević was in relaxed mood as he puffed on a cigarillo and leaned back into the sofa in his Knightsbridge hotel suite. It was August 1992, at the end of a global summit in London which was supposed to end the Bosnian war that had begun four months earlier.

I had spent the past couple of days vainly attempting to schedule a meeting with the Serbian leader, an elusive figure who rarely gave interviews. I had begun to accept it would never happen. But, as the conference ended and with nothing to lose, I turned up without an appointment at the president's hotel to try my luck one last time. I strolled with all the confidence I could muster past security and reception, went a few floors up to Milošević's suite – where Madonna once stayed, I was told – and claimed an appointment. Once I had got that far, nobody seemed to have sufficient interest or authority to throw me out. I waited. Eventually I was invited in to see the man himself.

Milošević, alone except for his bodyguards in the corner, was in good spirits. The conference had concluded with fine words about 'respect for the highest standards of individual rights and fundamental freedoms', 'total condemnation' of forcible expulsions, calls for 'compliance by all persons with their obligations under international humanitarian law', and more of the same. But, though the messages sounded strong, it all meant little in practice. Ahead of the conference, I met with Britain's foreign secretary Douglas Hurd, who told me of his hopes that the meeting would achieve 'peace with justice'; it didn't work out that way.

Milošević invited me to join him for a Scotch on the rocks. 'Why not?' he insisted when I initially refused. Feeling sullied by my willingness to accept his hospitality but relieved to be there, I took a tumbler of his whisky. I asked how he felt the conference had gone. Milošević exuded bonhomie. All had gone well. Any accusations were caused by misunderstandings. 'I think there must be some examples of this in every place – in England, too. But any violations of human rights are the subject of a penalty and not tolerated.'

The famously nationalistic Serbian leader explained: 'I strongly believe that nationalism has no part at the end of the twentieth century.' Then, after some back and forth on Bosnia and abuses in the Serb-ruled province of Kosovo, I asked the elephant-in-the-room question: what did he think about war crimes prosecutions, mentioned at the conference in the past two days? Some had accused Serb forces of committing crimes against humanity. The German foreign minister, Klaus Kinkel, even talked of genocide. In language reminiscent of the St James's Declaration fifty years earlier, Kinkel said: 'The community of nations will pursue all crimes no matter who has committed them. Let no one believe that these atrocities will be forgotten.'

Milošević was unfazed. Accountability for war crimes, he said, was an excellent idea. Indeed, 'If there is any citizen of Serbia who is involved in any crime, he will be the subject of a criminal prosecution, there is no doubt of that.' Then – tentatively, especially given that I was still drinking his whisky – I asked about his own role. Might he himself be prosecuted for war crimes one day? Milošević seemed astonished that I could suggest such a thing. 'We have a policy for peace. If anything stays the same, it is that. All our efforts in recent months have been oriented towards peace. I will not allow anything in my policies to be against peace.'

It was getting late. The bodyguards were restless, and so was their boss. Milošević's VIP police escort was waiting to take him to his plane for a midnight flight back to Belgrade. Milošević wondered if he would be permitted to fly through Austrian airspace, complaining that some countries made problems for him because of UN restrictions on flights to Serbia. And off he went, thus ending one of the more surreal meetings of my life.

I suspect that Milošević genuinely believed he would remain untouchable, despite all the war crimes that Serb and Bosnian Serb forces committed. Certainly, I did not imagine he would ever face justice. The conference in the Queen Elizabeth II Centre in Westminster was just across the road from Church House, where Robert Jackson and colleagues planned the Nuremberg indictments half a century earlier. But, despite Kinkel's fine-sounding words, there was little expectation that Nuremberg would be repeated, and there were plenty of precedents for looking the other way. I had asked the war crimes question only because the subject was in the air, not because I thought Milošević might ever end up in the dock. Only much later would it become clear how wrong both of us were.

Despite Milošević's talk about peace and human rights, there was no real question about what was happening in Bosnia at this time. The scale of the crimes was clear to anyone who was willing to see. There was, however, no will to respond. Politicians expressed regret, or organised humanitarian supplies, or – as at the London conference – expressed 'total condemnation'. And there it ended. In besieged Sarajevo, they talked of the UN peacekeepers as 'taxi drivers for the Serbs', shuttling politicians to and from unproductive peace talks in Geneva and elsewhere. On the desk in front of me is a copy of the Bosnian newspaper *Oslobodjenje* which I brought back to London after a visit to Sarajevo a few weeks before my meeting with Milošević. A courageous team of Bosnian Muslim ('Bosniak'), Serb and Croat journalists produced the paper in almost impossible circumstances out of a much-shelled building on the broad avenue in the Bosnian capital that became known as Snipers' Alley. Many of *Oslobodjenje*'s reporters lost their lives.

The paper's front-page cartoon shows world leaders throwing paper darts, with labels like 'declarations' and 'resolutions', from the hills around Sarajevo down onto the city. The politicians look pleased with the determination their paper darts convey. 'These declarations will make all the difference,' their satisfied expressions seem to say. The cartoon reminded me of a poem by the Polish poet Zbigniew Herbert, written under martial law in Communist Poland a decade earlier. 'I know they feel true compassion,' says the narrator of the timeless 'Report from a Besieged City'. After all, 'they send us flour sacks of comfort / lard and good counsel'. Bosnians recognised Herbert's description too well. They became used

to dodging bullets while receiving humanitarian aid, even as
the world looked elsewhere. A production of *Waiting for Godot*
directed by Susan Sontag in a besieged Sarajevo in 1993 – 'He
won't come this evening ... But he'll come tomorrow' – is
remembered in Bosnia to this day.

The British prime minister John Major talked of the Balkan
wars as 'age-old feuds and hatreds' which 'from time to
time break out'. But that wholly misunderstood the political
underpinning and desire for power that drove the conflict.
It was true that the wars in Yugoslavia did not come out of
nowhere. The strains on the multi-ethnic federation had been
endlessly discussed both before and after the death of Josip
Broz Tito, the country's long-term Communist leader, in
1980. After my first visit to Kosovo as a journalism student in
1982, I wrote of how recent riots sent 'shockwaves through
the entire federation'. At that point, though, few could have
imagined what was to come.

　　After 1945, Tito put in place a system under which each of
the federation's six constituent republics – Bosnia, Croatia,
Macedonia, Montenegro, Serbia and Slovenia – enjoyed
equal authority and a rotating leadership. (The province
of Kosovo, 90 per cent Albanian and belonging to Serbia,
did not form part of this Slavic carousel.) The system had
kept Yugoslavia more or less stable for forty years. But
Milošević, president of the largest republic, now argued the
Serbs had been short-changed. Croatia, Bosnia and other
republics had significant Serb minorities within their borders. As Communism melted away, Milošević promised he
would reclaim what he portrayed as Serbia's lost dignity and
authority.

　　By 1990, storm clouds were already gathering, following a
fiery nationalist speech by Milošević in Kosovo the previous

year. In a referendum in the small northern republic of
Slovenia in December that year, almost 90 per cent voted for
independence. Some already saw the still-existing Yugoslav
federation as mere history. A woman in the Slovene capital,
Ljubljana, told me regretfully but in a matter-of-fact tone:
'The sad thing is, it was a nice idea.' By spring 1991, scattered violence had begun. 'A nation at boiling point' and 'A
town just waiting to trigger a civil war' were headlines to
two of the pieces I wrote for the *Independent* after a visit in
April 1991, which talked of 'hundreds, probably thousands'
of deaths in a coming civil war. At the time, after decades of
peace in Europe, I could hardly believe what I was writing:
it still felt unthinkable. When I met Radovan Karadžić, the
bouffant-haired former psychiatrist and Bosnian Serb leader,
he warned: 'If there is a civil war, Serbs will gain victory.' I
feared what might come next, but felt Karadžić must surely
be grandstanding.

Even before the wars began, some argued for signs of
accountability that could help prevent the approaching bloodshed. Most visionary of all was the journalist Mirko Klarin,
who in May 1991 wrote an article in the Belgrade paper *Borba*
headlined 'Nuremberg now', arguing that a new body was
needed to help prevent future crimes:

Would it not be better if our big and small leaders were
made to sit in the dock instead of at the negotiating table?
And if, with the help of world-famous experts in international laws of war, we had a Nuremberg trial of our own,
no matter how small and modest? Not *when* 'this is all over',
but *instead* of whatever might soon befall us.

Few paid attention to Klarin's prophetic words. But the
descent into horror came soon afterwards. First there was a

short war in Slovenia. Then, two months after Klarin's call
for a new Nuremberg, violence began in Croatia. There were
massacres in the eastern town of Vukovar and elsewhere in
the months to come. Then, most brutally of all, Bosnia was
ripped apart.

As the war in Bosnia got under way in 1992, the country's
grandfatherly president, Alija Izetbegović, used an arresting
image to describe his country. He told me that Bosnia's
map was 'intermingled, like a painting by Jackson Pollock –
there are no ethnically pure regions'. Izetbegović was right.
Separating out the three main ethnic groups – 40 per cent
Bosniaks, 30 per cent Serbs, 20 per cent Croats – would be
impossible without bloodshed. What Bosnian Serb leaders
described as *etničko čišćenje* or 'ethnic cleansing' – tidying
Bosnia's chaotically Pollock-splattered ethnic map into neat,
separate blocks of identity – would soon form part of a deadly
new routine.

In April 1992, when roads into Sarajevo were still partly
open, I drove through the hills to the Bosnian capital, stopping off in Bijeljina. There had been killings in the town a
few days earlier. In the Krin Hotel, I found members of a
Serb paramilitary group, the Tigers. They were playing pool
and video games, Kalashnikovs draped over their shoulders
or propped on the floor beside their bulletproof vests.

The Tigers' leader, Arkan, who liked to pose with a pet
baby tiger, was already notorious for war crimes committed
in Croatia in the previous nine months. (Eight years later, he
would be machine-gunned to death in the lobby of the Inter-
Continental Hotel in Belgrade, apparently because he knew
too much.) Arkan's men told me they would stay in Bijeljina
'as long as is needed'. An award-winning photograph by Ron
Haviv which was used to illustrate one of my reports from

Bosnia at this time shows what Arkan and his forces felt was 'needed'. One of the Tigers, cigarette in hand, casually kicks a dying woman on the pavement, shot with her husband a few minutes earlier. (Haviv received death threats because of that powerful image, published in newspapers worldwide.) The Tigers killed around fifty people in the town. By the time that I arrived, many Muslims had already fled. Others hoped against hope. Samira, a medical student, described the impossible choice. 'We are afraid,' she told me. 'I want to stay, but I can't be cold-blooded about it. I know they might kill.'

Fear was everywhere. As I prepared to leave Sarajevo a few days later, a friend asked me to give a lift to her mother and her two children. In the hills outside the city, bearded armed men flagged the car down. 'Chetniks!' said the terrified woman – in other words, Serb nationalist forces. 'Where are you going?' Belgrade. 'What are your names?' The woman's name was obviously Muslim. 'What's happening in Sarajevo?' 'There's shooting,' my passenger whispered. 'Shooting? Who's shooting?' 'Everybody,' she breathed, desperate not to give an answer that might offend. As a foreigner, I was in no real danger. But I remember thinking, what if the militia demand that the woman and her grandchildren step out of the car? Civilian killings were already becoming common, as in Bijeljina and elsewhere. In the end, the men waved us on. But the sense of the gunmen's impunity remained with me. Even with my privileged passport, I had little power. Bosniak civilians had no power at all.

Within a couple of months, the noose around Sarajevo had tightened. The only way into the city was on UN flights bringing humanitarian supplies, where passengers were told to put on flak jackets as we landed. From the airport there was a high-speed drive into town, along a road notorious for its exposure to the Serb snipers. At the Holiday Inn, south-facing rooms were not recommended – they were open to the gunmen in the hills. I visited the hospital morgue, where a young girl lay on a slab; six years old, they said, though nobody knew her name. Her waxen expression meant she resembled a large doll, arms folded across her chest. The top of her head was missing, exploded by a Serb missile. The dead girl was wearing a pink T-shirt and flowery leggings; they reminded me of a pair that my five-year-old daughter liked to wear.

Tens of thousands of civilians lost their lives across Bosnia in the next three years. Sixteen hundred children were killed in Sarajevo alone. Even crossing the road or going to fetch water became a deadly risk. People sprinted across junctions to avoid the snipers. Shortly before my arrival in the city, twenty-six people were killed in a bread queue. Amir, who ran the nearby Café Ragusa with his sister, described the aftermath: 'When the fog and smoke lifted, there was just a mountain of people – like fresh meat. The blood was flowing like a stream, and I could hear screams.' Bad though things already were, Amir's prediction would turn out to be accurate: 'The worst is yet to come.' The mother of ten-year-old Ina Arnataulić wiped away angry tears as she remembered her daughter's question: 'What will I do if you are killed, Mama?'

In the countryside, Bosnian Serb authorities issued decrees which gave an indication of what was on the way. In Čelinac in northern Bosnia, instructions were published in July 1992 for Bosniaks in the town. Muslims were forbidden to:

- move around the town between 1600 and 0600 hours
- linger in the street, in catering facilities and other public places
- bathe in the Rivers Vrbanja and Jošavka, hunt and fish

- move or use cars
- gather in groups of more than three
- travel from their settlement to other towns without permission from the competent municipal authorities
- use communication systems apart from the post office telephone
- sell real estate and exchange flats without special permission from the municipal authorities

The instructions noted that Muslims were allowed to leave the town 'on condition that their departure is conducted in an organised fashion', in which case the authorities would 'ensure them safe passage'. Disobeying any of the rules would lead to being 'held accountable in accordance with current legal regulations'. By now, nobody could misunderstand the meaning. Just up the road from Čelinac were the detention camps of Omarska and Trnopolje, soon to become notorious. Across the country, Bosnian Serb forces committed rape, ethnic cleansing and genocide for the next three years.

So much happens in plain sight. A large part of Lemkin's landmark volume *Axis Rule* consists of decrees published by the occupying Nazi forces. Put together, those decrees – 'the imposition of the national pattern of the oppressor', in Lemkin's words – persuaded him of the need for his newly defined crime to be named. Fifty years later, Lemkin's word would have consequences in a court for the first time, when the Čelinac rules would help bring perpetrators to account for genocide.

Interviewing Radovan Karadžić was surreal. The Bosnian Serb leader liked to say that there were no snipers in the Serb-occupied hills around Sarajevo. He knew, and I knew – and we both knew that we both knew – that was a lie. But he insisted the ethnic cleansing of Muslims was all done humanely. 'We let them go,' Dr Karadžić said with a smile. 'With their luggage, and everything.'

Višegrad in eastern Bosnia was one of many places where atrocities took place. Nerma Jelačić, a teenager at the time, remembers how quickly the town was submerged in political darkness. She and her friends saw New Year 1992 in with cheerful normality. 'I didn't even know who was Serb or Muslim,' as Nerma remembers now. Then, a few months after the New Year celebrations, she was woken by the light and sound of crackling flames. Through the bedroom blinds, she saw neighbours' homes were ablaze. Many Muslims were detained in the days to come. Some came back beaten and bruised; some were never heard from again. At one point, Nerma and her family and thousands of others were taken to a football stadium, where men were separated from the women and children. (For a fifteen-year-old in a previously peaceful country, the dark significance of that moment was not immediately obvious; Nerma remembers her only thought was: That's a bit stupid and sexist.) Only a chance intervention from a Yugoslav army officer meant nobody was killed that day.

In the weeks that followed, bodies piled up near the town's famous Ottoman-era bridge; people had their throats cut and were tossed into the river. Nerma's art teacher was on the 'crisis committee' which oversaw the killings. Several of her relatives were killed. Bosnian Serb paramilitary forces ('charcoal-faced thugs', as Nerma remembers them) under the command of former policeman Milan Lukić burned hundreds alive in their homes. A local hotel became a recreation centre for Serb militias; hundreds of women and girls would be raped there in the next three years.

Those crimes in Nerma's home town would influence her work – not just in Bosnia and the former Yugoslavia, but investigating and holding to account war criminals in other conflict zones, too. At this time, however, it still seemed impossible to imagine there would be any consequences. Politicians had for years used the phrase 'Never again!' on the occasion of Holocaust anniversaries and to accompany the laying of wreaths. But time had drained the words of meaning. From Cambodia to Halabja, the injunction had been ignored. David Rieff summed up the dark absurdity of the phrase in his *Slaughterhouse: Bosnia and the Failure of the West*: 'We know what "Never again!" means. "Never again" simply means "Never again will Germans kill Jews in Europe in the 1940s." That's all it means.'

Changes were on the way, however, which might finally give meaning to the phrase. In May 1993, nine months after Milošević talked so enthusiastically in his London hotel suite about his love of peace, the UN Security Council created the International Criminal Tribunal for the former Yugoslavia. All fifteen Security Council members voted in favour of this first new war crimes tribunal since Nuremberg and Tokyo. In theory at least, the importance of justice was agreed by all.

One reason for the apparent unanimity was, perhaps, that politicians did not expect the tribunal to make any difference. Nor were they wrong about that – not least because they themselves had set it up that way. The tribunal's existence enabled politicians to give the impression of taking action, while in fact doing little. As one official told me later, the court was little more than a 'fig leaf' at the time of its creation. Antonio Cassese, the court's first president, made the same point: 'The Security Council thought we would never become operational. We had no budget. We had nothing. Zero.'

In 1994, one single war crimes suspect was arrested in Munich, after being spotted by former inmates of a Serb camp. Germany – which over the years had become one of the most committed supporters of global justice – delivered Dušan Tadić to The Hague. But that was it. It was not just that almost nobody was arrested. One reason for creating a war crimes court was to deter future crimes. Judged by that yardstick, the International Criminal Tribunal for the former Yugoslavia seemed to have failed miserably. The worst single episode in the three-year Bosnian war, the massacres in and around the town of Srebrenica in eastern Bosnia in 1995, took place two years after the Tribunal's creation. So much, it would seem, for deterrence.

In 1993, the UN Security Council had declared Srebrenica and other Bosnian towns to be 'safe areas'. As one resident of the town told me years later: 'I thought everybody should celebrate. It was like being born a second time.' Now, as Serb forces closed in on Srebrenica in July 1995, the phrase 'safe area' was as fatally vacuous as 'never again'. UN headquarters failed to send planes that could bomb Serb positions, as Dutch peacekeepers requested; one request was refused because it was submitted on the wrong form. The peacekeepers argued with Bosnian Serb forces. Then, as seen in Jasmila Žbanić's powerful Oscar-nominated film *Quo Vadis, Aida* – a story of terror, horror and international failure – they abandoned those they had pledged to protect.

The Serbs who slaughtered their Muslim neighbours in the days to come did so with a literal vengeance. General Ratko Mladić told his men: 'We give this town to the Serb nation . . . The time has come to take revenge on the Turks.' (The reference harked back to the period of Ottoman rule, when many in Bosnia converted to Islam. Bosniaks, like the Serbs, are ethnically Slav.) Troops handed out sweets to children even as the executions of their brothers and fathers got under way. Serb forces were unashamed in documenting their crimes. 'We're doing a little filming now,' a cameraman says to those who are about to be killed. At one point, the slaughter is briefly interrupted because a camera has run out of battery. In another haunting scene, a Bosniak shouts across the fields to urge his son and those with him to emerge from their hiding places in the woods. 'Come down, Nermin!' Ramo Osmanović cries, as his captors film him and tell him what to say. 'There is nothing to fear!' The bodies of both father and son were later found in mass graves. Eight thousand men and boys were killed in and around Srebrenica.

General Bernard Janvier, the French commander of UN peacekeeping in Bosnia, is generally reckoned to have been more responsible than any other individual for the deadly institutional decisions taken at this time. As the Pulitzer-winning reporter David Rohde put it in *Endgame*: 'More than any other UN official, [Janvier] betrayed the people of Srebrenica.' As so often, failure brought its own rewards. Just ahead of the first anniversary of the genocide, Janvier was made a Grand Officer of the Légion d'Honneur, one of the highest decorations of the French state.

The world's failure to respond was catastrophic. But that obvious failure also became a belated wake-up call. Bosnian Serb bases were targeted, forcing an end to the three-year siege of Sarajevo and paving the way for talks. In December 1995, all sides signed a peace deal at an airbase near Dayton, Ohio, marking an official end to the war. Even now, though, that didn't seem to bring accountability any closer – at least for those at the top. A few months after Dayton, Milošević authorised the delivery to The Hague of twenty-four-year-old Dražen Erdemović, who, racked by guilt, had sought out a French journalist to confess his part in the Srebrenica massacres. Erdemović was – to use the famous phrase from Nuremberg – only obeying orders. Like some of the young

Russian conscripts who would go on trial in Ukraine three decades later, Erdemović apologised profusely. 'They took them to the meadow. So we started shooting at those people … To be honest, I simply felt sick.' Accepting he was a 'mere footsoldier', the court concluded: 'He voiced his feelings, but realised that he had no choice in the matter: he had to kill or be killed.' Erdemović was jailed for five years. The bigger players remained free.

As part of the Dayton Agreement, the UN created a multinational 'stabilisation force' with thirty thousand Nato and Russian peacekeeping troops all across Bosnia. Officially, their orders were to arrest war criminals. Unofficially, their orders were to do the opposite. Graham Blewitt, a plain-speaking Australian who was deputy chief prosecutor of the Tribunal almost from the beginning, remembered afterwards how his request for the Nato-led force to make arrests had 'fallen on deaf ears'. The reason, he said, was simple: 'There was a policy: no apprehension under any circumstances.' In 1996, Louise Arbour, the quietly determined Canadian chief prosecutor, demanded Nato commanders arrest suspects in accordance with their obligations; that didn't happen.

In the first years after Dayton, Radovan Karadžić and his bodyguards liked to travel around Republika Srpska, the Bosnian Serb entity, in his distinctive black Audi A8 limousine. International peacekeepers literally looked the other way: on one occasion, Karadžić passed through six checkpoints in a single day. Troops admitted their orders were to 'steer clear' of the indicted leader. See no evil, prosecute no evil was, in effect, the new mantra. All of this, in the name of 'stability'.

A courageous Serb journalist highlighted the gap between ambitious words and deliberate inaction. Foča in

south-eastern Bosnia was notorious for the atrocities committed there. One of those held most responsible was Janko
Janjić, whose face was on 'Wanted' posters across Bosnia.
And yet, when Gordana Igrić visited Foča for the CBS programme *Public Eye*, she and producer Randall Joyce found
Janjić within a couple of hours. Indeed, he came and introduced himself. For a price, he was happy to confess to his
war crimes. 'Everything for five thousand Deutschmarks.
And you can tape me.' (Janjić didn't know they were already
recording him with a hidden camera.)

All the while, Nato soldiers sat chatting in the sunshine on
the café terrace next door. The French commanding officer in
Foča explained in an interview how hard it was to track down
war crimes suspects: 'Of course these people are hidden. It is
difficult – I've never found one.' Then, confronted with the
fact that the CBS team had found Janjić so easily, the hapless
officer blurted out the obvious truth: 'We must have good
relations with the population and not shock them.' Better, in
other words, for an indicted rapist and killer to walk freely in
the town he had terrorised than for the peacekeepers' 'good
relations' with Bosnian Serbs to be disrupted. Igrić received
death threats after the CBS report was broadcast; but change
was at last on the way.

Janjić's boasts for money suggested he was as confident as
Milošević had been that he would never face justice. Karadžić,
too, described the tribunal as 'ridiculous'. But the appointment
in 1997 of Robin Cook as Britain's new foreign secretary,
promising foreign policy 'with an ethical dimension', marked
a change of gear, as did the commitment of President Clinton's
Secretary of State, Madeleine Albright, who lived through the
Nazi occupation of Czechoslovakia as a child.

Back in 1995, General Radislav Krstić, military commander at Srebrenica, clearly believed there was no chance he

would be held to account. An intercepted exchange between
Krstić and Colonel Dragan Obrenović laid things out in plain
language:

> KRSTIĆ: Kill them all in turn. Fuck their mothers!
> OBRENOVIĆ: Everything is going to plan.
> KRSTIĆ: Don't leave a single one alive! Do not leave
>   anyone alive!
> OBRENOVIĆ: Everything is going according to plan,
>   everything.

Three years later, US troops arrested Krstić in a dramatic
ambush involving a spike mat and a stun grenade as he travelled along roads where he thought he was safe. The above
exchange would be played at the war crimes tribunal in The
Hague, where I saw him in the dock before his conviction
for genocide in 2001.

Six years after the creation of the tribunal, indictments
reached the top. In 1999, long-simmering violence in Kosovo
finally exploded. The explosion had been a long time coming;
it was in Kosovo that Milošević gave the nationalist speech
which helped bring him to power a decade earlier. Tensions
had grown steadily. As I wrote when I visited the province in
spring 1998: 'Another Balkan war is on the way . . . There is a
general expectation here – much stronger than ever before –
that Kosovo is on the edge of conflagration.' One Albanian
told me then: 'We live like dead people. We have nothing.
How can this go on?' The violence worsened, including
the massacre of forty-five Albanians, aged from fourteen to
ninety-nine, in the village of Račak in January 1999.

Prosecutor Louise Arbour arrived to investigate, but Serb
forces turned her back at the border. Kosovo peace talks

collapsed, and Nato airstrikes began. Serb forces killed thousands of Albanians in massacres; hundreds of thousands were driven or fled across the border into Macedonia. In May 1999, two months into the war, Arbour unveiled the indictment of Milošević for crimes against humanity, in connection with the ongoing killings and deportations. An arrest warrant had been issued for a serving head of state; the possibilities of international justice were changing as never before.

In July 1999, two months after the indictment and a month after the airstrikes ended with Milošević's defeat, I reported from Serbia on demonstrations against him across the country. Milošević claimed the Hague indictments were to punish him for his courage in standing up for the nation. For many Serbs, however, he was now a millstone around the country's neck. At a protest in Kragujevac in central Serbia, Silvana, a thirty-six-year-old secretary, echoed what others around her were saying: 'Milošević must simply go,' she told me. 'He just destroyed our country – and made us the worst country.'

A year later, presidential elections took place. Milošević was defeated, though he denied the result. For the next two weeks, huge crowds demanded recognition of the opposition victory. A friend in neighbouring Montenegro helped me slip into Belgrade on the overnight train, enabling me to witness the extraordinary scenes on 5 October 2000, when roads into Belgrade were jammed with cars and buses filled with people laughing and hooting their horns in celebration of a victory they believed would soon be theirs. The protesters' favourite slogan during those days was '*Gotov je!*' He's finished!' They were right: the end was near. As his own police deserted him, Milošević announced he had 'just received' information that his challenger had won. He would, he promised, return to political life soon.

It didn't work out that way. Shortly after 3 a.m. on 1 April

2001, Serbian police arrested Milošević in his villa on Užicka Street in the diplomatic district of Dedinje in Belgrade. It was almost straightforward, apart from Milošević's daughter wildly firing her pistol and narrowly missing one of the arresting party. (Both of Milošević's parents and an uncle had all committed suicide, so taking him alive was by no means seen as a given.) Endgame was now approaching.

A few weeks earlier, I had visited the International Criminal Tribunal for the former Yugoslavia that was awaiting the moment when the Serbian leader might be sent from Belgrade to The Hague. In storage rooms behind locked doors, rows of box files bore titles like 'Slobodan Milošević: statements in favour of deportations' and 'Slobodan Milošević: statements in favour of killings'. 'This tribunal should not be an alibi,' Switzerland's outspoken Carla Del Ponte, Arbour's successor as chief prosecutor, told me. 'It's important that powerful people cannot go unpunished. That's why it's important that Milošević should be transferred.' Soon enough he was. Two months later Milošević was flown from his prison cell in Belgrade to The Hague, still insisting 'This is an abduction!'

A former head of state would now be obliged to answer in court for his alleged crimes. It was, said Carla Del Ponte, 'the most powerful demonstration that nobody is above the law or beyond the reach of international justice'. Milošević died behind bars in 2006, awaiting judgment on charges of crimes against humanity and genocide. By this time, dozens of other perpetrators in the wars in Yugoslavia had been convicted.

Yet two of the main suspects remained at liberty. Radovan Karadžić and Ratko Mladić, who had lived almost in plain sight for two years after Dayton, had gone underground for the previous nine years. There had been creative attempts at arrest, including (as described by Julian Borger in *The*

Butcher's Trail, his account of the long search for accountability) a man in a gorilla suit who was supposed to confuse Karadžić's driver on the mountain roads. None came to anything. After years of no results, many were sceptical that either man would ever face justice. Eventually, however, their time came. Karadžić, sporting a ponytail and bushy white beard, had taken on a new identity as Dragan Dabić, an alternative healer who claimed to be able to rejuvenate the sluggish sperm of infertile men with a laying-on of hands. The quiet life of Dabić *né* Karadžić came to an end when a plainclothes policeman approached him on a Belgrade bus in 2008:

POLICEMAN: Dr Karadžić?

KARADŽIĆ: No, it's Dragan Dabić.

POLICEMAN: No, it's Radovan Karadžić.

KARADŽIĆ: Are your superiors aware of what you are doing?

POLICEMAN: Yes, fully.

In 2016, Karadžić, who told the court in The Hague that Srebrenica was 'a myth', was found guilty of crimes against humanity and genocide, and jailed for forty years (later increased to life).

And finally, Mladić. For many years he had a phalanx of guards, as well as a driver, a cook and a waiter. In 2011, his freedom ended too. An old man in a black baseball cap was found hiding behind the door of a farmhouse belonging to Mladić's cousin north of Belgrade. The exchange was brief:

'Who are you?'

'You have found who you are looking for.'

Boris Tadić, the Serbian president, said the arrest was needed both for reconciliation and for 'the moral dignity of our country'. In 2007, the International Court of Justice had ruled Serbia was in breach of the genocide convention, including for the failure to deliver Mladić to the Yugoslavia tribunal. In 2017 Mladić, like Karadžić, was found guilty of crimes against humanity and genocide, and jailed for life.

Others who had enjoyed impunity for many years found their time came to an end, too. Janko Janjić, the self-confessed rapist-murderer from Foča, blew himself up to avoid facing trial. Others, however, answered for their crimes.

Nerma Jelačić, who as a teenager escaped the terror in Višegrad, went on to become Bosnia director of the Balkan Investigative Reporting Network (created by Gordana Igrić, who interviewed Janjić while peacekeepers looked the other way). She helped track down Lukić, the killer from Višegrad. Lukić was arrested in Argentina and delivered to The Hague, where he was convicted of crimes against humanity in 2009. For war criminals in Bosnia and around the world, impunity was no longer a given.

———

The wars in the former Yugoslavia were not the only example of unspeakable violence unleashed by ruthless leaders during these years. As in the Balkans, the mass killings in Rwanda in 1994 — which began at the same time as South Africa's historic first free elections — were largely ignored until it was too late. Even as the worst killing was already under way, many governments were united in their eagerness to find excuses *not* to react.

A few did their best to prevent the nightmare. In January 1994, Roméo Dallaire, Canadian commander of the small UN force in Rwanda, learned of secret arms caches and death lists that had been drawn up in the capital, Kigali. He cabled UN headquarters in New York about his intentions to seize weapons and head off the murderous conspiracy, signing off with his old brigade motto: *'Peux ce que veux. Allons-y!'* – 'Where there's a will, there's a way. Let's go!' There was, however, no will, and therefore no way. Dallaire was forbidden to act and was slapped down when he appealed that decision. Rwandan activist Monique Mujawamariya wrote in March of the threat of 'an instantaneous, carefully prepared operation' and of the 'carnage which is to come'. The regime described her as 'a bad patriot who deserved to die'.

The mass slaughter of those whom the Rwandan Hutu government described as Tutsi 'cockroaches', along with Hutus who opposed the killings, began on 7 April 1994. Prime minister Agathe Uwilingiyimana, one of Africa's first women leaders, was among the first to be murdered. Monique Mujawamariya was on the phone to her friend Alison Des Forges of Human Rights Watch when the killers knocked at her door. Mujawamariya hung up the phone, telling Des Forges, 'Please take care of my children. I don't want you to hear this.' Miraculously, Mujawamariya survived after hiding in the roof of her house, and managed to travel to the United States to lobby the administration there.

But the politicians did not want to hear. Madeleine Albright told Mujawamariya, in response to her description of the genocide: 'Monique, that's not my struggle, that's your struggle. I have to do everything I can so that the decisions that are taken are to my country's advantage.' More than half a million would be murdered in the next three months. Ghanaian peacekeepers risked and lost their lives to protect Rwandans; Dallaire reckons their courage saved tens of thousands of lives. But the permanent members of the UN Security Council were resolved to do nothing, even as the mass killing of Tutsis

continued – close-up killing of neighbours, using machetes
and other farm tools. Alison Des Forges would later describe
the landscape of apocalypse in *Leave None to Tell the Story*, her
landmark account of the genocide:

> The sweetly sickening odor of decomposing bodies hung
> over many parts of Rwanda ... at Nyarabuye in eastern
> Rwanda, where the cadaver of a little girl, otherwise intact,
> had been flattened by passing vehicles to the thinness of
> cardboard in front of the church steps; on the shores of idyl-
> lic Lake Kivu in western Rwanda, where pieces of human
> bodies had been thrown down the steep hillside; and at
> Nyakizu in southern Rwanda, where the sun bleached
> fragments of bone in the sand of the schoolyard and, on a
> nearby hill, a small red sweater held together the ribcage of
> a decapitated child.

Smaller, non-permanent members of the UN Security
Council like New Zealand and the Czech Republic called for
action. But, like Czechoslovakia in 1938, Rwanda was treated
as (to quote British prime minister Neville Chamberlain at
that time) a 'quarrel in a faraway country between people
of whom we know nothing'. The Czech ambassador, Karel
Kovanda, complained that the Council's approach was like
'wanting Hitler to reach a ceasefire with the Jews'. British and
American diplomats rebuked him. The British ambassador
insisted the Security Council would be 'a laughing stock' if
it talked of genocide.

There followed what Samantha Power, in her Pulitzer-
winning *A Problem from Hell: America and the Age of Genocide*,
described as the 'two-month dance to avoid the g-word'. The
reluctance to call the crime by its name was in some respects a
compliment to the perceived power of Lemkin's convention.

One US memo warned: 'Be careful. Legal at State was worried about this yesterday – genocide finding could commit [the US government] to actually "do something".'

Commitments that the 'pest Lemkin' had persuaded governments to build into the 1948 convention now made America fearful of the obligations it had finally agreed to just a few years earlier, in 1988. If the United States and other governments acknowledged what was happening in Rwanda, they would be obliged to take action for the 'prevention and suppression' of genocide, as Lemkin always insisted. The governments did *not*, however, wish to take any action. Therefore, with impeccably brutal logic, they must refuse to acknowledge genocide. As the official instructions summarised it, US diplomats were 'not authorized to agree to the characterization of any specific incident as genocide or to agree to any formulation that indicates that all killings in Rwanda are genocide'.

A State Department spokesperson tied herself in knots as she gamely attempted to follow her bosses' instructions to dodge Lemkin's word. Two months into the killing, Christine Shelly acknowledged: 'We have every reason to believe that acts of genocide have occurred in Rwanda.' But, she continued: 'Clearly not all of the killings that have taken place in Rwanda are killings to which you might apply that label.' Reuters journalist Alan Elsner followed up: 'How many acts of genocide does it take to make genocide?' 'Alan, that's just not a question that I'm in a position to answer.'

Even the simplest actions were blocked. Hate radio was a central part of the genocide. The broadcasts of Radio Mille Collines directed killers in real time. Some US officials proposed jamming the broadcasts, which would send a strong message to the killers and could have saved lives. The Pentagon decreed, however, that at $8,500 an hour jamming was too expensive. An official reached for the gun lobby's favourite phrase when he rebuked deputy assistant secretary of state Prudence Bushnell for her supposed naivety in wanting to block the purveyors of hate: 'Pru, radios don't kill people. *People* kill people.'

Eventually, politicians could no longer look the other way. In July 1994, the UN Security Council called for a commission of inquiry to look into 'possible acts of genocide'. Then, once the killing was over, Rwanda became the issue that everybody cared about – the next subject for 'never again'. In November, the UN Security Council voted to create the International Criminal Tribunal for Rwanda, the second new international war crimes tribunal in two years. Those sponsoring the resolution included Russia, as well as Britain, France and the United States. The tribunal would share its headquarters with the Yugoslavia war crimes tribunal in The Hague, and its trials would take place in Arusha in Tanzania. From now on those responsible for the worst atrocities would, perhaps, be held to account.

In the years to come, politicians half-apologised for their failures on Rwanda, while continuing to insist that it really wasn't their fault. President Clinton, who had received regular and detailed updates from the beginning of the genocide, told Rwandans in 1998 he 'didn't fully appreciate' what was happening at the time. (As presidential candidate Clinton explained to President George Bush in 1992: 'If the horrors of the Holocaust taught us anything, it is the high cost of remaining silent and paralyzed in the face of genocide.') A sign on President Harry Truman's Oval Office desk proclaimed 'The buck stops here'. Clinton took the opposite approach, suggesting in effect that he had only been obeying orders. He said he would always regret 'that Rwandan thing'. But he blamed the failures on 'the people that were bringing these decisions to me'.

Over the next few years, dozens of key *génocidaires* were convicted at the Arusha tribunal, including prime minister Jean Kambanda and Théoneste Bagosora, chief architect of the genocide. Ferdinand Nahimana, historian and co-founder of the Mille Collines radio and television network, was convicted of inciting genocide. (There were precedents for this: Julius Streicher, publisher of the hate-filled *Der Stürmer* newspaper, was convicted at Nuremberg for crimes against humanity.)

In 1998, fifty years after Lemkin's convention, came the world's first conviction for genocide. The trial of Jean-Marie Akayesu, mayor of the commune of Taba, was historic in other respects, too. Rwandan women testified how they were subjected to repeated gang rape as Akayesu looked on. Those crimes were not initially included in the indictments. It took a South African woman judge, Navi Pillay – later UN High Commissioner for Human Rights – to focus on sexual violence as a crime against humanity. The Akayesu case was the first time mass rape and sexual violence were recognised as a means of committing genocide. 'From time immemorial, rape has been regarded as spoils of war,' said Pillay. 'Now it will be considered a war crime . . . Rape is no longer a trophy of war.'

Critics claimed the Rwanda tribunal was too expensive and convicted too few people for the money spent – a billion dollars for sixty trials. It was always going to be challenging to prosecute all the crimes committed when three quarters of the Tutsi population had been killed. In response, Rwanda created informal *gacaca* courts – literally 'justice on the grass' – which convicted more than a million people in a decade. *Gacaca* trials, based on the principles of community truth-telling and bearing witness, were widely criticised by defendants and accusers alike. Many argued that the process perpetuated divisions it was supposed to heal, rather than paving the way for restorative justice. Some said that the process became so politicised that it created collective guilt for all Hutus. Its defenders argued it was better than nothing.

But the problems of equality of justice were not just a problem with the *gacaca* trials. Paul Kagame, who has been Rwanda's leader for the past thirty years, was determined to exclude crimes committed by his own Tutsi forces from investigation by the war crimes tribunal in Arusha, even though his Rwandan Patriotic Front stood accused of committing massacres of its own. Carla Del Ponte, who had a dual role as prosecutor of the Rwanda as well as the Yugoslavia tribunal, later described how Kagame 'screamed' at her in 2002 for daring to investigate crimes by his forces, too. As Del Ponte remembered it: 'I admit that at times I can be gruff. But on this occasion I was reserved to a fault, almost reticent. It was President Kagame who launched into a diatribe.' The UN Security Council sided with Kagame and voted to relieve Del Ponte of her Rwandan responsibilities. The official explanation was that overseeing two tribunals was too much for one person, but the Security Council now saw Del Ponte as a difficult troublemaker.

Yet again, governments refused to acknowledge that picking and choosing which crimes you are willing to address can never be a recipe for stability. A year before the confrontation between Del Ponte and Kagame, I met Prudentienne Seward, a Rwandan survivor who lost dozens of Tutsi relatives in the genocide and who herself came close to death many times. She told me: 'They made us wait in line, they killed people, and then they put the bodies in the hole.' Then, as the genocide came to an end, her Hutu mother and her sister were both killed by Kagame's 'liberating' forces. Rwandan diplomats rebuked and threatened Seward for publicly raising such issues. But, she said, 'You can't just put soil on the volcano. If you do that, one day it will explode.'

That instability remains. Alison Des Forges, my late and much-missed Human Rights Watch colleague who had done more than anybody to press for a stronger response to the genocide in 1994, was banned from Rwanda in the months before her death in 2009 because she called for crimes on both sides to be addressed. Kagame's government harasses and kills its critics, as described in Michela Wrong's *Do Not Disturb: The Story of a Political Murder and an African Regime Gone Bad*. And yet, at a breakfast with Kagame in New York that I attended when I was UN advocacy director at Human Rights Watch, every question from government representatives in the room was a variation on the theme of 'Mr President, how do you succeed in being such a brilliant leader?' In 2020, Paul Rusesabagina, Schindler-style saviour of Tutsis as seen in the film *Hotel Rwanda*, was kidnapped and tortured for his later criticism of the regime. Wrong received death threats when her book was published in 2021. Governments remain shy of criticising Kagame, even today. Just as Benjamin Netanyahu likes to describe prosecutors or politicians who criticise Israel's crimes as antisemitic, so Kagame argues his critics must be 'genocide deniers'. In elections in 2024, Kagame gained '99 per cent' of the vote.

Meanwhile, prosecutions continue, including in France. (There is some irony in this: in 2021, a report commissioned by President Macron talked of France's 'overwhelming' responsibilities in connection with its support for the Francophone Hutu regime at the time of the genocide.) In 2023, a former Rwandan police chief was arrested in South Africa for genocide. Fulgence Kayeshima said: 'I have been waiting a long time to be arrested.'

*

The impact of the Yugoslavia and Rwanda tribunals was significant. The creation of two war crimes courts which prosecuted genocide meant the practical significance of Lemkin's legacy could be seen for the first time. But the two temporary 'ad hoc' tribunals also exposed a gap. How could and should crimes against humanity and genocide in conflict zones around the world be addressed more widely? Even as the work of the new tribunals got under way, some were already working to create a universal forum for prosecuting war crimes. An impossible idea would soon become real.

Chapter Four

'An Idea Whose Time has Come'

International Criminal Court, Pinochet, Charles Taylor, Hissène Habré (1998–2016)

As Russia and east Europe editor of the *Independent*, it was one of the privileges of my life to witness and report from Budapest, Vilnius, Warsaw, Tallinn, Berlin, Prague and across the region on the 'bonfire of the certainties' of 1989. The revolutions of that year did not come out of a clear blue sky. As I described the growing rumbles in my introduction to a two-page analysis in the *Independent* in January: 'The goalposts are on the move . . . All bets are off.' The changes that engulfed the continent in the next twelve months were, however, astonishing by any measure.

One after another, ninepins fell. In June, I reported from

Poland on elections where 99 per cent of the freely elected seats went to the Solidarity opposition, whose birth against the odds I had witnessed when living in Kraków in 1980. In 1981, the Polish Communist Party leader, General Wojciech Jaruzelski, had put tanks on the streets to stop change. He seemed to have swept opposition under the carpet. But, as I noted in an article written ten months after the declaration of martial law, his problem was how to remain on his feet as the carpet writhed under him. In the next few years, Poland's unloved rulers never quite succeeded in staying upright. Western politicians treated Solidarity as a mere historical footnote, defeated by tanks. In reality – to quote Yeats on Ireland's rebellion against British colonial rule, seventy years earlier – all had changed, changed utterly.

Adam Michnik, one of the country's leading opposition figures, wrote from his prison cell in 1985: 'What I saw after my release [for a brief period in 1984] exceeded not just my expectations but even my dreams.' Michnik predicted that Poland would emerge 'sooner or later, but I think sooner . . . on to the bright square of freedom'. Michnik was right: the continuing pressures from below led to Solidarity being re-legalised less than four years after he wrote those words. As strike-leader-turned-president Lech Wałęsa later told me: 'We finished off what Lenin promised to do but never achieved. The working class caused the system to change, and ruled.'

When I met Jaruzelski a few days after the June election, he admitted for the first time that the humiliating results meant the Communists were now in danger of losing power, despite having carefully fixed the rules to exclude such an outcome. In July, Michnik agreed to write a guest column for the *Independent*, summarised in the headline to my story that day about what until now had seemed so unthinkable: 'Solidarity states terms to form a government.' In Warsaw in

August, I watched from the gallery of the Polish parliament as MPs gave a standing ovation to the first non-Communist prime minister since 1945.

One day earlier, two million joined hands in a human chain that stretched for four hundred miles across the Baltic states of Estonia, Latvia and Lithuania, demanding restoration of the sovereignty that Moscow had stolen half a century earlier. For a film I made about the growing prospects for Baltic independence, I asked Estonia's deputy prime minister Edgar Savisaar if he wasn't frightened of Russian tanks. He pointed to the example of Poland and gave a simple answer: 'Nowadays, tanks can solve nothing.' He and others across the region would soon be proved right.

In Leipzig on 9 October 1989, on one of the most extraordinary evenings of my life, I witnessed peaceful protesters force a climbdown by the East German regime which days earlier had publicly hinted at a Tiananmen-style massacre ('if need be, with weapons in the hand'). The authorities hoped the threats meant everybody would be too scared to come out for the scheduled weekly protest. The opposite happened: many more came out that Monday evening than ever before. Initially, with a lump of dread in my stomach, I hid in an archway where I reckoned I could stay safe from the expected shooting. But tens of thousands of Leipzigers, chanting 'No violence!', refused to hide. It soon became clear that their courage had achieved a historic U-turn. Despite the trucks of armed militias I saw before the march began, despite the clearing of hospital wards for expected casualties, the protest went ahead peacefully in ways that the demonstrators themselves could scarcely believe. No shots were fired; there were none even of the familiar beatings and arrests. Instead, I watched a protester gently place a flower in the buttonhole of one of the men with guns. The Stasi secret police expelled

me from Leipzig later that night as punishment for what I
had seen, but I was happy to have witnessed the apparently
impossible.

There were so many retreats and U-turns in the following
days and weeks that the regime found itself, as I put it then,
in search of a King Canute, a leader who could stop the unstoppable. The world's politicians still failed to understand
what was happening: even after Poland's dash for democracy,
they believed all change came from the Kremlin and found it
difficult to conceive that the courage of seemingly powerless
individuals could cause huge monoliths to crack.

Despite what is sometimes said, what happened next was
not impossible to predict. It was simply that politicians were
looking through the wrong end of the telescope. The cascade
of retreats became a 'zigzag to the precipice', as the Polish
author Ryszard Kapuściński had described it in the context of
the Iranian revolution a decade earlier. One of Kapuściński's
most beloved authors was Herodotus, whose *Histories* he carried with him on his own travels. As Herodotus wrote 2,400
years earlier: 'The first lesson you should acknowledge is that
there is a cycle to human affairs, one that as it turns, never
permits the same people forever to enjoy good fortune.'

It was a lesson that East Germany's unelected rulers, celebrating the country's fortieth anniversary, were about to
learn. The Berlin Wall which divided Europe for decades had
come to seem a permanent feature of the landscape. Now the
fall of the Wall became, as I described it in the *Independent*,
not just a possibility but 'one of the few logical options left'.
My colleagues and I began to prepare a two-page 'obituary'
of the Wall which could be slipped in at short notice. We had
barely drawn up a list of contents and a rough design for the
planned spread before the Wall broke open, thirty-six hours
after that piece appeared.

Ten days earlier, over lunch in his favourite local restaurant, the endlessly-jailed Czech playwright Václav Havel – a hero of mine and author of a visionary essay on what he famously called 'the power of the powerless' – had talked to me of his country as 'a pressure cooker'. Two weeks after the Wall came down, I was back in Prague and saw Czechoslovakia, too, explode in its magical Velvet Revolution. Crowds jangled keys and rang little bells to signify that the rulers' time was up; the unelected leadership resigned, and Havel (officially dismissed as 'an absolute zero' just a few months earlier) became president.

In December, Mikhail Gorbachev summed up the new spirit of optimism at the end of a storm-tossed summit off Malta, declaring: 'We are at the beginning of a long road to a lasting peaceful era.' The threat of force, mistrust, psychological and ideological struggle should, the Soviet leader said, 'all be things of the past'.

The author and historian Timothy Garton Ash included a disclaimer in *The Magic Lantern*, his eyewitness account of that historic year: 'If things have gone badly in east-central Europe by the time you read this, you will probably find what follows absurdly hopeful . . . I would only say that this, too, belongs to the record. It felt like that at the time.' The caveats would soon be needed. But Garton Ash was right: this was a time when, to borrow from Seamus Heaney, hope and history rhymed.

Central-eastern Europe was not the only place where millions found new reasons for hope. In February 1990, three months after the fall of the Berlin Wall, Nelson Mandela was released after twenty-seven years of what was supposed to be a life sentence for daring to defy the apartheid system in South Africa. 'Our march to freedom is irreversible,' Mandela told cheering crowds. 'We must not allow fear to stand in our way.' A month later, Pinochet's seventeen-year dictatorship in Chile gave way to civilian rule. Seven months after that, fifteen years of civil war ended in Lebanon. In 1991, the Madrid Conference brought Israelis and Arabs together in what Washington and Moscow jointly described as a 'historic opportunity'. The head of the Palestinian delegation told the conference: 'We have had a prolonged exchange of pain; let us have hope instead.'

This was a time, in short, when anything seemed possible. That included one idea that had previously seemed unthinkable: the creation of a court that could prosecute war crimes anywhere in the world.

The proposal for an international criminal court was not exactly new. In 1872, eight years after the first Geneva Convention, Gustave Moynier – Henry Dunant's ally and then bitter rival – had unsuccessfully proposed an international tribunal that could punish infringements of the laws of war, as described in Chapter One. After 1918, the Romanian lawyer Vespasian Pella proposed an international criminal court and drafted a list of crimes. That, too, was buried. After the Second World War, the idea briefly returned. As proposed when Lemkin's convention was agreed, with its talk of 'preventing and punishing genocide', Pella and others worked on a draft statute after 1948. But that, too, faded away, a victim of the Cold War.

And yet, not everybody gave up. At Oxford in 1953, Arthur Napoleon Raymond 'Ray' Robinson, a student from Trinidad and Tobago, became friendly with the New Yorker Robert Woetzel. Woetzel was writing a thesis on the Nuremberg trials and international law. In their student rooms, the two men discussed the anti-colonial struggle, the east–west divide – and the creation of a permanent successor court to Nuremberg. Like Lemkin with his ideas thirty years earlier, Woetzel and Robinson never gave up on that vision.

In 1970, Woetzel – by now a law professor and secretary of the International Criminal Law Commission – published a collection of essays entitled *Towards a Feasible International Criminal Court*. The book pleaded against 'scoffers and cynics', and argued against 'total abandonment' of the idea of an international court. A. N. R. Robinson had in the meantime become a leading player in the politics of Trinidad and Tobago, becoming the country's first finance minister after independence in 1962. In 1971, Woetzel invited Robinson, now a parliamentary backbencher, to join a meeting at the Frank Lloyd Wright-designed Wingspread estate in Racine, Wisconsin, on Lake Michigan to discuss how, despite the 'scoffers and cynics', they might move the proposal forward. Robinson acknowledged, with some understatement, that the momentum towards an international criminal court had seen 'some degree of retrogression'. But, he argued in his summary of the meeting, there was a 'certain urgency' to the themes. We should not be disappointed, he said, 'if our effort sometimes seems to have some affinity to walking in space'. Robinson planted a blue spruce sapling in the Wingspread grounds and expressed his hope that the tree would in years to come 'spread its branches as a symbol of growth for international law'.

Woetzel and Robinson were not quite alone with their unlikely vision, even at this time. One of those who joined the Wingspread meeting was Ben Ferencz, who had led the *Einsatzgruppen* trials at Nuremberg. In 1980, he published *An International Criminal Court: A Step Toward World Peace*. The idea had, Ferencz said, been 'pushed aside like a piece of unripened fruit'. But, he argued, America's own recently concluded war was another argument in favour. 'As the war in

Vietnam intensified, the allegations of aggression, war crimes and crimes against humanity were increased ... If the laws of war were to be enforced, the existence of an independent international tribunal was essential.'

Throughout the Cold War, few politicians took such ideas seriously, just as they found it hard to believe in the possibilities of change itself. For a book that I later co-authored on protest and change, Václav Havel – former dissident, former president – described how he had been mocked for his ideas about the 'power of the powerless' that he first proposed in 1978. He was perceived, he said, as a Czech Don Quixote, 'tilting against unassailable windmills'. Ferencz, too, would describe himself as 'the man from La Mancha'. As he put it: 'You have to be able to live with the mockery.' In 1986, however, Robinson became his country's prime minister. In 1989, as the Berlin Wall came down, he asked for the creation of an international criminal court to be put on the agenda of the UN General Assembly. One focus was international drug trafficking, which was easy to agree on. But the uncontroversial framing also acted as a Trojan horse that smuggled in war crimes: Trinidad and Tobago's request referenced Nuremberg, international law and genocide. As Robinson had noted at Wingspread two decades earlier, developed countries might be more interested in drug trafficking, hijacking and similar themes; developing countries, he argued, would be more interested in 'genocide, racial discrimination, human rights and certain forms of ecological crimes'. Cherif Bassiouni, an Egyptian-American law professor who helped draft the resolution, concluded: 'If this tribunal, or court, can be achieved, then the dreamers of today will be the architects of the world of tomorrow.'

As early as 1795, Immanuel Kant argued that states should 'renounce their savage and lawless freedom' and, like individuals, should 'adapt themselves to public coercive laws'. Two centuries later, however, governments remained keen to exercise that savage and lawless freedom. They were, in Bassiouni's words, 'leery of supranational law'. One obvious example of that leeriness, as mentioned in the previous chapter, was Washington's refusal for forty years even to ratify the genocide convention, lest the United States might itself be in the frame. Given America's own track record, those fears were not necessarily groundless. Three years after the convention was agreed, W. E. B. Du Bois, Paul Robeson and others submitted and published a 250-page petition to the UN, *We Charge Genocide*, which quoted Robert Jackson at Nuremberg and talked of racist crimes by federal, state and municipal governments which were 'of the gravest concern to mankind'.

Only decades later did Washington finally relent. Not least as a result of the Lemkin–like tenacity of William Proxmire, a Wisconsin senator who made three thousand speeches over two decades about the country's 'national shame', the United States ratified the convention in 1988. There were less noble reasons why it happened, even then. In 1985, President Reagan had stumbled into a public-relations disaster when he paid his respects at a German war cemetery where many SS officers were buried. Ratification of the genocide convention became a belated reputation-cleanser – a way of proving the president *did* care about Nazi crimes, after all.

The creation of the Yugoslavia and Rwanda war crimes tribunals showed what could be done if the political will existed. It helped, too, that more people around the world were now engaged in the struggle for change. Lemkin had been a lone human-rights wolf with his stalking of the corridors of the UN, based until 1951 in the village of Lake Success on

Long Island's North Shore. In the 1990s, by contrast, many domestic, regional and global human rights organisations were part of the advocacy mix, working with sympathetic diplomats. Those two disparate groups, collaborating as never before, would play a key role in the historic establishment of a permanent war crimes court.

A key moment came in February 1995, when Bill Pace, unflappable head of the small but mighty World Federalist Movement, invited colleagues from two dozen non-governmental organisations to a meeting in the Dag Hammarskjöld Lounge on the twelfth floor of Church Center, a few minutes' walk from Le Corbusier's and Oscar Niemeyer's iconic UN headquarters building on the East River; those attending included Christopher Keith Hall of Amnesty International, who would make key contributions to the court's creation in the next three years. The World Federalist Movement was founded in 1947 and is dedicated to the pursuit of peace and justice through international law; historic supporters included Bertrand Russell and Albert Einstein. The agenda for the Church Center meeting, for discussion over coffee, pretzels and orange juice: how to turn the idea of an international criminal court into reality.

In addition to the NGOs, one diplomat was present: Silvia Fernández, legal adviser to the government of Argentina. Argentina's own trial of the juntas had played a historic role ten years earlier. In the years to come, Argentina, not least through Fernández herself, would give that energy for justice back to the world. There was enthusiasm at the Church Center meeting. But, as Bill Pace remembered later, 'Truthfully, most of us thought the ICC was more likely to be established in 2098 rather than 1998.'

The coalition for an international criminal court quickly expanded to include hundreds of non-governmental organisations worldwide. Initially, all five permanent members of the Security Council – Britain, China, France, Russia and the United States – were unenthusiastic or wanted to ensure any court would remain fully under the thumb of the Security Council itself through the exercise of their vetos. But the momentum for change continued to grow. In Africa, where many were unhappy with what was seen as the unequal application of justice over so many years, there was excitement about what a new, independent court might bring. South Africa and Senegal hosted regional meetings which sought to provide a counterweight to those governments – including and especially the former colonial powers – which still seemed determined to call the shots.

Finally, in June 1998 – twenty-seven years after the Wingspread meeting, nine years after Robinson's request to the UN, four years after the first draft statute and three years after the meeting at Church Center – delegates from 160 governments met in a sweltering Rome for the conference which would mark the grand finale, at least if agreement could be reached. Until the last moment, that remained a big if. Forty-five years after his first student conversations with Robert Woetzel, A. N. R. Robinson, now his country's president, warned there were 'many hurdles yet to be overcome'. He called for a court 'unfettered by the reality or the perception of subordination to the will of a few states' and with freedom of action 'unencumbered by states' vetos'. Those warnings would prove all too relevant in the years to come.

The next five weeks were filled with meetings until late into the evening in the lounges and corridors of the Mussolini-era headquarters of the UN Food and Agricultural Organisation near the Colosseum and in the nearby cafés and trattorias where diplomats and NGOs strategised, exchanged intelligence and tussled over details. (It wasn't all hard work.

Sometimes, delegates crowded into a specially erected tent to cheer on their teams in the FIFA World Cup; the France–Brazil final came five days before the end of the conference.) America, hustling to get its own way, ploughed a solitary furrow. US chief negotiator and war crimes ambassador David Scheffer later talked of the stream of 'stubborn and losing propositions' he received from Washington as part of a 'futile endgame'. Germany took as its motto in Rome a quotation attributed to Victor Hugo: 'Nothing is stronger than an idea whose time has come.' But the challenges remained. In the words of Silvia Fernández, who in 2015 would become president of the International Criminal Court, 'Many continued to think that an agreement was not possible, that the time for such an ambitious institution had simply not come.'

The Pentagon was determined that US forces should never be prosecuted, no matter what they had done – they remained dedicated to their 'savage and lawless freedom'. But the generals were not the only problem. Clinton's Secretary of State, Madeleine Albright, who had been a champion of human rights in other contexts, asked Scheffer: 'What can we do to blow up the entire conference?' (Scheffer was 'stunned' by the question.) Finally, however, a draft was agreed. America insisted on bringing the proposal to a vote – which served only to highlight Washington's unsplendid isolation. Late in the evening of 17 July 1998, 120 states voted for the creation of an international criminal court. Alongside the United States, just six governments – Israel and China, together with what David Scheffer later described as the 'rogues' gallery' of Cuba, Iraq, Syria and Yemen – voted against.

It was a moment as seemingly unimaginable as the agreement on Lemkin's genocide convention fifty years earlier. It marked the end of what my colleague Richard Dicker, who was leading the international justice work at Human

Rights Watch, remembers as 'an emotional and intellectual rollercoaster ride'. Diplomats and NGOs, traditionally on different sides of the advocacy barricades, embraced in disbelief at what they had jointly achieved. There were tears and a ten-minute standing ovation, even as America's delegation remained glumly in their seats. Richard talks of the sense that history was being made: 'Justice and accountability for the most serious crimes – that was in the wind, the sails were full of that. It was an extraordinary moment.' Canadian lawyer Philippe Kirsch, who chaired the negotiations and would become the court's first president, talked of 'humanity's finest hour'. UN Secretary-General Kofi Annan said the creation of the court was 'a gift of hope to future generations'. As German President Frank-Walter Steinmeier later told Ben Ferencz and others gathered in Nuremberg's historic Courtroom 600: the creation of the International Criminal Court meant 'the spirit of Nuremberg took tangible form'.

Even now, the White House couldn't decide if it wanted to be part of 'humanity's finest hour' after all. Bill Clinton spent the next seventeen months wondering how not to make his mind up. In mid-December 2000, as the final deadline of New Year's Eve approached, the still-energetic Ferencz helped tip the balance. Jointly with Robert McNamara, the US defense secretary during the Vietnam war, who had come to regret America's conduct during that conflict, Ferencz published an article in the *New York Times* calling on Clinton to 're-affirm America's inspiring role as leader of the free world in its search for peace and justice'. The purple language did the trick. Clinton, who had less than six weeks left in the Oval Office, scribbled on his copy of the article that he wanted to be 'kept informed'. ('Leave it to the wonders of a prominently published op-ed to finally awaken a president to action,' was Scheffer's reflection.)

As New Year's Eve dawned, Clinton still remained torn between bowing to the demands of the Pentagon on the one hand, and 'reaffirming America's inspiring role' on the other. There was heavy snow on the eastern seaboard; flights were cancelled and roads closed, so Scheffer boarded an early Sunday-morning train from Washington to New York, still not knowing if his journey had any purpose. Only as he rode up the escalators at Penn Station did he finally receive the phone call from his boss, Madeleine Albright: it was a yes from the president. At the signing ceremony at UN head-quarters, Scheffer wore the hiking boots in which he had trudged through the snow of midtown Manhattan. Those invited to the ceremony included Bill Pace, in recognition of his own contribution and the contribution of civil society more generally to making this moment happen. In an addi-tional twist, Israel and Iran both signed on the same evening, just hours before the final deadline. (Like America, neither Israel nor Iran ratified the treaty, so their membership never came into effect.)

'US signs treaty for world court to try atrocities,' the *New York Times* announced on New Year's Day 2001, which sounded like good news. But George W. Bush and his team arrived in the White House three weeks later. They hated everything the Court stood for and were determined to ensure it was stillborn. Bush's luxuriant-moustached under-secretary of state, John Bolton, a picture of opinionation who I met later when he was ambassador to the UN, wrote that America had 'no legal obligations'. He declared afterwards that 'unsigning' the treaty was his happiest moment as a dip-lomat. Other countries moved forward, however. America's attempts to kill the court failed. The usually cumbersome process of ratification – parliamentary approval of signatures appended to the treaty – happened more quickly than anyone had expected. Four years after the Rome meeting, the necessary sixty states had ratified, allowing the Rome Statute of the International Criminal Court to come into force in July 2002. A. N. R. Robinson, 'grandfather of the court', returned to the Wingspread estate for an event to celebrate the occasion and to honour his contribution. The sapling he had planted three decades earlier now stood thirty feet tall. It was, President Robinson said, 'a most satisfying moment'.

But the Bush administration wasn't finished yet. President Bush signed the American Service-Members' Protection Act, dubbed the 'Hague Invasion Act'. Dangerous and absurd in equal measure, the legislation authorised US forces to storm The Hague (using 'all means necessary and appropriate') to free any American or citizen of a US-allied country who might be detained or prosecuted by the new court. The apparent authority to invade a sovereign ally was, in truth, a mixture of empty bluster and an admission of failure. It was bluster because it was hard to imagine circumstances in which an attack on a Nato ally would become real. It was an admission of failure because the core principle of 'complementarity' means the ICC is a court of last resort: it becomes involved only when a state refuses or fails to organise credible investigations or prosecutions of its own.

More than half a century after his own prosecutions of Nazi crimes, Ben Ferencz was scathing about Washington's familiar exceptionalism and its suggestion that rogue prosecutors might target the United States: 'A frivolous prosecutor would be fired like a shot ... The "uncontrolled prosecutor" argument is made by those who are fools or liars or both,' Ferencz said. 'It is a shabby pretext by those who seek to avoid the rule of law.' (The issue of how to punish the court for daring to take an independent view – no longer theoretical, this time – would come to the fore again in 2024, when leaders of a key American ally were indicted for war crimes and crimes against humanity.)

In a policy that Bush's Secretary of State Condoleezza Rice later described as 'shooting ourselves in the foot', Washington sought other ways of sabotaging the court, too. It threatened smaller countries with the cancellation of millions of dollars in aid unless they signed agreements guaranteeing they would never turn an American soldier over to The Hague. It threatened a boycott of peacekeeping operations in Bosnia, forcing the UN Security Council to approve a special one-year agreement which offered immunity to US troops. That deal was renewed in 2003, in a pattern that might have continued indefinitely if not for a wake-up call that could not be ignored. In 2004, revelations of US torture at Abu Ghraib prison in Iraq made the idea of giving Washington new guarantees of impunity unthinkable. America eventually withdrew its request, to avoid what it called 'prolonged and divisive debate' (or: inevitable and humiliating defeat).

Lemkin noted the desire of governments to put the worst things always in the past, while not wishing to 'prevent and punish future crimes of the same type'. Samantha Power made a similar observation with reference to the Rwandan genocide, saying: 'We slotted [the Holocaust] in our consciousness as "history"; we resisted acknowledging that genocide was occurring in the present.' That same blindness would be repeated ten years after Rwanda, in Darfur.

Sudanese human rights defenders, global human rights groups, humanitarian organisations and UN officials all did their best in the early months of 2004 to raise the alarm on what Amnesty International described as a 'vicious, invisible war' where government-backed Arab Janjaweed militias attacked black African ethnic groups in Darfur in western Sudan; more than a million people fled their homes. The violence was supposedly to confront an armed rebellion; as so often, civilians suffered most. International Crisis Group warned of 'the potential horror story of 2004'. Human Rights Watch (where I was UK director at that time) published *Darfur in Flames: Atrocities in Western Sudan*, which talked of humanitarian catastrophe and crimes against humanity. Humanitarian agencies like Oxfam and Médecins Sans Frontières did everything possible to highlight the issues. Kofi Annan used a Rwandan-anniversary speech in April to highlight Darfur and say the risk of genocide was 'frighteningly real'. The *Financial Times* published an editorial which quoted Annan and concluded: 'International reflexes are still too slow.' Mostly, however, the catastrophe unfolded in what twenty signatories writing to the *Guardian* described as 'deafening silence' – the silence of murder, as Lemkin had put it sixty years earlier. I remember a meeting convened by one of the aid agencies in Church House where twenty or more non-governmental organisations strategised on what more we could do to ensure the crimes were addressed. None of us succeeded. Endless 'never again!' pieces marking the tenth anniversary of the Rwandan genocide in April 2004 failed to mention the nightmare unfolding, at the very same time, in western Sudan.

Politicians remained focused on peace talks in Naivasha, Kenya which aimed to end the long war between north and south Sudan. The Comprehensive Peace Agreement that would be signed at Naivasha the following year was historic. When I reported for the *Independent* in 1999 on a peace dialogue between civilians from the Dinka and Nuer tribes in the south of the country, helping to pave the way for the deal that came later, the war was already in its seventeenth year. Two million had died and millions had fled their homes. Salva Kiir, the Castro-bearded rebel commander (who would later become the first president of an independent South Sudan), had little to say when I asked him about the prospects for peace, but waxed enthusiastic when talking about a prolonged war. He told me at the conference near the village of Wunlit: 'We're prepared to take on the struggle for a hundred years.'

The Naivasha deal that would be reached six years after the Wunlit meeting and a year after some of the worst Darfur massacres was, in other words, a turning point which needed to be taken seriously. Less understandable was that policymakers seemed to believe that the importance of the north–south negotiations left no room to focus on ethnic cleansing, rape and murder in a different part of the country. I had a meeting in the early months of 2004 with a British government minister, where he and his adviser explained that, although they did not quarrel with the Human Rights Watch findings that I presented ('that all fits with what we have been hearing'), what they called a 'sequential' approach was essential. In effect: 'Let's get the peace deal tied up first – and then we can get round to these massacres of yours later.' Governments refused to accept the simple point that Kofi Annan and others had made: ignoring mass atrocities and postponing things until 'later' was only likely to make things worse.

The massacres themselves were not seen as important enough to focus on. But the attempted *suppression* in late April 2004 of a story about the atrocities suddenly made them newsworthy. A UN report which talked of a 'reign of terror' in Darfur was leaked, causing Sudanese indignation. The leaked report and official fury caused more media interest than all the un-leaked

reports from the past few months put together, even though
those earlier reports had essentially said the same thing. I
received a call from a former colleague at the *Independent*,
who I had previously emailed and talked to about Human
Rights Watch's concerns with little success. Following the
noise around the UN report, he wanted to know if we had
enough additional material to justify a front-page story. The
answer came with the *Independent*'s main headline next day, a
wake-up call for which I was grateful to my old paper: 'Rape,
torture, and one million forced to flee as Sudan's crisis unfolds.' The story spilled onto page two and the opinion pages.
In the days and weeks to come, reporters and television crews
were dispatched to the region. Powerful reports began to be
beamed daily into millions of living rooms. Politicians decided the massacres were important after all. US Secretary of
State Colin Powell visited Darfur in June, followed in quick
succession by his German, French, British and other coun-
terparts. In September, President Bush even used Lemkin's
word, so taboo in Washington during the Rwandan slaughter
ten years earlier, when he called for a full investigation of the
'genocide and other crimes' in Darfur.

During the Rwandan genocide, Clinton's National
Security Adviser, Anthony Lake, had told Alison Des Forges
of Human Rights Watch that she needed to 'make more
noise' if she wanted politicians to take any notice. The implication was that without such media 'noise', politicians' hands
were tied. The sudden change of heart on Darfur was a good
example of what Lake had talked about: the string of powerful television reports and front-page stories from late April
onwards helped change the political conversation. But it left
an uncomfortable paradox about what makes a story worth
addressing. In a piece for the *Financial Times* magazine a few
months later, I reflected on the catch-22 which can sometimes

apply even today, when endless social media commentary on what seems to be every possible theme would appear to have made gatekeepers obsolete. 'If newspaper editors do not see the story on TV, they do not believe it's news; if programme-makers do not read it in the newspapers, they do not believe it's news,' I wrote. 'And if politicians and officials don't see or read it except in reports thudding on to their desks from human-rights and humanitarian NGOs, then that doesn't quite count, either.' There was, in other words, little logic as to whose suffering counts and who is ignored.

Sudan now became what Rwanda had eventually become once the 1994 genocide was over: the issue everyone wanted to talk about. The United States led on a UN Security Council resolution which demanded accountability for the crimes committed, responding partly to a Save Darfur coalition which had been launched in Washington in July. The Security Council initiative was welcome, even if countries like China were not keen. But a contradiction went unnoticed, not least by Bush and his advisers. The obvious place for achieving accountability for the crimes in Darfur was at the new International Criminal Court, which the US still loathed with an unnatural passion. When the UN commission of inquiry which America itself had asked for published its 170-page report in February 2005, the recommendations were clear. The commission, led by a former president of the Yugoslav war crimes tribunal, concluded that the scale of the crimes meant referral to the International Criminal Court was the only appropriate action. The commission clearly had one particular audience in mind with its two curt sentences in paragraph 573: 'The Commission considers that the ICC is the only credible way of bringing alleged perpetrators to justice. It strongly advises against other measures.'

The Bush administration was caught in a chess-players'

zugzwang, boxed into a corner of its own making. Washington wanted to be seen to be taking a strong stance on Darfur. But it was also desperate not to cooperate with the new international court. In this unusual new goal – 'We want to see accountability anywhere but in the place which everyone agrees is most suited for it', a contorted diplomatic version of Twister – Washington needed a pliant ally. Sure enough, the UK began to insist that although it was a strong supporter of the International Criminal Court *in principle*, maybe the court didn't need to be involved on this occasion. Downing Street argued for 'consensus' at the Security Council. This meant everybody else should give up on the recommended solution, while, as I summarised it in an article then, 'one permanent member moves not an inch – that is hardly consensus'. US war crimes ambassador Pierre-Richard Prosper admitted this had nothing to do with the interests of the people of Darfur. It was simpler: 'We don't want to be a party to legitimising the court.'

Human Rights Watch and Amnesty International had a meeting at this time with the British foreign secretary, Jack Straw. We put forward our arguments as to why an ICC referral was essential, and why (on this occasion at least) the Americans must be persuaded to compromise. Usually, you can't be sure if your arguments have landed or have gone in the diplomatic trash. But we heard later that Straw spoke to his US counterpart, Condoleezza Rice, that same afternoon. She described the political embarrassment the administration would face if Washington allowed a referral to The Hague to be approved. Straw offered sympathy for Rice's difficulties, but added that his government, too, faced challenges. 'In fact, only today I had human rights organisations in my office who were pressing me on this very point . . .'

Eventually, following pressure from France, Germany

and other European allies, Britain decided it would stand up for the court after all, leaving America in a minority of one. And so, with no obvious options for how to get out of the fish-trap that it had so eagerly swum into a few months earlier, America agreed to give way, despite what Rice later described as 'much strong dissent' from her ever-rigid colleague John Bolton. On 31 March 2005, the UN Security Council voted for its first-ever referral to the ICC. The resolution referring Sudan to The Hague passed unopposed. France and Britain voted in favour, as did Russia. The Russian ambassador said the struggle against impunity was 'one of the elements of long-term stability' and that 'all those responsible for grave crimes must be punished'. America and China both abstained.

In the lead-up to the creation of the ICC, African governments had played a key role in pressing for an effective and independent court. Africa was disproportionately represented, too, among the first sixty countries to confirm their membership, thus allowing the court to come into existence. Within a few years, however, that would all go sour.

At the start, there were productive collaborations between African governments and The Hague. The court's first investigation came in response to a request from the government of the Democratic Republic of Congo, in the context of the conflict in eastern Congo in which millions had died. Greed for natural resources has been at the heart of violence in Congo since colonial times. King Leopold II of Belgium made obscene profits from rubber plantations at the cost of millions of lives, in what Joseph Conrad described as 'the vilest scramble for loot that ever disfigured the history of human conscience'. (Like other imperial powers, Belgium remained in denial for many years; not until 2018 did the vast

Royal Museum for Central Africa outside Brussels finally tear up the rosy narratives and confront the reality behind inscriptions like 'Belgium brings civilisation to Congo'. In 2022, King Philippe told the Congolese parliament of his 'regrets', while stopping short of an apology for earlier crimes.) With the end of colonial rule, abuses continued. President Mobutu Sese Seko, acclaimed by Western governments as a supposed bulwark against Communism, was notorious for his corruption in the country he renamed Zaire. In the twenty-first century, that same greed – for gold, diamonds, coltan, cobalt and more – has continued to have deadly impact.

In 2005, I visited Nyankunde in Ituri province in eastern Congo, three years after thousands were slaughtered in the town. My Human Rights Watch colleague Anneke Van Woudenberg and I were doing follow-up advocacy with an international mining company on her *Curse of Gold* report, which we had launched in Johannesburg a few months earlier, documenting the nexus between gold extraction and atrocities in the region. The hospital in Nyankunde had been a particular target: fourteen people hid in the ceiling of the operating theatre for days without food or water, before being dragged out to their deaths. An eight-month-old girl was killed in front of her mother; a two-week-old baby was thrown into a latrine. Even as the killing continued, an email was sent from inside the hospital – subject line: 'Nyankunde: on fire and in blood'. Church groups forwarded the message to the UN. They never received a reply.

At the time of our visit, Nyankunde still felt like a ghost town. But the mayor was determined to bring life back. He wanted truth and justice for survivors and for those who had died. A box beside Jean Gaston Herambo's house contained a collection of skulls, marked with gashes from the killers' machetes. Herambo wanted to build a memorial to the dead.

He hoped this might serve as evidence: 'It is important that [the killers] should be judged and brought to justice so that this can't happen again.'

At that time, it was hard to imagine any accountability being achieved for crimes committed here and across the region. Nine years later, though, I sat in a courtroom in The Hague to see at least a small measure of justice. In 2014, Germain Katanga, the warlord who liked to be known as 'Simba', and whose forces were responsible for the killings at Nyankunde, stood impassive as a judge at the International Criminal Court pronounced him guilty of war crimes and crimes against humanity (though he was never charged in connection with the worst massacres of all, at Nyankunde).

Another key warlord in the fight for control of the region's gold, Thomas Lubanga, was eventually convicted of recruitment of child soldiers and jailed for fourteen years – although, to the dismay of many victims and relatives, he was not charged with crimes of sexual violence or murder. Ben Ferencz, aged ninety-two, gave the closing speech for the prosecution. He talked of the 'slow awakening of the human conscience' and argued: 'The law can no longer be silent but must instead be heard and enforced to protect the fundamental rights of people everywhere.'

A third warlord, Bosco Ntaganda, was able to live freely in Goma in eastern Congo for years after he had been indicted, eating in the best restaurants while UN peacekeepers sat nearby. But Ntaganda's options eventually ran out. Seven years after his indictment, early one Monday morning in March 2013, he presented himself to a startled security guard at the US embassy in the Rwandan capital, Kigali, requesting transfer to The Hague. In 2019, the ICC convicted him of crimes against humanity.

*

Other early cases also came from Africa, as self-referrals or with African votes at the Security Council. In 2004, the Ugandan president Yoweri Museveni even held a controversial press conference with the court's chief prosecutor, at which they jointly announced the referral to the court of crimes committed by rebels of the Lord's Resistance Army in northern Uganda. In other contexts, too, African governments were supportive. In 2010, when President Omar al-Bashir was indicted for genocide in Sudan, Thandi Modise, deputy secretary-general of South Africa's ruling African National Congress, insisted her country would do everything possible 'to bring the culprit to The Hague' and that 'the perpetrators of war crimes should be tried at all costs'. In 2011, South Africa voted in favour of referring Gaddafi's Libya to The Hague. In 2012, Mali referred itself to the court, in connection with al-Qaeda-linked violence in west Africa; two jihadists have in the meantime been convicted of war crimes and crimes against humanity, including for torture, rape and destruction of sacred buildings.

But some began to argue that the court − co-created by Africans and with an outspoken Gambian deputy prosecutor and then chief prosecutor, Fatou Bensouda − was itself anti-African. That turnaround was partly down to what happened in Kenya, where more than a thousand people died in post-election violence in 2007 and 2008. A commission led by Judge Philip Waki called for a tribunal to prosecute perpetrators, and the new Kenyan government agreed. But Waki also organised a fallback scenario in case the politicians reneged on their commitments. If the promised tribunal was *not* created, a sealed envelope with the names of those suspected of being most responsible for the violence would be passed to the ICC. The tribunal didn't happen. In 2009, the Ghanaian former UN Secretary General Kofi Annan therefore handed the list of names to The Hague. Annan warned that without progress on confronting impunity, 'the reconciliation between ethnic groups and the long-term stability of Kenya is in jeopardy'.

Still, though, nothing happened. A year later, the International Criminal Court issued charges, including against Uhuru Kenyatta, deputy prime minister (and son of the country's first post-independence leader), and William Ruto, who had been a presidential candidate during the violence in 2007. Polls showed an overwhelming majority of Kenyans supported the court's move. The *Nation* newspaper talked in an editorial of 'slaying the dragon of impunity'. But the politicians unleashed their anger on the court. Kenyatta and Ruto, previously opponents, joined forces with a shared message that the ICC was biased. A British PR agency was appointed in order – as Bensouda described it to me a decade later – 'to discredit the court'. In elections in 2013, Kenyatta and Ruto emerged victorious, becoming president and deputy president respectively. Remarkably, both men travelled to The Hague to testify in their own defence. Kenyatta even temporarily stepped down from the presidency to attend a hearing in October 2014. But, following persistent reports of witness intimidation, charges against both men were dropped or set aside. Bensouda, now the court's chief prosecutor, said the dropping of charges against Kenyatta, just two months after his appearance in The Hague, marked 'a dark day for international criminal justice' and 'a painful moment for the men, women and children who have . . . waited patiently for almost seven years for justice to be done'.

When the Kenyan trials were still under way, I joined a meeting on behalf of Amnesty International in the Ethiopian capital, Addis Ababa, on the theme of Africa and the International Criminal Court under the headline 'Making International Justice Work Better for Africa'. I was struck by the division that ran through the room during the two-day meeting. African civil society groups remained broadly supportive of the court, though impatient with its failure to indict the most powerful leaders or prosecute the most serious crimes. By contrast, government representatives (including several from Kenya) talked as if the court itself were the problem – just as Western governments would complain about a different set of indictments in 2024.

It was hardly surprising that repressive leaders had little good to say about the ICC. Genocide indictee Omar al-Bashir, for example, described it as a 'colonial court'. It would have been more surprising if he had sounded supportive of the Gambian prosecutor in The Hague who wanted to see him behind bars.

But the court's opponents now included previous supporters, too. When the Sudanese leader arrived in Johannesburg for an African Union summit in 2015, his hosts proved eager to help him out. Civil society groups demanded al-Bashir's arrest in compliance with South Africa's obligations under the Rome Statute of the ICC. Judges ruled that, pending a final overnight decision, al-Bashir was forbidden to leave the country and the government must 'take all necessary steps to prevent him doing so'. The government responded with a judicial middle finger, allowing the indicted president to fly back to Khartoum from a South African airbase with little more than an 'Oops, sorry!' afterwards.

The Supreme Court of Appeal said the contempt for a judicial ruling was 'disgraceful' and called the excuses 'simply risible'. Angela Mudukuti, working at that time with the Southern Africa Litigation Centre which pressed for al-Bashir's arrest, told me later that the government learned lessons from the 2015 debacle: 'I think South Africa seriously had regrets. They completely underestimated us, our energy and our motivation.' The clash over al-Bashir would have implications ahead of another summit hosted by South Africa eight years later, where the indicted Russian president stayed at home rather than risk his luck by going to Johannesburg.

Eventually, there was a part-turnaround. When the first rumblings against the court began in 2009, Kofi Annan had asked: 'Do these leaders really want to side with the alleged perpetrators of mass atrocities rather than their victims?' Belatedly, his message began to be heard. In 2016, South Africa announced it would withdraw from the ICC – then changed its mind. Gambia, too, announced that it would leave – a decision that the country's new democratic government would soon reverse.

African leaders were not the only ones who accused the court of bias when it dared to investigate their alleged crimes. When the International Criminal Court announced an investigation into hundreds of extrajudicial executions in the 'war on drugs' in the Philippines in 2018, President Rodrigo Duterte withdrew from the court, complaining – as Vladimir Putin and Benjamin Netanyahu would also do, a few years later – that the court was 'a political tool'.

Meanwhile, one welcome consequence of the allegations of anti-African bias at the ICC was to increase pressure for domestic or regional prosecutions of the worst crimes. The arguments against the court had never been that justice wasn't needed, only that prosecutions belonged more properly in Africa. Nobody at The Hague – least of all Fatou Bensouda, herself a former Gambian attorney-general, or the court's five African judges – would disagree with that. On the contrary, as Annan pointed out, 'There will be less need for [the ICC] to protect African victims only when African governments themselves improve their record of bringing to justice those responsible for mass atrocities.'

Today, Bensouda is Gambia's high commissioner in London, after her seventeen years at the court. 'Well behaved women don't make history,' says a sign above her desk, a gift during her time in The Hague. Bensouda argues that African governments 'turned everything on its head' with their accusations of an 'anti-African' court in past years. There were 'tense moments', she tells me. But she never thought of backing down. Instead, she says, 'people said I should wear it as a badge of honour' that she was ready to investigate government leaders. African civil society groups, she points out, 'always wanted more' justice, not less. The veto system in New York meant that some of the worst crimes were not prosecuted, with Syria as the most glaring example of that. But the blame for that failure belonged to the UN Security Council, not to the court.

Like other tribunals, the International Criminal Court has been criticised for its expense and lack of impact: it has spent more than two billion dollars and has achieved only a handful of convictions, all of which so far have been of militia leaders, not national politicians. But if the court can act as a wake-up call for the importance of justice at home, that will be an achievement, too. Bensouda believes that process has already begun. 'The ICC has sparked more domestic prosecutions. I saw that already during my time, with governments coming to my office. We need to push more for those.' Her successor Karim Khan, too, says the International Criminal Court should not stand on a lonely mountain of its own. Instead, he tells me, 'We need to do it together. The ICC is not an apex of justice but a hub – we are building a common front, maybe capable of withstanding some of the counter-forces that we face.'

*

One key piece of unfinished business when the Rome Statute was agreed was the 'crime of aggression', described at Nuremberg as 'crimes against peace', or 'waging aggressive war'. Launching a war of aggression was, in the words of the Nuremberg judgment, the 'supreme international crime'. After 1945, however, the crime of aggression fell prey to what one commentator describes as 'a sort of international omertà'. In theory at least, the silence ended in 1998, when the crime of aggression was listed in the Rome Statute as a fourth category of core crime alongside war crimes, crimes against humanity and genocide. To be precise: it was both included and not included. The Rome Statute ruled that the crime of aggression could only be prosecuted once it had been defined. But it hadn't yet been defined. Until then, therefore, talk of prosecuting aggression was purely decorative. And so things rested, with the crime of aggression simultaneously on the books and not on the books, as negotiations began on hammering out a definition. That task was always going to be tricky. But defining the crime of aggression would become doubly fraught after the US- and UK-led invasion of Iraq in 2003, in what most international observers saw as a brazen flouting of international law.

Negotiations on defining the crime of aggression, on the one hand, and the Anglo-American drive to war, on the other, collided after prime minister Tony Blair commissioned advice in 2003 from his attorney-general, Lord Goldsmith, on military action against Iraq. A confidential thirteen-page memo from Goldsmith concluded that 'the safest legal course' would be to seek a fresh UN Security Council resolution before an invasion. But that wasn't what Downing Street or the White House wanted to hear. Just ten days later, Goldsmith offered Parliament a crisp new three-hundred-word statement which concluded instead that, because of three existing UN resolutions (two of which were twelve years old), a new authorisation of force could be dispensed with.

Elizabeth Wilmshurst, deputy legal adviser at the Foreign Office and Britain's lead negotiator on establishing the International Criminal Court, was unimpressed with that logic. A day after Goldsmith's new opinion was published, she wrote to request early retirement or resignation, pointing out that Goldsmith's statement contradicted earlier Foreign Office advice (and the attorney-general's own previous view). She argued that the invasion of Iraq without the proper authority would be 'detrimental to the international order and the rule of law'. In her letter, published in response to a freedom of information request two years later, Wilmshurst referred to the not fully defined crime which was due to be incorporated in the revised statute of the International Criminal Court, of which Britain claimed to be a proud member. An unlawful use of force on such a scale, she wrote, 'amounts to the crime of aggression' – just at the point when discussions on defining that crime, which Wilmshurst was due to lead on behalf of the UK, were about to get under way. The contradiction, she said, made her job untenable.

The shock-and-awe invasion of Iraq began two days later, on 20 March 2003. As Wilmshurst predicted, this did indeed make things tricky for her successors. Any consideration of the crime of aggression inevitably touched on the legality or illegality of an invasion which two permanent members of the Security Council had launched with such confidence and which had brought such catastrophic consequences. UN Secretary-General Kofi Annan would later echo Wilmshurst's view that the Iraq war was illegal; many governments around the world agreed. (George W. Bush, for his part, explained that God told him to do it.)

With this unhappy prologue, it is remarkable that a definition was ever agreed. In 2010, however, 120 members
of the International Criminal Court finally nailed down a
definition of the crime of aggression at a review conference
in the Ugandan capital, Kampala. The court's jurisdiction
over the crime finally came into effect in 2018 – eight years
after Kampala, fifteen years after the invasion of Iraq and
twenty years after the agreement in Rome to find the right
words.

Even then, some had in the meantime negotiated get-
out-of-jail-free cards for themselves or their friends. For the
original three core crimes – genocide, war crimes and crimes
against humanity – the International Criminal Court has
potential jurisdiction even if states involved have not ratified
the Rome Statute, as long as the offences were committed
in the territory of a state which is a party (thus including,
for example, unpunished US war crimes in Afghanistan).
But the United States, despite not being a member of the
court – and therefore needing the help of its wingmen,
especially in Paris and London – negotiated an additional ex-
emption for the crime of aggression. In the words of Jennifer
Trahan, my former colleague at Human Rights Watch and
now convenor of the Global Institute for the Prevention of
Aggression, 'Three of the four Nuremberg allies were evis-
cerating the jurisdiction of the court.' As would become clear
four years later, America would not be the main beneficiary
of the carve-out that Washington and its allies had pressed
for. Instead, the country which in 2022 would benefit was
another non-member of the court which, like the United
States, hates encroachments on its 'savage and lawless freedom' – Russia, the fourth prosecuting power at Nuremberg.

———

The creation of two new international war crimes tribunals in 1993 and 1994 had opened up the possibilities of justice in ways that previously seemed unthinkable. The 1998 agreement to create an international criminal court marked another leap forward. Then, just three months after the Rome Statute was agreed, came another historic moment for international criminal justice – this time in London.

Augusto Pinochet liked to say that Britain was his favourite country. After Chile's return to civilian rule, the former dictator enjoyed regular visits to London, where he would go shopping in Harrods, visit the waxworks at Madame Tussaud's and have cosy catch-ups with Margaret Thatcher at her grand home in Belgravia. In September 1998, the eighty-two-year-old general was once again in Britain. His back was giving him problems, and it was agreed that he should have surgery. He had to cancel his tea with Thatcher but found time to buy a Hitler biography and more books on Napoleon (adding to his collection) before his operation.

Eight years after stepping down from the presidency, Pinochet remained a power in the land. After giving up his role as head of the Chilean armed forces a few months before his latest visit to London, he was appointed senator for life, which appeared to give him immunity from prosecution. There had been talk of putting Pinochet on trial abroad in the previous two years. A case began in Spain in 1996, led by investigating magistrate Baltasar Garzón, which focused on the deaths of Spanish citizens in Operation Condor, a CIA-backed collaboration that enabled Chile, Argentina and other South American military regimes to work together to carry out disappearances, torture and murder. Garzón's initiative made headlines in Spain and Chile, and Pinochet was wary of visiting Madrid. London, though, was different: he felt safe to visit the sights, to have his portrait taken at the Dorchester

Hotel for a profile in the *New Yorker*, and to go into hospital. He told the *New Yorker*'s Jon Lee Anderson how he wished to be remembered: 'As a man who loved his fatherland, and served it all his life . . . I hope they do justice to my memory. Each person will interpret it as he wishes.'

After his operation, Pinochet recuperated in the exclusive London Clinic on Devonshire Place (previous patients: Elizabeth Taylor and Princess Margaret). It was here that legal history was made for a second time in quick succession. On 16 October, Garzón filed an urgent request for the general's arrest and his extradition to Madrid. A London magistrate approved the request. Pinochet was woken just after midnight, and – with the help of bodyguards acting as improvised translators – Metropolitan Police detectives informed the general he was under arrest for crimes against humanity. He was, he said afterwards, 'hurt and bewildered'. After all, 'I wasn't in England as a common bandit. I was here as a diplomatic figure and had been welcomed as such.'

Pinochet's bewilderment was understandable. His opponents never expected this moment either. Ariel Dorfman, who worked as an adviser to President Allende before the coup, believed Pinochet 'would mock us forever, that we would never be rid of his person or his legacy. Those hands shrouded in white would go to the grave without once having had to confront what they had done, what they had made other hands do.' Now, though, everything changed. 'Other hands, the hands of English policemen, had stormed into his life and ours; the hands of a Spanish judge had the tyrant cornered.'

The Pinochet arrest was an early example of 'universal jurisdiction', the principle which makes it possible to arrest somebody for serious crimes committed anywhere in the world. There were, however, still many twists and turns to come after that first moment of drama. Even as knots of Chileans gathered daily outside the clinic, chanting for justice, the UK High Court ruled Pinochet was immune from extradition. Pinochet's supporters celebrated. But that was still not the end. Prosecutors appealed to what was at the time Britain's highest court, a panel of senior judges in the House of Lords. On Pinochet's eighty-third birthday, 25 November 1998, the law lords delivered their decision. It was a nail-biting climax. The first two judges agreed Pinochet enjoyed immunity. At 2–0, the omens looked good for the general. The next two judges argued Pinochet had 'no immunity whatever'. With voting tied at 2–2, Lord Hoffmann was the last to speak. He agreed there was no immunity and allowed the appeal. On Parliament Square, demonstrators cheered as they heard the historic news. In Santiago, car horns sounded for hours in jubilation. Even now, this was not the end of the story. It emerged that Lennie Hoffmann's wife worked for Amnesty International, which had intervened in the case, and that Hoffmann himself was the unpaid chair of the organisation's fundraising arm. His fellow law lords said he had flouted the principle that 'justice must not only be done but must be seen to be done'. Everything started again from scratch.

That sounded like good news for Pinochet, now living in comfortable house arrest in suburban Surrey while complaining that he was 'the only political prisoner in England'. This time, though, there was to be no tie-breaker. By a majority of six to one and backed up by a 200-page judgment, the new panel of law lords agreed with the first judgment: Pinochet was *not* entitled to immunity. In the words of Lord Phillips, later Lord Chief Justice, 'An international crime is as offensive, if not more offensive, to the international community when committed under colour of office. Once extra-territorial jurisdiction is established, it makes no sense to exclude from it acts done in an official capacity.' In other words, echoing the words of Macaulay that Helmuth von Moltke quoted in Kreisau half a century earlier: if somebody has been in a position of power, that makes it *more* important, not less, that they should be held accountable. The implications of that ruling continue to ripple out today.

The judges had ruled on the principle, but that still left open the practicalities of whether extradition would actually go ahead. After a medical report suggesting Pinochet had suffered brain damage, the British government decreed that he should be allowed home. (Subsequent medical reports would reach a different conclusion.) So, after seventeen months of house arrest and endless reverses, Pinochet was put on a Chilean air force jet which flew him back to a hero's welcome led by the head of the armed forces in Santiago. Pinochet, no longer the frail invalid, stepped out of his wheelchair and proudly waved his walking stick in the air as a band played 'Lili Marlene'.

Some commentators had warned of the dangers for Chile's own stability if the former dictator were to go on trial. Former allies claimed that a 'giant bomb' had been dropped on the transition. In London, *The Times* said the fate of Chilean democratisation and democracy was 'disturbingly uncertain'. In reality, the discussion of a theoretical prosecution abroad energised the possibilities of actual prosecution at home. Chile's foreign minister, Juan Gabriel Valdés, said the welcome party was 'disgusting' and a national disgrace. Chilean courts overturned Pinochet's proclaimed immunity. 'If human rights abuses will not cease because of the General's exemplary punishment,' Ariel Dorfman wrote two years after Pinochet's return, 'a subtle displacement has nevertheless been validated in the way in which the world imagines power and equality and memory.'

The Supreme Court ruled that Pinochet's reported dementia made him unfit to stand trial. But that changed in 2003 after Pinochet gave an interview to a Miami TV station in which he explained that he had 'always acted in a democratic way', and that if anybody needed to apologise it was the Marxists. The courts were unimpressed with this new lucidity, given his supposedly 'irreversible' dementia. By now, many of his associates had been prosecuted and domestic support had dwindled. A new indictment was upheld. At the time of his death in 2006, just after his ninety-first birthday, six years after his return to Chile and sixteen years after the country's return to civilian rule, Pinochet was under house arrest awaiting trial for kidnap, torture and murder.

All these initiatives – the creation of new ad hoc war crimes tribunals, the agreement and creation of an international criminal court and the arrest of Pinochet under the principle of universal jurisdiction – combined to create a sense that everything was changing.

In the years to come, the idea of universal jurisdiction began to spread. In 2005, an arrest warrant was issued in the UK for General Doron Almog, former head of Israel's Southern Command, in connection with alleged war crimes in Gaza in 2002. Almog, who was due to give a speech in London, was tipped off and returned home without disembarking at Heathrow. It later emerged that British police didn't board the plane because they feared it could end in a gun battle with Almog's bodyguards. Four years later, an arrest warrant was issued for former Israeli foreign minister Tzipi Livni, member of the war cabinet during the Operation Cast Lead assault on Gaza in 2009. Israel, Livni said, 'is a country that when you fire on its citizens it responds by going wild – and that is a good thing'. Livni, too, got wind of the planned arrest; she cancelled her trip and the British government changed the rules to avoid such an unfortunate possibility in future. The foreign secretary, William Hague, said in 2011 it was 'an appalling situation' if 'people like Ms Livni' faced arrest for alleged war crimes. He insisted Britain wanted people who committed serious crimes, 'wherever in the world they took place', to be brought to justice. Clearly, though, 'wherever in the world' had its exceptions: Israel was an ally, and Britain would therefore do everything possible to stymie any attempt to hold its leaders to account.

Even if in some contexts the possibilities of justice still seemed blocked, new doors to accountability now began to open as never before. Ousted dictators had long been accustomed to the idea they could live out their lives in comfortable exile. After being driven out in 1979, Uganda's Idi Amin, famous for his unparalleled brutality, lived untroubled for years in Jeddah, Saudi Arabia. After an unsuccessfully stolen election in 1986, Philippines dictator Ferdinand Marcos went to Hawaii. In the same year, Haitian president-for-life Jean-Claude 'Baby Doc' Duvalier settled in a villa near Cannes after fleeing a popular uprising in his own country. The local police chief said, 'He bothers no one; no one bothers him. And we don't watch him.'

Liberia's warlord leader Charles Taylor no doubt thought he, too, would be safe from justice. The Liberian civil war that began in 1999 (three years after the end of a seven-year war) was notorious for its brutality. Government and rebel forces alike raped, maimed and killed with impunity. The courage of a remarkable group of women, the Women of Liberia Mass Action for Peace, put Taylor under pressure to end the conflict. The president mocked the women for 'embarrassing themselves'. But the momentum of the protests grew. 'We are taking this stand because we believe tomorrow our children will ask us: "Mama, what was your role during the crisis?"' protest leader and future Nobel Prize-winner Leymah Gbowee told Taylor when he finally agreed to meet. Taylor was eventually forced into exile in 2003. 'History will be kind to me,' he said as he left. 'I have fulfilled my duties.'

The Special Court for Sierra Leone, a UN-supported tribunal created in 2002 to prosecute war crimes and atrocities committed during that country's eleven-year war, indicted Taylor while he was still president for crimes that he facilitated, including support for rebel forces in Sierra Leone in return for blood diamonds that financed his own war. For three years, apparently untroubled by the indictment, Taylor lived undisturbed, playing tennis at his luxurious home in Calabar in south-eastern Nigeria. But in 2006, Taylor was arrested as he tried to slip unnoticed through a remote border post from Nigeria into Cameroon. Nigeria delivered him to Liberia, which in turn handed him over to the court in Sierra Leone. In 2013, Taylor was sentenced to fifty years behind bars for crimes which put him, the judge said, 'in a class of his own'.

It took ten years for Charles Taylor to be brought to justice, in ways that he never expected to see. Elsewhere, survivors have fought for longer and against even greater odds. Hissène Habré was president of Chad from 1982 until his overthrow in 1990. He presided over torture and tens of thousands of deaths. But, just as Saddam Hussein received billions of dollars in support from the United States because he was at war with Iran, the fact that Habré was in conflict with the Libyan leader Muammar Gaddafi was, for Western governments, the most important thing. Habré was the enemy's enemy, and therefore the West's friend. America funded and armed Habré; President Reagan said it was an 'honour' to receive him. President François Mitterrand provided him with weapons, advisers and military training, and invited him to the Bastille Day parade in Paris. As France's foreign minister Roland Dumas later acknowledged, with some understatement, 'We turned a blind eye to what he was doing in his country.' After he was overthrown, and following the familiar pattern, Habré fled into exile in Senegal, where he liked to watch re-runs of *Seinfeld* in his villa. Because of the courage and determination of Habré's victims and of activists in Chad, Senegal and internationally, that comfortable exile eventually ended.

Souleymane Guengueng was working as an accountant with the Lake Chad Basin Commission when Habré's secret police dragged him from his office and jailed him in 1988. While in detention, Guengueng made a resolution. If he survived, as many of the prisoners he shared a cell with did not, he would work to ensure accountability for those responsible for these crimes. After Habré's fall in 1990, Guengueng created a victims' association and assembled hundreds of files documenting the abuses. Habré's allies were still powerful at this time; Guengueng hid the documents in a trunk at his home.

The Pinochet arrest in 1998 seemed to open up new possibilities. Criminal proceedings were authorised against Habré in Senegal, the country of his exile, in 2000. One Senegalese paper concluded: 'The message is clear: those who commit, order or tolerate torture can no longer be assured of a peaceful retirement.' But those hopes were short-lived. In what Senegalese activist Alioune Tine described as 'shenanigans unworthy of Senegal's democracy', the government blocked legal proceedings.

Attempts to bring Habré to justice were dangerous for all

those involved. One key figure working to make prosecution happen was Chadian lawyer Jacqueline Moudeïna, founder of a human rights group which worked with victims of Habré's regime. In 2001, she was severely injured in a grenade attack on a peaceful protest in Chad, apparently organised by a police official who had been part of Habré's inner circle. Moudeïna spent a year on crutches – but continued her fight for justice.

The first setback in Senegal in 2000 suggested a local trial was no longer an option, so Moudeïna, Guengueng and others embarked on a decade of on-again off-again attempts to prosecute Habré in a European court. Among them was my colleague Reed Brody of Human Rights Watch, who had been involved with the attempts to bring Pinochet to justice in London and who came up with the phrase 'Africa's Pinochet'; the tagline stuck. The 'dictator-hunter', as headline-writers liked to call him (or 'the Indiana Jones of international justice', as he has also been described), would devote years of his life to trying to put Habré behind bars.

Senegal kept promising Habré would 'very probably' be delivered to Belgium, which said it was ready to prosecute. But that never happened. Gradually, it seemed only the naive could still believe Habré would ever face justice. I first met the quietly determined Souleymane Guengueng in 2008, eighteen years after his release. Poor health conditions in prison had damaged his eyes. Peering through his owlish glasses, he told me: 'I will not feel complete until Habré is in jail.' It was inspiring stuff but, despite all my admiration for their efforts, I don't think I truly believed that Guengueng, Moudeïna, Brody and others would ever achieve their goal. All the attempts to prosecute Habré seemed lost in what South Africa's Archbishop Desmond Tutu complained of as an 'interminable political and legal soap opera'.

In 2012, however, twenty-two years after Habré's oust-
ing, the judicial fog suddenly lifted. Following a request
from Belgium, the International Court of Justice ruled that
Senegal must either prosecute Habré 'without further delay'
or extradite him to a country willing to do so. Senegal's new
justice minister, former anti-corruption campaigner Aminata
Touré – Hurricane Mimi, as she was known – made the
prosecution happen, saying: 'We regret that for years this trial
did not take place.'

Now, everything changed. The Senegalese government
and the African Union jointly created the Extraordinary
African Chambers in the Courts of Senegal to prosecute
crimes committed in Chad under Habré's rule. One Sunday
morning, Habré was arrested at one of his two homes (one
for each wife) in the elegant Dakar district of Almadies..Like
Pinochet, Milošević and others, Habré complained of 'illegal
abduction' and 'kidnapping'. But his life of luxury was over.

Jacqueline Moudeïna talked at the trial of being 'the
mouthpiece of the voiceless, the missing, the dead, the tortured, all those who because of the crimes of Hissène Habré
can never come to testify before you'. Habré, dressed in traditional white *boubou* robe and turban, shouted 'This is a farce!'
The judge was unimpressed: 'The rule of law will prevail.' As
Reed Brody wrote in *To Catch a Dictator*, his account of the
long struggles to bring Habré to justice, 'Habré wasn't in the
dock because Chad's strongman [Habré's successor, President
Idriss Déby] had so decreed. He was there because a group
of brave citizens . . . had fought furiously for years to get him
there. The power of their achievement was nothing less than
revolutionary.'

In one of the most powerful moments of the trial, a prosecution witness described how Habré had raped her thirty
years earlier. Khadidja Zidane had said for years that if she

ever came face to face with Habré she would reveal something, without saying what. Now she told her shattering
story. 'The president himself raped me four times,' Zidane
told the court, standing a few metres away from her attacker.
'When I was finished,' she said after the hearing, 'I felt that a
great weight had been taken off me.'

On 30 May 2016, Habré was jailed for life for rape, torture
and crimes against humanity. An African court had convicted an African dictator. It was the first time a former head
of state had been convicted of rape anywhere. The courtroom erupted in weeping, ululation and cheers. Widows in
colourful outfits, whose husbands had died in Habré's jails
and who had travelled to Dakar for this moment of history,
symbolically threw down pieces of black cloth to mark the
end of their mourning.

Souleymane Guengueng declared before a forest of cameras outside the court, 'To all the dictators violating human
rights in the world: this can happen to you. To all their
victims: this means don't keep your mouth shut. Open it.'
UN Secretary-General Ban Ki-moon talked of a 'historic'
moment. US Secretary of State John Kerry described the trial
as 'an opportunity for the United States to reflect on, and
learn from, our own connection with past events in Chad'.
Jacqueline Moudeïna praised the 'heroes' who had given evidence, and concluded: 'For all the atrocities, the torture that
people endured, the disappearances – for all this, one person
is responsible. And that person is Monsieur Hissène Habré.'

Chapter Five

'The Rules of the Game are Changing'

Guantánamo, Iraq, Afghanistan (2001–).
Northern Ireland (1972–2010)

As the new millennium began, there were more reasons for optimism about global justice than at any time since Nuremberg. An international criminal court had been agreed. A Latin American dictator had been arrested (and his immunity was removed at home). Organisers of genocide had been convicted at an international court in Africa. A European government would soon deliver its own former president for trial at a war crimes tribunal in The Hague.

There would soon be reminders, however, that some governments still believed it was up to them to choose whether or not to comply with their obligations. That contempt for the law – Kant's 'savage and lawless freedom' to break the rules – would have dangerous consequences for the world.

In 1775, when Americans were fighting for independence from the British crown, the crimes committed by the redcoats shocked George Washington. King George III declared the American rebels to be guilty of treason, which meant captured soldiers were beaten, starved and killed instead of being treated as prisoners of war. George Washington insisted America must be different. Prisoners, he wrote, should be treated with humanity: 'Let them have no reason to complain of us copying the brutal manner of the British Army ... While we are contending for our own liberty we should be very cautious of violating the rights of conscience in others.' Washington believed there should be consequences if such orders were disobeyed: 'I do most earnestly enjoin you to bring him to such severe and exemplary punishment as the enormity of the crime shall require.' Anyone disobeying such orders would bring 'shame, disgrace and ruin to themselves and their country'.

Those humane principles – which were not universally applied, even in Washington's time; he was, after all, himself a slave-owner – were now tossed aside. George Washington was right to predict that if Americans committed 'base and infamous' abuses, that would bring shame to their country. In the twenty-first century, however, there was none of the 'severe and exemplary punishment' which the country's first commander-in-chief had called for.

In the wake of the attacks of 11 September 2001, few could doubt the scale of the challenge that the US and other governments faced. Al-Qaeda hijackers seized control of passenger planes and destroyed the World Trade Center skyscrapers and targeted the Pentagon in order to kill the largest number of people in the most spectacular fashion in the shortest possible time. The dust clouds of death where the Twin Towers once stood left the world reeling in disbelief. 'This is an attack on all of us,' signs of solidarity in India declared. In Beijing, thousands left letters of condolence outside the American embassy. Even Iran condemned the 'horrific' attacks perpetrated by those who 'could only communicate with perceived opponents through carnage and devastation'.

The scale of the horror led the leaders of the world's most powerful democracy to reach an extraordinary conclusion: that the attackers' rejection of humanity meant the US government, too, should abandon basic rules. Vice-President Dick Cheney explained: 'We have to work, sort of the dark side ... It's going to be vital for us to use any means at our disposal, basically, to achieve our objective.' White House counsel (later Attorney-General) Alberto Gonzales argued that the Geneva Conventions, strengthened in 1949 in response to the horrors of the Second World War, were 'obsolete' and 'quaint' because of restrictions they imposed.

Out of the reach of US courts, abuse was legitimised. That began with the CIA's use of 'extraordinary rendition' – abducting sometimes entirely innocent suspects and sending them to be tortured by others (including Assad's Syria). The abuses quickly came in-house, too. The US base at Guantánamo Bay, near the eastern tip of Cuba – a forty-square-mile anomaly, leased from Cuba under a deal struck in 1903 – took in hundreds of detainees US forces had picked up after the defeat of the Taliban regime in Afghanistan. Some in Guantánamo had supported terror attacks. But many had simply been in the wrong place at the wrong time or had been denounced by somebody with a score to settle.

For those and other detainees, the United States was determined to tear up the rules. In August 2002, a secret memo signed by assistant attorney-general Jay Bybee sought to redefine torture almost out of existence. From now on, only events such as organ failure, impairment of bodily function 'or even death' would count as torture. Anything else was deemed acceptable. Some raised their voices against such lawlessness. Alberto Mora, born of Cuban-Hungarian parents, was US naval counsel with a rank equivalent to a four-star general. He criticised the 'catastrophically poor legal reasoning' of a 2003 memo, and asked its author, deputy assistant attorney-general John Yoo (main author of the memo signed off by his boss Jay Bybee the previous year), 'Are you saying the president has the authority to order torture?' 'Yes,' Yoo replied. 'Otherwise criminal' conduct, another document suggested, could be rendered 'not unlawful' by decree. Mora pointed to the obvious conclusion: 'If everything is permissible and almost nothing is prohibited, it makes a mockery of the law.'

Mark Fallon, deputy commander of the Criminal Investigative Task Force which had a presence at Guantánamo, alerted Mora in December 2002 to his concerns about the growing permissiveness of torture. Fallon, one of America's most experienced counter-terrorism investigators, believed torture was morally wrong and practically unproductive. In one email in 2002, Fallon warned his colleagues: 'Somebody needs to be considering how history will look back at this.' But, as he wrote in *Unjustifiable Means*, an insider's account of how America lost its moral compass, 'The boulder kept rolling. The avalanche followed. America became just what its extremist enemies wanted – a fellow terrorist in a world where the established rules of war no longer applied.' When Fallon took his concerns to the Guantánamo commander, General Geoffrey Miller, Miller made clear he wasn't listening. 'If you want to be on the team,' Miller told Fallon, 'you've got to wear the same shirt. Hoo-ah.'

I got to know Mark Fallon years later, when he agreed to speak at a Freedom from Torture event in 2019. As he says now, looking back on the post-9/11 era, 'We embraced torture as a country. That's hard to swallow, but that's the truth. And embracing torture enabled the proliferation of terrorism.'

Some understood that rules matter – not just morally, but practically, too. In August 2003, five months after the invasion of Iraq, there was a showing at the Pentagon of Gillo Pontecorvo's film *The Battle of Algiers* (which had initially been banned in France, as described in Chapter Two). A flyer for the evening announced: 'How to win a battle against terrorism and lose the war of ideas.' The parallels were obvious – not just in the context of Iraq, but also in other conflicts where governments make choices about how to deal with violent armed groups and whether rules matter. As the Defense Department flyer put it: 'Children shoot soldiers at point-blank range. Women plant bombs in cafés. Soon the entire Arab population builds to a mad fervor. Sound familiar? The French have a plan. It succeeds tactically, but fails strategically. To understand why, come to a rare showing of this film.'

The Battle of Algiers includes graphic portrayals of torture. It begins and ends with a scene in 1957 in which French forces blow up a house where the FLN rebel leader is hiding. He is killed, as are sixteen innocent others. The French general is happy with a successful day and assumes the rebellion is now defeated ('the tapeworm no longer has a head'). As the film's closing titles remind us, five years later Algeria gained independence from France and the nationalists took power. Whoever had the idea for the film night (it seems reasonable to assume it wasn't Donald Rumsfeld), the choice was inspired. And yet, few lessons were learned.

*

On the inside, people like Mora and Fallon did their best to stop the dangerous juggernaut of illegality. On the outside, even as the evidence of torture and other abuses began to emerge, some people found it hard to comprehend the extent to which an elected government had already begun to trample basic rules of humanity and the rule of law.

In the *Columbia Journalism Review*, Eric Umansky would later highlight editors' reluctance to accept even their own reporters' findings where the evidence seemed too disturbing. Umansky gave the example of an investigation by Carlotta Gall, based in Afghanistan for the *New York Times*. In early 2003, just ahead of the invasion of Iraq, Gall – who had previously reported for the *Moscow Times* on Russian abuses in Chechnya – discovered that Americans had tortured and killed two detainees at Bagram airbase north of Kabul. Foreign editor Roger Cohen and investigations editor Doug Frantz believed the importance of the story meant it should run on the front page. As Frantz remembered later: 'On a scale of one to ten, Carlotta's story was nailed down to a ten. And if it had run on the front page, it would have sent a strong signal not just to the Bush administration but to other news organisations.' But senior executives at the *New York Times* believed the account of such serious abuse was, in Frantz's words, 'improbable; it was just hard to get their mind around'. Gall concluded that her bosses did not want to 'believe bad things of Americans'. Eventually Cohen gave up the argument; the story was buried on page fourteen and went mostly unnoticed. Only later did it become clear that not only was Gall's story correct in every important detail, but the full extent of torture and abuse at Bagram was worse than she or anyone else could have imagined at that time.

Even some whose job it is to shout about human rights violations found it difficult to believe that a government in a

democracy could lie so brazenly. In June 2003, eleven leading human rights organisations – including Human Rights
Watch, where I was working at that time – issued a joint press
release *praising* the White House for its willingness to disavow
torture, in response to an announcement that all interroga-
tions would be 'in a manner consistent' with international
obligations. President Bush went so far as to claim: 'The
United States is committed to the worldwide elimination of
torture and we are leading this fight by example.' Bush called
for others to join with the United States in 'prohibiting, investigating and prosecuting' acts of torture.

The issuing of an enthusiastic press release about the statement was internally controversial even at the time, with a
series of fierce exchanges on the arguments for and against.
Those who argued in favour of this verbal bouquet to the
White House ('Bush administration rules out using cruel
treatment', said the headline) saw the promise of compliance
with international obligations as a 'welcome message' which
deserved to be highlighted. Others – including and especially
those with personal experience of torture regimes and the
lies they love to tell – were wary of unreservedly praising
the government's words before we knew what was really
happening.

As would soon become clear: the sceptics were right, the
optimists were sadly and badly wrong. Even as the government published its fine-sounding words about compliance
with international law, it was secretly working to pick the
moral and judicial locks. As Anthony Lewis wrote in the *New
York Review of Books* after the torture memos quoted above
were published in 2004: 'The memos read like the advice of
a mob lawyer to a mafia don on how to skirt the law and
stay out of prison. Avoiding prosecution is literally a theme
of the memoranda.'

Some officials treated concerns about torture as a mere joke. When signing off a memo which authorised 'enhanced interrogation techniques' including twenty-hour inter-rogations, phobias and stress positions, Donald Rumsfeld scribbled at the bottom, 'I stand for eight to ten hours a day. Why is standing limited to four hours?' Colonel Lawrence Wilkerson, chief of staff to Secretary of State Colin Powell, put Rumsfeld's flippancy in the context of crimes commit-ted in Vietnam: 'It said, "Carte blanche, guys." That's what started them down this slope. You'll have My Lais then. Once you pull this thread, the whole fabric unravels.'

Unravel it did, most dramatically sixteen months after Rumsfeld signed that memo. In April 2004, CBS's *Sixty Minutes* programme showed the photographs from Abu Ghraib prison. A *New Yorker* article by Seymour Hersh, who had revealed the My Lai killings thirty-five years earlier, followed soon afterwards. The stories and accompanying images made headlines worldwide. Those now-notorious images from Abu Ghraib are a stark reminder of what hap-pens when rules are no longer believed to matter. In one photograph, twenty-one-year-old Private Lynndie England is seen holding a naked man on a leash. In another, twenty-five-year-old reservist Sabrina Harman grins from behind a pyramid of naked bodies. In a third, a hooded detainee stands precariously on a box, wires attached to his hands; he was told he would be electrocuted if he moved.

In response to publication of the photographs, President Bush spoke of his 'disgust' and Rumsfeld said he felt 'terri-ble'. After all, 'They're human beings.' Rumsfeld declared that he and Bush were 'blindsided' by what had happened, and promised consequences. 'What we believe in,' he told Congress, 'is making sure when wrongdoing or scandal occur that they are not covered up but exposed, investigated and publicly disclosed – and the guilty brought to justice.' Comedy Central's *The Daily Show* skewered the contradictions: 'There's no question that what took place in that prison was horrible. But . . . it's our principles that matter, our inspiring, abstract notions. Remember: just because torturing prisoners is something we did, doesn't mean it's something we *would* do.'

The satirical summary was accurate. The connection between earlier decisions taken in Washington and what happened at Abu Ghraib was clear. Geoffrey Miller, who had been so contemptuous of Mark Fallon's concerns at Guantánamo in 2002, visited Abu Ghraib shortly after Rumsfeld's 'enhanced interrogation techniques' memo and called for them to 'Gitmo-ise' their operation. He explained to the prison commander, Janis Karpinski, 'You're too nice to the prisoners . . . You have to treat the prisoners like dogs.'

And so it went. Treating prisoners 'like dogs' became the norm. Sabrina Harman had written emails home to her partner, Kelly Bryant, in which she expressed her concerns. Describing a detainee who had been beaten to death, Harman wrote: 'Not many people know this shit goes on. The only reason I want to be there is to get the pictures and prove that the US is not what they think. But I don't know if I can take it mentally. What if that was me in their shoes?' Long before the Abu Ghraib images became notorious, Harman told her girlfriend: 'These people will be our future terrorists. Kelly, it's awful.'

Harman, who had no legal training and no previous experience of war – she had worked in Papa Johns Pizza in Alexandria, Virginia before being deployed to Baghdad – understood clearly what she was seeing (and what she ended up appearing to condone). As Alberto Mora pointed out, 'The debate here isn't only how to protect the country. It's how to protect our values.' But politicians ignored that simple lesson.

Harman the not-quite whistleblower, Lynndie England and other junior soldiers were prosecuted and jailed for the abuse exposed at Abu Ghraib, just as junior soldiers had been prosecuted in connection with the My Lai massacre three decades earlier. Harman said: 'Not only did I let down the people in Iraq, I let down every single soldier that serves today.' Meanwhile, however, some who created the context for those crimes did not just go unpunished but were *rewarded*: General Geoffrey Miller was praised as an 'innovator' and received the Distinguished Service Medal when he retired in 2006.

As would gradually become clear, the abuses at Abu Ghraib were just the tip of the iceberg. The culture of impunity meant deadly abuse became widespread in Iraq, Afghanistan and elsewhere. Core values were abandoned even while that abandonment was denied.

For many years, waterboarding – creating the sensation of drowning through prolonged submersion – had been a notorious form of torture. At the Tokyo tribunal, American judges convicted Japanese soldiers who waterboarded prisoners during the Second World War ('did wilfully and unlawfully, brutally mistreat and torture … by beating and kicking him, by fastening him on a stretcher and pouring water up his nostrils'). Sixty years later, Vice-President Dick Cheney insisted the use of waterboarding was 'a no-brainer'. (He added the standard nonsensical rider: 'We don't torture. That's not what we're involved in.') CIA director George Tenet asked President Bush if waterboarding was acceptable. 'Damn right,' Bush replied.

This tearing-up of existing rules and obligations ran in parallel with a determination to avoid future accountability. Bush's 'Hague Invasion Act' against the International

Criminal Court became law two days after the Bybee torture
memo was approved in 2002. The closeness in time is partly
coincidental, since the existence of the memo was known
only to a handful of people at that time. But the torture
permissions and the moves against the ICC had one obvious thing in common: the belief that rules are for powerful
governments to impose but not to obey. There was little
understanding of how such lawlessness might backfire.

The 'Global War on Terrorism' declared after 9/11 – with
its own acronym and even its own GWOT military service
medal – became a free pass for those who wanted to set
long-standing obligations aside, all around the world. It was
unsurprising that repressive governments seized gratefully
on the excuse to lock up and torture people, everywhere
from Bahrain to Uzbekistan. 'In authoritarian states, anti-
terrorism has become a sledgehammer with which to smash
opponents of all shapes and sizes, from the genuinely violent
to the merely politically sceptical,' as Conor Gearty put it in
Homeland Insecurity: The Rise and Rise of Anti-Terrorism Law.

Even among democracies, however, America was not alone
in acting as though rules no longer mattered. There were
deadly attacks around the world at this time, from Madrid
to Mumbai. In London, fifty-two people were killed in a
series of bombings on the transport network in 2005. In
other words: as with 9/11, the security challenges were real.
But the British government responded not by strengthening
the rule of law but by calling it into question, including the
prohibition on torture and returning people to the risk of
torture. As prime minister Tony Blair summed it up, 'The
rules of the game are changing.'

In 2005, the government's annual human rights report
insisted: 'Torture is one of the worst human rights abuses . . .

When governments condone it, they risk losing their legitimacy and provoking terrorism.' True enough. And yet, Britain refused to criticise US abuses at Guantánamo, Abu Ghraib and elsewhere. It also became complicit in state-sponsored abduction and torture – a modern version of the Nazis' 'Night and Fog' disappearances which the Allies had prosecuted at Nuremberg.

This contradiction – simultaneously condemning torture and condoning it – tied the government in impossible knots. In 2006, I was involved in the publication of a Human Rights Watch volume of essays on torture. 'Does it make us safer? Is it ever OK?', the cover strapline asked. Human rights lawyer (and prime ministerial spouse) Cherie Booth, who had contributed an essay on sexual violence and torture, kindly accepted my invitation to give a lecture at the launch, to be hosted by the foreign affairs think tank Chatham House. Before 9/11, a talk condemning torture would have seemed uncontroversial. But times had changed. Torture was now a touchy issue. A few weeks later, Downing Street phoned to tell me the event would either have to be off the record (which, despite Chatham House being famous for its non-attributable 'Chatham House rule' meetings, was a non-starter for an event like this) or would not take place at all. Only when I pointed out that Chatham House had already notified journalists and that sudden cancellation would require an explanation – which I would not be able to give – did they reluctantly and irritably back down.

The same discomfort appeared in other contexts, too. Channel 4 Television organised an event in the Houses of Parliament which took the themes of the Human Rights Watch torture volume as its starting point. Conservative and Liberal Democrat representatives accepted invitations to take part; the government refused to provide a speaker until Channel 4 told them they would in that case be 'empty-chaired', thus high-lighting the refusal to answer key questions. My main memory of the day is that the minister who reluctantly appeared on the panel was in a foul mood throughout, essentially asking, How dare we question his government's obvious good faith? (His unhappiness was partly understandable: the title of the event was 'Torture: Bending the Rules', an accurate summary of what was happening at that time but not what the government wanted to hear.)

A few months later – and partly in response to the angry but implausible denials of culpability – I wrote a report for Human Rights Watch on British government attitudes to torture, called *Dangerous Ambivalence*. The government was unhappy with my conclusions; I was berated for the suppos-edly unfair criticisms I had made. And yet, looking back, I am struck mostly by how soft the conclusions were and how little we knew; the truth was much worse. A parliamentary inquiry chaired by former attorney-general Dominic Grieve later found 'inexcusable' acquiescence in torture as part of the war on terror, including global kidnap and hundreds of cases where Britain's intelligence agencies received information from prisoners who had been tortured.

In 2004, to take just one example of the moral collapse, the British intelligence services facilitated the kidnap of Libyan dissident Abdel Hakim Belhaj and his pregnant wife Fatima Boudchar on behalf of the Gaddafi regime. The couple were abducted and transported, trussed up and blindfolded, from Thailand to Libya, where Belhaj was duly tortured. MI6's di-rector of counter-terrorism, Sir Mark Allen, wrote a gushing note to Gaddafi's intelligence chief Moussa Koussa, telling him the illegal kidnap was 'the least we could do for you' to demonstrate the 'remarkable relationship we have built over recent years'. (Colleagues from Human Rights Watch stumbled upon an extraordinary cache of faxed messages, including the one quoted above, at the abandoned intelligence headquarters in Tripoli during the uprising against Gaddafi in 2011. Without that chance find, the story would presumably never have come to light.) In 2018, the British government finally agreed to apologise for what prime minister Theresa May described as the couple's 'appalling' treatment; the government had previously spent millions of pounds trying not to apologise. Fatima Boudchar received compensation for her suffering; Belhaj said he had never wanted money, only the apology. He was more gracious than Britain had been: 'A great society does not torture; does not help others to torture; and, when it makes mistakes, it accepts them and apologises. Britain has a made a wrong right today, and set an example for other nations to follow.'

Like others who have authorised or committed torture and other crimes over the years, politicians who had been involved in shaping the US torture programme were confident they would never face consequences. But the Pinochet precedent of universal jurisdiction – arrest while travelling – had begun to change the ground rules. In 2011, George W. Bush cancelled a scheduled visit to Switzerland, apparently rattled by a criminal complaint that human rights groups had prepared, which detailed the former president's responsibility for torture. (Eight years earlier, Bush had called on all 'law-abiding nations' to join in 'prohibiting, investigating and prosecuting all acts of torture', so they were only doing what he had asked for.) Other senior US officials were reported to hesitate over trips to Europe, too. Such initiatives were, admittedly, as much about headlines as about a likely arrest. In Washington, meanwhile, there was little sign of accountability of any kind – even after the arrival of a president who promised a new start.

During his presidential campaign in 2008, Barack Obama was eloquent in his commitment to the rule of law: 'In the dark halls of Abu Ghraib and the detention cells of Guantánamo,' he said, 'we have compromised our most precious values.' On election night, as it became clear that Obama would be the next president, prisoners at Guantánamo called his name from inside their cells. Defence lawyers for the detainees mamboed their way in provocative celebration through the prosecutors' quarters, chanting 'Hey, hey ... Goodbye!' That initial optimism seemed justified: within days of his inauguration in 2009, the new president promised the camp would be closed within a year. But that didn't happen.

Six years later, on the occasion of a scathing Senate report on torture, President Obama said one of America's strengths was its 'willingness to openly confront our past, face our imperfections, make changes and do better'. It was a bravely positive spin on a decade of attempts to block publication, as vividly portrayed in *The Report*, the 2019 film starring Adam Driver. Even today, only a summary of the 7,000-page Senate report has been published. Obama said he wanted 'to look forward, not backward', which meant there would be no attempt to prosecute those who might have broken domestic and international laws.

As Mark Fallon sums it up, 'We treated detainees as somehow subhuman, and in the process we became something less than human ourselves.' Bush and Rumsfeld pretended to condemn torture, even while encouraging it to happen. Obama acknowledged that 'we tortured some folks' – but made clear that there would be no consequences for those crimes. Donald Trump went further even than Bush and Rumsfeld had done: he publicly praised torture, saying it 'absolutely' works. Fallon has little time for such fantasies:

'In the movies, bad guys don't crack until their interrogators have them begging for mercy. But in the real world I had seen time and again that building rapport with detainees yielded far better actionable intelligence than the strong-arm approach, and prevented more attacks in future.' But in 2017 Trump came into office, as Fallon puts it, 'celebrating torture'. Gina Haspel, who Trump appointed as his new head of the CIA, had been in charge of a 'black site' in Thailand – an off-the-books torture site – where US interrogators waterboarded detainees. She was also involved in the destruction of ninety-two videos of CIA torture, which she justified by the difficulties that would be caused 'if the tapes ever got into the public domain'. Trump pardoned American soldiers who had been indicted or convicted by US courts for war crimes in Afghanistan. US defence chiefs, worried about discipline, were unhappy, but Trump didn't care: Navy Secretary Richard Spencer was sacked when he pushed back against the president's love of impunity.

Trump upped the ante on the International Criminal Court, too. In 2002, President Bush had approved the noisy but essentially empty 'Hague Invasion Act'. In 2020, Trump took this a step further by announcing personal sanctions against prosecutor Fatou Bensouda and others as punishment for the court's willingness to examine unpunished US war crimes in Afghanistan and to consider a Palestine investigation.

Trump's dangerous clownery and love of impunity could seem to be in a class of its own. Less heralded was the mini-Trumpery that sprung up on the other side of the Atlantic. In 2019, even as Trump pardoned US soldiers indicted for or convicted of war crimes, the British government put forward one of the most startling pieces of legislation seen in any parliamentary democracy in recent years.

The Overseas Operations Bill purported to protect British troops from 'vexatious' claims. In reality, the most obvious consequence of its 'presumption against prosecution' for war crimes would have been to provide effective immunity after five years – a blink of the eye in terms of investigations in conflict zones.

At the time, I was policy and advocacy director at Freedom from Torture, which campaigned against the global signal of impunity for torture and other war crimes the proposed legislation would send. Johnny Mercer, the minister who dreamed up the proposals, dismissed concerns expressed by torture survivors as 'garbage'. Others, however, saw dangers for potential victims of war crimes and for Britain's reputation alike: a former head of the armed forces, a former attorney-general and a former defence and foreign secretary all agreed to my request on behalf of Freedom from Torture to make their voices heard in protest at these extraordinary proposals. In the House of Lords, former Nato head Lord Robertson worked with former Supreme Court judges and others to vote the most dangerous elements down.

For a year, the government continued to insist it would never back down, despite repeated pushback from the upper house. And then, one Tuesday afternoon, prime minister Boris Johnson suddenly did just that. The bill survived in truncated form, but the impunity proposals were dropped. This unexpected defeat of official lawlessness was welcome. But how had we ever got to this place? Before the turna-round, I had talked about the problems with Stephen Glover, my first boss at the *Independent*, who had sent me to eastern Europe thirty years earlier and who was now a columnist at the conservative *Daily Mail*. A few days after our conversation, the *Mail* published an editorial which rightly concluded: 'Implying troops are untouchable sends a dangerous message about our values, giving rogue regimes carte blanche to commit war crimes.' Torture survivors and others who had protested across the country celebrated Johnson's U-turn, which came a few days after that piece was published. But it remained extraordinary to think that an elected government could ever have thought it was a good idea to send such a signal of entrenched impunity.

The dangers were not just hypothetical. Even as the government was trying to push its impunity proposals through, evidence emerged of alleged war crimes by British special forces in Afghanistan – and an apparent determination to cover up what had happened. The incidents included a night-time raid in February 2011 by the SAS in the village of Gawahargin in Helmand Province, with a series of what appeared to be executions. Officially, the killings were 'self-defence', but Afghan special forces who took part in the raid talked of assassination. British colleagues were sceptical, too. 'This is the eighth time this has happened,' one officer wrote. 'You couldn't MAKE IT UP!' Another asked, 'Why are we the only ones who see this bollocks for what it is?' An email on the Gawahargin killings talked of the 'latest massacre!'; nine Afghans had been killed in similar circumstances a week earlier and eight more would be killed two days later. Concerns that Britain's elite forces were operating an unofficial execution policy were raised at the top. Nothing happened.

In 2014, lawyers for Saifullah Yar – whose father, two brothers and a cousin were all killed that night in Gawahargin in circumstances of extraordinary improbability, if we were to take the official version at face value – called for his case to be investigated. The military police began a probe, including – unknown to the families of Afghans killed – the night raids. But that investigation, Operation Northmoor, was closed down in 2019 because there was 'no evidence of criminal behaviour'. Saifullah Yar refused to accept these findings and challenged the UK's failure to investigate. The government said there was nothing to investigate, because none of those involved could 'specifically remember' the operation. By a mixture of chance and dogged determination, those failures would eventually be exposed. A High Court judge, sceptical of what he called 'collective amnesia', gave the go-ahead for a judicial review, whereupon the Ministry of Defence had to admit that it did in fact have thousands of pages of highly relevant materials. A previously hidden trove of documents (including the emails quoted above) was suddenly disclosed.

Eventually, the UK government was forced to allow some light in. In 2022, a year after the withdrawal of the impunity proposals which would have made investigation of these and other well-documented crimes impossible because of the time elapsed, the government settled the legal proceedings and announced a public inquiry to look into the Gawahargin and other killings. In the Royal Courts of Justice on the Strand in 2024, I listened to hours of astonishing testimony from a tetchy Johnny Mercer. Mercer, who had served as an army captain in Afghanistan, told the inquiry how, as veterans' minister, he had expressed private concerns about a possible cover-up of war crimes based on what he had heard from others. So far, so admirable. And yet: he hadn't been worried enough to jettison the impunity proposals he was trying to push through at the same time.

Lord Justice Haddon-Cave, chair of the Afghanistan inquiry, was unimpressed by Mercer presenting himself as a courageous voice of truth while refusing to share the names of those who might have evidence of crimes; Mercer said he was 'not prepared to burn them' and rejected the judge's calls for him to show 'moral courage'. Mercer said he was ready to go to jail rather than hand any names over (even though any witnesses would be guaranteed anonymity). In July 2024, a few weeks after elections in which the country and his constituency ended Mercer's time as minister and member of parliament respectively, Haddon-Cave let him off jail 'for the time being'.

We can hope the inquiry establishes at least some of the truth. That, in turn, may lead to prosecutions. But such an inquiry should never have been needed. The apparent willingness to cover up crimes had practical as well as moral implications, which the government seemed reluctant to acknowledge. As Frank Ledwidge, a former military intelligence officer, told the BBC's *Panorama* programme as the evidence of extrajudicial killings mounted in 2019, 'Aside from alienating our Afghan allies, the narrative of murderous British forces played right into the hands of the insurgents.'

In terms of the readiness to let difficult truths be heard, developments in Australia came, by comparison, almost as good news – though it might not sound like that at first. Australian special forces stood accused of murdering thirty-nine Afghans in twenty-three incidents between 2005 and 2016. The crimes were shocking. But the Australian reaction was remarkable, too, especially by contrast with the whitewash that the British government had apparently tried to engineer. In 2020, Australia published a report by Major-General Paul Brereton which said that the soldiers' actions were 'disgraceful and a profound betrayal' of all that the Australian armed forces stood for. The chief of the defence force said the revelations in the Brereton Report were 'shameful' and 'appalling', and promised consequences. At the time of writing, at least one trial is getting under way. The alleged crimes, in other words, were serious. But potential punishment is taken seriously, too.

Sometimes, civilian deaths have been denied, against all evidence. Barack Obama declared in 2011: 'We're a nation that brings our enemies to justice while adhering to the rule of law, and respecting the rights of all our citizens.' But truth is an essential starting point for justice. Drone attacks by US forces on Islamic State targets in Iraq and Syria killed thousands of civilians in what Obama described as 'the most precise air campaign in history'. But a Pulitzer-winning investigation by Azmat Khan and others in the *New York Times* in 2021 revealed the 'many, often disastrous ways the military's predictions of the peril to civilians turn out to be wrong' – unacknowledged by Washington. As one former Pentagon adviser told Khan, 'We develop all these capabilities, but we don't use them to buy down risk for civilians. We just use them to make attacks that maybe we couldn't do before.'

For all its problems, the United States was, however, a model of transparency by comparison with its allies in the UK. America acknowledged 1,400 civilians had died in attacks on ISIS targets between 2014 and 2017. Britain, by contrast, insisted it had caused not a single civilian death. In 2016, the official Chilcot Report on the war in Iraq criticised the government's apparent lack of interest in civilian casualties and concluded: 'A government has a responsibility to make every reasonable effort to understand the likely and actual effects of its military actions on civilians.'

Chilcot's recommendations were ignored, as Emma Graham-Harrison of the *Guardian* and Joe Clark of the nonprofit watchdog Airwars revealed with their 2023 investigation in Mosul in northern Iraq. They showed Britain's supposed zero civilian casualty figures (or, when that was challenged, 'one' death) were purest fiction. Graham-Harrison and Clark met with Enam Younis, whose six-year-old daughter Taiba was killed, whose toddler son Ali lost part of a foot and hand, and whose then three-year-old daughter Zahra has shrapnel embedded in her skull which cannot be removed. The pain associated with that day means that Younis, even years later, cannot bear to return to her home town: 'I didn't even visit my daughter's grave. I can't do it.' The 2016 drone attack which had such devastating consequences came just four months after the Iraq inquiry had called for 'every reasonable possibility' to investigate civilian deaths. Nobody from the British government ever tried to find out what had happened that day, even though drone operators knew civilians had been hit. Enam Younis's case was just one of many.

The refusal to tell the truth about civilian lives destroyed is an obvious moral and legal failure. As with the Gawahargin killings, there are practical implications, too. As Emma Graham-Harrison pointed out, 'In the past twenty years, civilian deaths have again and again proved one of the most powerful recruiting sergeants against western armies, from Iraq to Afghanistan.'

———

Too often, governments refuse to take responsibility for crimes their forces have committed. The proclaimed need for 'security' trumps everything else. But in one area at least, the British government gradually took responsibility and eventually apologised for its past crimes. Partly through that acknowledgement of wrongdoing, a previously unimaginable degree of stability has been achieved.

The killings of fourteen people at a single demonstration, three years after the 'Troubles' began in Northern Ireland in 1969, caused waves of increased violence in the province for years to come, not least because of the official lies that were told about Bloody Sunday, as it came to be known. A peaceful protest against internment without trial was planned in the Catholic-majority city of Derry (Londonderry) on 30 January 1972. The Northern Ireland Civil Rights Association, noting that the proposed rally defied a blanket ban on protests, called on participants and security forces alike to ensure this would be an 'incident-free day'.

Ten thousand people joined the march, which initially passed off peacefully. As the rally neared its end, youths threw stones; soldiers dispersed them with water cannon. And then, just after 4 p.m. on that sunny winter afternoon, paratroopers opened fire. Thirteen unarmed Catholics died that day; a fourteenth died later. A famous image shows Father Edward Daly, Catholic priest and later Bishop of Derry, waving a bloodied white handkerchief as he leads a small and terrified group carrying the fatally wounded Jackie Duddy, aged seventeen. 'Am I going to die?' Jackie asked the priest. Daly told him no, then administered last rites. (The handkerchief is now in a Derry museum; in 2022, fifty years after Bloody Sunday, Derry Playhouse staged *The White Handkerchief*, a play about the events of that day.)

The soldiers of 1 Para, the 1st Battalion of the Parachute Regiment, claimed they opened fire in response to sustained attack from nail bombs and bullets. The Lord Chief Justice, Lord Widgery, was appointed to chair an inquiry. At a meeting in Downing Street, prime minister Edward Heath told Widgery that Britain was fighting 'not only a military war but a propaganda war'. Sure enough, the Widgery Report published three months later concluded that protesters were to blame for their own deaths, because defiance of the protest ban was 'highly dangerous'. Widgery took no testimony from survivors but concluded there was 'no reason' to suppose the soldiers would have opened fire unless they had been fired on first. He boldly and implausibly argued that the only reason why no British soldiers were hurt must have been down to their 'superior fieldcraft and training'.

Anger over the killings of Bloody Sunday and the subsequent cover-up became a key recruiting tool for the Provisional Irish Republican Army in the years to come. As Bishop Daly said later, 'Many young people I have talked to in prison have told me they would have never joined the IRA had it not been for what they witnessed, and heard of happening, on Bloody Sunday.' Three thousand would die in Northern Ireland in the next three decades – Catholic, Protestant and members of the security forces. Even on the less dangerous British mainland, anyone who lived through that time remembers the bombs and bomb scares in pubs, department stores and shopping centres. For decades, insecurity remained the norm: prime minister Margaret Thatcher was almost killed in Brighton's Grand Hotel in 1984 (five others died that night); a mortar shell exploded in the garden of 10 Downing Street during a cabinet meeting in 1991.

Many Catholics distrusted and disliked the violence of the IRA, which claimed to represent them. But, in the words of the narrator of Anna Burns's 2018 Booker Prize-winning novel *Milkman*, 'No matter the reservations held then – as to methods and morals and about the various groupings that came into operation . . . if we hadn't had the renouncers [the IRA] as our underground buffer between us and this overwhelming and combined enemy, who else, in all the world, would we have had?'

For some, the jump from blaming the IRA to blaming all Catholics was tempting. In words that have echoes in conflicts elsewhere today, Protestant politician Jean Coulter argued after one especially horrific firebombing of a hotel near Belfast in 1978 that there were 'no innocent people' in the 'Republican ghettoes', and that, in order to end terror attacks by the IRA, it was necessary to bomb Catholic areas from the air. It can only be imagined what the deaths of hundreds or thousands of men, women and children would have achieved if anybody had taken Coulter's idea seriously. Luckily, they didn't. Instead, change gradually came. John Major, who became prime minister in 1990, began secret talks which led to a ceasefire in 1994. His successor Tony Blair picked up the baton in 1997. The Good Friday Agreement of 1998 would change Northern Ireland for ever.

Even as history was being made, I heard much pessimism, when I reported from the province for the *Independent on Sunday* at this time, from those whose hopes had been battered too often. By the morning of 10 April 1998, negotiators, led by President Clinton's special envoy George Mitchell, were dotting the final i's and crossing the final t's on the deal that was about to be signed. There was, however, a dissonance between what politicians were saying and the reactions on the streets. Comments I noted down from the radio and television news that day – 'historic', 'without parallel', 'like the Berlin Wall' – sat in my notebook alongside a string of weary remarks from those who continued to feel that a happier ending was impossible. Just days before the deal was finally done – and when it was already in sight – one man pointed at a concrete bollard and promised me he would 'eat that pillar' if agreement were achieved. Others were equally doubtful. In many respects, the scepticism was justified. A few weeks after the Good Friday Agreement, controlled explosions defused a 700-pound car bomb in Lisburn, south of Belfast. 'It's good to have peace, isn't it?' a policeman said to me deadpan as we stood amidst the shards of broken glass that covered the road. Then came a huge bomb in Omagh, where twenty-nine people were killed. This was, however, almost the last gasp for the mostly defeated men of violence. There was at least a rocky road to peace.

Acknowledging past failures was a key part of the strategy. Ahead of the Good Friday negotiations, Tony Blair announced an inquiry that would look again at what happened on Bloody Sunday. Establishing the truth could, he suggested, be an important part of 'building a secure future' for Northern Ireland. The inquiry led by Lord Saville, a senior judge, was criticised for its length and expense. It took twelve years to complete, cost almost £200 million and was eventually published thirty-eight years after the events took place. But its impact was huge. Saville concluded soldiers had 'knowingly put forward false accounts'. He was as clear in his exoneration of those who died as his predecessor had been eager to blame the dead and exonerate the soldiers who fired the lethal shots.

On 15 June 2010, the day the Saville Report was to be published, crowds gathered in Derry's central square. The first hint of Saville's conclusions came when a thumbs-up from a family member with early access to the report was spotted through the window grilles of the nineteenth-century Guildhall. There was a brief moment of confusion before the crowds exploded in celebratory disbelief. As remarkable as the conclusions of the inquiry was the response of the British prime minister. David Cameron's speech to a packed House of Commons was broadcast live on the square: 'There is no doubt, there is nothing equivocal, there are no ambiguities. What happened on Bloody Sunday was both unjustified and unjustifiable. It was wrong.' The crowds cheered a British prime minister in ways that perhaps neither they nor he could ever have imagined. A copy of the Widgery Report was torn into confetti. Fists punched the air.

Simon Winchester, who reported on Bloody Sunday for the *Guardian* in 1972, was back in Derry in 2010:

> It was as though they could scarcely believe what they had just heard, a British prime minister, a Tory at that, offering a formal and sincerely-meant apology for what his soldiers had done near four decades ago to men and women who were guilty only of protesting at the excesses and longevity of British colonial rule in Ireland.

In the words of Bishop Daly: 'There was no triumphalism — just unadulterated delight. The Trojan efforts of the families of the dead and injured in pursuit of justice over so many years deserved such a result.'

Military attitudes changed, too. In 2000, my *Independent* colleague Kim Sengupta and I interviewed General Mike Jackson, commander of Britain's land forces, who had been present as press officer and adjutant on Bloody Sunday. When we asked questions about that day he was defensive, emphasising (as Widgery had) the 'rapidly deteriorating situation' the army had to cope with. Ten years later, though, Jackson praised Cameron's 'fulsome apology'. General David Richards, head of the armed forces, said there had been 'serious mistakes and failings'.

The Saville Report was of historic importance, and families welcomed its conclusions. But, in ways that were reminiscent of My Lai and Abu Ghraib, Lord Saville, too, seemed eager to absolve the senior leadership of blame. Ignoring Macaulay's dictum (as quoted by Helmuth von Moltke in 1943, when he proposed trials in The Hague after the war) that 'the men of rank' are the 'proper objects of severity' when it comes to accountability for crimes committed, Saville insisted that the killings on Bloody Sunday could never have been 'foreseen by the authorities as likely to happen'.

That is, at the very least, debatable. Bloody Sunday did not come in a vacuum. Five months earlier and out of sight of the cameras, there had been an almost equally violent and lawless prologue – *The Ballymurphy Precedent*, as a Channel 4 documentary by Callum Macrae described it in 2018. In August 1971, British troops killed ten people on the Ballymurphy estate in west Belfast; the dead included a priest as he administered the last rites and a mother who was searching for her children. The commander of the British troops in Belfast was Brigadier Frank Kitson, later commander-in-chief of land forces, who had developed his skills in Britain's brutal counter-insurgency in Kenya and who believed the law could be 'tied into the war effort in as discreet a way as possible', in order to make it more difficult to prosecute crimes by the armed forces.

The Paras were known as 'Kitson's private army' and were notorious for their violence. Given what had already happened at Ballymurphy, what they did when they were sent to Derry to sort things out should not have come as a surprise. Callum Macrae argues: 'It wasn't the "bad apples" or the junior officers of the Parachute Regiment who decided to go to Derry less than six months after they had killed so many innocent people in Ballymurphy. It was their commanders. And if those commanders did not know what the paratroopers were likely to do, they certainly should have.'

The official version of the Ballymurphy massacre was that 1 Para targeted only gunmen who had fired or were about to fire. That lie was widely reported. As with the My Lai headlines in 1968, which boasted of how many 'Reds' had been killed, the headlines reporting on Ballymurphy were triumphal in tone. 'In the early morning two gunmen die' and 'Chief of staff says major defeat was inflicted: We have wiped out IRA hardcore, claims the army' were two of the stories in the *Belfast Telegraph*, based on press briefings by Captain Mike Jackson, as he then was. 'In retrospect, I should have said "alleged",' General Jackson told an inquest into the deaths almost fifty years later, in 2019. It took until 2021 for the truth to be officially proclaimed: the coroner, Justice Siobhan Keegan, found at the end of her three-year inquiry that all those who died were 'entirely innocent of any wrongdoing' on that day. The government apologised 'unreservedly' to the families on behalf of the state. The Northern Ireland Secretary, Brandon Lewis, said: 'Part of reconciliation is the ability to understand what happened . . . but it is also about accountability.'

Prosecutions have been delayed and few, but even those have been praised. In 2023, former soldier David Holden was given a suspended sentence for killing twenty-three-year-old Aidan McAnespie thirty-five years earlier. McAnespie's brother Sean said the verdict counted for more than a tough sentence: 'We weren't looking for a pound of flesh. We were just looking for truth and justice.'

In the same year, and contradicting the talk of the need for accountability, Rishi Sunak's Conservative government passed a law that sought to make further prosecutions and inquests more difficult. Ireland promised to challenge Britain's 'Legacy Act' at the European Court of Human Rights in Strasbourg, but the new Labour government in 2024 in any case promised to overturn the legislation, which all five main parties in Northern Ireland had opposed. Just before the general election in 2024, one of the Bloody Sunday soldiers appeared in a Derry court, accused of two murders and five attempted murders, after decades of campaigning by the dead men's families. At the time of writing, it is unclear if a full trial of 'Soldier F' will be allowed to proceed.

Those who believed that covering up official killings was the way to achieve security have been proved wrong. Northern Ireland is now immeasurably safer than many in the province believed was possible at the time of the Good Friday Agreement, let alone in the decades before that. Between 1969 and 1998, there was an average of more than a hundred security-related deaths a year. In the year after Ballymurphy and Bloody Sunday, five hundred died. In 2023, for the first time since records began in 1969, the number of security-related deaths fell to zero.

Chapter Six

'I am Glad to be Deceived'

Putin and Assad: Chechnya, Georgia, Ukraine (1999–2014). Syria, open-source investigations, Koblenz (2011–22)

On 9 August 1999, President Boris Yeltsin named Vladimir Putin, forty-six-year-old director of Russia's security services – the FSB, formerly known as the KGB – as his new prime minister. Putin was Yeltsin's fifth prime minister in seventeen months. Most observers assumed Putin, too, would not last long. 'Who will take a prime minister seriously if they change them like gloves?' Communist Party leader Gennady Zyuganov asked.

This was a time of instability, especially in the north Caucasus. Islamist rebels from Russia's southern republic of Chechnya had in recent months made incursions into the neighbouring republic of Dagestan. In the six weeks following Putin's appointment, there was a series of deadly bombings which were blamed on Chechen extremists. Sixty-four people died in a car bomb explosion in Dagestan. Two hundred died in explosions which destroyed apartment buildings in Moscow. Seventeen were killed by a truck bomb in the southern town of Volgodonsk.

Unsurprisingly, the attacks put Russia on edge. Yeltsin's new prime minister made clear that he was the man to keep the country safe. 'We will pursue the terrorists everywhere,' Putin announced. 'Excuse me for saying so: we'll catch them in the toilet. We'll wipe them out in the outhouse.' On 30 September, Putin launched a devastating ground and air assault on Chechnya to follow up on his promise.

Civilian deaths at the hands of Russian forces in Chechnya were nothing new. Four years earlier, in the town of Argun, I had talked to the despairing neighbours of a man who died trying to protect them from Russian gunfire. A Chechen woman, whose children the dead Russian neighbour had helped save, asked: 'How can they think of an action like this?' Between 1994 and 1996, there was much criticism of what the headline to my story from Argun that day called a 'dirty war'. But Yeltsin's actions in Chechnya would seem child's play by comparison with what his protégé now unleashed. Leaflets dropped from planes onto the Chechen capital, Grozny, declared: 'Those who remain will be viewed as terrorists and bandits . . . All those who do not leave the city will be destroyed.' Two hundred thousand fled their homes. Thousands of civilians were killed. Grozny was bombed to ruins.

On New Year's Eve 1999, Yeltsin resigned, naming the 'intelligent, strong, energetic' Putin as interim president until elections in three months' time. At two in the morning on New Year's Day, Putin flew from Moscow down to

Chechnya, where he drank champagne in a helicopter over the combat zone and handed out engraved hunting knives to the supposed heroes. Russian forces went on killing sprees in the weeks to come – *zachistki*, or 'cleansing operations', a term that would become notorious as part of the Russian invasion of Ukraine two decades later. Sixty civilians were killed in a single day in the district of Novye Aldy on the edge of Grozny. Women were raped; grenades were thrown into basements. Moscow denied it all, and complained of 'fairy tales'.

On 21 February 2000, Moscow declared victory with a fly-by and a military parade at Grozny airport. Defence minister Igor Sergeyev handed out awards, saying, 'For there to be peace in this long-suffering territory, there has to be total victory.' From the Kremlin, Putin assured Chechens, 'History teaches us to cherish the traditions of good neighbours, which have helped us for centuries to live in a multi-ethnic state. We have one country, and this is where we and our children shall live.'

The war strengthened Putin's support at home. Internationally, too, there were few expressions of concern. Indeed, Britain's prime minister became a willing participant in Putin's election campaign. Putin and Tony Blair were photographed chatting in the state box at a performance of Prokofiev's *War and Peace* in St Petersburg. Blair and other politicians saw Putin as a 'liberal moderniser' who, in addition, was battling terrorism. In the presidential elections a fortnight later, Putin delivered a knock-out blow to his rivals in the first round.

It needs no hindsight to suggest the Western adoration of Putin was inappropriate. Russian activists and journalists risked their lives to make that clear; they were ignored. From the outside, the problems were obvious, too. While writing this book, I found an *Independent* editorial I wrote after the elections in March 2000. I began by quoting French President Jacques Chirac on what he described as a 'brilliant' Putin victory, and went on to argue: 'The Western enthusiasm for Putin is difficult to understand ... Only on one issue can we see where Putin stands ... His conduct of the war in Chechnya has been a cynical disgrace ... Killing civilians in order to win an election is a poor start.' My observations were self-evident, given everything that had already happened. But Western politicians weren't interested. With their help, Putin was here to stay.

A key justification for the assault on Chechnya that would help Putin to power in the March elections was the spate of deadly bombings which shocked the country shortly after his appointment as prime minister the previous year. Putin blamed those attacks on Chechen militants and few initially saw any reason to question that narrative. But things were not necessarily what they seemed. On the evening of 22 September 1999, Alexei Kartofelnikov, a driver for Spartak football club, noticed suspicious movements outside his home in Ryazan, south-east of Moscow. A car pulled up near the entrance to his apartment block. He watched as three people carried heavy sacks from the car down into the basement before quickly driving away.

Given the recent terror bombings, Kartofelnikov was suspicious. He jotted down the number on the partly covered registration plate and phoned the police, who discovered three fifty-kilogram sacks attached to a timing device. Residents were evacuated. Bomb disposal experts established that the device had been set to explode overnight. State media broadcast the dramatic news: a terrorist bombing had been foiled. Kartofelnikov would receive a colour television set from the city of Ryazan as a reward for his quick reactions. Two days later, the Russian interior minister confirmed what media had already reported: a tragedy had been averted.

Two official narratives would, however, now diverge and crumble into chaos. The left hand of the security services (FSB headquarters in Moscow) had apparently failed to inform the right hand (the regional FSB in Ryazan) what they were up to. In Ryazan, law enforcement and security services worked to track down the perpetrators of this attempted outrage. Soon, they were ready to pounce. According to a statement from the local FSB, 'The [Ryazan] department of the FSB identified the residences in Ryazan of those involved in planting the explosive device and was preparing to detain them.' At which point, Moscow suddenly changed its story. Putin's successor as head of the security services jumped in to explain it had all been an unfortunate misunderstanding. 'The incident in Ryazan was not a bombing, nor was it a foiled bombing,' FSB boss Nikolai Patrushev announced. 'It was an exercise. It was sugar; there was no explosive substance there.'

The popular *Moskovsky Komsomolets* newspaper summed up the contradictions the government had created for itself: 'On 24 September 1999, the head of the FSB, Nikolai Patrushev, made the sensational announcement that the attempted bombing in Ryazan was nothing of the sort. It was an exercise ... The same day, Minister of the Interior Vladimir Rushailo congratulated his men on saving the building in Ryazan from certain destruction.' This was, in short, what former KGB agent Alexander Litvinenko later described as 'the FSB fiasco'. (Litvinenko co-wrote a book called *The FSB Blows Up Russia*, which the Kremlin banned; some believe the book is one reason why two FSB agents poisoned Litvinenko with polonium in a London hotel in 2006.) At a time when alternative views could still be expressed, Russian papers reported that 'in the opinion of highly placed employees of the interior ministry', the action involved not just genuine explosives but even 'the same detonators' as had been used in the deadly attacks in Moscow. As a former prosecutor general summed it up, the FSB in Moscow seemed to be 'making very clumsy excuses when they were caught out'.

Putin later described such conclusions as 'utter nonsense' and 'totally insane'. According to him, 'No one in the Russian special services would be capable of such a crime against his own people.' Insane or not, a planned 'crime against their own people' appeared to be the only plausible explanation for the foiled Ryazan bombing – which, in turn, raised questions about the earlier incidents. The journalist Anna Politkovskaya compared the bombings to a presumed act of provocation in Hitler's Germany: 'The tragic terrorist bombings,' she wrote, 'are rapidly coming to resemble another distant event: the burning of the Reichstag.' For Putin, it seemed that Russian deaths did not matter; they were a means to an end. Gaining and retaining power was what mattered.

In June 2001, fifteen months after Putin's first election victory, I was one of a group of journalists invited to attend a black tie caviar, vodka and champagne dinner and White Nights ball (named after St Petersburg's fabled midsummer, when darkness never falls) in the magnificent Catherine Palace outside Russia's former capital. The event, lit by thousands of candles, matched Tolstoy's description of a grand ball in *War and Peace*, with its 'brilliantly lighted rooms, the music, the flowers, the dances of the emperor, all the dazzling people of Petersburg'. There were diamonds, bouquets, footmen in blue tricorn hats and scarlet breeches, dancers from the Mariinsky Ballet, fireworks and a performance of Tchaikovsky's *1812* overture conducted by Valery Gergiev. Putin was by now the unchallenged leader; all mockery was forgotten. As he entered the vast ballroom under the Triumph of Russia ceiling fresco, everyone rose to give him an ovation. 'Our president!' one woman near me murmured, eyes shining. War crimes in Chechnya were not a topic of conversation that evening.

But it was not just in Russia that the president was seen as the conquering hero. Western politicians remained determined to treat the new Russian leader as the man with whom (to quote Margaret Thatcher on Mikhail Gorbachev) they could do business. In 2003, Putin arrived in London for the first state visit by a Russian leader since Tsar Alexander II in 1874. He rode in a gold-trimmed carriage with Queen Elizabeth II and was toasted at a banquet in Buckingham Palace. Blair announced: 'The leadership of Putin offers not just tremendous hope for Russia, but also for the wider world. I would pay tribute to him as a partner and as a friend.' Anna Politkovskaya, invited to a journalists' lunch with the prime minister in London, challenged him over braised salmon and potatoes to explain why he found the Russian leader so appealing. Blair had a simple answer which made clear he did not believe war crimes were his business. He told Politkovskaya, 'It's my job as prime minister to like Mr Putin.' Politkovskaya's own more prescient analysis: 'He sees us as a means to his own ends, a means for the achievement and retention of personal power, no more than that ... In Russia we have had leaders with this outlook before. It led to tragedy, to bloodshed on a huge scale, to civil wars. I want no more of that.'

During the Putin visit, my colleague Anya Neistat, who studied law at Moscow University before joining the Russian office of Human Rights Watch, published an article which drew on her own and colleagues' work documenting torture, executions and forced disappearances in Chechnya. She called on the British government to condemn Putin's crimes. But, she noted, 'Tony Blair seems determined not to admit the truth – let alone act on it.' Anya quoted a couplet from a well-known Pushkin poem, written in the voice of a credulous lover: 'It is easy to deceive me, / For I am glad to be deceived.'

Blair, with his talk of 'tremendous hope', was not alone in his gladness to be deceived. George W. Bush looked Putin in the eye and found he was able to 'get a sense of his soul'. German Chancellor Gerhard Schröder declared Putin to be a 'flawless democrat'. Jacques Chirac awarded him the Grand Cross of the Légion d'Honneur. All this, while the evidence of crimes was in plain sight.

Even after the first full flush of the 'I am glad to be deceived' love affair with Putin was over, governments remained reluctant to confront the Russian leader. In 2006, Putin introduced the first of a series of laws to clamp down on independent non-governmental organisations. The direction of travel was unmistakable and needed to be called out. But, it became clear, the British government did not wish to criticise or even be perceived as indirectly criticising the Russian leader.

A few weeks after the Chatham House talk on torture which Downing Street had tried to block, Anya Neistat and I met with Cherie Booth in the prime ministerial flat above Downing Street. We discussed Putin's new crackdown on civil society, and asked the human rights lawyer and prime minister's spouse if she might, as a sign of solidarity, meet with human rights groups during an upcoming G8 summit in St Petersburg. 'Happy to do anything that can be helpful,' she replied. In the next two months, I liaised with the Foreign Office and Downing Street to nail the practicalities down.

And then, just before the summit in July 2006, a Blair

adviser called me. The meeting, he told me, could not happen; there was 'nothing more to discuss'. Months of planning had gone to waste; beleaguered Russian activists would, I knew, feel betrayed and disappointed. There was nobody I could appeal to. But then I remembered: Downing Street, eager to maintain a political firewall, had kept telling me that this was 'Cherie's decision', not theirs. So I called the prime minister's wife herself, asking if she was still happy to go ahead. She said yes, absolutely. I then wrote to the prime ministerial adviser, treating our phone call from a few minutes earlier as if it had never happened. I thanked him for always reminding me that this was a personal decision, and added 'thanks to Cherie [cc'd on the email] for confirming in our conversation now that she would like the meeting to happen'. I re-shared details of the venue and of my Human Rights Watch colleagues in Moscow who were coordinating the meeting, hosted by a St Petersburg NGO, Citizens' Watch. The visit went ahead as if there had never been any issues; none of the reporters who wrote sympathetic stories about the encounter could have guessed how eager the government had been to prevent the meeting from ever taking place.

Blair was not alone in remaining eager not to offend Putin. President Bush no longer talked of being able to see into the Russian leader's soul. But he talked in St Petersburg of a 'strong friendship' and expressed understanding for Putin's 'Russian-style democracy' with 'different traditions'. Three months later, the nature of Putin's 'different traditions' – and the urgent need to support Russians who dared to speak out – became clear. On 7 October 2006, Anna Politkovskaya – rebuffed by Blair three years earlier, when she challenged him to explain his admiration for the Russian leader – was murdered in the elevator of her Moscow apartment block. For two days, Putin said nothing; he then described Politkovskaya's role and influence as 'extremely insignificant'.

More such killings would follow. At an event in New York that I attended which honoured Politkovskaya's life, Natalia Estemirova of the Russian human rights group Memorial – who, like Politkovskaya, had documented Putin's crimes in Chechnya from the beginning – paid tribute to her friend's work and legacy. Three years later, Estemirova would herself be abducted and murdered.

Two years after Politkovskaya's murder, it became clear that even the invasion of a neighbouring country was not enough to derail diplomatic relations, so desperate were governments to remain on good terms. The conflict in Chechnya at the beginning of the century was just the first of Putin's wars. Next in line was the southern republic of Georgia.

Already in the Soviet era, Georgia had been punished for wanting to break free of Moscow's rule. I first visited Tbilisi shortly after the Kremlin crushed pro-independence protests in the Georgian capital in 1989. Twenty-one people had been killed with gas and sharpened spades; 9 April, the day of the massacre, is now commemorated as the Day of National Unity. Here in Georgia, I concluded at that time, was 'an unstoppable force preparing to collide with the (almost) immovable object that is Soviet power'. Georgia, like other Soviet republics, gained independence from Moscow two years later. But instability, conflict and Russian resentments only grew in the years to come – culminating in the seizing by Russian-backed forces of Georgian territory in 2008.

In April of that year, Russia voted with the rest of the UN Security Council to reaffirm the territorial integrity of Georgia 'within its internationally recognised borders'. Four months later, Moscow led an armed intervention in the Georgian region of South Ossetia, supposedly (using the same language it would use in Ukraine fourteen years later) to protect Ossetians from 'genocide'. Moscow recognised South Ossetia's 'independence' from Georgia as 'the only possibility to save lives' – just as it would do in eastern Ukraine. The International Criminal Court opened an investigation into crimes committed. In 2022, the court issued arrest warrants for three South Ossetian officials with ties to Russia for war crimes including torture and unlawful transfer of civilians 'in the context of an occupation by the Russian Federation'. Governments, though, did not wish to think about such things. Seven months after the annexation of South Ossetia, Hillary Clinton, Obama's newly appointed Secretary of State, presented her Russian counterpart, Sergei Lavrov, with a huge red 'reset' button for a smiling photo opportunity. Clinton declared this would be a 'fresh start' for US–Russia relations. It was time to move on.

Five years after the post-Georgia reset button came another annexation. In November 2013, Ukraine was about to sign a historic pact with the European Union when President Viktor Yanukovych, under pressure from Moscow, suddenly abandoned the deal. Ukrainians were enraged that key decisions about their country's future were still being made in Moscow. Huge protests erupted on Maidan Square in the centre of Kyiv, filled with Ukrainian and European Union flags, in what came to be known as the Revolution of Dignity. In the months to come, riot police and snipers would beat and shoot demonstrators. More than a hundred protesters were killed ('the heavenly hundred') especially on 18 February 2014 and the days that followed. On the night of 21 February, Yanukovych, abandoned by his own police, fled to Russia while still declaring himself to be the legitimate president. Crowds wandered in dazed disbelief through the 300-acre estate where Yanukovych had a petting zoo, private golf course and replica galleon. A Ukrainian court later convicted the former president *in absentia* of treason. It seemed that Ukraine would, from now on, be able to make its own decisions.

Revenge was, however, not long in coming. Within days, Russian forces (initially wearing no identifying insignia and described only as 'little green men') raised the Russian flag and installed a new government in the Crimean peninsula. A few weeks later, Putin signed a bill declaring Crimea to be part of the Russian Federation. 'Crimea has always been an integral part of Russia in the hearts and minds of people,' Putin told an audience in the Kremlin, in a speech interrupted by enthusiastic applause.

Crimea, which the Soviet leader Nikita Khrushchev 'gave' to Ukraine in 1954, had long been a subject of resentment for Russian nationalists. I visited the port city of Sevastopol in 1993, two years after the collapse of the Soviet Union. The previous year, the Russians had fired warning shots when a Ukrainian ship ran up the blue and yellow national flag. Those disagreements had supposedly been ironed out, but the situation remained fragile. These were strange between-times, when rules both existed and didn't exist. Sevastopol was theoretically still closed to foreigners, as in the Soviet era. But the occupants of a military vehicle from the formerly Soviet and now Russian Black Sea Fleet offered me a lift into town, cheerfully bluffing their way through a checkpoint where passes were scrutinised. 'Have we any foreigners aboard? Yes, I'm an American spy!' one passenger declared amidst much laughter. Boris Kozhin, admiral of the new Ukrainian fleet, told me it was 'a pity' that Russians had boycotted the ceremony for the arrival that day of a formerly

Soviet ship, now flying the flag of independent Ukraine. 'Of course, I am at home here, so I didn't need anybody to come,' Kozhin said. 'But it is a celebration, after all.'

Not everybody saw it that way. The Russian nationalist leader in Crimea, Yuri Meshkov, warned of violence to come, comparing the situation to another civil war then under way. He told me: 'Maybe we're different from Yugoslavia. But the strength of the explosion will be greater than in Yugoslavia.' As I wrote then, the tensions on the Crimean peninsula gave an idea of 'what could yet explode'. I tentatively concluded: 'Some of the politicians who want to replace Yeltsin might find such a confrontation convenient, to distract from the domestic problems yet to come.' Even then, however, despite all the rhetoric, war still didn't seem the most likely outcome. In the years that followed, tensions dwindled and the threats from Meshkov and others came to seem a mere historical footnote. It would be twenty years before the convenient confrontation came. After Putin's annexation in 2014, Meshkov returned from Russia to Crimea; he talked of 'the joy of this entire region'.

In the months after the occupation of Crimea, Russian and Russian-backed forces took control of Donetsk, Luhansk and other towns in the Donbas region, supposedly to save the area 'from chaos'. Three thousand civilians would die in the next few years. But, as with Georgia, governments quickly adjusted to the new status quo and the de facto annexation of eastern Ukraine. There was talk of the need for 'de-escalation', and self-congratulation when that seemed to have been achieved. In 2016, two years after the annexation of Crimea and the stealth invasion of the Donbas, a leading German-American think tank published a report entitled *Transatlantic Success Story*. This proclaimed success included that the West's response had 'very likely' prevented further Russian advance in Ukraine by 'changing Moscow's calculus'.

Ukrainians, living in a country that their giant neighbour had sliced in two while the rest of the world looked on – a modern version, it could be said, of Hitler's seizure of the Czech Sudetenland in 1938, followed by Chamberlain's 'peace for our time' – might be forgiven if they did not perceive things in such rosy terms. In 2020 the International Criminal Court found there was a 'reasonable basis' to believe war crimes and crimes against humanity had been committed in eastern Ukraine. But Putin's war continued undisturbed.

———————

It was not just in the territories of the old Russian empire and the former Soviet Union that Putin's forces committed war crimes with impunity. The early months of 2011 were a time of astonishing change across the Middle East and North Africa. The 'jasmine revolution' in Tunisia forced dictator Ben Ali to flee after twenty-three years in power. Huge protests in Tahrir Square in Cairo and across Egypt – 'eighteen golden days', in the words of novelist Ahdaf Soueif – led to the resignation of President Hosni Mubarak after thirty repressive years in power. Protests began in Gaddafi's Libya and then in Syria, too. 'It's your turn, doctor!' graffiti declared, with reference to the London-trained ophthalmologist-president, Bashar al-Assad. The protests grew steadily in the next few months – as did the violence used to suppress them.

Assad denied it all. 'No government in the world kills its people,' the Syrian leader insisted, 'unless it's led by a crazy person.' It was an interesting caveat. In reality, the killings got worse. Harshly repressed peaceful protests gradually descended into civil war. As Mazen, an engineer turned protest leader, later remembered, 'People waited, and waited, and waited for the West to pay attention to our fate. We waved olive branches, and got shot at, and nobody said a word. We tried to resist, to protect ourselves, and got labelled terror-ists ... What could be a more fruitful ground for the Islamists to come and take over?'

The UN High Commissioner for Human Rights, Navi Pillay (previously a judge at the Rwanda war crimes tribu-nal), called for the UN Security Council to refer Syria to the International Criminal Court, as had happened with Sudan and Libya. A UN Commission of Inquiry, headed by Carla Del Ponte, former chief prosecutor at the Yugoslavia and Rwanda war crimes tribunals, echoed those calls. But it was never going to happen. In 2014, thirteen out of fifteen members of the council voted for a referral of Syria to The Hague. But Russia and China both wielded their vetoes, and the resolution foundered. Del Ponte resigned from her post in 2017, complaining the existence of her role had become 'an alibi' for inaction.

For both Assad and Putin, lying about their crimes comes nat-urally. In that respect, little has changed from repressive rulers in the past. One thing that is new, however, is the use of digital tools to defeat official lies and establish undeniable truths.

In 1982, during the presidency of Bashar al-Assad's father Hafez, government forces crushed an uprising of the Muslim Brotherhood in Hama in central Syria. Hafez al-Assad's brother, Rifaat, oversaw the destruction and terror that followed. Tens of thousands were killed. Scattered reports reached the outside world, but nothing could be verified. The Syrian information minister insisted Hama was 'more quiet and stable and secure than a number of American cities' and invited the US State Department spokesman to come on vacation to see for himself. Journalists asked if they, too, might visit Hama. 'Of course,' came the answer – but not yet.

The denials of 1982 bore as much relation to the truth as the insistence by Bashar al-Assad thirty years later that his forces did not kill Syrian civilians. But there was a difference. At the time of the Hama massacre, government denials were hard to disprove, however implausible they might seem. There were no images from inside the city. By contrast, when al-Assad unleashed violence against Syrians in Hama and across the country in 2011, thousands of videos appeared on YouTube and Twitter. The killings in Syria by the forces of Assad senior happened in near silence. The killings by his son's forces were front-page news around the world.

In the age of the internet, pinning down facts is in some ways harder than ever. Things that never happened are discussed by millions as if they had. Things that *did* happen are flatly denied. Both Putin and Assad seek to turn the truth upside down. This is a world where, to quote the title of a 2015 book on Russia by Peter Pomerantsev, 'nothing is true and everything is possible'. The Syrian authorities (and their useful idiots on the internet) suggest the White Helmets rescue teams, who have risked and lost their lives to save those injured in bombing attacks, are part of a terrorist group. In response to images of civilians killed in Bucha, the Kremlin talked of 'monstrous forgery'. Russian television showed video of a mannequin being dressed, with the comment 'This is how the Ukrainian armed forces prepare their staged videos.' (The images came from a film set near St Petersburg.)

Moscow's version of what happened at Bucha is (to quote an official statement in 2024, on the second anniversary of what was described as a 'goodwill gesture' to withdraw Russian troops from the area), that 'the Zelensky regime and its Western handlers staged a bloody mass murder'. Any blame attached to Moscow is, according to the Kremlin, part of a 'propaganda-driven disinformation campaign'. Moscow described reports of the targeted attack on a maternity hospital in Mariupol in March 2022 as a 'completely staged provocation' (while also claiming that Ukrainian armed forces had taken over and were firing from the hospital). But even as false claims and denials continue, the possibilities have also multiplied for how to disentangle truth from lies – even without a physical presence on the ground.

A month after the Srebrenica genocide in 1995, the US showed satellite images at the UN Security Council, revealing patterns of freshly disturbed soil where Bosnian Serbs had dug mass graves, thus providing clear evidence of the massacres. In the years to come, satellite imagery, previously the preserve of governments, would become a standard human rights tool across the world, from Darfur to Myanmar, revealing everything from burned villages to mass graves.

The arrival of smartphones changed things, too. In 2009, at the end of a bloody twenty-eight-year war against Tamil rebels, the Sri Lankan government talked of 'zero civilian casualties' even as its armed forces targeted hospitals and killed tens of thousands of civilians. When human rights organisations and aid agencies sounded the alarm, we were ignored. The UN Security Council failed to pass a single resolution condemning the slaughter. As with Rwanda and Darfur, the international reaction to this spiralling disaster could, as I wrote at the time, be summed up as: 'Don't bother us now, we're a bit busy.'

There were many reasons for governments' failure to speak out on the civilian killings, from geopolitics to a dislike of armed groups. (The rebel Tamil Tigers committed serious crimes, including suicide bombings and the use of human shields; as in Gaza today, those crimes were used to justify a government policy that killed so many who bore no responsibility for those crimes.) But there was one key reason for the lack of interest: the fact that there were no images from inside what the Sri Lankan authorities, with boundless cynicism, described as a 'no-fire zone'. The deadly catastrophe that unfolded on and around the sandy beach at Mullaitivu in the north-east of the country was mostly invisible to the outside world. In that sense, little had changed since Hama in 1982. Only with the broadcast in 2011 of *Sri Lanka's Killing Fields* and two other Channel 4 documentaries which included trophy atrocity videos and other phone video material, did the conversation change.

In 2013, four years after the end of the war, I was in Colombo on behalf of Amnesty International, attending a Commonwealth summit in the Sri Lankan capital. President Mahinda Rajapaksa had planned the conference as a post-war victory lap. Instead, he found that his alleged crimes – 'an assault on the entire framework of international law', as a UN report described the killings of 2009 – were under greater scrutiny than ever before. The Sri Lankan government distributed a dossier to correspondents, intended to disprove Channel 4's 'lies'. The tactic may have backfired. At one press conference to highlight the achievements of the summit, the spokesman eventually asked: 'Are there any questions which are not on human rights?' There weren't.

It was in 2011 that digital possibilities began to come of age. In Cairo, the 'We are all Khaled Said' Facebook page – named after a twenty-eight-year-old who plainclothes police had dragged out of an internet café and beaten to death; images of his battered body went viral – was just one example

of the social media accounts which fuelled change. When I
was in the Egyptian capital a few months after the revolution
of Tahrir Square and the fall of Mubarak, graffiti were still
visible: 'Thank you, Facebook!'

But the new developments did not just help energise rebellion against tyrants. Digital technology provided investigative
tools, too. Until now, governments had always been able to
brush away the evidence of crimes without fear that their lies
would be exposed. From now on, that would not be so easy.
In Syria, Ukraine and other conflicts in the years to come,
assembling digital evidence into a compelling whole – confronting disinformation and documenting the truth – would
play an ever more important role.

The digital sleuthing skills of open-source investigations
do not require a presence on the ground. They do, however,
require dogged determination. Eliot Higgins, a business
administrator from Leicester, had plenty of that. Posting as
Brown Moses, a reference to a favourite Frank Zappa song,
Higgins began blogging on Libya in 2011. It was two more
years before his work broke into the mainstream.

In August 2013, Assad's forces fired sarin-filled rockets
into the opposition-controlled Damascus suburb of Ghouta,
killing more than a thousand people. It was the worst
chemical attack since Saddam Hussein's genocide in Halabja
twenty-five years earlier. People stumbled through the streets,
frothing at the mouth, convulsing, suffocating to death. The
evidence was, in the words of UN Secretary-General Ban
Ki-moon, 'beyond doubt and beyond the pale'. Assad denied
responsibility, saying, as always, that the idea 'insults common
sense'. Russian reports said variously that rebels had fired the
rockets, or that everything was faked.

Amid all the contested narratives, Higgins and others
wanted to see if they could establish a single, incontrovertible

truth. They geolocated, measured and analysed internet images of the tubular rockets embedded in the ground. They examined munitions and delivery systems, looked at what materials were available to whom, and calculated trajectories, distances and where the missiles had been fired from. The findings were conclusive: Syrian government forces had fired the missiles.

Press TV, run by Syria's ally Iran, dismissed Higgins as a 'UK-based armchair observer'. That was true enough, as far as it went. Higgins had never visited Syria and did not claim to be a weapons expert (though he drew on the expertise of others). The implication was that somebody sitting thousands of miles away from the events described could have no way of knowing what they were talking about and must be making it all up. And yet, a report from UN experts who visited the area would in due course reach almost identical conclusions.

In 2014, Higgins and his colleagues created an organisation which they named after one of Aesop's fables, in which a community of mice wonder how to protect themselves from the cat that threatens all their lives. One mouse comes up with a solution: put a bell on the cat so they will be alerted when danger approaches. The proposal gains support, apart from one mouse who points to a flaw: 'Who will bell the cat?' Bellingcat and other similar organisations could now place a bell around the cat's neck – revealing undeniable facts, even when governments thought they would remain obscured.

One example of such open-source intelligence – OSINT, to use the military-style acronym – came shortly after the creation of Bellingcat. On 17 July 2014, a Malaysia Airlines plane en route from Amsterdam to Kuala Lumpur was shot down over the cornfields of eastern Ukraine. All 298 passengers and crew on flight MH17 were killed. Russian armed groups were initially heard boasting to each other about downing the plane. But when it became clear that MH17 was a civilian plane, the story changed. Russia now insisted Ukraine was responsible, and that a video showing a Buk missile launcher on a flat-bed truck was filmed in Ukrainian-held territory, not (as the Ukrainians said) on its way back to Russia.

Only a few years earlier, such claim and counter-claim would have been impossible to disentangle with any confidence. Now, online investigations made it possible to check (and find flaws in) every element of Russia's narrative. One of Bellingcat's collaborators was Iggy Ostanin, a Russian-born student in Amsterdam. Ostanin spent hours searching social media for video clips that might provide clues. In Higgins's words, 'He dived into the haystack, searching for needles nobody else knew about.'

Ostanin found video and still images which traced the path of the convoy carrying the missile launcher on its 350-mile journey from the Russian city of Kursk to the Ukrainian border in the days before the plane was shot down. Through a detailed comparison with Google Street View scenes, he and Bellingcat colleagues were also able to show that photographs and video which Russia said were taken in Ukrainian-held territory were in fact in Russian-held Luhansk. As one headline summed it up: 'Group of bloggers unearthing MH17 intel quicker than US spies.'

A Dutch-led international investigative team concluded in 2018 that it was indeed Russian forces which had shot MH17 down. Those findings led to a trial in a Dutch court and the conviction *in absentia* in 2022 of three of those held most responsible.

———

One powerful example of the growing impact of open-source investigations came in 2018. A video that was widely shared in Cameroon and across west Africa was shocking in its documentation of casual murder. A group of soldiers chat as they lead two women, with a young girl and a baby, along a dusty track. The group stops. The men blindfold the women and push them to the ground. They pull the girl's T-shirt over her head. Then they shoot the women and both children at close range. One soldier keeps shooting until his comrades eventually tell him, 'That's enough. They're dead now.' The video caused uproar in Cameroon. Complaining of 'fake news', the government insisted it had been filmed in Mali, a thousand miles to the west. According to Cameroon's version, the weapons were wrong, the uniforms were wrong, everything was supposedly wrong. Blaming Cameroon was an attempt to 'distort actual facts and intoxicate the public'.

Investigators at Amnesty International and then the BBC's *Africa Eye* programme were determined to nail down facts which could help establish responsibility for the killings. They wanted to answer three key questions: where, when, who. For the 'where', they managed to match the profile of hills seen in the video to landscapes on Google Earth, thus provisionally locating it to a village in northern Cameroon. They further checked that against satellite imagery: aerial images of buildings, trees and bushes all matched up with identical objects seen at ground level in the video.

Then came the 'when'. By looking through historic Google Earth images, investigators narrowed down the timeframe. It had to be after one set of walls (visible in the video but not in earlier Google Earth images) had been built, and before another structure (visible in the video but not in later Google Earth images) was demolished. Then they used SunCalc, an app which analyses the length and direction of shadows to calculate the time of day, in order to pin the date down more precisely. By combining those two sets of calculations, they established with a high degree of certainty that the killings had taken place within a two-week period in late March or early April 2015.

Finally, after matching names mentioned in the video with a search of social media, they were able to provisionally name the killers. Put together it was, as the *Columbia Journalism Review* put it, 'a masterclass in how to verify a video'. The digital detective work forced a U-turn from the Cameroon government. Just a few weeks after the dismissive statements about 'fake news', seven soldiers were arrested. Four were later jailed for ten years, while the soldier who filmed the video was jailed for two years.

Such investigations have been repeated many times over. The use of open-source material is now part of the main-stream, as indictments by the International Criminal Court of a Libyan militia commander in 2017 and 2018 made clear. The evidence of the murder of forty people included video and Facebook posts. There were, the indictments said, 'no traces of forgery or manipulation'.

Establishing robust standards of proof is a key challenge when using such material. Open-source experts, lawyers, UN officials and human rights advocates worked together in recent years to create the Berkeley Protocol, which identifies agreed standards and recommends best practice on obtaining and preserving tamper-proof electronic evidence. The protocol, published in 2020, reflects what Alexa Koenig, director of the Human Rights Center at Berkeley Law, describes as the 'dawning realisation' of how much has changed. It has quickly become a global yardstick: in 2023, a Ukrainian prosecutor was quick to assure me that digital information his team had gathered on war crimes was all handled 'according to the Berkeley Protocol'.

———

It is not just at the Security Council in New York that Putin's support has played a key role in helping Assad. In 2015, when the Syrian leader seemed to be on the ropes, Russia launched air strikes against rebels and sent in ground forces to keep its ally safe. In 2016, Russian bombs destroyed the opposition stronghold of eastern Aleppo in what the UN described as 'a complete meltdown of humanity'. (Russian foreign minister Sergei Lavrov called for an end to the 'whining'.) In 2021, Memorial and other Russian human rights groups published their own report, *Devastating Decade*, about Russia's role. The 200-page report concluded: 'Unfortunately, the overwhelming majority of our [Syrian] interviewees do not see Russia as a saviour, but as a destructive foreign force whose military and political intervention helped bolster the war criminal heading their country.' Memorial was closed down shortly afterwards, after four decades of consistently speaking truth to Kremlin power.

Russia's protection at the Security Council seemed to mean there was no chance of accountability for the crimes committed in Syria. There are, however, chinks in the judicial armour. The Pinochet precedent has provided a window of legal opportunity.

Dictatorial regimes sometimes have in common a similar weakness in their armour. Governments that commit the worst crimes also threaten or kill witnesses to ensure the truth will never be known. When challenged, they lie brazenly. And yet, along with the denials and suppression of the truth, perpetrators of mass murder are often also meticulous record-keepers. At Auschwitz, pre-printed forms helped the Nazis keep tally of how many gold teeth they had ripped out of the mouths of the people they had just killed. Ben Ferencz's prosecution at Nuremberg of SS murder squad commanders was based entirely on the Nazis' own documentation. The regime of Bashar al-Assad, too, has eagerly documented its own crimes in ways that have significant implications for achieving justice.

Before 2011, it was the job of a middle-aged Syrian military police photographer to photograph crime scenes. For security reasons he can still be known only by his pseudonym: Caesar. From 2011 onwards, Caesar was required to record the state's own crimes. He photographed the tortured and mutilated bodies of 'terrorists' – those who were seen as having criticised the regime in any way – laid out in lines in the courtyard of 601 Military Hospital in Damascus. Each corpse had three separate labels – prisoner number, branch of the intelligence services and medical report number, with causes of death like 'cardiac arrest' or 'respiratory problem'. Caesar took the required photographs and clipped them to the documentation. He said nothing. As he put it later: 'If we expressed the way we felt, we could have been arrested and tortured to death and ended up as one of those bodies.' And yet, Caesar took extraordinary risks. He transferred images to thumb drives which he smuggled home hidden in his socks or inside his belt, past body searches on the way out of the office and at checkpoints on the way home.

Over the next two years, with the help of his friend Sami, Caesar collected and stored tens of thousands of images of official murder. He had no idea whether the risks he was taking would ever achieve anything. But he believed he *might* make a difference. 'Our work was terrifying,' he tells me.

We were terrified of what might happen to us, and what might happen to our families. If anybody from the security services figured out what we were doing, that was the end. But that fear was also mixed with a feeling of hope and happiness – that we could show the world what was happening inside the murderous regime cells, and that we could help families know the fate of their loved ones.

When Caesar eventually fled Syria, his images were separately smuggled out at the same time. The photographs were published in 2014; for many families, this was the first confirmation of the fate of their loved ones. Fourteen-year-old Ahmad al-Musalmani, for example, was pulled off a minibus while travelling to his mother's funeral. Soldiers were suspicious of the fact that Ahmad was in tears. They seized his phone. A single anti-Assad song became his death warrant. Ahmad was beaten to death soon after he was arrested. (Even then, the cynical brutality continued: Ahmad's father handed over thousands of dollars for his son's promised release but, as Caesar's photos later revealed, Ahmad was already dead.)

The Syrian authorities denied everything. Caesar's images were 'fake'. They bore 'no relation' to prisoners or detainees in Syrian prisons. Assad asked: 'Who took these pictures? Who is he? Nobody knows . . . It's all allegations without evidence.' In reality, few photographs have ever been so closely scrutinised. Researchers examined metadata, cross-checked images, found families and even tracked down those who had worked in the detention centres. The real question was not 'Are these photographs real?' but 'Can any of this make a difference?'

An answer came partly as the result of a chance encounter in the Marienfelde refugee camp in Berlin a few months after Caesar's photographs were published. The Syrian lawyer Anwar al-Bunni, newly arrived in Germany as a refugee, spotted a familiar face. He said to his wife, 'I know this man.' But he couldn't place him. Only a few days later did al-Bunni realise who he had run into. The haircut and glasses had changed. But there was no mistaking him: this was Anwar Raslan, former head of investigations at the notorious al-Khatib branch, Branch 251 of Assad's General Intelligence Service in Damascus. Al-Bunni knew Raslan from when he himself had been detained eight years earlier.

Al-Bunni, quiet-spoken with a wiry moustache and a mischievous smile, created the Syrian Centre for Legal Studies and Research in 2004, four years after President Assad came to power. The organisation's wordy name was intended to sound innocuous, but that didn't work for long. Al-Bunni was jailed and tortured for spreading 'false information harmful to the state'. When he first arrived in Germany in 2014, al-Bunni remained focused above all on what was happening at home. 'I had only just arrived, I had left my life behind, I was in a strange country,' he tells me in his office, tucked away in one of the endless mazes of courtyards in east Berlin. But al-Bunni learned from colleagues at the Berlin-based European Center for Constitutional and Human Rights that German police were interested in prosecuting Raslan using the principle of universal jurisdiction. He could help make that happen.

Al-Bunni tracked down survivors and witnesses. Caesar's photographs provided evidence of the crimes described. In 2020, Raslan went on trial in the Rhineland town of Koblenz, charged with the murder of fifty-eight people and the torture of thousands more. On 13 January 2022, he was sentenced to life imprisonment for crimes against humanity including torture, rape and murder. It was, said UN human rights commissioner Michelle Bachelet, a 'landmark leap forward' in pursuit of truth. Al-Bunni says, 'This sent a message to criminals all around the world: your safe zone is no longer a safe zone.'

The jailing of Raslan had implications that went beyond this one case. 'It gave hope to Syrians, so many people contacted us after that,' al-Bunni says. 'And not just from Syria. They got in touch from Yemen, from Egypt, from Iraq, from everywhere. I always believed that day would come. But I was so happy. The message was clearly delivered – to the criminals, to the victims, to the whole world.' Caesar, too, was proud that his work had made a difference: 'These trials are a new nail in the regime's coffin,' he told me, 'because the regime feels scared of the implications. Escaping accountability is now impossible.'

Even if the International Criminal Court could do nothing about Syria because of the Security Council vetos, its sister court in The Hague could speak out. In November 2023, in language that would find echoes in a ruling two months later on Israel and allegations of genocide, the International Court of Justice demanded that Syria take 'all measures within its power' to prevent acts of torture and other abuses. The ruling, in response to a request from Canada and the Netherlands, came five months after Assad was invited to rejoin the Arab League. Ahmad Helmi, a survivor of Assad's jails, argued the court's ruling sent a message: 'Whoever wants to re-normalise the Syrian regime, they will have this tag on their forehead that you are normalising with a state that is torturing people round the clock.'

Meanwhile, there have been other ways of seeking to hold Syrian war criminals to account. In 2019, the United States introduced the Caesar Act (officially, the Caesar Syria Civilian Protection Act), which imposed sanctions on Assad and others around him for war crimes. In the same year, a US court ordered the Syrian government to pay $300 million for the death of *Sunday Times* journalist Marie Colvin, killed for the power of her reporting from the besieged city of Homs in 2012. In her last interview, with Anderson Cooper of CNN, Colvin said, 'The Syrian army is simply shelling a city of cold, starving civilians . . . The terror of the people and the helplessness of these families hiding on the first floor. All they can do is hope it doesn't hit them. That's very, very difficult to watch.' On the basis of the evidence presented, the court concluded her death was a 'targeted murder' – partly in punishment for the power of that final interview, seen around the world. The ruling was, Colvin's family said, a 'legal rejoinder' to Assad's 'war on truth'.

In 2023, the *New York Times* reported on a five-year FBI investigation into the involvement of Ali Mamlouk, Assad's intelligence chief, in the death under torture of a Syrian-born US aid worker in 2016. In Paris in 2024, Mamlouk and two other senior Assad officials were convicted *in absentia* of crimes against humanity and sentenced to life imprisonment for the deaths of a twenty-year-old French-Syrian student and his father, an adviser at the French Lycée in Damascus. France's top appeals court even gave the go-ahead for an arrest warrant for Assad himself, following an application from survivors of the 2013 chemical gas attack in Ghouta. Two weeks after the Paris trial ended, the man who had run one of Syria's most notorious jails was arrested at Los Angeles airport in July 2024. Samir Ousman al-Sheikh, who had bought a one-way ticket back to Beirut, was charged initially with immigration fraud, after declaring on his visa application that he had never been involved in persecution or killing; his lawyer said it was all 'a simple misunderstanding'.

Sometimes, governments wait until it is too late. TRIAL International, a non-governmental organisation based in Geneva, called in 2015 for the arrest of Rifaat al-Assad, uncle of Bashar al-Assad and known as the Butcher of Hama for his role in the massacres of 1982. Swiss police knocked on the door of Assad's luxury suite in Geneva's Hotel Metropole and briefly detained him – then released him again. An arrest warrant was ordered in 2021, by which time Assad was safely back in Damascus; in 2024, Switzerland announced that the eighty-six-year-old's trial would go ahead *in absentia*.

At least Switzerland eventually issued an arrest warrant. For many years, one European government has seemed more eager to protect a war crimes suspect than to indict him, as the case of Khaled Halabi, a former senior Assad official, makes clear.

As described in Chapter Three, Nerma Jelačić escaped atrocities in the Bosnian town of Višegrad as a teenager; her work when she became Bosnia director of the Balkan Investigative Reporting Network helped put a key war criminal from her home town behind bars. In 2012, she took her justice work global when she went to work for the newly created Commission for International Justice and Accountability, formed to bring Syrian and other war criminals to justice worldwide. As she summarises CIJA's work: 'If shit happens, something should happen as a result. We can secure enough evidence that nobody could say: "We didn't know." If nothing happens – it's because you didn't want it to happen.'

The founder-director of CIJA is the cheerfully no-nonsense Bill Wiley, ex-military and a former investigator at the International Criminal Court and the Yugoslavia and Rwanda tribunals. He describes himself as an 'idealistic realist'. CIJA's focus is above all on 'linkage evidence' – evidence which helps join the dots, linking the crimes committed with the political leaders or military commanders ultimately responsible for those crimes. Such connections can be hard to prove. But, Wiley emphasises, they are essential. 'Everything is linkage. You want to prosecute those most responsible, as set out in the ICC statute. Chain of command, links in the chain – that's what you need.'

To that end and despite all the difficulties, CIJA gathered a million pages of documents revealing structures of power in Assad's Syria. Syrian activists have repeatedly risked their lives to secure those documents and smuggle them out of the country, one package at a time. In CIJA's inconspicuous offices in a European city, a locked room contains shelf after shelf of files crammed full of evidence that Wiley, Jelačić and their colleagues hope can, like the Milošević files I saw in The Hague two decades earlier, lead to prosecutions for crimes committed in Syria. Against unlikely odds, they have assembled similar dossiers on Myanmar.

The treasure trove of Syrian documents enabled CIJA to reconstruct the chain of command in forensic detail, analysing the responsibilities of those around the president. One of those they focused on was Assad's former director of intelligence in Raqqa in north-east Syria, Brigadier-General Khaled Halabi. Nadim Houry, then of Human Rights Watch and now director of the Arab Reform Initiative, describes entering Halabi's offices shortly after Raqqa fell to the rebels in 2013, where he saw for himself what he calls 'the bureaucracy of death'.

In his work for Human Rights Watch, Nadim had for years documented torture by Assad's regime. Now, Nadim saw for himself the place where the horrors he had so often heard about took place. 'The mental image I had formed was like in *Midnight Express*, all dungeony,' he tells me. 'But the building is banal-looking, the ground floor and first-floor offices are like any bureaucratic building in the Middle East.' And then, in the basement: the torture devices were still in place. That included the notorious *bsat al-reeh* or 'flying carpet', a wooden plank which immobilises detainees while they are being beaten and which folds in the middle, allowing guards to inflict excruciating pain. All this was Halabi's domain.

In 2015, CIJA discovered Halabi was living in France. He was seeking political asylum and tried to deploy the defence that Nazi leaders used at Nuremberg. 'When you receive an order,' he told French officials, 'as a soldier you have to carry it out.' France was unenthusiastic about Halabi's application, noting there were 'serious reasons' to believe that he was implicated in repression, so he tried his luck elsewhere. He vanished from Paris. After months of searching, CIJA identified some of Halabi's social media profiles. Via an IP address used for his Skype account, they worked out he was now in Vienna.

Wiley and colleagues approached the Austrian justice ministry to request the arrest of Halabi under the principle of universal jurisdiction that had begun with Pinochet and was now increasingly common in courts in Europe and around the world. The Austrians thanked CIJA for their visit but gave little away. In particular, they failed to mention one significant detail: Austrian intelligence didn't need anybody to tell them Halabi was in Vienna. They knew that already. In collaboration with the Israeli intelligence service, Mossad, Austria had provided Halabi with a paid-for apartment; two weeks before the meeting with CIJA, they had taken him shopping for furniture in Ikea.

CIJA had hoped the meeting would trigger the investigation or arrest of a key war crimes suspect. Instead, the Austrians put CIJA themselves under surveillance. Two agents were dispatched to The Hague to bring back insights such as: 'At lunchtime, food was brought into the building. Obviously, food was ordered.' (The organisation whose lunch habits the agents secretly surveilled had no connection to

CIJA.) Wiley's colleagues – still unaware that Austria was more interested in supporting a war crimes suspect than prosecuting him – kept checking to see if an arrest was imminent. It wasn't. Instead, in 2017, shortly after Russia's destruction of Aleppo, Halabi flew to Moscow on a new Austrian passport for talks with the Russian deputy foreign minister.

And there the story might have rested, if not for the work of CIJA and a series of journalistic follow-up investigations in Austria, Germany and the United States. Eventually, the embarrassment became too much even for apparently unembarrassable Austria (whose foreign minister, Karin Kneissl, danced with Putin at her wedding in 2018; Kneissl moved to Russia in 2023, with her ponies following in a Russian military transport plane from Syria). In 2023, four Austrian intelligence officials went on trial in connection with concealing Halabi from justice; Halabi appeared not as a defendant but as a witness. All four officials were acquitted. At the time of writing, Halabi is still at liberty, reportedly in Austria; the justice ministry in Vienna assures me an 'investigative procedure' remains open.

For the most powerful of all, apparent impunity continues, for the moment at least. In 2024, a year after Assad's re-admission into the Arab League, Putin – who in 1999 had been predicted to last for just a few months – was re-inaugurated for a fifth presidential term. He gained '87 per cent' of the vote, record-breaking even by his standards; by now key potential challengers were all in jail or dead. Margarita Simonyan, head of the RT television network, didn't see a problem with her president's unchallenged candidacy: 'Is there a need for a serious opponent?' she asked. 'Why?'

Chapter Seven

'If Not Now, When?'

Ukraine (2022–)

only women testify in this strange town
one speaks of a missing child
two speak of the tortured in the basement
three repeat what rapes and avert their eyes
four speak of the screams from the military headquarters
five speak of the executed in their own yards
six speak but are incomprehensible
seven check food supplies counting out loud
eight call me a liar because there is no justice
nine talk on their way to the cemetery
I'm also on my way because I know them all
in this town
its dead are my dead
its survivors are my sisters

From 'Testimonies', by
VICTORIA AMELINA (1986–2023)

'First, they would electrocute me on my ears. Then it was the genitals. Often I lost consciousness. They would give me another shock to the genitals. That would wake me. The pain was unbearable.' Oleksiy, a Ukrainian merchant seaman, is telling me of his treatment at the hands of Russian soldiers who seized him from his home in the southern port of Kherson in August 2022, put a bag over his head and drove him to a city-centre office block, where he was locked along with others in the basement. Oleksiy was tortured repeatedly in the months to come. 'They didn't seem to want to know anything. They just kept saying "Talk, talk! Tell us everything you know!"' The answers he and his fellow prisoners gave didn't halt the unremitting violence. 'They beat you to start with, with truncheons. You are asked a question – but they have already started to beat you again.'

My meeting with Oleksiy comes a few months after Ukraine drove out the Russian forces which had occupied Kherson from March until November 2022. Earlier that day, together with Ukrainian prosecutors, I saw the basement where Oleksiy was held. In the room where he was tortured stands a desk and a broken chair. Elsewhere, dried blood is sprayed across the walls, along with scribbled messages of despair. Oleksiy did not expect to survive. There seemed to be no reason why he would. 'We didn't think about tomorrow. We didn't even think about the evening. Anybody who ended up in there didn't expect ever to return home.'

One of the detainees' core offences, in the eyes of their captors, was the very fact of their Ukrainian identity. Russia, the torturers assured their prisoners, 'is here for ever'. Prisoners were ordered to chant 'Glory to Putin! Glory to Russia!' If they refused, they were beaten again. In September 2022, Kherson 'voted' to join the Russian Federation in a referendum staged by the occupiers. Six weeks later, Ukrainian forces recaptured the city and Russian forces fled in disarray. They tried to destroy incriminating documents as they left – with only partial success.

By the time of my visit to Kherson in April 2023, the city is still far from safe. Russian forces regularly shell the city from across the Dnipro river. Sixteen people were killed near the central square on Christmas Eve; remains of the missile are still embedded in the road. In the weeks after that, a maternity hospital, a school and a health clinic were targeted. In the spring sunshine, I drink coffee with the prosecutors outside a café which has fresh flowers on the tables and serves home-made cakes. But Kherson, a once thriving port of three hundred thousand people, is now a ghost city with less than one in five of its pre-war population.

Oleksiy's torture is one of more than a hundred thousand war crimes documented in the first year of Russia's war against Ukraine. He cannot understand how ordinary life could be so suddenly and viciously overturned: 'We can travel to other planets – and things like this happen here on earth.' Oleksiy is clear about what he wants: 'Those people need to see justice. They mustn't go unpunished.'

Even before the full horror of the Russian occupation became clear, achieving accountability was a central theme for Ukrainians. At the heart of the Geneva Conventions and the Rome Statute of the International Criminal Court is the prohibition on targeting civilians. And yet Russian forces seemed determined to do just that. When I meet Ukraine's head of war crimes investigations, Yuri Belousov, in a café near the prosecutor's offices in Kyiv, he tells me he has been re-reading Raphael Lemkin's original writings on genocide – including his essay on the Holodomor, the politically created famine which killed millions in Ukraine in 1933, as described in Chapter One. For Belousov, previously head of a human rights organisation, there are clear parallels. 'It was so interesting. It fitted the historical relationship. What we see today is the prolongation of what we have seen over so many years.' Like millions of Ukrainians – including President Volodymyr Zelensky himself – Belousov used Russian as his main language until the invasion of 2022. Now, though, he concludes: 'Russians want to destroy us as a separate country. They see Ukrainians as "spoilt" Russians.'

After the collapse of the Soviet coup in 1991, 90 per cent of Ukrainians voted for separation from Moscow. When I was in Ukraine shortly after the coup and a few days after a parliamentary declaration of independence in Kyiv, politician and human rights activist Mykola Horyn told me, 'The last collapse of empire has happened. Now, there's no return.' But some Russians have never accepted that. In a rambling seven-thousand-word essay written in 2021, Putin insisted Russia and Ukraine were 'a single whole' and that the sovereignty of Ukraine was possible 'only in partnership with Russia'. That mindset gives context to the invasion itself.

Belousov asks: 'What will we say about Ukraine in years to come? I think we will talk about genocide. It's not about killing the whole group. It's not about numbers. It's about intent.' Others have drawn similar conclusions. An investigation into the Kherson torture chambers by Global Rights Compliance, a Kyiv-based group led by British lawyer Wayne Jordash, concluded the patterns of abuse meant 'genocidal tactics are baked into Putin's plan to extinguish Ukrainian identity'.

The attempted extinction of identity takes different forms. In the chapter on genocide in *Axis Rule*, Lemkin quotes a German newspaper on the reported destruction of a Jewish library in Lublin in eastern Poland. 'For us, it was a matter of special pride to destroy the Talmudic Academy which was known as the greatest in Poland,' Lemkin quotes the *Frankfurter Zeitung*. 'We threw out of the building the great Talmudic library and carted it to market ... There we set fire to the books. The fire lasted for twenty hours ... Then we summoned the military band and the joyful shouts of the soldiers silenced the sound of the Jewish cries.' Eighty years later, books again became a target. The occupiers destroyed Ukrainian schoolbooks and replaced them with Russian ones. Russia has destroyed more than 170 Ukrainian libraries; Volodymyr Yermolenko, president of the Ukrainian branch of the writers' organisation PEN, talks of 'librocide'. In response to the destruction of a key printing plant in Kharkiv, Anna Gyn, an author in Ukraine's second-largest city, wrote: 'I always adored the smell of books. Now, probably, they will always remind me of ashes and blood.'

Those who tortured Oleksiy were confident no one would be held to account. A key question in the next few years will be whether that confidence was misplaced – and what consequences achieving justice, or failing to achieve justice, may have.

As in Chechnya, Syria and elsewhere, the standard Russian response to accusations of war crimes in Ukraine is denial. The crimes were staged or never happened; the other side committed them; the target was legitimate (sometimes, all three explanations are presented at the same time). Many Ukrainians have, however, worked since the beginning of the full-scale invasion to ensure that truths will be known and crimes will have consequences. The scale of the crimes committed by Russian forces in Ukraine has sometimes seemed unimaginable. Equally remarkable is the determination to achieve accountability for those crimes.

Early attempts came with startling speed. Ukraine's first war crimes trial began three months after the invasion, in May 2022. A Russian soldier, Vadim Shishimarin, had shot dead a sixty-two-year-old unarmed civilian, Oleksandr Shelipov, as he rode his bicycle through a village in north-east Ukraine. The killing was an obvious war crime, but the twenty-one-year-old Shishimarin was no obvious war criminal. 'I realise that you can't forgive me,' he told the murdered man's widow, 'but I'm pleading to you for forgiveness.' Shishimarin told the court: 'I wasn't trying to kill him. I just wanted everyone to get off my back.' Prosecutors accepted he had indeed been unwilling to shoot, and had fired only when repeatedly ordered to do so. Shishimarin was jailed for fifteen years. Many more trials have happened since then, the majority conducted *in absentia*. But a key question remains: how were such crimes permitted or encouraged, and who bears ultimate responsibility?

One of the most remarkable books on the Holocaust, Christopher Browning's *Ordinary Men*, documents how an unexceptional group of middle-aged Hamburg policemen are gradually transformed from reluctant killers to hardened murderers. It was all about normalisation of the unthinkable. Eighty years later, that same pattern is relevant for understanding Russian crimes in Ukraine, too. The basement where Oleksiy and others were tortured was no freelance operation. There were twenty such sites across Kherson. The men in charge reported to a more senior commander, who in turn reported to a commander more senior still. None of these crimes happened by chance. This was a context where anything and everything was permitted or encouraged from on high.

Andriy Kovalenko, head of war crimes investigations in the Kherson region and a bundle of buzz-cut energy, is clear on what he and his team need. In their evacuated offices in Mikolayiv, an hour up the road from embattled Kherson, he shows me an organigram of the Russian regional command structure, complete with names and nicknames, from brigade commanders all the way up to the generals. Kovalenko says he is determined that those responsible for the suffering of Oleksiy and others will face justice some day. He insists: 'The information is growing, all the time.'

Sometimes, evidence available to prosecutors is clear. In intercepted radio traffic near Bucha, a Russian commander gives orders as unambiguous as similar instructions issued during the genocide at Srebrenica: 'First question the soldiers, then shoot them.' One soldier tells his mother about an eighteen-year-old Ukrainian who was shot in the leg. 'Then his ears were cut off. After that, he admitted everything, and they killed him.' In another call, a soldier tells his mother: 'We have the order to take phones from everyone and those who resist – in short – to hell with the fuckers. We have the order: it doesn't matter whether they're civilians or not. Kill everyone.'

When Russian forces retreated from Bucha after their month-long occupation, there was a list of urgent issues to address. Bodies had to be identified; electricity had to be restored; there was a shortage of everything from coffins to drinking water. From day one, however, there was another focus, too: securing evidence for future prosecutions. 'We don't know what Putin's plans are,' Kyiv regional police chief Andriy Niebytov said during those early traumatised days, while decaying corpses were still being collected and buried. 'So we are working as quickly as possible – in case he drops a bomb and destroys all the proof.' Investigators set up office in a schoolroom; people queued up to give testimony.

It is not just those directly impacted by crimes who want to see consequences. Oleksandra Matviichuk, chair of Ukraine's Nobel-winning Centre for Civil Liberties, notes that two thirds of Ukrainians say accountability for crimes matters most to them when the war finally ends. A huge poster on Khreshchatyk avenue in the centre of Kyiv shows bewigged judges looking down on a handcuffed Putin who is wearing a prisoner's orange jumpsuit; Ukrainians stop in front of the picture to take selfies. People want the truth, too. One woman in Bucha told me: 'It's important that the Russian people understand what has happened here. Too many Russians don't believe. That must change.'

She is right that Russia needs to find ways past its many layers of denial, but that change will take time. Russians who condemn Putin's lawlessness suffer harsh consequences. After Moscow's invasion of Czechoslovakia in 1968, the poet Natalia Gorbanevskaya was one of a tiny group of Russians who went out on to Red Square with a banner declaring 'For your and our freedom!' They were jailed, sent to labour camps or, in Gorbanevskaya's case, committed to a 'special psychiatric hospital' (a de facto prison) for 'enemies of the people'. But the courage of that small band had impact in the years to come; Gorbanevskaya would be celebrated as a hero in a free Prague.

In Russia in 2022, protests were almost as harshly repressed as in 1968. Twenty thousand people were detained. Even carrying a sign with no obvious slogan spelt trouble: placards declaring '*** *****' were interpreted as нет войне – *nyet voine*, meaning 'No to war' or, in an alternative reading of the asterisks, 'Fuck war'; those eight stars could get you arrested. Artist Aleksandra Skochilenko, who replaced supermarket price tags with messages calling for an end to the war, was jailed for seven years. Opposition activist Ilya Yashin was jailed for eight years for 'fake news' for a YouTube post describing the 'apocalyptic scene, like in a horror movie' of corpses with their hands tied in Bucha. Vladimir Kara-Murza, a Russian-British former journalist, was jailed for twenty-five years for 'treasonous lies' after he condemned the bombing of maternity hospitals and schools.

Oleg Orlov, co-chair of the banned Memorial human rights group which was joint recipient of the Nobel Peace Prize in 2022, was jailed for 'discrediting the armed forces', after telling an obvious and painful truth: 'It isn't just about the destruction of the principles of international law. The war also deals a very heavy blow to Russia's future.' On the day that Orlov's second trial opened in February 2024 (prosecutors claimed a previous sentence had been too lenient and started again from scratch), opposition leader Alexei Navalny, who four years earlier had been poisoned with novichok, died in a Siberian prison at the age of forty-seven.

Orlov, who during the proceedings sat reading Kafka's *The Trial*, described his case as 'absurdity and tyranny dressed up as formal adherence to some pseudo-legal procedures'. He asked the judge and prosecution, 'Doesn't the obvious occur to you? That sooner or later, the machine of repression may roll over those who launched it and drove it forward?'

Those who were jailed asked their compatriots to believe in a different future. Yashin begged the country not to 'retreat in the face of evil'. Kara-Murza, echoing Chilean leader Salvador Allende before his death in 1973, declared, 'I know the day will come when the darkness over our country will dissipate ... This day will come as inevitably as spring follows the coldest winter. Our society will open its eyes and be horrified when it realises what crimes were committed on its behalf.'

In August 2024, Kara-Murza, Yashin and Skochilenko were all released and expelled, together with *Wall Street*

Journal reporter Evan Gershkovich who had been falsely accused and convicted of espionage. The arrest of Gershkovich was a barely concealed form of hostage-taking; the releases came as part of a complex international swap. Those who Putin got back in return for Gershkovich and others included Vadim Krasikov, an FSB agent who was serving a life sentence for a murder in broad daylight in Berlin; Putin thanked Krasikov, his former bodyguard, for his patriotic act.

Kara-Murza has not lost his belief in the future. On the plane from Moscow, an FSB agent told him to look out of the window because it was the last time he would see Russia. Kara-Murza replied: 'I'm a historian, so I am sure I will be back in my country – and it will be much quicker than you think.'

In the first days and weeks after Russia's full-scale invasion, the world seemed ready to speak almost with one voice. The UN General Assembly called for Russia's withdrawal; only a traditional rogues' quartet of Belarus, Eritrea, North Korea and Syria voted in solidarity with Moscow (thirty-five states abstained, a silence that would get louder in the next two years). As Russia's threats against Ukraine had multiplied ahead of the invasion, Kenya's ambassador to the United Nations, Martin Kimani, said it was essential to recover 'from the embers of dead empires' in a way that 'does not plunge us back into new forms of domination and repression'. Kimani said Russia's actions meant multilateralism was 'on its deathbed'. But he had criticisms for some of Ukraine's supporters, too. Pointedly referring to the invasion of Iraq twenty years earlier, he condemned the trend of 'powerful states, including members of this Security Council, breaching international law with little regard'. The ambassador's accusation of double standards was a message that some people didn't want to hear.

It would, however, have damaging consequences – including, in due course, for Ukraine.

Despite the challenges, initiatives to hold perpetrators to account quickly multiplied. Russia would clearly veto any attempt by the Security Council to refer the crimes in Ukraine to the International Criminal Court, just as it had vetoed attempts to hold Assad to account in Syria. But Ukraine had already pledged to 'cooperate with the court without delay or exception' and to accept the jurisdiction of the court in connection with crimes in Russian-occupied eastern Ukraine and Crimea. That earlier agreement was now re-affirmed. Within days of the invasion, the ICC's newly appointed chief prosecutor, Karim Khan, sought authorisation for an investigation and encouraged governments to refer the case to accelerate the process. Forty-three countries (though only three from the global south and none from Africa) obliged with unprecedented speed.

Khan visited Ukraine three weeks after the invasion. He was back a few weeks later to visit a newly liberated Bucha, where he declared: 'Ukraine is a crime scene.' In May 2022, the court announced it would send its largest-ever team to Ukraine. Khan talked of his hope that there could be 'a dawning realisation that the rule of law is not a passive spectator, but an intrinsic part, an intrinsic buckle to keep us together'.

The International Criminal Court was not the only venue in The Hague where Russia might face consequences for its crimes. Even as the ICC began its investigations, Ukraine brought a parallel case at the International Court of Justice, a couple of miles across town from its sister court. The immediate trigger was Putin's claim that Ukraine was committing 'genocide' against Russian-speakers in eastern Ukraine.

Those false allegations had been used as a pretext for the invasion. The ICJ made a provisional ruling in favour of Ukraine, calling for 'immediate suspension' of military operations. To nobody's surprise, Russia ignored the ruling. There were, however, implications in the court of world opinion, too. As the judges put it, in words that would be relevant in its judgments against Israel two years later, 'Whether or not they have consented to the jurisdiction of the court, states remain responsible for acts attributable to them that are contrary to international law.'

In addition to the International Criminal Court (prosecuting individuals for war crimes, crimes against humanity and genocide) and the International Court of Justice (ruling on inter-state disputes, including breaches of the conventions on torture or genocide), a third possibility now came into play, reviving an idea that had long seemed moribund.

At Nuremberg, Moscow had pressed for crimes against peace to be part of the indictments. As described in Chapter Four, the crime of aggression was then set aside for half a century before being revived and eventually included in the revised Rome Statute of the International Criminal Court in 2018. Once again, however, the insistence on privileged rules for some countries had unforeseen consequences. Because of the pressures from America at the Kampala review conference in 2010, the leaders of countries which were not members of the ICC could not be prosecuted for the crime of aggression. Russia now looked set to benefit from this.

In the weeks after the invasion, the 102-year-old Ferencz joined with others to call for a re-examination of the carve-outs that America (and its French and British friends on the Security Council) had pushed for. That proposal didn't get anywhere – though pressure continues, with potential revisions due in 2025. But the Ukrainians embraced an alternative suggestion, floated shortly after the invasion by lawyer and author Philippe Sands. Sands argued for the creation of a new tribunal which would investigate the crime of aggression as a leadership crime, as Moscow had pressed for in 1945.

Sands was already well known in Ukraine, especially for his acclaimed *East West Street*, which tells the stories of Lemkin, Lauterpacht and their contributions to international law, interwoven with stories from the Holocaust of some of Sands's own Jewish relatives, born in what is now western Ukraine. Translations of *East West Street* are piled high in Ukrainian bookshops today. Sands's idea quickly gained traction in Kyiv. From the Ukrainian perspective, Russia's unprovoked assault was indeed what Nuremberg judges had called the 'supreme international crime'.

It would have been understandable if, at this moment of existential crisis, Ukraine's leadership remained focused only on the challenge of driving the invaders back from the gates of Kyiv. Even at this early stage, though, Ukraine devoted attention to the possibilities of future accountability, as an event just eight days after the invasion made clear. On 4 March 2022, Ukraine's foreign minister, Dmytro Kuleba, joined a virtual meeting hosted by Chatham House, focused on the proposal for a new tribunal.

'I'm sorry, I may not look like a foreign minister,' Kuleba introduced himself with a tired smile. Sitting in his car in sweatshirt and winter jacket, he looked like a foreign minister whose country's survival was hanging by a thread. Kuleba referred back to the St James's Declaration of 1942 which paved the way for Nuremberg – the declaration was, I learned later, a theme of Kuleba's doctoral thesis at the University of Kyiv. As Polish prime minister General Władysław Sikorski had told the meeting in St James's Palace, a few minutes' walk from Chatham House, the invaders needed to 'clearly understand that there can be no crime without punishment'. Eighty years later, Kuleba echoed Sikorski's words. He acknowledged: 'When bombs fall on your cities, when forces rape women in your cities, it's difficult to speak about the efficiency of international law.' He insisted, however, 'This is the only tool of international civilisation which is open to us to make sure that all those who made this war possible will be brought to justice.'

Many governments were wary of creating yet another legal mechanism. In the months to come, however, Kyiv made the same arguments that the Russians themselves had used in 1945. None of the murders in Bucha nor the brutal destruction of Mariupol would have taken place if Putin had not launched his illegal war in the first place. In that respect, the act of invasion did indeed contain within itself, as the Nuremberg judges put it, 'the accumulated evil of the whole'. As described later in this chapter, Ukrainians would continue to push for a special tribunal for the crime of aggression – sometimes with success, sometimes buffeted by apparently unrelated military and political storms elsewhere in the world.

In the lead-up to the full-scale war, the Kremlin mocked those who suggested Russia might be about to invade its neighbour. In November 2021, Putin's spokesman Dmitry Peskov declared: 'Russia doesn't threaten anyone. The movement of troops on our territory shouldn't be a cause for anyone's concern.' The denials continued in the months to come, though sounding less and less convincing. Finally, on 21 February, it became clear that a deadly turning point had been reached. Putin declared 'independence and sovereignty' for the occupied Donetsk and Luhansk regions in eastern Ukraine and condemned the 'aggressive and nationalistic regime' which had 'seized power' in Kyiv. (The centrist Zelensky had been elected by a landslide in 2019.) Responsibility for any bloodshed, Putin said, would 'lie entirely on the conscience of Ukraine's ruling regime'.

Across the country, millions of Ukrainians understood that life as they knew it was about to end. Olha Reshetylova heard Putin's speech while giving her son Ostap his bedtime bath. 'I sat on the bathroom floor as I listened,' she tells me when we meet in Kyiv. 'I didn't sleep all night.' Reshetylova is co-founder of Ukraine's Media Initiative for Human Rights, which has documented forced disappearances and other crimes by Russian forces in eastern Ukraine since 2016. After Putin's speech she made arrangements for her team's safety. She wrote to donors, explaining that promised work would need to be 'postponed'. And, at the same time, life continued. It would be Ostap's second birthday on 24 February. Reshetylova went to the market to buy balloons.

The first explosions came just before dawn. Olha recalls: 'I grabbed my two sons. My older son is eleven. I remember his eyes.' Explosions shook the apartment windows as the family hung up the balloons, took pictures and sang 'Happy Birthday' to Ostap (there was a cake, too, but that got forgotten amidst the bombing). 'I had to save the mental health of my children,' Olha says. 'It was important not to be scared.' The family managed to drive out of Kyiv to the relative safety of western Ukraine. Within a few weeks, Olha returned to Kyiv to continue her work. Across the country, millions of Ukrainians faced similar challenges – trying to rebuild elements of normality, even as their lives and country were ripped apart.

In his invasion-day speech, Putin praised the 'high values of human rights and freedoms' and insisted: 'It is not our plan to occupy Ukrainian territory. We do not intend to impose anything on anyone by force.' He repeated the familiar mantra: 'All responsibility for the possible bloodshed will lie fully and wholly with the ruling Ukrainian regime.' Putin even spoke of the need for justice, promising to prosecute Ukrainians for 'numerous bloody crimes against civilians'. Ukrainians saw it differently. They repainted road signs with a message for any Russian tanks that might pass that way: 'GAAGA', or The Hague. Straight on for The Hague, turn right for The Hague, all roads lead to The Hague.

Putin's casting of the aggressors as victims had earlier parallels. When announcing the invasion of Poland in 1939, Hitler explained how the Poles had obliged him to destroy their country: 'Germans in Poland are persecuted with bloody terror and driven from their houses ... In order to put an end to this lunacy, I have no other choice than to meet force with force from now on.' Like Putin eight decades later, Hitler emphasised that his armed forces would, naturally, obey the laws of war. 'I will not wage war against women and children,' he said. 'I have ordered my air force to restrict itself to attacks on military objectives.' (Behind closed doors, Hitler was frank with his generals: 'Destruction of Poland is in the foreground ... I shall give a propagandist cause for starting the war, never mind whether it be plausible or not.') In Germany in 1942, a leaflet published by the non-violent White Rose resistance group (whose members were later executed) quoted Aristotle on how 'the tyrant is inclined to constantly foment wars' in order to retain his grip on power. Eighty years later, Aristotle's words were again applicable.

For Putin, too, truth was irrelevant – and some were happy to take anything he said at face value. In 2024 Putin told Donald Trump's favourite interviewer, Tucker Carlson, 'We don't attack anyone.' Carlson – like Trump himself, fawning in the presence of authoritarian power — expressed surprise that Putin had been so patient with his Ukrainian neighbours for so long, instead of simply marching in: 'You have nuclear weapons, they don't. It's actually your land. Why did you wait so long?'

Putin seemed confident that Russia was too powerful to be bothered by any of the legal initiatives — the International Criminal Court, the International Court of Justice or the proposed new crime of aggression tribunal. After all, nobody had seriously challenged him over Chechnya, Georgia, Crimea or eastern Ukraine. Why should this be any different? As Putin might have said, echoing Hitler on the Armenians, 'Who remembers the Chechens now?'

The Ukrainians were, however, determined that this time things would be different. A year after the full-scale invasion, in January 2023, I met with Ukraine's war crimes ambassador, Anton Korynevych, in Kyiv. He remembered the scepticism Ukraine faced when the crime of aggression tribunal was first proposed. 'Governments told us: "Nothing can be done, stop playing!"' Now, though, he told me: 'There is an acceptance, there must be accountability. The question has become not if but how. We have walked a long road.'

The optimism seemed justified. A few days before our conversation, the European Parliament had backed the creation of a new tribunal, referencing Nuremberg and the St James's Declaration. A few days later, Ursula von der Leyen, President of the European Commission, used the occasion of a visit to Kyiv to promise the creation of an International Centre for the Prosecution of the Crime of Aggression in The Hague. Even Washington, initially wary, seemed to warm to the idea. At a conference in Lviv in March to discuss plans for future accountability, US war crimes ambassador Beth van Schaack talked of 'truly a historic moment', which could ensure that 'the promises of Nuremberg are not mere history'. Van Schaack told Congress she looked forward to 'the first prosecutions of the crime of aggression in the modern era'.

The momentum would slow in the months to come, with arguments over whether it was better to have fully international backing for the planned tribunal (as Ukraine wanted, which would ensure that Putin and other senior leaders could not claim immunity), or whether a more 'local' form of tribunal would suffice (as America argued). In the meantime, however, an unprecedented judicial detonation was on its way.

For me, the names of Putin and Vermeer will now always be intertwined. On the afternoon of 17 March 2023, I was queuing outside the Rijksmuseum in Amsterdam, waiting to see the biggest-ever exhibition of the master from Delft. As I contemplated standing in a few minutes' time in front of *Girl with a Pearl Earring*, my phone rang. It was a radio producer from London: 'The International Criminal Court has just issued an arrest warrant for Putin.'

It was one of those moments that is simultaneously astonishing and entirely predictable – predictable at least in retrospect. Holding the most powerful people in the world to account was what the ICC had been created for. Given all that had happened in the past year, how could the court *not* indict Putin? And yet, many of us who had observed the slow-turning wheels of justice had over the years become conditioned to assume prosecutors would always begin with small fry. It took six years for the Yugoslavia war crimes tribunal to indict Slobodan Milošević. It was four years before the ICC indicted Sudanese leader Omar al-Bashir. To the frustration of victims and their families, indictments for top leaders often never happened at all. This time, those cautious expectations were all overturned. An international court had charged the head of state of one of the most powerful countries in the world with grave crimes. There had been nothing like it since 1945.

The charges did not focus, as many had expected, on the most obvious crimes of the past year – the atrocities in Bucha, say, or the destruction of Mariupol – but on a subset of crimes which the Russians had made their own. The charges against the president and his children's commissioner, Maria Lvova-Belova, were simply described:

Mr Vladimir Vladimirovich Putin, born on 7 October 1952, President of the Russian Federation, is allegedly responsible for the war crime of unlawful deportation of population (children) and unlawful transfer of population (children) from occupied areas of Ukraine to the Russian Federation (under articles 8(2)(a) (vii) and 8(2)(b) (viii) of the Rome Statute).

The charges against Lvova-Belova – former singer in a church choir, philanthropist and wife of an Orthodox priest – were similar. The indictments talked of 'at least hundreds of children' taken from Ukraine to Russia.

Some thought the numbers were conservative. Ukraine's chief prosecutor, Andriy Kostin, had talked of sixteen thousand children being deported through 'filtration points'. Whatever the actual figure, the evidence was hard to deny. Maria Lvova-Belova had herself described Ukrainian children being taken to Russia after being 'found in basements' in Mariupol. She did not mention the three-month siege which reduced the city to rubble and forced people to take shelter in cellars in the first place. She did, however, acknowledge that the separation of children from their families was not necessarily what the children wanted. 'Maybe in the beginning,'

Lvova-Belova said, there was 'some negativity' from them, including that they wanted to sing the Ukrainian anthem, or said 'Glory to Ukraine!' In due course, however (as she explained), those negative feelings were transformed into 'love for Russia'.

The president and his children's commissioner held a winsome televised dialogue about the joys of bringing up somebody else's children in another country. The removal of children was presented as if it were a generous humanitarian gesture.

> PUTIN: You adopted a child from Mariupol, right?
> LVOVA-BELOVA: Yes, Vladimir Vladimirovich, thanks to you.
> PUTIN: Is he little?
> LVOVA-BELOVA: No, he is fifteen years old. Now I know what it is like to be a mother of a child from Donbas – it is complicated, but we love each other for sure.
> PUTIN: That's the most important thing.
> LVOVA-BELOVA: It is. I think we will manage everything, won't we?
> PUTIN: Of course.

Even ahead of Putin's arrest warrant, Russian television presenters warned viewers of the dangers which prosecutors in The Hague allegedly posed to all Russians. Margarita Simonyan of the RT broadcasting network said, 'They will come even for a street cleaner who is sweeping the cobblestones behind the Kremlin.' Television host Olga Skabeeva warned that 'the carefree existence of every citizen of the Russian Federation' was on the line. Her solution was not to stop killing Ukrainians, but to kill more: 'In order to avoid the Hague tribunals, the initiation of criminal cases, compensation, reparations – in order to avoid all this, we need a total intensification of military actions, we have to squeeze and pressure them so much that they approach us about a truce or a peace process.'

When the indictments were unveiled, Russian commentators went almost literally nuclear. Margarita Simonyan said: 'I'd like to see the country that arrests Putin according to The Hague's ruling. Eight minutes later – or whatever the flight time to its capital is.' Russia said Karim Khan was now on a wanted list, for 'criminal prosecution of a person known to be innocent'. Lvova-Belova, meanwhile, said she was simply baffled: 'It all looks like a farce without specifics and is incomprehensible.' She was astonished at the suggestion she might be a war criminal: 'I'm a mother. That says it all. A war criminal? What are you talking about?'

Putin was due to attend the annual summit of the five BRICS nations – Brazil, Russia, India, China, South Africa – in Johannesburg in August 2023. As a result of the indictment, South Africa was obliged to arrest Putin if he arrived in the country. That presented hosts and guest alike with difficult choices. First, Putin could choose to play the martyr card by being arrested as he walked off the plane. That, to be fair, never seemed likely. Few reckoned Putin had a political death wish. The second option – to which both Moscow and Pretoria devoted much energy in the months to come – was for Putin to travel to Johannesburg after negotiating guarantees of safe passage. That would echo what had happened in 2015, when, as described in Chapter Four, the South African government smuggled the indicted Sudanese leader Omar al-Bashir out of the country. Even in the case of al-Bashir, however, the contempt for the rule of law had come at a cost. Judges complained of the government's 'disgraceful' action and 'risible' excuses; civil society groups were furious. If such defiance were repeated on Putin's behalf, that would have consequences. The third possibility was that Putin would stay at home. That would keep him safe.

The South African government ducked and dived for months before finally announcing that Putin would join the meeting by video link. Moscow insisted the decision was made from a position of strength. 'Putin will not go to Africa. Africa will come to Russia,' one headline declared, referring to a conference of African leaders that Putin was due to host in St Petersburg. But there was no way of disguising the truth: the Russian leader's travel plans would from now on be uncomfortably constrained.

The Putin indictment was a dramatic first shot from the prosecutors, but it did not stand alone. A year later, in March 2024, the International Criminal Court unveiled a second set of arrest warrants, this time against Admiral Viktor Sokolov, commander of Russia's Black Sea Fleet, and Lieutenant-General Sergei Kobylash, commander of long-range aviation, in connection with attacks on Ukraine's energy infrastructure in the winter of 2022–3. Details of the charges remain secret, but the court said the existence of arrest warrants was revealed in order to 'contribute to the prevention of the further commission of crimes'. Three months later, there were two further indictments, this time against then defence minister Sergei Shoigu and General Valery Gerasimov, commander of Russian forces in Ukraine. There has been talk of further indictments in connection with, for example, the torture and execution of prisoners of war.

Ukrainian state prosecutors, in collaboration with investigators from the ICC and with other international lawyers, lead the attempts to nail down responsibility for the hundred thousand-plus war crimes that have been identified. But they are not alone. Civil society groups play a more active role in seeking war crimes justice in Ukraine than in any other conflict in history.

Traditionally, human rights groups and elected governments have a complicated relationship. Non-governmental organisations criticise the authorities for doing the wrong thing or failing to do the right thing. Governments grumble that their difficult choices and magnificent achievements are insufficiently recognised. All this is normal and beneficial, even if politicians do not always see it that way. After Russian forces occupied Crimea and eastern Ukraine in 2014, Ukrainian human rights groups continued to criticise the authorities in Kyiv on some issues. Thus, for example, Kyiv failed for years to ratify the statute of the International Criminal Court which it claimed to support so strongly; Ukrainian NGOs repeatedly criticised Zelensky's government on this and other failures. (In 2024, ten years after Ukraine first accepted the ICC's jurisdiction, Ukraine finally bowed to the pressures and ratified the Rome Statute. Even now, however, echoing America's unhelpful approach to impunity, Kyiv insisted there would be no jurisdiction 'when, likely, the crime was committed by [Ukraine's] citizens'.)

Meanwhile, in parallel to the standard and healthy criticisms of the government, the scale of the crimes committed against Ukraine means that a new and unusually collaborative relationship has also emerged between the authorities and civil society. Within weeks of the full-scale invasion, dozens of groups formed the '5AM coalition', named after the time the invasion began. One key focus was on the collection and securing of evidence that could help future prosecutions, supporting the efforts of the state. At the beginning, none of those involved knew if they might be arrested or dead in a few days' time. But they were determined to do whatever was needed and to continue for however long it took. As Tetyana Pechonchyk, head of Zmina ('Change'), a founding member of the 5AM coalition, put it: 'We understand this task will not be completed in just a few years. I am preparing myself to continue working on this until the end of my life.'

In parallel, another coalition was created, to support the proposed crime of aggression tribunal. A founding member of the Tribunal for Putin initiative is the Nobel Prize-winning Centre for Civil Liberties, created in 2007 with an initial aim of strengthening Ukraine's democracy after the Orange Revolution of 2004. Oleksandra Matviichuk, the centre's chair, notes the connection between past failures to react and the brazenness of crimes committed now. 'This hell we see now is the result of complete impunity over many years,' she tells me when we meet in her office in central Kyiv, ten minutes' walk from Maidan Square. In her Nobel acceptance speech a few months earlier, Matviichuk argued that we may be at a turning point: 'Dictators are afraid that the idea of freedom will prevail ... Yes, the law doesn't work right now. But we do not think it is for ever. We have to break this impunity cycle and change the approach to justice for war crimes.'

Many of the war crimes investigations are connected to places where the horror has made international headlines – murder in Bucha in the north, torture in Kherson in the south, or hundreds of mutilated bodies in shallow graves in Izyum in the east. But less high-profile deaths are also part of the mosaic. On a drizzly spring day, I join Matviichuk's colleagues on a drive south from Kyiv through villages where peace and war intersect – tank traps, storks on telegraph poles, checkpoints. Our destination is the small town of Rzhyshchiv, where Iranian-made drones recently hit a residential catering college.

On arrival, everything at first looks normal. But, just around the corner, tattered fragments of clothing dangle from branches high in a tree beside a fifth-floor room whose contents have been blown into the sky. The assembly hall is missing its roof; velvet curtains flap as a dog chases through the rain and rubble. The dead included an ambulance driver who came to rescue the injured and was himself killed a few minutes later by a second drone – the 'double-tap' that Putin's and Assad's forces have used so often and to such deadly effect in Syria in past years. The nine deaths in Rzhyschchiv went mostly unreported: the international news that day focused on Putin toasting a 'new era' with Chinese president Xi Jinping in Moscow. But the details collected will all feed into a shared database cataloguing damage to infrastructure and civilian lives lost across the country; the information can be accessed and cross-checked by domestic and international prosecutors alike.

Truth Hounds, one of Ukraine's best-known investigating groups, first emerged after the Revolution of Dignity in 2013–14 and Russia's subsequent occupation of Crimea and eastern Ukraine. Roman Avramenko, the organisation's co-founder, describes this as 'the best documented conflict we have ever seen'. Achieving accountability is at the heart of the work. In Avramenko's words: 'Many people have lost everything. I have interviewed people where they describe how everything is destroyed in seconds. The possibility of justice gives them hope and fills life with some meaning.' In addition to the witness testimonies which remain the bedrock of traditional human rights reports, Avramenko and his colleagues gather evidence from satellite imagery, mobile phone videos, text messages, abandoned materials and more. Olha Opalenko, head of evidence, talks of the 'spider's web' which brings it all together.

Above Opalenko's desk in the Truth Hounds office in the buzzy Podil district of Kyiv is a drawing by the daughter of a colleague: a blue-and-yellow Ukrainian flag and a blue-and-yellow heart, enclosed in another pink heart. On the wall hangs a Sakharov Freedom Award. Perched on the back of the sofa is a row of protective helmets. On a group video call, Opalenko and her colleagues discuss evidence they have gathered in a town that was occupied by Russian forces in 2022. A database lists crimes associated with a suspect they are looking into – 'illegal detention and torture of a civilian', 'illegal arrest of family and subsequent disappearance of civilian', 'brutal murder of a civilian grandfather', 'destruction of critical infrastructure facilities', and more.

Opalenko shakes her head in disbelief as she scrolls through the entries: 'Torture, shelling, sexual violence, civilian killings, disappearances, crimes against children – there's such a wide range of crimes, it's just crazy.' But she insists there are reasons for hope amidst the darkness. 'We have this piece, this piece, this piece – and we can put it all together. These are reasons for unprecedented hope and belief.'

Most of the investigations in Ukraine – by non-governmental organisations, state prosecutors and international investigators alike – are into crimes such as the killing of civilians and the targeting of infrastructure which have long formed part of the Geneva Conventions and, more recently, the Rome Statute. But Truth Hounds and others have also begun to focus on another theme. The word 'ecocide' was first used in the 1970s in connection with America's use of the defoliating herbicide Agent Orange in Vietnam. It has gained a new relevance in Ukraine. Russia's destruction in 2023 of the Kakhovka dam upstream from Kherson caused hundreds of deaths and will have impact for years to come, an incident that Ukrainian officials have compared to Chernobyl. (Russia denies responsibility, though Russian commentators previously described dams as a 'legitimate military objective'.)

Because of the Chernobyl disaster (Chornobyl, in Ukrainian) and now Kakhovka, Ukraine has been ahead of other countries in defining ecocide as a crime. But others are moving in that direction. The European Union agreed in 2024 to criminalise behaviour 'comparable to ecocide'. There is pressure, too, for ecocide to be included as an additional core crime in the next round of amendments to the Rome Statute of the International Criminal Court.

Much of the Truth Hounds' research on the Kakhovka dam could be done in areas that are now under Ukrainian control. But even without access to areas where crimes have been committed, open-source research can assemble a detailed picture of facts on the ground in ways that would have been impossible until recently. Truth Hounds also joined with Human Rights Watch and the New York-based SITU Research who worked for two years with satellite imagery, 3D reconstructions and hundreds of geo-tagged videos to produce a detailed picture of the Russian destruction of the port city of Mariupol, published in 2024. The project includes powerful stories of life and death. It also includes calculations of damage caused, minimum numbers of deaths (with the help of ultra-high-resolution satellite imagery showing burial patterns in five Mariupol cemeteries) and the names of commanders who the investigators believe bear the greatest responsibility for thousands of civilian deaths. All this was put together through digital research; on-the-ground investigations were impossible.

Sam Dubberley, previously at Amnesty International and

now leading open-source investigations at Human Rights Watch, sums up the significance: 'Do we know who pulled the trigger? No. But we can say: these commanders were in charge. That's a massive contribution, which we hope will be picked up. All this has only become possible in the past few years.'

The row of protective helmets in Olha Opalenko's office is a reminder that those who document war crimes also put themselves in harm's way. One of the Truth Hounds investigators was Victoria Amelina, novelist and creator of the New York Literature Festival in the small town of New York in eastern Ukraine. I had seen her posts on social media; I admired her courage and dry humour; I made a note to get in touch and looked forward to hearing more about her work.

Indirectly, Raphael Lemkin was responsible for Amelina going to work with Truth Hounds. In her home town of Lviv, she noticed the modest plaque at 21 Zamarstynivska Street which commemorates Lemkin and his achievements. 'That made me stop and think that maybe I can do more than moving the boxes of humanitarian aid,' she told Joanna Kakissis of National Public Radio in June 2023.

Amelina's work with Truth Hounds included meeting the parents of Ukrainian writer Volodymyr Vakulenko and promoting his legacy. On 23 March 2022, Vakulenko, knowing the dangers he faced from the occupiers, buried his diary in the garden of his home near Izyum in the Kharkiv region of north-east Ukraine. Russian soldiers seized him the next day. When Vakulenko's mother asked about her son, they told her, 'Don't worry, we'll let him go, we're not Nazis.' It was another lie. Vakulenko was tortured, executed with two pistol bullets and buried in a mass grave. When the Ukrainians recaptured Izyum after six months of occupation, the body of the forty-nine-year-old poet and children's author was found in grave no. 319 in the woods outside the town. In the words of his fellow author Andrey Kurkov, 'He was killed because he loved Ukraine and the Ukrainian language, culture and history. They killed him because they saw strength in him. They killed him because he did not kneel before them.' Kurkov, himself one of the millions of Ukrainian Russian-speakers, compared Vakulenko's fate to those who have become known as Ukraine's 'Executed Renaissance', murdered in the Stalinist 1930s: 'This is how Russia kills, how it has always killed Ukrainian culture.' Amelina made the same comparison: 'My worst fear was coming true: that I was in the middle of a new Executed Renaissance, just like in the 1930s, when Ukrainian artists were being murdered, their manuscripts disappearing and their memory wiped away.'

Amelina and Vakulenko's father dug for hours together until they eventually found the diary, wrapped in a plastic bag and buried under a cherry tree. The final entry reads: 'Now I have pulled myself together, even worked in the garden a little and brought potatoes into the house . . . And today, on the Day of Poetry, a small flock of cranes called from the sky, seeming to say: "Everything will be Ukraine! I believe in victory."' On 22 June 2023, Amelina spoke at the Book Arsenal literary festival in Kyiv, presenting the diary that she had helped bring into the light. She was finishing a book of her own, too, later published as *Looking at Women, Looking at War: A War and Justice Diary*.

On 27 June, Amelina and colleagues were eating dinner in the popular Ria pizza restaurant in Kramatorsk, an hour's drive south of Izyum. One of those with her was the Colombian writer Héctor Abad, whose own father had been killed by paramilitaries in 1987. A Russian missile targeted the busy restaurant. Amelina died of her injuries four days later. She was one of thirteen people who lost their lives. 'We were having a laugh,' said Abad, 'and suddenly we found ourselves in hell.' The head of Russia's parliamentary defence committee, General Andrei Kartapolov, praised the attack, whose victims included two fourteen-year-old twin sisters, as 'very chic'. He said on a popular television show: 'I take my hat off to those who planned it. It rejoices my old soldier's heart.' Most obviously, the general's reaction, which went down well with the studio audience, lacked humanity. It was also revealing: Russian state media treat the killings of Ukrainian civilians as an outcome to be celebrated. This was not the first time Kramatorsk had mourned such an attack. A year earlier, cluster munitions killed fifty-eight civilians at the railway station as thousands tried to flee the Russian assault (Moscow called the deaths a 'Ukrainian hoax').

Will anybody be held to account for all those killed at the Kramatorsk station, for the killing of Vakulenko and hundreds of others in Izyum, for the killings of Amelina and others while they ate dinner? In the words of Nataliya Gumenyuk, who shared a stage at the Book Arsenal festival with Amelina just before her death, 'We can't save those who have already died, but at least this plague of impunity may be punished.'

For some of the members of the 5AM coalition, the cross-over between journalistic reporting and the search for justice lies at the heart of the work. The Reckoning Project emerged from conversations in the days after the invasion between award-winning veteran war correspondent Janine di Giovanni, Soviet-Ukraine-born British writer Peter Pomerantsev (who has written widely on disinformation and is author of *This is Not Propaganda*) and Nataliya Gumenyuk. Di Giovanni, founder and executive director of the

Reckoning Project, has said that her experience of giving tes-timony at the Yugoslav and other war crimes tribunals made her realise her carefully labelled notebooks were not enough when questioned about all that she had seen and reported on. As she put it later, her memory was foggy, her notebooks disorganised. Di Giovanni, Gumenyuk, Pomerantsev and colleagues are determined this time will be different.

The evidence gathered by the Reckoning Project is intended to be robust enough to stand up in any court. Gumenyuk, who reported on Putin's earlier wars in Georgia and eastern Ukraine, notes the 'incredible level of detail' it assembles. One example was what happened in the village of Yahidne, eighty miles north-east of Kyiv, where in March 2022 Russian occu-pying forces held hundreds, aged from six weeks to ninety-two years old, in a school basement. 'We came to free you from the Nazis,' the occupiers said. Ten villagers died in the basement in the four weeks before the Russian forces withdrew on 30 March. The Reckoning Project evidence contributed to fifteen prosecutions and convictions.

The trials were held *in absentia*, like many of those now taking place in Ukraine. It was, however, another signal for the future. As another indication of the unusually close collaborations between state structures and civil society organisations in Ukraine today, di Giovanni and chief prose-cutor Andriy Kostin signed a formal collaboration agreement between the Reckoning Project and the prosecutor's office in 2024. As Nataliya Gumenyuk points out, Ukraine – in contrast to many other conflict zones – still enjoys the rule of law. That, she argues, gives reasons for hope. 'Civil society in Ukraine is strong, and there is international will. Russians don't really hide their acts. If not now, what ingredients do you need?'

*

The unpunished crimes of Syria in recent years are an ever-present backdrop to what is happening in Ukraine today. Russia's crimes against alleged 'terrorists' in Aleppo (anybody who was critical of Assad) would be used again, sometimes by the same commanders, in Putin's next war, against the 'fascists' in Ukraine (anybody who believes Ukraine is entitled to its own identity and borders). When General Alexander Zhuravlyov took command of Russian forces in Syria in 2016, he oversaw an eightfold increase in the use of cluster weapons to terrorise the residents of east Aleppo. (These are banned under the 2010 Cluster Munitions Convention – an international treaty which neither Russia nor Syria has signed – because of the disproportionate civilian deaths they cause.) Six years after Aleppo, Zhuravlyov, now commander of Russia's western district, oversaw the assault on north-east Ukraine, where cluster munitions again killed hundreds in Kharkiv and elsewhere. General Sergei Surovikin, known in Russia as 'General Armageddon' for the ferocity of the assault he oversaw in Syria in 2017, later became commander of Russia's forces in Ukraine. When I meet Zelensky adviser Igor Zhovkva in his office in the sprawling and sandbagged presidential complex in central Kyiv, he echoes Oleksandra Matviichuk and others on the consequences of earlier failures: 'If you kill civilians, if you kill women and children, if you carry out carpet bombing, and nothing happens, this is the result. It's some of the same people, like Surovikin. They bombed in Syria, then they did the same in Ukraine.'

The siege and starvation of east Aleppo in 2016 marked what UN human rights commissioner Zeid Ra'ad al-Hussein of Jordan called 'crimes of historic proportions'. Six years later, those tactics would be repeated with deadly effect as part of the destruction of the once-handsome city of Mariupol on the Sea of Azov in the north-east corner of the Black Sea.

Mariupol was encircled, its infrastructure destroyed and aid withheld. To quote the Rome Statute of the International Criminal Court: 'Extermination includes the intentional infliction of conditions of life, *inter alia* the deprivation of access to food and medicine, calculated to bring about the destruction of part of a population.'

In Mariupol, as in Aleppo, thousands of civilians died as a result of the destruction and the siege. Angelina Kariakina of the Reckoning Project, co-founder with Nataliya Gumenyuk of Ukraine's Public Interest Journalism Lab, directed the film *Grozny-Aleppo-Mariupol*, which joins the threads between three of Putin's wars in the past twenty years, where Russian forces targeted maternity and other hospitals. Hamza al-Kateab worked as a hospital doctor during the siege of Aleppo, in which tens of thousands of civilians lost their lives; his wife Waad al-Kateab made the Oscar-nominated documentary *For Sama*, named after their daughter who was born during the siege. Hamza al-Kateab described to Kariakina — who herself found out she was pregnant while investigating the siege of Mariupol — the Russian and Syrian tactic of targeting hospitals to bring a population to its knees. 'If there are no hospitals in your area, you will flee. They don't really need to shell your home to make you leave it. They will just target the healthcare system, destroy it and then people will leave. That's an easy win for Russia and the regime.' That tactic was used in Aleppo and Mariupol alike.

For one member of the Reckoning Project team, the connections between crimes in Syria and Ukraine are especially personal. The organisation's legal counsel is Ibrahim Olabi, a British lawyer of Syrian heritage. Olabi has been engaged on justice issues since the beginning of the war in Syria: he was still a law student at Manchester University when he first crossed into rebel-held areas in 2012 to meet with human rights activists and to advocate with rebel groups on compliance with the laws of war. He founded the Syrian Legal Development Programme, of which he remains director, working with Syrian NGOs to build understanding of international law. When we meet near his legal chambers in the tranquil setting of the gardens of Inner Temple in London, Olabi talks of the 'odd kinship – a common perpetrator' that he felt between Syria and Ukraine. 'Emotionally, I felt a sense of solidarity I hadn't felt with anything else. We Syrians didn't have freedom – and Russia and the regime didn't want to give it. The Ukrainians had freedom – and Russia was trying to take it away . . . If our Syrian pain and suffering help prove that what Russia is doing is a matter of policy, not just individual cases, that's important.'

For some foreigners working in and on Ukraine, the personal relevance of the work is closer still. Anya Neistat, my Russian-born colleague at Human Rights Watch and then Amnesty International, tried to persuade Western governments to wake up to Putin's abuses in Chechnya at the beginning of the century, as described in Chapter Six. She went on to document war crimes in Georgia, Sri Lanka, Syria and elsewhere. In 2020, she became legal director of the Docket initiative at the Clooney Foundation for Justice, which seeks to trigger prosecutions of mass atrocities using the principle of universal jurisdiction. Her work, and that of her Ukrainian colleagues, includes documentation which can be used to build cases against Russian war crimes suspects anywhere in the world.

In 2022, a documentary film crew captured the moment when Anya and her Ukrainian colleague Solomiia Stasiv, searching by torchlight because of the Russian forces who are still in the vicinity, stumble on what Stasiv describes in startled tones as 'a freaking goldmine'. That includes abandoned documents, with lists of call-signs and more, which can help identify those responsible for the murder of Volodymyr Vakulenko and others. They have submitted details to prosecutors in Germany and elsewhere, and hope for indictments in connection with Vakulenko's execution and other crimes.

In May 2023, Anya and I first talked about the investigations over a bowl of borscht in her Parisian home office; a few months later, she moved to Kyiv to be closer to the work. She echoes Ukrainians in pointing to the consequences of the failure to react to Russian state crimes. 'If they woke up earlier, we wouldn't be dealing with what we see in Ukraine today. It wasn't just Chechnya. Then it was Georgia in 2008. What Russia did was the same playbook – executions, torture, cluster munitions, annexation of territory.' But she, like Gumenyuk and others, believes new possibilities are opening up: 'We are at a pivotal moment for international justice. Everything put in place since World War Two is now put to the test.'

Achieving accountability in Ukraine has become both more difficult and more necessary in the time I have been writing this book. During three visits to Ukraine in the first four months of 2023, I found optimism even as the bombs fell. There were non-stop air alarms. Russian attacks continued in the south and east, and worries were constant. Solomiia Stasiv, whose brother is serving on the front line, described a daily routine of family WhatsApp exchanges made up of simple + signs, a one-character message of reassurance that the sender is still alive. 'I realised how little words mean,' she tells me when we meet in Kyiv. 'The pluses are all I need to feel happy.' Another friend told me: 'Every day I am so afraid

to open my Facebook. Every second post is honouring somebody who is missing or killed.' In addition to all the reasons
for worry, however, I also found pride at what Ukraine had
already achieved.

In February 2022 Western governments assumed the huge
Russian army would need just a few days or a couple of weeks
at most to crush Ukraine's resistance; on that point at least,
they agreed with Putin. Kyiv proved all of them wrong.
President Zelensky rejected offers of evacuation to safety, telling the Americans, 'I need ammunition, not a ride!' (I asked
Igor Zhovkva, Zelensky's adviser, if the famous story was
really true. 'Of course!' he said – and pulled out a notebook
with his boss's quote emblazoned across the front.)

Russian forces never reached the centre of Kyiv, despite
what Putin had hoped for with his planned Hitler-style
victory parade. In less than nine months, Ukrainians drove
Russian forces out of Bucha and the Kyiv region in the north,
out of much of the Kharkiv region in the north-east, and
out of Kherson in the south. In early 2023, there were high
hopes for what the endlessly discussed spring offensive might
bring and for victories yet to come. By the time I returned
in the autumn, however, the mood was more sombre. The
counter-offensive had gone slowly. Weapons and ammunition
were in short supply. There were fears, too, of what a Trump
presidential victory in 2024 might mean.

Even before Donald Trump arrived back in the White
House, some Western politicians began to suggest – to the
angry despair of the Ukrainians – that Ukraine should make
the best of a bad lot and give Putin what he wanted in order
to gain 'peace'. From the perspective of Ukraine and its immediate neighbours, that fails to understand the implications
of Putin's assault for the rest of the world. In the words of
Estonian prime minister Kaja Kallas, 'The lesson from 1938

and 1939 is that if aggression pays off somewhere, it serves as an invitation to use it elsewhere.' Or, as Polish foreign minister Radek Sikorski put it, 'Ukraine has bought us time. Will we put it to good use?'

In August 2024, Ukraine sought to confound the pessimists when it occupied a few hundred square miles of territory and took prisoners of war in Russia's Kursk province, thus putting unexpected pressure on Moscow. But the military challenges remain as great as ever. The key eastern Ukrainian town of Pokrovsk, for example, came under renewed pressure from Russian forces in late 2024 and was widely predicted to fall.

At the same time, the determination to achieve accountability has remained as strong as it was when I was in Kharkiv in October 2023. Regional prosecutor Oleksandr Filchakov shows me a ten-foot-long panel in his office, a more ambitious version of the organisational chart I saw in Kherson six months earlier. At the bottom are the small fry – those who Filchakov's team believe may be implicated in crimes but who bear little command responsibility. In the middle are more senior officers. Finally, at the top of the pyramid is a row of photographs of the men in charge, including the minister of defence Sergei Shoigu, armed forces head Valery Gerasimov and Putin himself. (I don't immediately notice that Filchakov's colleagues have given the president a digital tweak: Putin is dressed in Nazi uniform, complete with swastika armband.)

'We are here,' says Filchakov, pointing at the bottom of the board. 'Or maybe [pointing to the middle of the pyramid] here.' But, he concludes, jabbing at Putin and his comrades: 'We want to be *here*! That's what we are heading for.' The prospect still seems distant. But Filchakov is determined justice must be achieved. 'Our people should feel that, whatever happens, they are under the protection of the state. And the world needs to see what happened.'

For some prosecutions, the pieces are already in place. Spartak Borysenko, head of war crimes investigations in Kharkiv, shows me evidence his team has assembled on crimes committed across the region, reflecting the pyramid of responsibility in Filchakov's office. One person of interest is the military commandant who was in charge in Balakliia, sixty miles south of Kharkiv, during the Russian occupation. Torture and killing were common in the town; many detainees were never seen again. Victims knew the commandant only as 'Granit'. But abandoned and partly charred documents make it possible to identify the man behind the nickname. Borysenko shows me a document naming Lieutenant-Colonel Valery Buslov as military commandant, together with his signature. (Other documents are signed, in the same handwriting, as 'V. Granit'.) Buslov is just one of many suspects whom Filchakov and his colleagues hope one day to put on trial for crimes committed by the officers themselves and by those under their command.

The morning after my arrival in Kharkiv, I join members of Filchakov's and Borysenko's team for one of their daily visits to the region, which includes areas occupied by Russian forces in 2022. Air alarms sounded almost non-stop through the night; I have barely slept. Many have left the city, and those who remain are taking a risk; a few months after my visit, a thirty-five-year-old district prosecutor, her husband and their three young children were all killed in a Russian drone attack. On our way out of the city we drive past Drobytsky Yar, site of a massacre which formed part of the historic Kharkiv war crimes trial in 1943. 'This is the place where the dead teach the living,' says the inscription in Latin, Ukrainian and Hebrew. A Russian missile has torn one of the arms off the massive menorah-shaped monument. (The Drobytsky Yar massacre of fifteen thousand Jews in 1941 is second in scale only to the better known Babyn Yar massacre in Kyiv. Prosecutors erased victims' Jewish identities at the trial in 1943, talking only of 'Soviet civilians' being killed. This was part of a wider pattern of Kremlin denial: publication of Vasily Grossman and Ilya Ehrenburg's 500-page *Black Book*, chronicling the Nazis' mass murder of Jews in the region, was cancelled and printer's plates destroyed in 1948 because it gave a 'distorted picture' and was 'anti-Soviet'.)

Our first stop is the village of Hroza, an hour's drive east of Kharkiv. A few days earlier, forty-nine-year-old Andriy Kozyr, killed on the front line the previous year, was reburied here. After the ceremony, family and friends gathered for a memorial lunch in the village café. Then, shortly after the meal began, a targeted Russian attack destroyed the café and everything around it. The fifty-nine people who were killed included the dead man's widow; his daughter; his son and daughter-in-law; his parents-in-law; his brother- and sister-in-law; and a cousin's eight-year-old son. Standing amid the rubble where the café used to be – somebody's shoe is still lying on the ground – one of the prosecutors shows me photos on his phone from when he arrived here just after the explosion. The images are of unrepeatable horror; many bodies could only be identified through DNA analysis. A villager gazes at his phone address book, numb with disbelief: 'Half of the numbers in my phone are dead now,' he tells me. 'But I won't delete them.' In the cemetery, a series of back-to-back funerals is taking place. The young gravedigger dug nine graves yesterday; he will do the same again today. His former maths teacher, sixty-one-year-old Tamara Solyanyk, will be buried in the grave in which he is now standing. 'They were all peaceful people. She was always so kind.'

As so often, Russia had two explanations for this attack which destroyed a community of a few hundred people in an instant. The victims included 'men of military age'. And, at the same time, any suggestion of Russian responsibility was 'fake news'. Russia's ambassador told the UN Security Council: 'Russia does not carry out strikes against civilian objects and does not target civilians.'

Those held to be most immediately responsible for the attack have already been identified. As we leave Hroza, the prosecutor is finalising a press release announcing arrest warrants for two brothers, former police officers who worked for the occupiers last year and who are now in Russian-held territory. On the basis of text messages sent before and after the attack, the brothers stand accused of helping Russian forces target the café and kill their former neighbours. The village has no military significance. Those who died were all civilians, with one former soldier. Assuming the brothers remain in Russian-occupied territory, they won't face justice soon. But this did not take place in a vacuum: Russian military commanders planned and authorised the slaughter. One of the prosecutors lists some of the questions they want to answer: 'Where did the missile come from? Which military formations are based there? Who was the commander of that division? Who has Iskander missiles? We hope to work all that out.'

Hroza is twenty miles from the front line. Few expected a rocket to land here. But the prosecutors' investigations regularly take them closer to the front line, too. From Hroza we travel east to Kupiansk, which has been partly surrounded by Russian forces since they were driven out of the town a year earlier and which in recent weeks has increasingly come under attack once more. There is regular shelling, and puffs of smoke are visible on the other side of the river. We stop to put on flak jackets before driving into the town. But – the familiar paradox of war – the most vulnerable enjoy no such protection. Civilians have been told to evacuate. Some, especially the elderly, defy orders. An old lady walks slowly up the deserted main street – past the ruined museum, past the partly destroyed hospital where abandoned equipment and dead pot plants stand behind flapping net curtains in empty rooms.

In Kupiansk, too, the theme of justice is never far away. Outside the mayor's building, a 'Wanted' noticeboard includes photographs of Putin and Maria Lvova-Belova, his indicted children's commissioner, alongside pictures of those accused of collaborating with the Russian forces during the occupation of the town last year. 'You can see what Russian "peace" has brought to our population,' says the mayor, Andrii Besed, once we have made our way past the sandbags to his basement office. 'People must go to The Hague for this. There must be just punishment. The museum was hit. The hospital almost doesn't exist any more. It's directed genocide – against museums, the hospital, the house of culture – whatever allows citizens to live.'

Above Besed's desk, a map shows the area from which Russian forces are shelling the town; it is labelled 'Mordor' in pink marker pen. A year after my visit, Kupiansk again looked set to fall to Putin's forces, for the second time in two years. It can seem that defeating contemporary Mordor, and holding accountable those who are responsible for killing civilians in Hroza, Kupiansk and across Ukraine, belongs only to the realm of fantasy fiction. For millions of Ukrainians, however, belief in that possibility remains as essential as belief in life itself.

*

The overlapping initiatives for justice for such a huge number of crimes can make for a confusing mix – the International Criminal Court, the International Court of Justice, Ukrainian domestic courts, universal jurisdiction and a potential tribunal to prosecute the crime of aggression. But they all send the same underlying message. Identifying perpetrators and addressing crimes committed matters for Ukraine – and beyond Ukraine.

When I was in Kyiv in January 2023, Anton Korynevych, the country's ambassador-at-large for war crimes, was understandably proud of the progress he and his colleagues had achieved in pressing against the odds for a tribunal that could punish Putin and other Russian leaders for the crime of aggression. When I saw Korynevych again nine months later, he was more cautious. He told me: 'You can't do this job as a pessimist. We need to find a solution.' He still hoped a deal would be done by the end of the year. And yet, a year after that conversation, the format of a special tribunal is still not agreed. The forty-six-member Council of Europe – from which Russia simultaneously jumped and was pushed in March 2022 – backs the idea in principle. But, almost three years into the war, the proposal is still not finalised.

The reduced international momentum for an accountability mechanism has nothing to do with a less urgent need for justice in Ukraine. On the contrary: Russia's lawless attacks continued more fiercely than ever, even as the country's indicted leader embraced everyone from Indian prime minister Narendra Modi to North Korean leader Kim Jong Un. On the same day in July 2024 that Putin and Modi were hugging in Moscow, dozens of Ukrainian civilians were killed in a series of attacks that included a Russian cruise missile fired into Kyiv's main children's hospital (Moscow, as always, denied it); this was one of the deadliest days there had been.

Especially since 7 October 2023, however, the belief of some governments that one set of rules should apply here (where the government killing civilians and attacking hospitals is our enemy) and a different set of rules should apply over there (where the government killing civilians and attacking hospitals is our friend) has become a bleeding wound in international relations. That obvious asymmetry has challenged and damaged the idea of universal justice as never before.

Chapter Eight

'Remember Amalek'

Israel/Palestine (2023–)

Horror takes many forms. In March 2024, I stand in a field in southern Israel, site of the Supernova music festival five months earlier. I am surrounded by hundreds of smiling and laughing memorial photographs of those who were kidnapped, raped and slaughtered in the hours after sunrise on 7 October 2023. A few miles from the festival site, I walk along the tree-lined paths of the once-idyllic and now deserted Be'eri kibbutz, where portraits of the dead are pinned on the walls of charred and abandoned homes.

One former resident who has returned for a visit shows me some of the places where more than a hundred of her friends and neighbours died. Among them was seventy-four-year-old Vivian Silver, Canadian-Israeli co-founder of Women Wage Peace and former board member of the Israeli human rights organisation B'Tselem. Three days before the attack, Silver helped organise an Israeli–Palestinian women's joint rally for peace. Her portrait hangs on the wall of her destroyed house; a carpet of vibrant yellow nasturtiums grows beside the path leading to where her front door used to be. Silver sent a last WhatsApp message to her son Yonatan from her hiding place: 'I love you. They're inside the house. It's time to stop joking and say goodbye.'

Fighters from Hamas's Qassam Brigades and other armed groups broke through the border fence from Gaza and spent hours hunting down and abducting more than two hundred and killing twelve hundred men, women and children. A key aim of Operation Al-Aqsa Flood was to instil terror. Hamas, which demanded the release of Palestinian detainees, acknowledged 'some faults' may have occurred; stories of civilians being targeted were, however, 'lies and fabrications'. Those denials were themselves the lie. A video showed Hamas gunmen cheering as they paraded the partially clothed and splayed body of twenty-two-year-old Shani Louk, a German-Israeli tattoo artist from Tel Aviv, remembered by her family as 'a peace-loving person who loved music, dancing and life'. There were countless such examples. One in ten of the festival-goers was kidnapped or killed. Hamas claimed it was 'committed to respecting international and human rights law'. In reality, as one survivor of the festival massacre remembered afterwards: 'It's like seeing a horror film with your own eyes.'

The events of that day were shocking. Equally shocking was the response of the Israeli government. In 1955, as described in Chapter Two, the French killed thousands of Algerian civilians after rebels killed a hundred Europeans; those revenge massacres by the French in and around Philippeville (now Skikda) are remembered in Algeria to this day. Seventy years later, the Israeli government seemed to feel similarly entitled to abandon all restraint. Prime minister Benjamin Netanyahu had been happy to let Hamas flourish because, he believed, increased divisions between the Palestinian Authority in the West Bank and Hamas in Gaza would 'prevent the establishment of a Palestinian state'.

Now, Netanyahu responded to Hamas's criminality with apparent criminality of his own. At Nuremberg, Robert Jackson talked of the need to 'stay the hand of vengeance'. Netanyahu took the opposite approach. He quoted one of the more blood-curdling passages from the Hebrew Bible: 'You must remember what Amalek has done to you, says the Bible.' The reference was to Deuteronomy and the Book of Samuel, and recommendations of unlimited revenge on the tribe described as the enemy of Israel: 'Now go and smite Amalek, and utterly destroy all that they have, and spare them not; but slay both man and woman, infant and suckling, ox and sheep, camel and ass.'

That prescription to 'utterly destroy' summarised what came next. The Israeli army spokesperson explained that, when balancing accuracy and the extent of damage, 'right now we're focused on what causes maximum damage'. People were told to leave their homes, then killed in areas that had been declared 'safe'. More than half the buildings in the Gaza Strip were damaged or destroyed. As in Syria and Ukraine, hospitals were a target. Within a few months, two thirds of Gaza's hospitals were no longer functioning. All of this was supposedly to punish Hamas. And yet, defence minister Yoav Gallant made little distinction between civilians and Hamas fighters or leadership when he announced after the 7 October attack: 'There will be no electricity, no food, no fuel, everything is closed. We are fighting against human animals and are acting accordingly.'

Gaza overflowed in the months that followed with

examples of what 'acting accordingly' would mean. On 19 October, twenty-seven-year-old physiotherapist Suha Nasser lost her husband, five-month-old baby Ahmed and thirty-one relatives when their house was bombed. 'I painted a beautiful future for my child in my imagination,' Nasser said later. 'I want to wake up from this nightmare.' On 2 December, twelve-year-old Alma lost her parents, her fourteen-year-old brother, her eleven-year-old sister, her six-year-old brother and her eighteen-month-old brother Tarazan. All were buried beneath the rubble. After Alma was rescued, she lifted the blanket that covered her baby brother. Tarazan's head had been severed. 'I wish for death after seeing my brother like that,' Alma told the BBC. 'What has he done in this war?' Alma's family had fled their home. The area they fled to was then bombed, and they fled again. The second place they fled to was also bombed and they fled once more. At the third attempted place of refuge, they were killed. As UN Secretary-General António Guterres put it, 'The people of Gaza are being told to move like human pinballs – ricocheting between ever-smaller slices of the south, without any of the basics for survival.'

Refaat Alareer, a poet and professor of English known as 'the voice of Gaza', said in an interview, 'I am an academic. The toughest thing I have at home is an Expo marker.' He remained defiant: he would, he said, throw that in the soldiers' faces if they stormed his home, 'even if that is the last thing I would be able to do'. He wrote a poem which concluded: 'If I must die, let it bring hope, let it be a tale.' On 6 December, Alareer was killed, together with his brother, his sister and four nephews and nieces. Four months later, the poet's daughter, son-in-law and three-month-old grandson were also killed, while sheltering in a building belonging to an international relief charity.

Those who tried to rescue others were themselves targeted. On 29 January 2024, six-year-old Hind Rajab pleaded on the phone with emergency workers to rescue her from the bullet-riddled car where she and her family had been trying to escape the Israeli bombardment. An Israeli tank killed Palestinian Red Crescent paramedics who came to save her. Hind's body was eventually found two weeks later, alongside the body of her fifteen-year-old cousin Layan and five other family members. Layan had been killed while calling for help. 'They are shooting at us,' she told the operator, 'the tank is next to me.' After a series of shots, Layan's screams can be heard before the line goes dead. Israel said its forces had not been in the area at the time; subsequent investigations by Forensic Architecture and others showed that was untrue.

Five months into the assault, the UN children's agency, Unicef, reckoned thirteen thousand children had been killed; thousands more have been injured or orphaned. Medical teams in Gaza came up with a new acronym, WCNSF, because the category was so horrifyingly large: Wounded Child, No Surviving Family. In August 2024, after ten months of bombardment, the death toll passed what UN human rights chief Volker Türk called the 'grim milestone' of forty thousand, one in fifty of the Gaza Strip's pre-war population. That number does not include those still buried under the rubble, or those who died because of no access to healthcare. A year into the assault, a UN inquiry found that Israel had carried out 'a concerted effort to destroy Gaza's healthcare system'.

Every building hit – including hospitals, schools and places of worship – was supposedly occupied by Hamas. The Israeli-Palestinian *+972 Magazine* and the Hebrew-language *Local Call* revealed the existence of an artificial intelligence-based program called Lavender which was used to select targets; Lavender's outputs were treated 'as if it were a human decision'. (The Israel Defense Forces said Lavender was 'neutral'.) The Israelis created what one former intelligence officer described to Yuval Abraham, author of a series of investigations for +972 and *Local Call,* as 'an assassination factory'.

At the heart of the Geneva Conventions is the concept of 'proportionality' to reduce to a minimum the incidental loss of civilian life. 'Indiscriminate attacks' are prohibited. 'Constant care' must be taken to spare civilians. As with Putin's tactics in Grozny in 1999 (and the slaughter at May Lai and Philippeville before that, at a time when an international court to punish such crimes still seemed unachievable), those injuctions were now ignored. The word 'proportional' was interpreted in ways reminiscent of the most brutal wars in history. Abraham's sources told him how the Israeli military command had, for example, authorised the killing of hundreds of Palestinian civilians in an attempt to kill a single Hamas commander. That pattern became standard. As one security source summarised it: 'When a three-year-old girl is killed in a home in Gaza, it's because someone in the army decided it wasn't a big deal for her to be killed – that it was a price worth paying.'

Bombing was not the only weapon. António Guterres talked of 'the highest number of people facing catastrophic hunger ever recorded by the [UN] system – anywhere, any time'. The UN blamed the hunger on 'Israel's extensive restrictions on the entry and distribution of humanitarian aid ... as well as the destruction of crucial civilian infrastructure'. Six months into the assault, B'Tselem published *Manufacturing Famine,* which concluded: 'Israel is guilty of a war crime no one believed possible in the twenty-first century: intentional starvation.'

The Geneva Conventions forbid collective punishment: 'No protected person can be punished for an offence he or she has not committed . . . Reprisals against protected persons and their property are prohibited.' But Israeli politicians seemed to believe collective punishment was the most appropriate response to Hamas's own lawlessness. In 1978, a Protestant politician in Northern Ireland had said in response to an IRA atrocity that there were no innocent people in 'Republican ghettoes'; she recommended that the Royal Air Force should bomb Catholic areas. As described in Chapter Five, Jean Coulter's advice was ignored; it is not hard to imagine how prospects for peace in Northern Ireland might have looked if anybody had taken seriously her recommendation that all Catholics should be targeted in punishment for the crimes of the IRA. In Israel, however, a version of Coulter's 'kill-them-all' now became official policy.

President Isaac Herzog said the 'entire nation' of Palestine was responsible for Hamas's crimes. 'This rhetoric about civilians "not aware", "not involved", it's absolutely not true.' Former prime minister Naftali Bennett asked an interviewer: 'Are you seriously asking me about Palestinian civilians? What is wrong with you?' The deputy speaker of the Knesset, Nissim Vaturi, said: 'We are too humane. Burn Gaza now.' (When criticised, he doubled down, explaining 'There are no innocents there.') Crimes by others were seen as an example to follow, too. Today, it is generally accepted that (to quote Hans-Peter Kaul, former deputy president of the International Criminal Court) the firebombing of Dresden would count as 'an especially serious war crime'. And yet, Israel's ambassador to London, Tzipi Hotovely, treated the killing of more than half a million civilians in the 1943–5 Anglo-American bombing campaign as a precedent to be admired in 2023. 'Was it worth it?' she asked. 'The answer is yes.' Israeli soldiers in Gaza posted videos mocking terrified civilians and celebrating everything from the destruction of food supplies to the blowing-up of residential buildings (one such video of death was lovingly dedicated to the soldier's two-year-old 'princess' daughter).

Netanyahu kept repeating, meanwhile, that the Israel Defense Forces are 'the most moral army in the world'. President Herzog echoed that, saying Israel was acting 'unequivocally' in accordance with international law. Herzog's great-uncle was Hersch Lauterpacht; we can guess that the giant of international law might have reached a different conclusion from his great-nephew. As Lauterpacht noted in 1950, in a twenty-fifth anniversary lecture at the Hebrew University of Jerusalem, 'The legal duty to promote human rights includes the legal duty to respect them.'

Israeli leaders now seemed to treat Lauterpacht's simple message with contempt. Instead of respecting human rights, they condemned those who themselves dared to condemn lawlessness. 'The grievances of the Palestinian people cannot justify the appalling attacks by Hamas. And these appalling attacks cannot justify the collective punishment of the Palestinian people,' said António Guterres as the assault got under way. 'Let me be clear: no party to an armed conflict is above international humanitarian law.' The attack, he said, 'did not happen in a vacuum'. The statement was unexceptionable in its condemnation of crimes on both sides, framed by a statement of the historically obvious. But that was not how Netanyahu and his colleagues saw it. Israel accused the UN Secretary-General of 'justifying terrorism' and demanded his resignation.

There were Israeli voices of disquiet throughout this time. Ambassadors, former members of parliament and a former director-general of the Israeli foreign ministry wrote a letter to the attorney-general which used Lemkin's word, that most sensitive term of all in the context of Israel. They warned of the 'absolute silence of the judicial system' in the face of 'extensive and blatant incitement to genocide'. Gideon Levy, columnist in the liberal *Haaretz* newspaper, condemned the refusal to confront the scale of suffering Israel had unleashed: 'A country lies in ruins and all its residents are in hell, and the generator of this hell bears no guilt, not even a tiny bit, not even together with Hamas' guilt.' As in Putin's Russia, wanting people to live in peace became an arrestable offence: two activists from the grassroots movement Standing Together were detained for displaying posters saying 'Jews and Arabs, we will get through this together'. In her office in Tel Aviv, Tania Hary of the human rights group Gisha tells me of the 'skewed logic' which brings 'disproportionate violence for the sake of it being disproportionate'. She worries: 'If we lose respect for international law, we're going back to the times that permitted atrocities.'

Even some of those who have most reason to want revenge argue against the senseless brutality of Netanyahu's policies. After Vivian Silver's murder, her son, Yonatan Zeigen, gave up his full-time job to be a peace activist. 'What we are doing now is not constructive, it's not in our interest,' he tells me a few months after his mother's death. 'Killing countless people in order to bring down Hamas is not acceptable. It's not moral, it's not constructive.'

Such views are compelling. But, as Zeigen acknowledges, he and others with similar views are 'an extremely isolated minority' in Israel. More representative was my fellow passenger one afternoon when I was on the comfortable fast train that zips between Jerusalem and Tel Aviv. When I checked Wi-Fi networks, I noticed the name someone had chosen for their phone: 'Destroygaza'. Who, I wondered, felt the need to proclaim the desire to kill men, women and children? The quiet older Orthodox woman opposite? The young woman in the stylish jacket? The soldier cradling his gun? It could have been any or all of them. Polls showed half of Israelis thought the level of firepower against Gaza was appropriate. More than 40 per cent believed the IDF had used too little force. (That last sentence may need reading more than once.) Fewer than one in thirty worried the scale of the assault was too harsh.

With good reason, pictures of the hostages seized by Hamas are displayed on lamp posts and billboards across Israel with the slogan 'Bring them home now!' But Israeli viewers do not see or hear from grieving mothers or injured Palestinian children in Gaza. 'We don't see the atrocities, the rubble, the destruction and the humanitarian crisis. The world sees something completely different,' said Anat Saragusti, director of press freedom for the Union of Journalists in Israel. 'We need to deal with it.' Haggai Matar, executive director of +972 Magazine (named after Israel's international calling code), tells me when we meet in Tel Aviv: 'You don't see the human cost. It's all stripped down.' Yuval Noah Harari, author of Sapiens and professor of history at the Hebrew University of Jerusalem, wrote about the impact on Israeli society at large of this failure to show the whole picture: 'When they encounter reports about the devastation, carnage and hunger in Gaza, they claim it is fake news, or they find moral and military justification for Israel's behaviour.' That denial is mirrored by attitudes on the other side. More than 90 per cent of Palestinians believe Hamas committed no atrocities on 7 October (those who have watched videos of that day are many times more likely to believe that atrocities took place; but few have done so).

On both sides, some have long believed that they are in any case entitled to commit crimes because of the crimes of the other side. In 2002, I was involved in the launch in the West Bank of a Human Rights Watch report on suicide bombings, after hundreds of Israeli civilians were killed in a series of attacks by Hamas and other armed groups on buses, in cafés, at family celebrations. My most vivid memory of the press conference in Ramallah is of the man who stood up to announce that, under international law, all forms of resistance are permitted in response to an illegal occupation. The *Erased in a Moment* report addressed this popular misconception in some detail and I started replying to that effect – but the speaker had already walked out without waiting for an answer. There has been a similar we-are-always-right blindness on the Israeli side. In reality, as António Guterres pointed out: 'International humanitarian law cannot be applied selectively. It is binding on all parties equally at all times, and the obligation to observe it does not depend on reciprocity.'

Many Israelis, encouraged by Netanyahu's narratives, believe the crimes of Hamas eclipse or justify any and all deaths caused by Israeli forces. In the acid summary of Omer Bartov, an Israeli-American professor of genocide studies who served in the IDF in the 1970s, 'Thousands of children were killed? It's the enemy's fault . . . If Hamas carry out a massacre in a kibbutz, they are Nazis. If we drop two-thousand-pound bombs on refugee shelters and kill hundreds of civilians, it's Hamas's fault for hiding close to those shelters.' As a result of that philosophy, Gaza came to resemble the ruins of Mariupol. In the words of Russian-Israeli artist Haim Sokol, 'In both cases, Goliath is kicking David's ass. The destruction of cities that leads to killing their residents – that is impossible to rationalise.'

It is indeed hard to rationalise. But might-is-right is baked into Israeli policy. Israeli leaders like to talk of 'mowing the grass' – summarised by an Israeli critic as 'periodic slaughter of Palestinians to return them to a state of submission'. There is the 'Dahiya doctrine', too, named after the suburb of south Beirut that Israeli jets bombed into rubble in 2006, which the commander of Israeli forces in Lebanon described as the need to 'wield disproportionate power and cause immense damage and destruction'. This, said General Gadi Eizenkot (who later became head of the armed forces), was a 'plan that has been approved'. Ehud Olmert, prime minister in 2006, was reported as saying he wanted Palestinians to know 'the landlord has gone crazy', a phrase revealing in its explicit reference to the imbalance of power and the implied possibility of expulsion at any time.

In the context of official statements like that – and many similar statements since the assault on Gaza began – a phone named 'Destroygaza' does not feel like an aberration. It reflects a normality, where the suffering of others doesn't count, or where everything can be blamed on Hamas. Professor Yuval Shany, Hersch Lauterpacht Chair in International Law at the Hebrew University of Jerusalem, tells me of what he sees as 'unrealistic expectations that the world will look at things from the perspective of our own victimhood – and not look at what we ourselves have done'.

Former UN human rights commissioner and Jordanian diplomat Zeid Ra'ad al-Hussein, who worked in Bosnia during the 1990s, warns of the dangers of what he calls 'tribalised pain'. Some want to focus on the crimes of 7 October and are unbothered by what happens to civilians in Gaza. Others believe the scale of crimes committed in Gaza means the horror of Hamas's crimes can be set aside. But, said Ra'ad al-Hussein, 'If we are to build trust and peace, we need to be as morally consistent as we can.' It is a simple message, with ethical and practical value. That moral consistency is, however, too often in short supply.

Double standards are not new, as the behaviour of the

former Allied prosecuting powers made clear after 1945. But the Western reaction (and lack of reaction) to so many civilian deaths in Gaza have brought charges of double standards to what Chatham House director Bronwen Maddox calls 'a new heat'.

In 2022, to take just one example, Ursula von der Leyen, president of the European Commission, rightly condemned Russia's attacks on civilian infrastructure in Ukraine. She told the European Parliament: 'The international order is very clear. These are war crimes.' And yet, when Israel destroyed apartment blocks, bombed hospitals and killed thousands – it would soon kill more civilians than Putin had killed in his prolonged and brutal war on Ukraine – von der Leyen said nothing during a visit to Israel about what, in the context of Ukraine a year earlier, she had described as 'acts of pure terror'. *Le Monde* pointed out that the implications of von der Leyen's silence went beyond Palestine: 'She sent a disastrous message to the global south, countries that refuse to condemn Russia's invasion of Ukraine: Jerusalem could exempt itself from the international law to which the West wants to subject Moscow.'

Many had come to believe that the selective approach to justice could and would never be addressed. Seven months into the assault on Gaza, however, came an announcement from The Hague even more dramatic and with even further-reaching implications than the historic indictment of Vladimir Putin a year earlier.

For months there had been swirling rumours that the International Criminal Court was ready to indict senior Israeli officials, even while the court itself remained tight-lipped. In many ways, given what the UN and others had documented, such a move seemed logical. But – as with the

Putin indictment in April 2023 – it also seemed unthinkable. Many of those I talked to in Israel, in the West Bank and internationally were sceptical, and their arguments seemed persuasive. Nothing like this had ever happened and there seemed to be many reasons why it never would. On 20 May 2024, however, everything changed.

On that Monday afternoon, chief prosecutor Karim Khan announced that he had asked a pre-trial panel of judges to issue two sets of arrest warrants. First came three of Hamas's most senior leaders: Yahya Sinwar, head of the organisation inside the Gaza Strip; Mohammed al-Masri (known as Mohammed Deif, 'The Guest'), head of Hamas's military wing, the al-Qassam Brigades; and Ismail Haniyeh, the group's political leader. Khan talked of crimes that inflicted 'unfathomable pain through calculated cruelty and extreme callousness'. All three were charged with crimes against humanity. The requested arrest warrants were important – and mostly uncontroversial. (All three men would be dead or thought to be dead within a few months. Israel assassinated Haniyeh in Tehran in July; the prosecutor cancelled his requested indictment because of 'changed circumstances'. Deif was also reported killed in July. Sinwar was killed in a chance encounter with Israeli forces in Gaza in October.)

The second set of requested indictments was politically explosive as no previous Hague announcement, not even the indictment of Putin, had been. Khan accused Yoav Gallant, the Israeli defence minister who had announced there would be 'no electricity, no food, no fuel'. More dramatically still, he requested an arrest warrant for Benjamin Netanyahu. The prosecutor alleged war crimes and crimes against humanity on seven separate charges, including starvation, directing attacks against a civilian population, persecution, extermination and murder.

As with the Putin indictment, there was, theoretically, nothing surprising about any of this. From a purely legal perspective, the proposed indictments of Israeli leaders could even be described as uncontroversial, given everything the UN and others had documented in the past seven months. Ahead of the announcement, Khan had asked a panel to advise him on whether or not he should go ahead with the request for an indictment. The distinguished group included two of Khan's special advisers, the Israeli-American Theodor Meron – Holocaust survivor, former Israeli government legal adviser and former president of the Yugoslavia war crimes tribunal – and Amal Clooney, co-founder of the Clooney Foundation for Justice. He also brought in Adrian Fulford, former judge of the International Criminal Court; Elizabeth Wilmshurst, former British government legal adviser; Baroness Helena Kennedy, director of the International Bar Association's Human Rights Institute; and Danny Friedman, a senior British Jewish lawyer who has served as a judge in Northern Ireland. In an attempt to pre-empt the criticisms, the group emphasised the unanimity of their recommendations to the prosecutor.

None of that protected Karim Khan and his colleagues from the condemnation that rained down in the days and weeks to come. Netanyahu said the accusations were 'blood libels' and would cast 'an everlasting mark of shame' on the international court. Khan insists the opposite is true: this is about individual responsibility for crimes committed. 'That's one purpose of accountability and the ICC,' the chief prosecutor says when we meet in his offices in The Hague a few days after the dramatic announcement. 'It's not to castigate a country or a people, but to look at individuals and separate them from the people.'

Some of Israel's allies were almost as indignant as

Netanyahu himself. When Karim Khan announced the requested indictments, he was flanked by two of his most senior advisers, both with experience of tribunals worldwide. Brenda Hollis is a former US air force colonel who as prosecutor at the Special Court for Sierra Leone put Charles Taylor behind bars for fifty years. Andrew Cayley is a former director of service prosecutions in the UK, who also drafted the genocide indictment of Ratko Mladić, the Bosnian Serb military commander, at the Yugoslavia tribunal in The Hague. But that did not diminish the criticism that followed. President Biden said the request for indictments was 'outrageous'; British prime minister Rishi Sunak, theoretically supportive of the court, complained that Khan's request was 'deeply unhelpful'.

Biden, like Netanyahu, complained of the supposed equivalence that Khan had made: 'Let me be clear: whatever this prosecutor might imply, there is no equivalence – none – between Israel and Hamas.' On that point at least, there was a convergence of views. Hamas also complained that the prosecutor's statement 'equates the victim with the executioner'.

In reality, Khan never suggested equivalence. The idea was, he told me, 'absolute nonsense'. In our conversation, Khan wondered if the 'acerbic reaction and vitriol' in response to his announcement has a different agenda: 'Is it manufacturing a stick to beat the living daylights out of an institution dedicated to justice? The unarticulated complaint is that there shouldn't be justice here at all because the interests are too strong. "Don't you dare!"'

In his announcement, Khan did not compare the two sets of proposed indictees. Instead, he laid out 'reasonable grounds' for believing that each of the individuals was separately responsible for crimes against humanity. The problem was with those who did not like that approach, and who believed that one set of grave charges deserved to be taken seriously, while another set of grave charges – committed by those with powerful friends, wearing Shakespeare's 'robes and furr'd gowns' – could be dismissed as 'outrageous' or, in that very British formulation, 'deeply unhelpful'.

Khan's historic step served as a reminder that nothing and nobody should be taken for granted. Khan is a British Muslim from the minority Ahmadi group (which has suffered persecution especially in Pakistan), who previously led a UN team investigating Islamic State crimes against Yazidis in Iraq. He was said to have been Israel's favourite candidate to be prosecutor when he was appointed in 2021, somebody who 'shies away from politicisation'. From an Israeli government perspective, that meant somebody who wouldn't rock the boat by investigating allegations against Israel. Palestinians took the same word and gave it the opposite meaning, while drawing the same conclusion as the Israelis. The Palestinians claimed Khan was indeed 'politicised' – by which they meant he was too reluctant to investigate Israeli crimes. Three years later, Khan showed both sides how wrong they had been.

Some politicians reacted to Khan's request for indictments with shocked disbelief, as if it had come out of nowhere. In reality, the announcement had been a long time coming – fifteen years, in all. In December 2008 and January 2009, fourteen hundred Palestinians (including three hundred children) were killed in Operation Cast Lead, launched in response to Hamas rockets fired into Israel; Hamas rockets killed three Israeli civilians during those three weeks. The Palestinian Authority, faced with the familiar challenge that America would block any and all actions at the UN Security Council in New York, decided to try rattling at a legal side door instead. Palestine recognised the jurisdiction of the International Criminal Court and asked the prosecutor to open an investigation – which automatically includes consideration of alleged crimes by both sides.

A decade-long diplomatic dance followed. In 2012, the court said no, because Palestine did not (yet) have sufficient status as a recognised observer state. The UN General Assembly duly upgraded Palestine's observer status from 'entity' to 'non-member state'; Mahmoud Abbas, president of the Palestinian Authority, described the vote as a 'birth certificate' for the state of Palestine. (The United States was one of just nine countries that voted against.) Armed with its new credentials, Palestine became a state party to the International Criminal Court, and re-applied for an investigation. This time, it was a half-yes. In 2015, the court opened a 'preliminary examination'. In December 2019, chief prosecutor Fatou Bensouda announced there was a 'reasonable basis' to believe war crimes had been or were being committed in Gaza and the West Bank, and that, subject to a final decision on jurisdiction, an investigation could proceed; she confirmed that a few months later. An enraged Benjamin Netanyahu declared the court to be one of Israel's main 'strategic threats', along with Iran.

Even now, however, nothing was fully confirmed. The court wanted to check it did indeed have jurisdiction, so judges continued to chew that question over. Finally, in 2021, Bensouda announced the conclusion: yes, the court had jurisdiction, for crimes causing 'deep suffering and despair on all sides'. Bensouda pleaded for 'some measure of reason and balance' in response to the announcement. As she well knew, there was little chance of that.

The Israeli government said the announcement was 'scandalous' and 'an act of moral and legal bankruptcy'. Netanyahu told television viewers: 'The state of Israel is under attack this evening.' Ignoring the court's references to Palestinian crimes, the prime minister complained (as he and his colleagues would again complain three years later) of 'undiluted antisemitism and the height of hypocrisy'. But, despite all the sound and fury, it was still unclear if the announcement would result in anything more than words. Bensouda herself seemed eager to manage expectations, insisting the ICC was 'not a panacea'; priorities, she said, would be decided 'in due time'.

Appropriate responses to Netanyahu's perception of a 'strategic threat' from the ICC could have included, for example, seriously investigating or punishing war crimes. Following the principle of 'complementarity' – in other words, The Hague as a court of last resort – that meant the International Criminal Court would no longer be involved. Netanyahu took the opposite approach. He declared war on the court itself, saying, 'The ICC proved once again that it is a political body and not a judicial institution.' The government acted, meanwhile, to neutralise organisations which might provide credible evidence of Israeli crimes. In October 2021, defence minister and former head of the armed forces Benny Gantz designated the Palestinian human rights group al-Haq ('Truth') and five other civil society organisations as 'terrorists'. Ten months later, Israeli forces smashed their way into the offices of al-Haq and other groups in the middle of the night in an essentially punitive raid. In al-Haq's headquarters in Ramallah, they trashed office space and bathrooms, tore down maps of 1948 Palestine, took trophy photographs and removed an international human rights award honouring the organisation's work before sealing the offices with a welded metal sheet. This was above all performative destruction, a display of power: despite the continuing threats, al-Haq and others got back into their offices and resumed their work.

Even at the time, there was speculation that the 'terrorist' label was above all connected to Israel's desire to discredit those who might provide valuable evidence to the ICC. In 2024, it became clear that Israel's attempts to damage the court's work were more serious than anybody could have imagined at the time. An extraordinary set of investigations published by *+972 Magazine*, *Local Call* and the *Guardian* revealed that Israel had for years routinely spied on Fatou Bensouda and her successor Karim Khan, as well as launching a crude smear campaign against Bensouda. The prosecutor's communications were intercepted, and on one occasion an envelope stuffed with dollars was delivered to her home address in The Hague with an Israeli telephone number inside, as part of an apparent attempt to intimidate or compromise her, or both. In one bizarre episode, the director of Mossad, Yossi Cohen, ambushed Bensouda by suddenly appearing from behind a door during a one-on-one meeting that Congolese President Joseph Kabila had requested in his Manhattan hotel suite. Israel's attempts to interfere with the court's investigation came from the top: *+972 Magazine* quoted one source as saying that Netanyahu was 'obsessed, obsessed, obsessed' with finding out what materials the ICC was receiving. Bensouda alerted ICC officials to continuing pressures from Cohen, a former Netanyahu adviser who was said to be the prime minister's 'unofficial messenger'.

Shortly after Bensouda's announcement of an investigation in 2021, Karim Khan became the new chief prosecutor. For the next two years, little seemed to happen; Palestinian groups grumbled at the prosecutor's perceived reluctance to act. As the Israeli destruction of Gaza got under way after 7

October, however, things moved into a different gear. Three weeks after the assault began, Khan visited the Rafah checkpoint between Gaza and Egypt. Then, in December 2023, he visited Jerusalem and Ramallah, meeting with hostages' families and Palestinian groups in Israel and the West Bank respectively. In addition to condemning the 'repugnant' Hamas attacks, Khan had words for Netanyahu and his colleagues: 'Israel has clear obligations in relation to its war with Hamas: not just moral obligations, but legal obligations that it has to comply with the laws of armed conflict. It's there in the Rome Statute. It's there in the Geneva Conventions. It's there in black and white.' Israel's leaders, the prosecutor said, 'will be under no misapprehension as to their obligations, or that they must be able to account for their actions'.

In February 2024 Khan emphasised, in language that was hard to misread, that he had not seen 'any discernible change' in Israel's conduct. 'Those who do not comply with the law should not complain later,' he said, 'when my office takes action pursuant to its mandate.'

Murmurings grew about what might come next. Israeli media reported that the IDF had appointed dozens of new lawyers in preparation for a possible 'legal onslaught'. And yet, it remained unclear whether even a battalion of lawyers could do much if Israel remained wedded to the 'landlord-gone-crazy' philosophy which had by now caused thirty thousand deaths, including thousands of children, in just a few months – what António Guterres described as an 'unparalleled and unprecedented' level of deaths since his time as Secretary-General. Six leading aid agencies said they had seen 'nothing like the siege in Gaza', noting that 'more children were reported killed in this conflict than in all major global conflicts combined last year'. Michael Sfard, one of Israel's leading human rights lawyers, offers a blunt summary of the challenge when we meet in his office in Tel Aviv: 'The IDF have very talented lawyers, they are very high-quality. But: they have a shitty client.'

As rumours multiplied, Netanyahu – never one to use diplomatic language where vitriolic abuse will do – warned that indictments against Israeli officials would be 'an outrage of historic proportions', a 'scandal' and 'an antisemitic hate crime'. Netanyahu said he expected 'the leaders of the free world . . . to use all the means at their disposal to stop this dangerous move'. It is sometimes suggested that an International Criminal Court investigation has no real meaning unless or until the suspect is behind bars; Netanyahu's undiluted fury in response to the court's actions serves as a reminder that some politicians, at least, do not see things that way.

The Israeli leader might perhaps more usefully have paid attention to the recommendations of his president's great-uncle. As Hersch Lauterpacht had written seventy years earlier (in the context of rulings from the International Court of Justice, but his words apply equally to any international court): '[The court] cannot refuse to give an opinion on the ground that to do so would be inconvenient, inopportune or politically embarrassing.' That is, courts need to go where the facts lead them. Generally speaking, it is not a good idea to threaten independent prosecutors, and Khan made clear he was no exception to that rule. A terse statement from his office noted that all threats against court officials were prohibited under article 70 of the court's own statute and warned: 'The Office insists that all efforts to impede, intimidate or improperly influence its officials cease immediately.'

Most obviously, the 'back off!' message was directed at the Israeli prime minister himself. As significant, however, were those in Washington and elsewhere who were watching (and seeking to intervene in) the legal process. It turned out that a dozen Republican Senators – including Senate minority leader Mitch McConnell and former presidential candidates Marco Rubio and Ted Cruz – had written an extraordinary letter to Khan nine days earlier, warning him that arrest warrants for Israeli leaders would 'expose your hypocrisy and double standards'. In sub-*Godfather* language, the senators threatened: 'Target Israel, and we will target you ... You have been warned.'

When I talked to Michael Sfard in March 2024, as the rumours swirled and the pressures were ramped up, he described this as an existential moment for the court. Sfard indirectly echoed Lauterpacht's earlier warning that a court cannot hold its tongue only because speaking out would be 'politically embarrassing'. In Sfard's words: 'The only way for the International Criminal Court to be strong is to remain true to the moral and legal values that it was set up to follow. If there is credible evidence that grave crimes have been committed and no local jurisdiction is willing and able to provide accountability, they should pursue it.' The prosecutor must, he said, ignore all pressures, 'or it will colour the institution that he serves'.

Ignoring those pressures is easier said than done. While writing this book, I lost count of the well-informed people who assured me that neither Khan nor any other prosecutor could or would ever be so bold as to indict an Israeli leader. Extremist West Bank settlers, maybe – but an elected Israeli politician? It seemed to break every rule that we had got used to over the decades.

There were, however, hints of optimism, too. Shawan Jabarin, director of the respected al-Haq human rights group that Israel chose to target as 'terrorists', was frustrated at what he saw as the court's lack of interest when he and his colleagues first submitted evidence a few years earlier. He tells me, when we meet in the organisation's offices in Ramallah: 'I challenge any institution to say they lack information. We gave them information for arrest warrants. Why did they delay?' Now, though, he is wondering if things have changed. 'Can you imagine what it will mean if the ICC moves forward? That would be big – that's what you are hoping and looking for.' He said he 'kept the hope' and sounded pessimistic and hopeful in the same breath. 'I don't know what despair means. The question is when. Gaza is waking the conscience of the world.' When I spoke to him again two months later, after the requested indictments in May, Jabarin felt 'more is still needed', including on continuing crimes in the West Bank. He was clear, however, that the prosecutor's request was 'a historic move'.

Even after the arrest warrants, there were continued attempts to put history into reverse. When I meet Khan a few days after his announcement, he talks of the ongoing pressures for him to back down. 'There's a lot of "good cop, bad cop" going on,' he says with a weary smile and a shrug. 'Every lever available is being used to pressure or threaten or to give us fig leaves to not act.' He is not inclined to follow that advice. 'I have told leaders: "I'm not clever enough to be a diplomat or a politician, I'm a simple lawyer. I just do my day job, to look at the facts, incriminating and exonerating evidence."'

By requesting the Netanyahu and Gallant indictments, the prosecutor was doing what he was appointed to do: he acted without fear or favour. Some governments had always been wary lest a prosecutor show too much independence – even though judges scrutinise every prosecutor's request, making it impossible for any prosecutor to 'go rogue'). Judging by the reactions to Khan's announcement, those same governments were still worried.

Not everybody jumped to attention, however, in response to Khan's requested warrants in the way that Netanyahu demanded, and that Washington and London at first seemed ready to do. France initially said it supported the independence of the ICC, and noted that it would take into account 'the principle of complementarity'. In other words, if the Israeli courts were to take significant action in connection with crimes committed, the ICC's indictments would no longer be relevant.

Meanwhile, in the wake of – and indirectly responding to – Netanyahu's belligerent response, some countries made clear they were unimpressed by such threats: Ireland, Norway and Spain issued co-ordinated declarations saying they would now recognise Palestine as a state. Israel withdrew its ambassadors from all three countries and announced there would be 'other severe consequences'. By now, though, such threats were less effective than they had once been.

When Keir Starmer arrived in Downing Street two months after Khan's request for arrest warrants, the new prime minister cancelled Rishi Sunak's challenge to the court's authority to even consider indicting Netanyahu and others (the issue that the ICC's judges had already spent so many years reflecting on). Impunity and pressures for impunity were, it seemed, no longer in fashion in quite the same way. Richard Hermer, who became Keir Starmer's new attorney-general, is a distinguished international human rights lawyer who I worked with when he did powerful pro bono work for Freedom from Torture a few years earlier. A trenchant legal analysis, of which he was the lead author, played a key role in defeating Boris Johnson's proposals for war crimes impunity for British troops, described in Chapter Five. Shortly after 7 October, Hermer was one of the signatories of an open letter from a group of senior

Jewish lawyers, including a former president of the UK Supreme Court. The letter emphasised the importance of Israel not committing crimes of its own in response to the atrocities committed by Hamas: 'The notion that there are laws that we must all live by is challenging but essential. Jewish history teaches us that we cannot give up on them.' From now on, it seemed, Benjamin Netanyahu would not necessarily get the easy international ride he was used to.

Complications with the arrest warrants continued. As this book was going to press, one of the three pre-trial judges who was to make the decision resigned on 'health grounds'. Israel implied that her replacement on the panel was herself compromised because of previous work in the prosecutor's office (the new judge gave a detailed response to those suggestions). The chief prosecutor faced allegations of sexual misconduct, which he denied; an external inquiry was created. On 21 November 2024, however, following a maelstrom of speculation – and after a plea from the prosecutor on the 'utmost urgency' of his request – the judges finally confirmed warrants for Netanyahu, Gallant and the one remaining maybe-not-yet-dead Hamas indictee, Mohammed Deif.

It was an extraordinary moment. The unanimous judges' ruling defied the will of the most powerful country in the world, whose leaders still found it hard to accept that Washington would not necessarily always get its way. Joe Biden's White House complained of the 'rush to seek arrest warrants' – thus ignoring the fact that the judges had spent a full seven months deliberating on the prosecutor's request (the Putin indictment, for comparison, took just three weeks to decide on). Trump's national security adviser, Mike Waltz, too, threatened a 'strong response'. A number of European governments, too, were suddenly eager to hedge their bets. From this day on, however, we were not in a world of unchallenged impunity any more.

The International Criminal Court has regularly been in the headlines over the years, on subjects ranging from Sudan and Libya to Ukraine. But the assault on Gaza meant that, four months before the ICC's requested indictments, the court's older and traditionally quieter opposite number, the inter-governmental International Court of Justice, found itself in the limelight as never before. Just after Christmas 2023, South Africa dropped a legal bombshell no less remarkable in its way than the ICC's indictment of Putin nine months earlier. South Africa made a submission to the International Court of Justice asking it to rule on possible Israeli genocide and on another central feature of Lemkin's convention: incitement to genocide.

In 2021, the mere announcement that the International Criminal Court was examining Israel's behaviour led to Netanyahu declaring Israel was 'under attack'. It was, therefore, hardly surprising that Israeli politicians now ramped up the volume. Israel said South Africa's ICJ submission was an 'absurd blood libel'. President Herzog said it was 'atrocious and preposterous'. *Haaretz* pointed out that one way to undermine the filing would be to remove from the government those who incite war crimes: 'This is the only way to persuade the world that the deranged ideas they are spreading do not reflect reality.' Netanyahu and his colleagues did the opposite. They doubled down on those same 'deranged ideas'.

Israel said the first hearing at the International Court of Justice in January 2024 was 'one of the greatest shows of hypocrisy in history', based on 'a series of false and baseless claims'. Like Russia, which called for a 'hopelessly flawed'

Ukraine case to be thrown out in 2022, Netanyahu presumably felt he had no choice but to come out fighting. But it was not just Israel. Israel's friends seemed equally determined to condemn the submission even before judges at the UN's highest court had spoken. President Joe Biden's National Security Council spokesperson declared South Africa's submission to be 'meritless, counterproductive, completely without any basis in fact whatsoever'. In London, Rishi Sunak complained, 'There is a horrific irony in Israel, of all countries, being accused of genocide.' There was indeed an obvious irony – but not necessarily in the way that Sunak and other politicians were trying to suggest.

Sunak, with his determination to remove difficult questions from the table, was following the example of Boris Johnson three years earlier. In 2021, when the International Criminal Court first confirmed an examination of alleged crimes in Gaza and the West Bank, Britain's then prime minister took it upon himself to explain why the judges had got it wrong. Part of his argument was that they had misunderstood the Rome Statute of the ICC (which Johnson himself may or may not have read). Johnson was also worried, however, that the ICC was seeking to investigate 'a friend and ally of the UK's'. Those reasons for disquiet were now extended to another international court.

For Johnson – and for others today, though they do not always put it in quite such unvarnished terms – the question was not whether Israel had committed war crimes, nor whether Israel was prepared to investigate and prosecute war crimes (in which case the ICC would not get involved) but only this: was the government concerned a friend and ally? If the answer was yes, Johnson believed that investigation by an independent court was inappropriate or unfair. With his criticism of the 'horrific irony' of the genocide case at the International Court of Justice, Sunak appeared to subscribe to the same logic. In effect: 'How dare anybody scrutinise the behaviour of our friends?' That remarkable approach – pushing down hard on one side of Lady Justice's scales – summarises one of the key challenges in seeking justice today.

The scornful words from Jerusalem, Washington, London and elsewhere ahead of the International Court of Justice hearing made it all the trickier for Israel, and especially for its loyal friends, to cope with the ruling of the independent judges when it came. Friday 26 January 2024 was one of the most remarkable days in the eighty-year history of the world court. Ahead of the ruling, two groups of demonstrators gathered outside the red-brick neo-Renaissance Peace Palace that Ambassador White persuaded Andrew Carnegie to fund a century earlier. On one side of Carnegieplein, a group with Israeli flags showed videos of the 7 October attacks on a large screen. A hundred yards along the road, a second group waved Palestinian flags and held banners with hashtags like #GazaGenocide. Inside the building, a line of white-bibbed judges filed into the Great Hall of Justice, with its vast chandeliers and cathedral-like 'Evolution of the Peace Ideal' stained-glass windows. The judges' near-unanimous 'provisional measures' took forty minutes for Joan Donoghue – president of the court for the past thirteen years and a US government legal adviser before that – to read out.

The rulings made nonsense of Washington's claims that the submission was 'meritless' and 'without any basis in fact whatsoever'. Instead, the court ruled there was a 'real and imminent risk that irreparable prejudice will be caused to the rights claimed before the court gives its final decision' – in

other words, the plausible right to be 'protected from genocide'. The judges ordered (following the terms of Lemkin's
convention of which Israel was one of the earliest signatories)
that Israel must prevent genocidal acts, prevent and punish
incitement to genocide, and report back on its actions within
a month.

Netanyahu's security minister, Itan Ben-Gvir (previously
convicted in Israel for inciting racism and supporting a terrorist organisation), quickly responded: 'Hague schmague.'
Other responses were not much more polite. Five years
earlier, Netanyahu had boasted of his friendship with Putin;
election posters showed the two men exchanging firm handshakes and gazing into one another's eyes. Now, they shared
something else in common: the UN's top court had sharply
criticised the actions of both.

This was, by any measure, a historic moment. Many
Palestinians had given up believing they would ever hear
such plain truths spoken by those with power and authority
in the world. A few weeks after the Hague ruling, I meet
the soft-spoken Orwell Prize-winning author, lawyer and
activist Raja Shehadeh for mint tea in a café near his home
in Ramallah. Here in the West Bank, Gaza is on everybody's
minds: a blackboard in the corner declares 'Gaza Under
Attack'; an exhibition of paintings and videos downstairs
is devoted to Gaza. Shehadeh describes watching the live
transmission of the world court ruling in January. 'I held
my breath. I thought I will be disappointed. When I wasn't
disappointed, I almost had a heart attack. I never imagined
anybody would be able to stand up to Israel.'

Others had similar reactions. Shawan Jabarin of al-Haq
(which Raja Shehadeh founded) tells me of a Palestinian who
lost relatives in Gaza. The man told Jabarin the court helped
him deal with his grief, saying, 'I know they cannot get my

loved ones back. But this is the first time I felt this can repair something.'

The South African government which brought the case at the International Court of Justice is by no means a champion of justice in all contexts. Nine years earlier, after all, South Africa had helped Sudanese president Omar al-Bashir escape arrest on charges of genocide, as described in Chapter Four. Now, a week before the first hearing at the UN court in January 2024, South Africa rolled out the red carpet for the Sudanese warlord known as Hemedti, whose forces stand accused of crimes against humanity; South Africa seemed eager to treat him as de facto president. Pretoria has been reluctant to criticise Putin's crimes in Ukraine, too. But if South Africa was no moral angel, the double standards its case highlighted were also undeniable. The submission served as a reminder that UN Security Council resolutions are no longer the only fruit when it comes to pressures for change.

The International Court of Justice began to monitor Israel's compliance (and lack of compliance) with the court's rulings. In March 2024, the court determined that Palestinians in Gaza 'are no longer facing only a risk of famine . . . but that famine is already setting in'. The ICJ demanded Israel 'take all necessary and effective measures' to ensure the 'unhindered provision at scale by all concerned of urgently needed basic services and humanitarian assistance'. Two months later, the court said the situation had deteriorated further and was now 'disastrous', meaning that previous measures were insufficient. By a 13–2 majority, the judges called on Israel, 'in conformity with its obligations under the convention on the prevention and punishment of the crime of genocide', to halt its assault on Rafah.

When the court placed similar obligations on Myanmar

four years earlier (telling the Burmese government it must 'take all measures within its power' to prevent genocide), European members of the UN Security Council reminded Myanmar of the need to comply with those compulsory rulings. When the court issued its rulings on Israel, those same governments were notably silent.

Netanyahu, meanwhile, showed little interest in compliance with judges' rulings. Instead, he and his government put their energies into blocking the possibility that Israel's crimes might be addressed. In September 2024, Israel requested its missions in the United States to identify politicians who would put pressure on South Africa to withdraw its case, saying South Africa must understand that a refusal to back down would 'come with a heavy price'.

The disconnect in terms of international pressures on Israel was especially conspicuous in a country which prides itself on being a global voice for human rights but whose support for justice was now revealed as uncomfortably context-specific. For thirty years, Germany has been one of the strongest champions of an international criminal court. A German court made history by jailing a Syrian torturer for life in 2022. Germany has been outspoken in its condemnation of Russian crimes in Ukraine. At the same time, Germany makes choices as to which crimes it is willing or unwilling to criticise. Chancellor Olaf Scholz, echoing his predecessor Angela Merkel's description of Israel as Germany's *'raison d'état'*, told the Bundestag as the assault on Gaza got under way: 'There is only one place for Germany: on Israel's side.' The good intentions of that approach are obvious. But a new set of contradictions now arose: those who criticised Israel's actions in Gaza were silenced or even arrested. Iris Hefets, a German-Israeli woman, for example, was detained for holding a one-person protest in Berlin. The slogan on her placard which caused offence (and which also declared her Israeli identity), said 'Stop the genocide in Gaza'.

Even high-profile public figures felt the consequences of speaking out. In December 2023, the award-winning Russian-born Jewish journalist Masha Gessen was due to receive Germany's Hannah Arendt Prize – named after the taboo-breaking author of *Eichmann in Jerusalem* and *The Origins of Totalitarianism* – for their writing about Putin's war in Ukraine. But Gessen then did the unthinkable: they published a *New Yorker* essay on the assault on Gaza, including the line 'The ghetto is being liquidated.' A torrent of abuse in Germany followed, and the award ceremony for Gessen, some of whose own relatives had been killed in the Holocaust, was cancelled (it was eventually rescheduled in a less public context).

Such contradictions became the next focus at The Hague. South Africa's case alleging genocide by Israel broke one significant taboo. Three months later, Nicaragua broke another by bringing a different Israel-related case at the International Court of Justice, this time against Germany as the unquestioning friend of Israel. Nicaragua argued Berlin was 'facilitating' genocide through its arms exports to Israel in 2023. Nicaragua is one of the least appropriate countries to bring a human-rights related case anywhere in the world. Just one day earlier, a UN report concluded that Nicaragua's own human rights violations were 'tantamount to crimes against humanity'. Nicaragua was one of four countries (along with North Korea, Syria and Belarus) to vote in solidarity with Russia on Ukraine in a UN vote in 2022. But even a hypocrite can sometimes speak the truth. As *Der Spiegel* pointed out, 'Germany's international reputation, after all, is partially based on the fact that it has drawn credible lessons from its criminal past . . . But since 7 October, accusations have been swirling that Berlin is applying a double standard.' In April 2024, the ICJ refused Nicaragua's request for 'provisional measures'. But it did not let Germany (or, by extension, Israel) off the hook, warning that it was 'particularly important' to remind states of their international obligations with regards to the transfer of arms to areas where they might be used to breach the genocide convention or the laws of war.

Most obviously, the selective attitude of Germany, America and other Western governments – in effect 'these crimes we care about – those other crimes, not so much' – has had deadly implications for Palestinians, who continued to be bombed and starved. It has been dangerous for Israelis, too, in ways that Netanyahu and his colleagues have been reluctant to acknowledge. John Sawers, who was British ambassador to the UN when I was working for Human Rights Watch in New York and who later became head of the MI6 foreign intelligence service, noted that 60 per cent of Hamas fighters are said to be orphans from previous wars. He added the obvious rider in connection with Israel's assault on Gaza: 'There are going to be a lot more orphans.' Israeli political scientist Yagil Levy made a similar point: 'The Gazans who will emerge from the ruins of their homes and the loss of their families will seek revenge that no security arrangements will be able to withstand.'

But it is not just those in the immediate region who are likely to suffer. A selective approach to justice creates other victims, too – victims of unintended consequences. In 2022, Ukraine enjoyed wide support in calling for accountability for Russia's full-scale invasion and subsequent war crimes. Only a handful of governments stood in solidarity with the Kremlin. After 7 October, that changed. Western governments which

had condemned Putin's crimes in Ukraine bent over back-
wards to avoid criticising Israel. South Africa and other
countries in the global south, meanwhile, condemned Israel's
crimes and – in apparently gleeful payback for the Western
reluctance to criticise Israel – increasingly gave a free pass to
lawless Moscow.

Only a small number of countries – including Ireland,
Spain and Chile, each with a history of their own suffering –
called out war crimes regardless of who committed them.
In the words of Irish prime minister Leo Varadkar: '[The
Israelis] do have the right to defend themselves. But they
don't have the right to breach international humanitarian
law.' Others, meanwhile, chose their camp by manifesting
Zeid Ra'ad al-Hussein's 'tribalised pain'.

Muslims and Jews alike suffered the brunt of this approach,
including thousands of miles from the conflict zone, as a result
of those who felt outrage at one set of crimes but were indif-
ferent to others, and who poured blame and hatred on those
who bore no responsibility for crimes committed elsewhere.
In Britain and across Europe, antisemitic and Islamophobic
attacks alike jumped sharply in the year after 7 October.

The damage to Ukraine's case did not begin on 7 October.
Seven months before the Gaza attacks, I spoke to Dapo
Akande, British–Nigerian professor of international law and
adviser to the government of Ukraine (who Britain would
later nominate to be a judge at the International Court of
Justice). Akande warned of the dangers of seeing things too
much from a northern perspective: 'There needs to be a
broader coalition [on Ukraine] beyond the Western states,'
he told me then. 'It's not just about Western states, but a
bigger consensus. A trick has been missed.' That failure would
become especially striking in the next two years.

Ukraine had long seen itself as a victim of Moscow's colonial attitudes, even if too few in the global south saw it that way. As the north–south divide deepened in 2024, President Zelensky indirectly acknowledged the dangers for Ukraine as he argued for increased global solidarity: 'We reject the colonialist view of the world that divides the nations between so-called "great powers" and geopolitical poles,' he told a conference in South Korea. 'Justice must become the new global rule supported by global unity with sufficient force. Is it possible without the global south? Definitely not.' Even the master communicator Zelensky has a tough challenge, however, in seeking to persuade governments in Africa and Asia to ignore the starkly contrasting approaches to two different conflicts.

As Indian opposition MP Saket Gokhale put it, when responding to criticism of the embrace between Putin and Narendra Modi in July 2024: 'Every sincere person would condemn this brutality and unprovoked attack by Russia on a sovereign nation.' On behalf of 'those of us in non-aligned countries', however, Gokhale added: 'Ethics demand that what's bad for the goose must also be bad for the gander. Bear-hugging Mr Netanyahu while condemning Mr Putin reeks of hypocrisy.' (The Indian leader, meanwhile, seemed eager to prove himself an equal-opportunity hugger: six weeks after embracing Putin, Modi travelled to Kyiv and embraced Zelensky, too.)

The widespread perception of Western hypocrisy, including Joe Biden's description of the Netanyahu indictment request as 'outrageous' – in effect, 'how dare you criticise my friends?' – paved the way for an act of defiance against The Hague which sent a damaging signal on Ukraine and on justice more broadly.

Mongolia has been a member of the International Criminal

Court from the start. In 2023, the court appointed its first Mongolian judge. A few weeks after the Netanyahu indictment, Mongolia added its signature to a letter which proclaimed the determination to 'stand united against impunity'. And yet, in September 2024 Mongolia (which is heavily dependent on Russia for its energy supplies) rolled out the red carpet for a Putin visit, thus ignoring the arrest warrant which it was theoretically obliged to execute.

It was an obvious boost for Putin, cocking a snook at those who wanted him to be held accountable for the crimes in Ukraine. It showed, too, how things had changed. Only a year earlier, Putin had been obliged to stay at home for the BRICS summit in South Africa because of the pressures that the ICC arrest warrant had created. Now, however, after eleven months of the assault on Gaza, the Kremlin was able to happily proclaim that it had 'no worries' about a presidential visit to Mongolia. The following month, Putin basked in the spotlight as host of the 2024 summit of the now-enlarged BRICS club; thirty governments joined the meeting in Kazan. Not least because of Gaza and the problematic Western responses to Gaza, the Russian leader now received an easier ride on his own crimes. South Africa and others condemned Israel and praised Moscow as 'a friend'. To Ukraine's anger and dismay, even UN Secretary-General António Guterres travelled to the summit and met with Putin for the first time in two years.

The continuing Israeli crimes have not just been in Gaza. Attacks in the occupied West Bank spiralled and went unpunished after 7 October. Five hundred Palestinians were killed in just a few months, as well-armed Israeli settlers acted in concert and in greater numbers than ever before. As *+972 Magazine* put it, six months after the assault on Gaza began: 'Pogroms surge across the West Bank.' Illegal settlements, roadblocks and barriers have multiplied faster than ever. Major-General Yehuda Fox, head of Israel's Central Command, acknowledged (in a classified document obtained by the *New York Times*) that any effort to clamp down on illegal settlement construction has dwindled 'to the point where it has disappeared'.

As I drive with Shawan Jabarin of al-Haq through the West Bank, he shakes his head in disbelief at the new structures and barriers that keep appearing. 'I'm updating myself,' he says. 'Their bulldozers never stop. Every day they create new facts on the ground.' In July 2024, Peace Now, an Israeli group which tracks development in the settlements, revealed that Israel had just approved the largest seizure of land in the West Bank for more than thirty years.

There has been a sharp increase in violence against detainees in Israeli prisons, too; prisoners who refused to kiss the Israeli flag were beaten (just as Oleksiy and other Ukrainian prisoners were beaten if they refused to sing the Russian anthem), and blindfolding was widespread. A string of UN and other reports documented torture at the Sde Teiman detention centre in the Negev desert and elsewhere. The UN high commissioner for human rights, Volker Türk, talked of the 'staggering number' of people, including doctors, journalists and human rights defenders, who had been detained since 7 October, mostly without charge or trial. A report by the Israeli group B'Tselem described the Israeli prison system as a 'network of torture camps'.

Some governments had long made clear that they wanted Israel to avoid scrutiny. In July 2024, the judges of the UN's highest court officially found those arguments to be without merit. Britain, the United States and others had argued that the International Court of Justice should refuse a request from the UN General Assembly for an advisory opinion on Israeli policies in the occupied territories. The UK claimed that the requested opinion would undermine an 'established process' and an 'agreed negotiation framework'. When we meet in Tel Aviv, Israeli lawyer Michael Sfard is unimpressed with such arguments: 'What "process"? What "negotiation"? Your government has no shame, absolutely no shame. Even when you're hypocritical, you shouldn't be *so* shameless.'

A few months later, Hersch Lauterpacht's successors in The Hague made clear that they, too, were unimpressed by the attempts to get Israel off the hook. In a searing opinion, the ICJ judges concluded: 'The sustained abuse by Israel of its position as an occupying power ... violates fundamental principles of international law and renders Israel's presence in the Occupied Palestinian Territory unlawful.' The court said Israel should move settlers out of the West Bank and East Jerusalem, and pay reparations to Palestinians.

There was little chance that Netanyahu's government would comply with the world court's advisory opinion, let alone that it would agree that the treatment of Palestinians was 'tantamount to the crime of apartheid', in the summary of the court's president. Instead, Netanyahu complained of an 'absurd' opinion; his national security minister Itan Ben-Gvir (of course) called it antisemitic. President Herzog, too, condemned the 'ill-judged' opinion, seemingly untroubled by his great-uncle's warning that the International Court of Justice should not duck difficult issues simply because they were 'politically embarrassing'.

Despite and because of Israeli leaders' noisy rejection of the ICJ's findings, the opinion of the world court helped confirm Israel's isolated lawlessness. It had implications for the actions of other countries, too. The Hague judges called on all states to help 'ensure an end to Israel's illegal presence' in the occupied territories and to press for 'the full realization of the right of the Palestinian people to self-determination'. The ICJ findings also had implications for its sister court in The Hague. As former Human Rights Watch executive director Ken Roth pointed out: 'The court's ruling is more than a legal setback for Israel. It is a virtual invitation for ... the International Criminal Court to prosecute the officials behind the settlements.' Alon Pinkas, a former adviser to prime minister Shimon Peres, wrote that Israel was 'walking straight into pariah status, with eyes wide shut'.

Even ahead of the world court's ruling, Israel had become more isolated. Britain, Canada, the European Union, Japan, the United States and others all issued sanctions against far-right settlers in the first half of 2024. In April, the US was reported to be ready to impose additional sanctions in connection with beatings and killings in the West Bank by the ultra-Orthodox Netzah Yahuda battalion. Netanyahu called that idea 'the height of absurdity and a moral low', and the far-right Ben-Gvir said it 'crossed a red line'. Biden duly blinked: an announcement on sanctions was 'delayed'; three months later, CNN reported that commanders of the unit had been promoted, not punished. When Washington imposed sanctions on another group of violent government-funded settlers a few months later, Netanyahu warned that he viewed the decision 'with utmost severity'.

But red lines and warnings now began to go both ways. A Dutch court ordered a stop to exporting fighter jet parts to Israel because of the danger that it was in breach of international humanitarian law or the laws of war. (The Dutch government appealed the ruling to the country's Supreme Court.) Spain said it would ban ships carrying weapons to Israel from docking at Spanish ports. Britain's new government suspended some arms export licences to Israel, based on the 'clear risk' that the military aircraft components and other items might be used in 'serious violation' of international humanitarian law. President Emmanuel Macron, with a dig at his allies in Washington, called on countries to 'stop supplying weapons' that would be used in Gaza.

Even in the United States, domestic pressures for a tougher line increased, including after the discovery in April 2024 of hundreds of bodies, some with their hands tied behind their backs, in mass graves at the Nasser and al-Shifa hospitals, which had been besieged by the Israelis. Some bodies had gunshot wounds to he head and marks of torture, others had catheters still attached. The Israeli government said the raid on al-Shifa was 'precise and surgical', and 'set the gold standard of urban warfare', with 'not a single civilian casualty'. An IDF officer, looking at the ruins of the hospital, told a reporter from the *Washington Post*, 'This is what they made us do.'

National Security Adviser Jake Sullivan said, 'We want answers.' By comparison with words like 'barbaric', which was how Joe Biden had described the Russian bombing of Ukraine, 'we want answers' was not exactly hard-hitting; it was, however, perhaps the beginning of change.

Many US politicians have long seemed determined not to acknowledge the nature of Israel's actions. In an extraordinary 'see no evil, hear no evil' move in June 2024, the US House of Representatives even voted to ban the State Department from quoting the Gazan health ministry's casualty statistics, generally agreed by the UN and other independent observers to be the most accurate figures available.

The White House closed its eyes to apparent crimes under international law, even in the face of evidence from its own experts. Secretary of State Antony Blinken rejected the conclusions of a seventeen-page memo from the US Agency for International Development. The memo documented

Israel's 'arbitrary denial, restriction, and impediments' of US humanitarian assistance into Gaza, and called for weapons deliveries to be frozen, following requirements under US law. USAID's sister agency, the Bureau of Population, Refugees and Migration, made similar recommendations. In May 2024, however, Blinken said the government did not 'currently assess' that there were restrictions on humanitarian aid; among the new commitments to supply weapons was a $20 billion multi-year deal, agreed in August.

As with Russia's continued crimes in Ukraine, Israel behaved as though a requested arrest warrant for the prime minister could and should be ignored. In the months after Khan's request, the scale and seriousness of IDF crimes seemed to multiply. Doctors working in Gaza described a pattern of children being targeted with gunshots to the head. It seemed unbelievable – and Israel denied it, just as Russia had denied the crimes of Bucha and Mariupol – but the evidence was overwhelming. As Feroze Sidhwa, a trauma surgeon normally based in California, summed it up: 'Nearly every day I was there, I saw a new young child who had been shot in the head or the chest, virtually all of whom went on to die.' Israel used Palestinians as human shields in their fight with Hamas, too – the illegal tactic it rightly condemned Hamas for, but which it now adopted as its own. (Again, Israel denied doing so, but the evidence published by Haaretz and others was clear.) Civilians, as always, were the ones who suffered most. In October 2024, an Israeli airstrike set dozens of tents ablaze in a hospital courtyard, injuring and killing displaced Palestinians who were sheltering there. Video of the nineteen-year-old Shaaban al-Dalou being burned alive shocked millions around the world. His aunt remembered how Shaaban, a software engineering student who dreamed of finding a better life outside Gaza, would tell her: 'Be optimistic, all will be well. God willing, God will help us, auntie.' Shaaban's ten-year-old brother died in the same attack.

In Israel, the deaths went mostly unnoticed because of what Noa Landau, deputy editor of *Haaretz*, called the country's 'voluntary, invisible firewall'. Human feelings were punished: a twelve-year-old Arab-Israeli girl was suspended from school after she expressed sympathy with children dying of hunger in Gaza. She was told: 'Your village should be burned down.' Elsewhere, however, it was no longer possible to look away. Linda Thomas-Greenfield, US ambassador to the United Nations, said the world 'watched in horror' as Shaaban burned in agony. She told the Security Council: 'There are no words, simply no words, to describe what we saw.' The ambassador said that a proposed surrender-or-starve policy in Gaza ('the generals' plan') would be 'horrific and unacceptable' and would have implications 'under international law and US law'. Antony Blinken and US defense secretary Lloyd Austin, too, finally began to warn that Israel would face restrictions in US military aid unless the humanitarian situation improved.

Still, though: the man named by the prosecutor in The Hague as bearing the greatest responsibility for the crimes committed in Gaza had already received the red-carpet treatment in Washington. Less than three months before Blinken's announcement (itself 'a thimble for an inferno', as one Israeli commentator described it), Benjamin Netanyahu addressed a joint session of both houses of Congress – the same honour that was previously extended to Winston Churchill, Volodymyr Zelensky and the pope.

Netanyahu used his speech not to look dignified but to attack the International Criminal Court. He accused the prosecutor of 'fabrications' and told his audience not to be fooled when 'blood libels' come from those who 'wear fancy silk robes and speak about law and justice'.

Not everybody was impressed by the honour that was paid to the Israeli prime minister and prospective Hague indictee. Vice-President Kamala Harris, president of the Senate and presumptive presidential candidate after Joe Biden dropped out of the race a few days earlier, found she had an unmissable appointment in Indiana that day; Palestinian-American Representative Rashida Tlaib held up a placard saying 'war criminal'; thousands gathered to protest outside. Most of those who were inside the chamber, however – especially but not only Republicans – greeted Netanyahu with a series of ovations.

The politicians on Capitol Hill were not alone in applauding a war crimes suspect at this time. In North Korea, Kim Jong Un gave an equally enthusiastic welcome to Vladimir Putin; the indicted Russian leader gave Kim a luxury car in which the two men drove around Pyongyang. Like Netanyahu in Washington a few weeks later, Putin thanked his hosts for supporting his war.

Politicians and policymakers often treat those who raise human rights issues as 'naïve' in failing to understand how the world really works. They regard themselves as the 'pragmatists', who know how to get things done. I remember a senior British diplomat explaining to me in 1994 that I should understand that Slobodan Milošević, though not a nice man, was 'very useful' in peace talks, and that too much pressure on the Serbian leader would therefore be unhelpful. A senior German official made similar arguments when we met in Tashkent in 2008: he told me that a notorious massacre in which hundreds of unarmed protesters had been killed should be seen 'in perspective' and that too much criticism

of Uzbek President Islam Karimov (whose regime was notorious for torture and who had given Germany the use of an
airbase for neighbouring Afghanistan) would not be helpful.
As described in Chapter Six, Tony Blair explained to Anna
Politkovskaya, later murdered for telling too many truths
to power, that it was 'his job' to like Putin; the implication
was that Politkovskaya was, by contrast, a political innocent.
Too often, those self-proclaimed 'pragmatists' have in reality
proved merely to be shortsighted – displaying what I described, in a piece written after my visit to Uzbekistan, as an
odd blend of cynicism and naivety.

Daring to criticise politicians who have committed
war crimes, from Chechnya to Gaza, can obviously prove
tricky for building cosy relationships. *Not* speaking out can,
however, have equally serious consequences, as the 'glad-
to-be-deceived' silence on Putin and others made clear.
Arguably, that same logic applies to Netanyahu today. Those
who unquestioningly back the Israeli leader argue that they
are supporting the people and security of Israel by doing so.
Eran Yashiv, economist and former chair of public policy at
Tel Aviv University, sees things differently. He argues that
the widespread reluctance to acknowledge the similarities
between Putin and Netanyahu – 'more and more deaths of
soldiers and civilians, the destruction of the economy, and
the emigration of the strong segments of society, leaving the
younger generation without hope' – is problematic for Israel
itself. Israel's future, Yashiv says, 'rests on the West treating
Netanyahu like Putin'.

That is no longer unthinkable. Despite the continued willingness of some in Washington to roll out the red carpet for
an ally who stands accused in an international court of committing crimes against humanity, a broader shift had begun
by mid-2024. More than half of American voters disapproved

of Israeli action in Gaza. The number of Americans under thirty who believed the nature of the Israeli assault was unacceptable was twice as many as those who thought it was acceptable. Thousands were arrested in protests on college campuses across America.

Wholehearted support for the Israeli government in all circumstances was once a safe bet for Democrat and Republican politicians alike. No longer. As a result of Netanyahu's perceived criminality, much else had changed. Four months into the Gaza assault and with nine months to go before the US elections, a senior Democrat in Michigan – a swing state with two hundred thousand Arab-American voters – expressed concerns that the leadership in Washington was 'in total denial' about the dangers of remaining silent. In February 2024, Andy Levin told Andrew Marantz of the *New Yorker*: 'They go, "What are these people gonna do? Stay home?"' Marantz described Levin's response to that complacent analysis, as he 'widened his eyes and smacked a palm against his forehead: Yeah, no shit they will.'

At the Democratic National Convention in Chicago in August, protesters chanted 'Genocide Joe' against the outgoing president, who had just bowed out in favour of Kamala Harris. Harris was under pressure to break with Biden's steadfastly pro–Israel stance, but was reluctant to do so. As Yousef Munayyer of the Washington-based Arab Center think tank put it, 'In the US, politicians kissed babies, petted dogs, loved baseball and unequivocally supported Israel. That last part isn't quite what it used to be.'

Many in the Democratic leadership were, however, reluctant to acknowledge how much had changed. A few days before polling day, *Haaretz* warned that Harris and her surrogates had 'done nothing but stick a finger in the eye of her disillusioned base' by being so reluctant to condemn

Israeli crimes. Sure enough: in the Arab-American majority city of Dearborn, Michigan, the Democratic vote crumbled by almost two thirds between Biden's victory in 2020 and Harris's humiliation in the same city four years later; the state of Michigan fell to Trump. There were many reasons for Harris's failure to beat Donald Trump in November 2024. But the refusal to condemn crimes committed by a key ally was one element contributing to this historic defeat – a defeat which has such significant implications for Ukraine, the Gaza war and more. The obvious irony that Trump was likely to prove worse for the Palestinians than President Harris would have been lost on nobody.

The final judgment of the International Court of Justice in South Africa's genocide case, following on from the provisional measures announced in 2024, is likely to come long after the publication of this book. At the risk of easily being proved wrong (the reader will be wiser than the author), there are plenty of reasons why the court may rule that Israel has not in fact committed genocide. ('Incitement to genocide' is different, and also serious. Language advocating the destruction of Gaza remains common and unpunished in Israeli political discourse.) The bar of 'special intent' for committing genocide is high, no matter how cruel and disproportionate (and therefore criminal) Israel's response has been.

Some analysts, including UN special rapporteur Francesca Albanese, Human Rights Watch co-founder Aryeh Neier and Professor Amos Goldberg of the Hebrew University of Jerusalem, have argued that Israel's actions do indeed meet the definition of genocide. It is entirely possible that the judges will, in the end, agree with that conclusion. Above all, however, it is important to remember that genocide does not stand alone among terrible crimes. We should not fetishise

Lemkin's word when Lauterpacht's 'crimes against humanity' are themselves so serious, as the International Criminal Court's list of alleged crimes – including starvation, persecution and murder – made clear in 2024. There is the danger of getting lost in what Professor William Schabas, a leading authority on the ICC, describes as the 'sterile debate' about whether to characterise acts as genocide or 'as "mere" crimes against humanity'.

Lauterpacht himself remained wary of the concept of genocide and published a mostly dismissive review of Lemkin's *Axis Rule* as the Nuremberg trials got under way in 1945. He conceded that Lemkin's book included 'interesting and sound observations' and showed 'prodigious industry'; he did not believe, however, that the book was 'a contribution to the law of belligerent occupation'. Writing ten years later about the genocide convention, Lauterpacht was sceptical of the 'disquieting incongruity between the enormity of the crime and the sanction provided for its suppression'. (On that point at least, Lemkin would have agreed: governments' failure to agree a tribunal which could prosecute genocide was one reason he felt his work had fallen 'on a fallow plain', since follow-up was impossible.) Lauterpacht thought the concept of genocide, by emphasising the importance of groups, was in danger of reinforcing the mindset – 'tribalised pain', to quote Zeid Ra'ad al-Hussein's formulation – that can pave the way for such crimes in the first place.

It is, however, not necessary to take a view on the Lauterpacht–Lemkin rivalries (which played out in drafted and redrafted prosecutors' speeches at Nuremberg) to see it is unhelpful for one word to eclipse all others. It is natural for us to be shocked, as Lemkin was, at the idea of a planned assault on a specific ethnic or religious group – Armenian, Jewish, Tutsi, Bosniak, Yazidi, Rohingya or other. But the killing of thousands or millions where the drive is political not ethnic – because the victims would like to keep their own cow or till their own field, because they remain loyal to an elected president who has been overthrown in a coup, or because they are held responsible for crimes committed by others – does not need to be seen as a 'lesser evil'. The ICC definition of crimes against humanity is widespread or systematic attack directed against any civilian population, including murder, rape, torture, forced disappearances and extermination. Genocide does not, in other words, have a monopoly on horror. It was, after all, only the targeting of some ethnic Vietnamese that makes it possible to define what happened in the killing fields of Cambodia between 1975 and 1979 as genocide, as described in Chapter Two: otherwise, the political madness which killed two million people in four years would 'merely' have counted as crimes against humanity.

In short, those who care about Palestinian suffering should be careful not to see as 'a sellout' a potential future ruling which stops short of a finding of genocide. Conversely, a ruling that the killing of tens of thousands of civilians is *not* genocide (while leaving open the possibility of crimes against humanity) would not mean declaring Israel innocent of serious crimes, as some might like to imply.

Justice, including the prosecution of those responsible for the worst war crimes, is not an answer to everything. It can, however, be an ingredient in seeking future stability – 'one link in a long chain', to quote Hebrew University law professor Yuval Shany. War crimes that go unpunished, meanwhile, are a recipe for more violence yet to come if, to paraphrase Robert Jackson, the hand of vengeance is unstayed.

Those governments which want themselves or their friends

to be protected from accountability for all time should understand they are damaging prospects for a stable future for themselves, for the region and for the world. Netanyahu may be eager to unleash destruction and shout into the void in order to maintain his hold on power – as Milošević did in the 1990s and as Putin does today. (One poll suggested that only 15 per cent of Israeli voters wanted Netanyahu to remain prime minister after the assault on Gaza is over.) The Israeli leader shows little interest, however, in identifying a framework which might provide the beginnings of a more stable future for Israelis and Palestinians alike. In *What Does Israel Fear from Palestine?*, published in 2024, Raja Shehadeh reflects on whether the current darkness may also pave the way for change:

> For the majority of Palestinians, who are not part of Hamas; for those Israelis who could only watch with dismay at what their government was doing, powerless to stop the horror; for those of us who know with unshakeable certainty that the only future is for the two peoples to live together – the future might seem bleak. And yet, looking back at the history of the region, it is only after great upheavals that hopeful consequences follow.

A year into the assault on Gaza, such an outcome feels distant. When Israel assassinated Hizbollah leader Hassan Nasrallah in Beirut in September 2024, it boasted of having cut off 'the head of the snake' – the same phrase used when Nasrallah's predecessor was killed, thirty years earlier. Nasrallah's death led to a renewed flurry of attacks on Israel.

As always, it was not Hizbollah's armed militias but above all defenceless civilians who lost their homes and their lives. Israeli bombing raids killed five hundred Lebanese in a single day; 1.2 million people, one in four of the population, were displaced. Even ever-reluctant Germany found its voice; Berlin joined the condemnation of Israeli attacks on UN peacekeepers in southern Lebanon. The region seemed to spiral into a wider war, both with slow-motion inevitability and at dizzying speed. In September, Netanyahu warned of the destruction of Lebanon, 'like Gaza'. In October, Israel attacked Iran and Iran threatened a 'crushing response'. Neighbouring Jordan talked of the 'abyss' of regional war and the UN warned of a 'spiral of doom'. Even if full-scale international war does not come, the impact of the current violence will not quickly subside.

If the hopes of Shehadeh and others for a more stable future can eventually become real, however, global pressures for justice – including the rulings of two international courts – can and must form part of that, by paving the way for future accountability and truth.

Yonatan Zeigen, who seeks to honour the memory of his mother, the murdered Israeli activist Vivian Silver, partly echoes Shehadeh in his hope that the horror might, under a different leadership, become a prologue to change: 'We need leaders to create a vision of security and freedom – security for us, freedom for the Palestinians. Public opinion is very dynamic. Now, you see "Israelis want blood!" But history tells us the greatest catastrophes can create the biggest changes. Things can change all the time.'

Chapter Nine

'I am Smelling Justice'

'The old era of impunity is over,' UN Secretary-General Ban Ki-moon told the review meeting of member states of the International Criminal Court in Kampala in 2010. 'In its place, slowly but surely, we are witnessing the birth of a new age of accountability . . . Those who commit the worst of human crimes will be held responsible.'

Ban's words can sound like the distant memory of a now-vanished era of hope. From Syria to Ukraine, Gaza and beyond, governments have committed grave crimes in recent years, apparently confident there would be no consequences. Still, though, the changes that began at Nuremberg and developed with new energy at the end of the twentieth and the beginning of the twenty-first centuries continue to have rippling impact today in what author and scholar Kathryn Sikkink has described as 'the justice cascade' – an idea that 'started as a small stream but later caught on suddenly, sweeping along many actors in its wake'. Around the world, despite all the obstacles, people have begun to believe.

The global consensus that existed for the war crimes

tribunals on Rwanda and the former Yugoslavia – approved by the UN Security Council unanimously or with near-unanimity thirty years ago – now seems to belong to a different universe. But the possibilities of justice that the ad hoc tribunals and the International Criminal Court unlocked can no longer be unseen. 125 countries are now members of the ICC. The creation of a range of new institutions – some successful, some less so – has gone in parallel with an increased desire and determination for justice in different contexts around the world. The fact that international courts are ready to challenge powerful governments and their friends, including both in Washington and in Moscow, is a reason for hope – even if some remain determined to punish that boldness or to side with the abusers. The return to the White House of Donald Trump, who has been so eager to ensure impunity in a range of different contexts, may seem to block the prospects for future change. Martin Luther King Jr's famous declaration that 'the arc of the moral universe is long, but it bends towards justice' was, however, made more powerful, not less, by the fact that he affirmed that faith at a time of political darkness and even as he predicted his own assassination. In today's context, too, it is no longer possible to put all the changes of recent years into reverse.

The demand for universal jurisdiction cases has dramatically increased, following the example set by the arrest of Pinochet a quarter of a century ago. Mazen Darwish, former inmate of Assad's jails and director of the Syrian Center for Media and Freedom of Expression, regrets that most of the cases are still in Europe and argues: 'We need to make this movement truly universal.' Darwish, who played a key role in the conviction of the Syrian torturer Anwar Raslan in Germany in 2022, is right to highlight that obvious problem. But the direction is clear. There have been hundreds of prosecutions, for crimes committed everywhere from Ethiopia to Afghanistan. At the beginning of this century, the Pinochet-loving Henry Kissinger responded to the arrest of the former Chilean leader by complaining that universal jurisdiction was 'judicial tyranny'. But the value of international jurisdiction has increasingly been recognised. Governments have promised to make such prosecutions simpler and more effective: a treaty agreed in 2023 commits states to cross-border collaboration in investigating war crimes, genocide and crimes against humanity. (The initiative was led by the former Yugoslav republic of Slovenia, which briefly suffered Slobodan Milošević's aggression before slipping out of the collapsing federation in 1991.)

In 2024, governments agreed to open negotiations on crimes against humanity, too, that would work along similar lines to Lemkin's 1948 genocide convention and the 1984 UN convention against torture – another 'milestone treaty', in the words of Amnesty International. Building on Lauterpacht's contribution at Nuremberg, the proposed new convention would create the obligations of prevention, prohibition and punishment of crimes against humanity for the first time, enforceable at the International Court of Justice in The Hague. For years, such a treaty had seemed unachievable. Now, like the International Criminal Court thirty years earlier, it was an idea whose time had come.

The possibilities have multiplied in different contexts. As former Rwanda prosecutor and former US war crimes ambassador Stephen Rapp told me when we met in Kyiv in 2023, 'There's more attention to war crimes and accountability now than at any time in my lifetime – even more than in former Yugoslavia.'

In 2002, an Afghan warlord told his men that researchers

from Human Rights Watch who had published a report on war crimes in Afghanistan were 'very dangerous' because they could 'take you to an international court' if you committed atrocities. At the time, that line was mostly grandstanding, of which the warlord was fond. 'If any of my commanders commits these kinds of acts,' Abdul Rashid Dostum declared, 'I will kill him tomorrow.' In the meantime, however, much else has changed. In 2018, Dostum himself was identified as somebody the International Criminal Court should investigate.

In 2019, a former Iranian prosecutor was arrested on arrival at Stockholm airport and later jailed for life in connection with the execution of thousands without trial thirty years earlier. (Five years later, Hamid Noury was released back to Iran as part of a 'hostage diplomacy' deal which saw two Swedish citizens freed.) In 2021, a Swiss court convicted a former Liberian rebel commander of crimes against humanity; Liberian human rights groups hoped the sentence would help end impunity for other former warlords inside Liberia, too.

In 2024, Gambia's former interior minister, Ousman Sonko, went on trial in Switzerland, following years of work by Gambian activists and the Swiss non-governmental organisation TRIAL International. 'I am smelling justice,' said sixty-seven-year-old Madi Ceesay, arrested and tortured for his journalism in the 1980s, as the trial got under way. Ceesay's optimism was justified: four months later, Sonko was jailed for twenty years. Gambia wants to see the former dictator, Yahya Jammeh — currently in exile in Equatorial Guinea — put on trial, too. 'Impunity is a kind of incentive that we are not prepared to serve perpetrators,' says Gambian justice minister Dawda Jallow. 'Their resolve to commit these atrocities cannot be stronger than our collective will as a society to hold them to account.'

In Germany, the Netherlands and elsewhere there have

been prosecutions and convictions for genocide and crimes against humanity in connection with the rape, enslavement and murder of Yazidis in Iraq and Syria in 2014. Not everybody has absorbed the lessons of the Rwanda and Yugoslavia war crimes tribunals, where Judge Navi Pillay and others ruled on rape as genocide. In *Our Bodies, Their Battlefield*, Christina Lamb quotes an Iraqi judge who tells her that rape does not deserve to be considered as a separate crime: 'When these terrorists join ISIS they are killing, raping, beheading so it all counts as terrorism ... There is no need to worry about the rape.' Lamb pointed out that it does indeed matter to those who have been raped, enslaved and sold – but the judge wasn't interested. Nadia Murad, Nobel Prize-winning Yazidi survivor and advocate, is clear: 'Every Yazidi wants ISIS prosecuted for genocide.' In the words of Amal Clooney, who has worked with her to achieve justice for Yazidis, Murad is 'the voice of every Yazidi who is a victim of genocide, every woman who has been abused, every refugee who has been left behind'.

In some respects, the existence of an international criminal court, and the need for universal jurisdiction, can be seen as an admission of defeat – acknowledgement that domestic justice has failed or is likely to fail. The court's first prosecutor, Luis Moreno Ocampo, argued that the fewer cases the ICC deals with, the better the system is working: 'The absence of trials before this court, as a consequence of the regular functioning of national institutions, would be a major success.' Arguably, that still holds true. Chief prosecutor Karim Khan sees the court as 'a catalyst' for justice. He tells me: 'I have met people who have lost everything, but still believe in justice, that it's not a pipe dream. They are struggling for it, they are demanding it, with maybe no food in their mouths, no clothes on their backs, no roof over their heads. But they believe justice is their birthright. That's the triumph of the human spirit.' Khan says that the very existence of the court in The Hague means there is a new belief in what can be achieved: 'People are demanding that the light of justice shines even in places that have been in the dark.' When I ask Khan about his legal heroes, his answer focuses instead on a different kind of courtroom hero: survivors who are determined to testify against their abusers, hard though that may be, and whose courage makes it possible for justice to be achieved.

Increasingly in recent years, justice has been coming home. Argentina, with its historic 'trial of the juntas', was an early trailblazer. The 1985 trial, at which Luis Moreno Ocampo was a prosecutor, came at the end of an almost complete drought for accountability worldwide (there had been limited trials in 1975 and 1976 after the collapse of far-right regimes in Greece and Portugal). The trial is a source of pride in Argentina today, and in 2022 became the subject of *Argentina, 1985*, an Oscar-nominated film that was the country's biggest box-office hit that year. In the words of the *Buenos Aires Herald*, 'The film brought back not only the horror suffered by the junta's innocent victims but also a sense of pride in being the first nation to prosecute a military dictatorship since Nuremberg.' After 1985, there were moves to nullify the impact of the trial. As described in Chapter Two, the *punto final* marked an apparent legislative full stop that would block prosecutions for all time. In reality, however, these were only temporary victories for the generals. The world was changing.

In 2003 – eighteen years after the trial in Buenos Aires, five years after the Pinochet arrest and a year after the creation of the International Criminal Court – Congress repealed the

punto final law. In 2005, the Argentine Supreme Court sealed
that decision by ruling the earlier law to be unconstitutional.
'The impunity granted by those laws overwhelmed us,' said
Estela Carlotto of the Grandmothers of the Plaza de Mayo,
whose daughter was disappeared and whose baby grandson
was stolen by the military to be raised as their own. 'We
have been living with thieves and murderers in our midst.'
(In 2014, Carlotto was united with the grandson she had
never met.)

Jorge Videla, the junta leader who declared in 1975 that 'as
many people will die in Argentina as is necessary to restore
order', was sentenced to fifty years in jail in 2012, including for
the theft of babies. One trial in 2017, almost forty years after
the crimes committed, ended with twenty-nine life sentences
for those involved. More than a thousand people have been
convicted for crimes during the period of military rule.

I spoke to Juan Méndez, former UN adviser on the prevention of genocide and himself a survivor of torture in the
Argentine junta's jails, who highlighted the achievement:
'Predictions were repeatedly made about a return to dictatorship if there were trials. But that didn't happen.' The journey
has not been simple. There are fears that the self-described
'anarcho-capitalist' Javier Milei, who became president in
2023, could roll back the moves towards accountability. But
huge crowds turned out in 2024 to protest Milei's 'denialism';
Argentine courts made clear that they would not reopen the
door to impunity. Argentina has also played a key role in
seeking justice for crimes committed elsewhere in the world,
opening universal jurisdiction cases for cases ranging from
Ukraine to Myanmar.

The same pattern of change can be seen elsewhere. In 1974,
Uruguayan president Juan María Bordaberry was confident
that there would be no punishment for any crimes committed

during the military dictatorship: 'It would be like assuming you could judge a man who broke the formal law to defend his mother, in this case his motherland. And this stance cannot be the object of a judgment.' Like so many others who believed in the possibilities of impunity for all time, the president was wrong. In 2010, a Uruguayan court convicted the eighty-one-year-old Bordaberry and sentenced him to thirty years in jail.

In 1998, critics claimed that Pinochet's arrest would 'destabilise' Chile. In reality, the arrest increased the impetus for the truth to be heard and justice to be achieved. Truth commissions addressed the themes of disappearances and torture. After Pinochet's death in 2006, the pressures for justice increased, with hundreds more convictions in the years since then. Manuel Contreras, the former head of the Dina secret police who said people should not think war was fought in 'gentlemanly uniforms and white gloves', was jailed for a total of five hundred years (unsurprisingly, he died behind bars). In 2023, former army officer Pedro Barrientos was extradited from the United States to stand trial for the murder of the singer Victor Jara, shot in the back of the head in the Chile Stadium in Santiago five days after the coup. (The stadium now bears Jara's name.) Jara's British widow Joan, who died just days before the announcement, had campaigned for justice for fifty years.

Chile, like Argentina, has also helped deliver justice elsewhere. In 2005, former Peruvian president Alberto Fujimori was returned to Peru, where he was jailed for human rights violations including kidnap and murder. (Fujimori was controversially released in 2023, to the anger of the Inter-American Court of Human Rights, which complained of contempt of court; he died, aged eighty-six, in 2024.)

In 2021, following calls from Argentina, Chile, Peru and

others, the International Criminal Court began an investigation in Venezuela (a member of the court from the start)
in connection with alleged crimes against humanity by
the government of Nicolás Maduro, including torture and
killings during anti-government protests in 2017, when a
hundred people died. There was renewed repression in 2024,
after Maduro claimed what Chilean president Gabriel Boric
and other Latin American governments described as a stolen
election. Reliable figures showed the opposition gained two
thirds of the vote. Maduro talked, however, of 'demonic
forces' ranged against him and vowed: 'I will never surren-
der.' The UN talked of 'unprecedented repression'. The ICC
investigation remains open.

Those pressing for justice have often fought against the
heaviest odds. In Guatemala in 1998, a *Nunca más* ('Never
Again') report for the 'recovery of national memory' was
launched at an emotional event chaired by Bishop Juan
Gerardi in the Metropolitan Cathedral in Guatemala City.
'Truth is the primary word,' Bishop Gerardi said, 'that makes
it possible for us to break this cycle of death and violence and
to open ourselves to a future of hope and light for all.' Two
days later, he was bludgeoned to death in his home; junior
military officers were eventually prosecuted. But Gerardi's
assassination did not stop demands for change. A truth commission concluded the worst crimes took place 'with the
knowledge or by the authority of the highest authorities of
the state'. In 2013, General Efraín Ríos Montt, who President
Reagan had found to be a man 'of great personal integrity',
was convicted of genocide and crimes against humanity (Ríos
Montt said he knew nothing, he ordered nothing). The verdict was overturned on a technicality but was followed by
a second trial. Ríos Montt died awaiting his verdict, again
facing charges of genocide. The challenges from those who

want to block justice remain strong, but so, too, are the grassroots pressures for justice. In 2024, Guatemala's new president Bernard Arévalo came to power with a promise to increase victims' rights. The 'subversive criminals' were now very differently defined from when I was in Guatemala four decades earlier. A few months after Arévalo's inauguration, the ninety-one-year-old General Benedicto Lucas García, former head of the army – who shouted 'Give it to them! Give it to them!' as civilians were mown down, as described in Chapter Two – went on trial for genocide.

In Europe, too, countries which have lived through authoritarian rule on both sides of the old Iron Curtain have found their own ways of processing memory and truth. In central and eastern Europe, there have been a variety of sometimes controversial 'lustration' laws which seek to ensure that politicians' past collaborations with the secret police are exposed and that dictatorships do not return. In 2022, forty-seven years after the end of the Franco era, Spain introduced a Democratic Memory Law to ensure truths could be told about the Spanish Civil War and the four decades of dictatorship that followed. As in Latin America, arguments continue about amnesty laws that were put in place after Franco's death in 1975. But even without prosecutions of the now elderly perpetrators, truth-telling has value.

Crimes which at the time they were committed seemed set to remain unpunished forever – including because the US and other governments were determined to look the other way – eventually had consequences. Pol Pot, the Khmer Rouge leader who presided over two million deaths in Cambodia, died in 1998 saying his 'conscience was clear'. In 2003, however, the Extraordinary Chambers in the Courts of Cambodia were created. The former head of state, Khieu

Samphan, and Pol Pot's number two, Nuon Chea, were both convicted of crimes against humanity and genocide. The tribunal, a collaboration between Cambodia and the UN, was ponderous; it took nine years for the first case to come to trial. There was strong early support for the idea of accountability, though that dwindled as the tribunal was widely perceived as being subject to political pressure from prime minister and former Khmer Rouge commander Hun Sen, who seemed determined to cut deals that protected perpetrators. Brad Adams of Human Rights Watch argued that decisions about prosecutions should be 'based on evidence, not politics'.

In the two decades since its creation, the International Criminal Court has achieved just five convictions for atrocity crimes, three of which have been in the Democratic Republic of Congo. Many Congolese felt those convictions did not reflect the gravity of the crimes committed. But the result of that disillusion has not been a desire to abandon the aspirations for justice. Instead, hundreds of perpetrators have been convicted in Congo in recent years, with more trials all the time. Toussaint Muntazini, a Congolese prosecutor who now leads a special war crimes court prosecuting atrocities in the neighbouring Central African Republic, believes: 'As long as justice is not served, it is not possible for a country to recover.' To make the process in Congo more accessible, some trials are in mobile courtrooms. That included the conviction in 2017 of a member of parliament and eleven others, jailed for life for the rape of children in eastern Congo. Reparations were paid to victims and families – an outcome that would have seemed unthinkable only a few years earlier. Guy Mishiata, a Congolese lawyer working with TRIAL International, says, 'The efforts sometimes feel like only a tiny drop in the ocean. But if I look back over the past twenty years, I'm proud of the progress. The Congolese have shown they can bring justice closer to the affected communities.' In 2024, Uganda saw its first conviction, in a court in the north of the country, of a rebel commander of the Lord's Resistance Army, twenty years after the crimes of the LRA were first referred to the International Criminal Court.

In the Balkans, too, prosecutions have partly moved from The Hague to the region, including dozens of convictions in Bosnia and a special war crimes chamber in Serbia. In 2024, a Belgrade court convicted Serbs of massacres in Kosovo villages twenty-five years earlier. There have also been attempts to show that justice is indeed blind. When I was in Kosovo after Milošević's forces were driven out in 1999, I was struck by the reluctance of Western politicians to take note of crimes committed by both sides. Under the headline 'Serbs are victims, too', I wrote that the failure to act against widespread Albanian intimidation and murder of innocent Serbs in Kosovo would be 'an obvious carte blanche for the committing of further acts of murder'. That self-evident truth was for many years largely ignored. But in 2023, Kosovo's former president, Hashim Thaçi, went on trial (in a court created by Kosovo, based for security reasons in The Hague), charged with responsibility for alleged crimes a quarter of a century earlier.

After long years of impunity, domestic and regional war crimes and human rights trials of former leaders have multiplied everywhere from Guinea and Burkina Faso to Suriname. Many of these trials have been messy and imperfect. But survivors and relatives welcome the fact that they are happening at all. As Alexander Hinton, director of the Centre for the Study of Genocide and Human Rights, argued in the context of the Cambodian verdicts in 2018, 'Justice is not perfect. But it is better than no justice. And what's the alternative? Impunity for mass murder.'

There have been attempts to chip away at the veto system at the UN Security Council, which has long enabled the most powerful governments to shield themselves and their friends from criticism. In 2022, tiny Liechtenstein gained widespread support for an initiative which requires the five permanent members of the security council to come to the UN General Assembly to justify any use of the veto. It was a blow for sanity – in Liechtenstein's own words, 'a little more than can be expected of us because of our small size' (Liechtenstein has a territory of sixty square miles and a population of just forty thousand.) The change does not abolish the veto itself. It does, however, help shine a spotlight on those who otherwise cannot be held accountable for their actions. In the words of Christian Wenaweser, Liechtenstein's ambassador in New York for the past two decades and a champion of global justice throughout that time, 'It resonates very strongly and positively. I didn't necessarily expect that ... The veto just hits a nerve.'

There have also been initiatives to pave the way for future accountability even in seemingly impossible contexts. When I visited Myanmar in 1998, I met – with difficulty, because of ubiquitous surveillance – Aung San Suu Kyi, the banned Burmese opposition leader. Aung San Suu Kyi's main offence was that her party had won an election eight years earlier, leading to years of house arrest and jail at the hands of the military junta. Ordinary Burmese and millions around the world saw her as a courageous heroine; the glowing magazine profile I wrote at that time reflected that. 'This is not what you would call a sustainable situation,' Aung San Suu Kyi told me as the monsoon rains beat down outside. 'Change will come.' It was a surreal few days. One of the plainclothes officers who detained photographer Tom Pilston and me after the interview explained, 'You can talk to anybody. But you can't talk to Aung San Suu Kyi. It is not permitted.' Why not? 'She disagrees with the government.' And why is that forbidden? 'I can't explain.' I felt honoured that, as punishment for our unauthorised interview and after a pre-deportation body search to the sound of the Spice Girls, we were put on a visa blacklist which would remain in force for the next fourteen years.

Change did indeed come. I met Aung San Suu Kyi again in 2012, when she travelled to Oslo to accept the Nobel Peace Prize she had been awarded twenty-one years earlier. In 2016, she became her country's de facto prime minister. This was, however, no human rights happy ending. In 2016 and 2017, the Myanmar military unleashed huge violence against Rohingya Muslims in the north-western Rakhine state, following years of repression. Hundreds of villages were burned; torture and rape were common; hundreds of thousands fled into neighbouring Bangladesh. By now, the human rights halo was no more than a memory. Aung San Suu Kyi complained of a 'huge iceberg of misinformation' which was supposedly aimed at promoting 'the interest of the terrorists'. But many saw similarities to the patterns of crime that Lemkin had identified. Senegalese lawyer Adama Dieng, UN adviser on prevention of genocide, said that Rohingya had been tortured, raped and burned alive 'solely because of who they are'. Dieng concluded that the perpetrators intended 'to cleanse northern Rakhine state of their existence, possibly even to destroy the Rohingya as such', as part of a 'predictable and preventable' scorched earth campaign.

Despite the mounting evidence, it seemed that the world would do nothing. At the Security Council, Beijing was ready to use its veto to protect the generals in Myanmar, just as Putin protected Assad. In 2018, however, the UN appointed Nicholas Koumjian, former Cambodia prosecutor and grandson of Armenian genocide survivors, to lead an 'independent investigative mechanism' on Myanmar along the same lines as the 'international, impartial and independent' mechanism created in 2016 to investigate crimes in Syria. Like the War Crimes Commission which led to Nuremberg, the mechanism gathers evidence with a view to future prosecutions, whenever those may be. Koumjian insists: 'The cycle of impunity will end, and there will one day be accountability and justice for these heinous crimes.'

In November 2019, Gambia, on behalf of fifty-seven Muslim countries around the world (the Organisation of Islamic Cooperation), broke new legal ground by bringing a case against Myanmar at the International Court of Justice under the terms of Lemkin's genocide convention. This was the first time a country had brought a case at the world court on behalf of the population of another state – the model South Africa would follow with its case against Israel four years later.

Four weeks later, Aung San Suu Kyi travelled to The Hague to give testimony. She praised Lemkin's convention as 'one of the most fundamental multilateral treaties of our time'. The one-time human rights heroine said international law was 'our only global value system' and international justice 'a practice that affirms our common values'. But she denied the relevance of any of this for Myanmar. The country's forces were, she said, dealing with an internal armed conflict; they were not committing genocide.

The court's unanimously agreed provisional measures, issued in January 2020, gave her arguments short shrift. Without taking a final position on whether or not genocide had been committed, the court (using language similar to what the judges would say on Israel four years later) talked of the danger of 'irreparable harm', and ordered Myanmar to prevent genocidal acts, to ensure its forces did not commit genocide, to preserve evidence of genocide and to report back on its compliance. It was a powerful warning shot, even while the UN Security Council remained silent. In the overflowing camps in Cox's Bazar in Bangladesh, Rohingya refugees held up signs: 'Thank you Gambia.'

Even in the context of criminal accountability, and despite China's role, it seemed there might be possibilities of change. As this book was going to press, the International Criminal Court's prosecutor requested the issue of an arrest warrant for the Burmese junta leader, General Min Aung Hlaing, with more requested warrants to come. Karim Khan announced the request from Bangladesh, and referred to his meetings with Rohingya survivors in Cox's Bazar. The court's work, he said, 'seeks to vindicate their resilience and their hope in the power of the law'.

At least until we see a radical reform of the UN system (in other words, not any time soon, despite a 'Pact for the Future' that was agreed in 2024), there is no possibility that a Security Council resolution will condemn China's crimes against Uyghur Muslims – torture, sterilisation, re-education camps, forced labour – in the western province of Xinjiang. But that hasn't stopped people ensuring the scale of those crimes is documented. In 2021, an international 'people's tribunal' – chaired by Geoffrey Nice, former Milošević prosecutor – found China guilty of genocide. Like the Russell Tribunal on war crimes in Vietnam half a century earlier, the Uyghur Tribunal – which met, as did the planners of the Nuremberg trials, in Church House in Westminster – has no immediate practical consequences. But the furious reaction from Beijing ('a farce carried out by a small number of anti-China elements') suggested the tribunal's very existence caused discomfort. Huge pressure was put on witnesses not to testify.

In 2022, the publication of a key UN report on Xinjiang was repeatedly delayed because of pressures from Beijing. UN human rights commissioner Michelle Bachelet, former president of Chile and herself a survivor of Pinochet's jails, promised publication before her term ended on 31 August. Bachelet's last day came and almost went with no sign of the report. I assumed Beijing had won and the UN's findings were buried for all time. It turned out, however, that arguments were continuing until literally the eleventh hour. 'Wait!' a friend in Bachelet's office texted that evening when I asked what had happened. The report, with its references to crimes against humanity in Xinjiang, was finally released just before midnight. Beijing complained that the report 'wantonly smears and slanders China', was 'based on disinformation and lies' and 'interferes in China's internal affairs'. But the UN report, like the Uyghur Tribunal, forms part of the historical record. Beijing's angry responses do not make the truth unheard.

Sometimes, even the first steps towards accountability and justice have been difficult to achieve. A hundred thousand were killed in the war in Ethiopia's Tigray region in 2022. Amnesty International and Human Rights Watch found evidence that government forces had committed rape, ethnic cleansing and murder. But governments did not wish to criticise the Ethiopian prime minister, Abiy Ahmed, recipient in 2019 of the Nobel Peace Prize for a deal reached with neighbouring Eritrea. There was, in the words of Tom Gardner, author of *The Abiy Project*, a 'collective entrancement', with Abiy treated, as one observer put it, 'like a rock star'. Mohamed Othman, Tanzanian chair of a UN inquiry, argued, 'Victims' demands for justice are clear and unwavering. Without accountability, serious crimes are likely to be repeated, as Ethiopia's history has shown.' But he and his colleagues were ignored. The inquiry was dissolved.

As Othman points out, one danger is that moving on paves the way for new violence. After Omar al-Bashir was overthrown in a popular uprising in 2019, Sudan's new rulers promised to deliver him to the ICC in The Hague. That never happened; in recent years, he has spent time in jail in Khartoum on corruption charges or in a military hospital. In the meantime, successive layers of impunity have been strengthened. A coup in 2021 and fighting that began in 2023 between the Sudanese army and the paramilitary Rapid Support Forces – successors to the Janjaweed militias, responsible for the worst massacres in Darfur twenty years earlier – now make the prospect of accountability seem more distant than ever. More than twenty thousand – many times that, according to some estimates – have been killed. Ten million have been forced to flee their homes. Alice Wairimu Nderitu, UN special adviser on prevention of genocide, echoes Othman in saying: 'When perpetrators of past atrocities are not held accountable for their action, we are doomed to see history repeat itself.'

Even in the context of Sudan – in most respects, an epidemic of impunity – new initiatives have sought to hold to account some of those whose actions or complicity may have enabled grave crimes. That has included an emphasis on corporate accountability – not completely new, but with new energy and determination in recent years. Following a decade-long investigation, a historic trial began in Sweden in 2023, involving the company previously known as Lundin

Oil and its exploration fields in an area of what is now South Sudan, where government-backed militias burned villages; thousands of civilians were killed and more than a hundred thousand were displaced. 'I have been waiting for this moment since the case started almost twenty years ago,' Pastor James Kuong Ninrew, several of whose relatives were killed, told the court in Stockholm. The former chair and the former chief executive of Lundin Oil are accused of complicity in war crimes committed between 1999 and 2003; they deny the charges.

In connection with Syria, too, there have been moves to hold a Western company to account. In 2024, the French supreme court confirmed that the cement maker, Lafarge, is potentially liable for crimes against humanity in connection with millions of dollars paid to Islamic State and other terror groups in exchange for keeping their factory open in northeast Syria. (In 2022, a US court fined the company three quarters of a billion dollars for its payments to ISIS.) These are some of the first cases which seek to hold Western companies and their executives to account for alleged complicity in war crimes; they will not be the last.

As this partial list and the earlier chapters in this book make clear, we have many more possibilities of achieving truth and justice than existed in Lemkin's and Lauterpacht's lifetimes. But the effectiveness of those mechanisms is diminished or erased if governments reject the simple and compelling message that the balanced scales of Lady Justice seek to convey. That challenge must be accepted and addressed.

Chapter Ten

Balancing the Scales

This book is partly a homage to those who in the past hundred years have paved the way for extraordinary change against all odds. It is a tribute, too, to survivors and activists who work, often at risk to their own lives, to ensure justice can be achieved today and in the years to come. I am privileged to have met or worked with some of those I have written about. I met many more inspiring people while writing this book. But the challenges they face are huge. During the past few years, the dangers of a pick-and-choose approach to justice, which some governments still seem determined to maintain, have become more glaring than ever.

Prosecutions of the powerful are not a cure-all. They do not end the pain of the crimes committed. They do not wave a magic wand and create world peace. Justice can, however, provide at least the beginnings of a framework for stability. Conversely, lack of justice, and the festering resentments which result from that sense of injustice, provide fertile soil for insecurity and renewed cycles of violence.

With the right leadership, domestic and international

courts can help achieve an acknowledgement of truth which otherwise may remain missing. With the wrong leadership, denial and instability continue to thrive. Zoran Djindjić, the Serbian prime minister who delivered Slobodan Milošević to The Hague in 2001, understood the importance of a country confronting its own history. After Milošević's indictment but while he was still in power, Djindjić told me of his fears of a 'flight into a historic world' and the dangers of the belief that Serbs 'have been victims for six hundred years, and we can do what we want'. Djindjić was assassinated in 2003 by those who did not want such uncomfortable truths to be spoken; a few weeks earlier, he had told Hague prosecutor Carla Del Ponte that he knew he would be killed. Serbian and Bosnian Serb leaders in the years since have often been less willing to confront history and responsibility.

When I visited Srebrenica twenty years after the massacres, I was struck by the continuing refusal of many Bosnian Serbs living there even to acknowledge what had happened. One woman told me that Karadžić and Mladić (who had been or soon would be convicted of genocide) had merely been 'defending the country'. We were standing just a few yards from a farm building where thirteen hundred Bosniak men and boys had notoriously been executed in 1995; the walls were still pockmarked with bullet holes. In the town of Srebrenica, I heard similar explanations. Such denial comes from the top; it does nothing for stability on either side.

Elsewhere, however, truth has been a stepping stone to the future. In South Africa, the Truth and Reconciliation Commission became an alternative to prosecutions after the end of the apartheid era. In Latin America and around the world, truth commissions have often served not as an alternative but as a prologue, helping to ensure that perpetrators are eventually held to account, sometimes decades after the event.

The existence of international courts has spurred energy for those seeking new forms of accountability across the world. The voices of survivors are heard more clearly than ever, influencing the shape of justice itself. When the International Criminal Court began its work at the beginning of this century, it was often criticised for being distant from those who were most directly affected by the crimes. But, not least as a result of untiring advocacy such as the 'pest Lemkin' might have appreciated, the survivors' perspective is now embedded in the court's strategies, including for the prosecution of crimes of sexual violence. Nadine Tunasi, a Congolese-born former colleague at Freedom from Torture who advises the British government on its Preventing Sexual Violence in Conflict Initiative, praises the increased awareness of survivors' needs: Things, she says, 'have definitely changed'.

Still, however, some governments seem reluctant or unable to acknowledge the dangers they create for themselves and others if they try to prevent crimes from being addressed. Few today would argue that French atrocities in Algeria, British cover-up in connection with army killings in Northern Ireland or US abuses at Guantánamo and Abu Ghraib made anybody safer from attacks by lawless armed groups. The opposite is clearly true. As former US counter-terror investigator Mark Fallon points out, 'Whether you go to the Battle of Algiers or examples throughout history, such tactics backfire and embolden your adversary. They make you less safe.' Equally, when America and Russia today share a determination to protect their friends from being held accountable for mass killings, they are jointly responsible for making the world a more dangerous place.

It was unsurprising that Benjamin Netanyahu would in 2024 condemn his indictment for war crimes and crimes against humanity by the prosecutor of the International Criminal Court. He was hardly likely, after all, to praise his own arrest warrant. But the apparent determination of the United States, which sees itself as a voice for justice world-wide, to protect Israeli politicians from judicial scrutiny is both disturbing and foolish. When an elected US president describes the indictment of the Israeli prime minister as 'outrageous', and when his successor in the White House tells that same leader, 'Do what you have to do', regardless of the consequences, that tramples Palestinian aspirations for justice and stores up yet more problems for the future. It also ignores the voices of courageous Israelis who point out that telling truth to power is just what Israel needs most in order to address what Avner Gvaryahu, director of the Israeli veterans' organisation Breaking the Silence, calls a 'pattern of moral deterioration'.

In 1948, Hersch Lauterpacht was invited to draft language for Israel's declaration of independence. His Declaration on the Assumption of Power by the Provisional Government of the Jewish Republic, just five pages long, talks of 'justice, international peace and respect and equality for all dwellers of our land regardless of race and religion'. Within the short document, Lauterpacht finds room to emphasise that the newly created state should respect the world court created three years earlier in The Hague. His proposed declaration promises that Israel's international conduct 'shall be subordinated to the generally recognized law of nations' and 'shall adhere permanently ... to international instruments conferring compulsory jurisdiction upon the International Court of Justice'. In the end, partly because of administrative confusions, his language wasn't used. But Lauterpacht's great-nephew President Herzog and other Israeli leaders might usefully go back to those core principles of international good citizenship that Lauterpacht recommended.

At Nuremberg, Robert Jackson said we cannot allow crimes to be ignored because we cannot survive their being repeated. We must ask ourselves: what will it mean if there are no consequences for Putin's crimes across Ukraine in the past few years? What will it mean if there are no consequences for Israeli leaders for the deaths of tens of thousands of civilians in Gaza today?

We can now hold the worst war criminals to account in ways that once seemed unthinkable. That sends a signal that such crimes can be addressed in the future, too. Prosecuting the powerful is not just about accountability for past crimes, though that matters, too. It is about securing our future. Given how much has already been achieved, there are reasons for hope. We owe it to those who have suffered most to follow through on the opportunities that have been created. But governments need to encourage, not block, ways of balancing the scales better for the sake of all.

Notes

A number of books have influenced my thinking on the themes of *Prosecuting the Powerful* over many years. I first read Samantha Power's Pulitzer-winning *A Problem from Hell: America and the Age of Genocide*, which addresses the repeated failure to confront genocide and other grave crimes, as I arrived at Human Rights Watch in 2002. Philippe Sands's *East West Street: On the Origins of Genocide and Crimes Against Humanity* powerfully interweaves the stories of Lauterpacht, Lemkin and more personal themes. Geoffrey Robertson's *Crimes Against Humanity: The Struggle for Global Justice*, first published in 1999, is a valuable overview. For current updates, the *Asymmetrical Haircuts* podcast (Janet Anderson and Stephanie van den Berg), EJIL:Talk! (Blog of the European Journal of International Law, ejiltalk.org), justiceinfo.net, justsecurity.org, opiniojuris.org (in association with the International Commission of Jurists) and Ukraine Justice Report (Institute for War and Peace Reporting, iwpr.net) have all been valuable. *Haaretz* (facing sanctions from the Israeli government, at the time of writing) and the Israeli–Palestinian *+972 Magazine* are essential reading for their quality reporting, thoughtful analysis and humane perspectives.

Introduction

2   **colonial erasure of the local language:** *Translations* was originally
           performed in the midst of another conflict with identity at its heart.
           In Northern Ireland in 1980, during the euphemistically named
           'Troubles', there were standing ovations for Friel's play even as British
           army helicopters circled overhead. Ireland's RTÉ radio later described
           the premiere at Derry's Guildhall as 'one of the most remarkable and
           important theatrical events' in the country's history. (Brian Friel,
           Translations (London: Faber and Faber, 1981). '25th anniversary of
           Brian Friel's *Translations*', Rattlebag, RTÉ, broadcast 23 September
           2005.)

4   **'I stopped breathing':** Emma Bubola, 'A make-up artist recognized this
           Bucha victim's picture by her manicure', *New York Times*, 6 April 2022.
           Stefanija Bern and Janis Laizans, 'Friends, family mourn Bucha victim
           who became symbol of Ukraine's year-long war', Reuters, 22 February
           2023. Youser Al-Hlou and others, 'Caught on camera, traced by phone:
           The Russian military unit that killed dozens in Bucha', *New York Times*,
           22 December 2022.

6–8   **'crumbling', 'kill us all', 'Behind the scenes':** Steve Crawshaw: 'The
           crumbling of an empire', *Independent*, 11 April 1989; '"They'll kill us
           all one day. I'm so afraid"', 12 July 1991; 'Unfinished business: Behind
           the scenes at the new Nuremberg', *Independent on Sunday* magazine, 8
           April 2001.

6–7   **impending collapse, 'genies couldn't be enticed back':** The book
           proposal is quoted in the foreword to the paperback edition of Steve
           Crawshaw, *Goodbye to the USSR: The Collapse of Soviet Power* (London:
           Bloomsbury, 1993; first published 1992). Yuri Karyakin in *Moscow News*,
           quoted in *Goodbye to the USSR*. Steve Crawshaw, 'The Kremlin cannot
           put the lid back on: In Moscow, tanks will solve nothing', *Independent*, 1
           February 1991 (this article led to an invitation to write a book on those
           themes).

8   **'the hour of Europe':** Jacques Poos, foreign minister of Luxembourg,
           led a 'troika' peace mission of three European Community leaders
           to Yugoslavia in June 1991. Alan Riding, 'Conflict in Yugoslavia:
           Europeans send high-level team', *New York Times*, 29 June 1991.

11   **'built for Africa':** Ivana Kottasová and Madalena Araujo, 'Exclusive
           interview: ICC prosecutor seeks arrest warrants against Sinwar and
           Netanyahu for war crimes over October 7 and Gaza', CNN, 20
           May 2024.

13   **'real and imminent risk':** Application of the Convention on the
           Prevention and Punishment of the Crime of Genocide in the Gaza Strip
           (South Africa v. Israel), ICJ, 26 January 2024.

14   **'infamous German judges':** Statement by Prime Minister Benjamin
           Netanyahu, Ministry of Foreign Affairs, 20 May 2024.

14   **'If we do not demonstrate':** Karim Khan statement, ICC, 20 May
           2024.

15   **'presumably immovable order of things':** Czesław Miłosz, foreword to
           Adam Michnik, *Letters from Prison and other Essays*, trans. Maya Latynski
           (Berkeley: University of California Press, 1985).

16   **'stay the hand of vengeance':** Robert H. Jackson, 'Opening statement

before the International Military Tribunal', 21 November 1945, via Robert H. Jackson Center.

Chapter One: 'This is Most Inconsistent'

17–19   **Dunant, Solferino:** Henry Dunant, *A Memory of Solferino* (Washington DC: American National Red Cross, 1959; first published 1862), Caroline Moorehead, *Dunant's Dream: War, Switzerland, and the History of the Red Cross* (New York: Carroll & Graf, 1999). Corinne Chaponnière, *Henry Dunant: The Man of the Red Cross* (London: Bloomsbury, 2022).

19   **to Moynier's annoyance:** Moynier was, in Caroline Moorehead's words, 'unbearably jealous' of Dunant. After Dunant's bankruptcy and financial disgrace, Moynier had him thrown out of the Red Cross. Dunant became 'like a wolf ejected from the pack, to haunt the fringes of the growing Red Cross movement ... travelling from one end of Europe to the other to talk about his book and the Geneva Convention and to urge governments to sign'. (Moorehead, *Dunant's Dream*.)

19–20   **Abu Bakr, Christine de Pizan, Henry V:** David M. Crowe, *War Crimes, Genocide and Justice: A Global History* (New York: Palgrave Macmillan, 2014). Sherifa D. Zuhur and Youssef H. Aboul-Ehein, *Islamic Rulings on Warfare* (Carlisle, PA: US Army War College Press, 2004). Immi Talgren (ed.), *Portraits of Women in International Law: New Names and Forgotten Faces?* (Oxford: Oxford University Press, 2023). Anne Curry, 'The military ordnances of Henry V: texts and contexts', in Chris Given-Wilson, Ann Kettle and Len Scales (eds), *War, Government and Aristocracy in the British Isles c. 1150–1500: Essays in Honour of Michael Prestwich* (Woodbridge: Boydell & Brewer, 2008). Lawrence Weschler's essay 'Henry V at Srebrenica', in *Vermeer in Bosnia: Selected Writings* (New York: Vintage 2004; originally in the *New Yorker* in 1996), includes conversations with Theodor Meron, author of *Henry's Wars and Shakespeare's Law: Perspectives on the Laws of War in the Later Middle Ages* (Oxford: Clarendon Press, 1993). Meron, who later became president of the Yugoslavia war crimes tribunal (and who later still became an adviser to ICC prosecutor Karim Khan), speculates that, in his description of the order to slaughter prisoners in *Henry V*, Shakespeare may indirectly have been reflecting on the executions, just a decade before he wrote the play, of hundreds of shipwrecked sailors from the Spanish Armada. Meron told Weschler: 'His implied criticism of Henry's behavior can be read as a sort of rearguard defense of the kinds of chivalric norms that were already fast receding.'

20   **von Hagenbach:** Gregory S. Gordon, 'The Trial of Peter von Hagenbach: Reconciling History, Historiography and International Criminal Law', in Kevin Heller and Gerry Simpson (eds), *The Hidden Histories of War Crimes Trials* (Oxford: Oxford University Press, 2013).

21   **'short and pregnant and weighty':** Quoted in Moorehead, *Dunant's Dream*.

21–2   **'best interests of humanity', 'happy presage':** A. Pearce Higgins (ed.), *The Hague Peace Conferences and Other International Conferences concerning the Laws and Usages of War: Texts of Conventions with Commentaries* (Cambridge: Cambridge University Press, 1909), via Online Library of Liberty. 'Peace Conference at The Hague 1899: Rescript of the Russian

Emperor', 24 August 1898, via the Avalon Project, Yale Law School Lillian Goldman Law Library.

22   '"Let there be light"': *The Hugo Grotius celebration at Delft, July 4 1899* (The Hague: Martinus Nijhoff, 1899). 'Homage to Hugo Grotius', *New York Times*, 5 July 1899.

23   'purely moral sanction': Quoted in Christopher Keith Hall (Amnesty International), 'The first proposal for an international criminal court', *International Review of the Red Cross*, 322, March 1998.

23   poison gas: The German scientist Fritz Haber, who in 1918 would be awarded the Nobel Prize in Chemistry, described poison gas as 'a higher form of killing' and said it was 'a way of saving countless lives, if it meant that the war could be brought to an end sooner'. British newspapers complained of German 'frightfulness'. But, despite the clear Hague prohibition, British and French forces themselves began to use poison gas. As a correspondent of the *Berliner Tageblatt* described an attack in 1915: 'Behind the gas and smoke cloud there suddenly emerged Englishmen in thick lines and storming columns. They rose suddenly from the earth wearing smoke masks over their faces and looking not like soldiers but like devils.' Sir John French, commander of the British Expeditionary Force, boasted of 'marked success' with the use of gas. The Allies' justification – which can still be heard in different contexts in some of the most deadly conflicts today – was, in effect: 'The other side ignored the rules first, so we should, too.' (Diana Preston, *A Higher Form of Killing: Six Weeks in the First World War that Forever Changed the Nature of Warfare* (London: Bloomsbury, 2015).)

23   Leipzig trials: Gary Jonathan Bass, *Stay the Hand of Vengeance: The Politics of War Crimes Tribunals* (Princeton: Princeton University Press, 2000).

24   'kidnapping the Kaiser' and other details: Willian A. Schabas, *The Trial of the Kaiser* (Oxford: Oxford University Press, 2018).

24   'most intriguing hypotheticals': Geoffrey Robertson, *The Trial of Vladimir Putin* (London: Biteback, 2024).

24–5   *New York Times* on Armenians, Morgenthau: Samantha Power, *A Problem from Hell: America and the Age of Genocide* (New York: Basic Books, 2002).

25   'crimes against Christianity': Bass, *Stay the Hand of Vengeance*. Schabas, *The Trial of the Kaiser*.

25   'Nuremberg that failed': Bass, *Stay the Hand of Vengeance*.

25   'Who, after all speaks': Adolf Hitler, Obersalzberg, 22 August 1939, quoted in Louis Lochner, *What about Germany?* (New York: Dodd, Mead & Co., 1943). Earlier attempts to discredit Lochner's account of the speech to Hitler's generals have themselves been discredited. See e.g. Norman Domeier, 'Das Kriegsziel besteht in der physischen Vernichtung des Gegners', *Der Spiegel*, 22 August 2022 and Norman Domeier, 'World domination and genocide: The "Lochner Version" of Hitler's speech on 22 August 1939, a key document of national socialist ideology', George L. Mosse Program in History lecture, University of Wisconsin-Madison, 12 July 2023.

26   'I have lived only to avenge': 'Assassin boasts of Talaat's death', *New York Times*, 17 March 1921.

26   **'a statistic'**: Kurt Tucholsky, 'Französischer Witz', *Vossische Zeitung*, 23 August 1925.

27   **'inconsistent'**: Most Lemkin quotations in this chapter come from his autobiography, Donna-Lee Frieze (ed.), *Totally Unofficial: The Autobiography of Raphael Lemkin* (New Haven: Yale University Press, 2013). Lemkin's story is also told in Samantha Power, *A Problem from Hell: America and the Age of Genocide* (New York: Basic Books, 2002) and Philippe Sands, *East West Street: On the Origins of Genocide and Crimes against Humanity* (London: Weidenfeld & Nicolson, 2016). Also: John Cooper, *Raphael Lemkin and the Struggle for the Genocide Convention* (Basingstoke: Palgrave Macmillan, 2008) and Douglas Irvin-Erickson, *Raphaël Lemkin and the Concept of Genocide* (Philadelphia: University of Pennsylvania Press, 2017).

27–8   **'counter-revolutionary bourgeoisie', Ukraine famine, 'fight to the death'**: Irvin-Erickson, *Raphaël Lemkin and the Concept of Genocide.*

28   **'ubiquitous odor'**: Anne Applebaum, *Red Famine: Stalin's War on Ukraine* (London: Allen Lane, 2017).

29   **'thought I was exaggerating'**: Interview with Associated Press, 1995 (quoted in *Guardian* obituary of Karski, 15 July 2000).

29   **'methodical, merciless butchery'**: Prime Minister Winston Churchill's broadcast to the world about the meeting with President Roosevelt, 24 August 1941, via Ibiblio digital library and archive.

29   **'decisive operations elsewhere'**: David Wyman, 'Why Auschwitz wasn't bombed', in Yizrael Gutman and Michael Berenbaum (eds), *Anatomy of the Auschwitz Death Camp* (Bloomington: Indiana University Press, 1998).

32   **'until the day of final victory'**: *Punishment for War Crimes: The Inter-Allied Declaration Signed at St James's Palace, London, 13 January 1942* (London: HMSO, 1942).

32   **'politely and nicely'**: Eichmann trial testimony (19 April 1961), quoted in Mark Roseman, *The Wannsee Conference and the Final Solution: A Reconsideration* (New York: Henry Holt, 2002).

33   **War Crimes Commission, 'in for a very thin time'**: Telford Taylor, *The Anatomy of the Nuremberg Trials: A Personal Memoir* (New York: Knopf, 1992).

33   **von Moltke, Hague tribunal, ignored, beehives**: Ger van Roon, *German Resistance to Hitler: Count von Moltke and the Kreisau Circle* (New York: Van Nostrand Reinhold, 1971). Michael Balfour and Julian Frisby, *Helmuth von Moltke: A Leader against Hitler* (London: Macmillan, 1972). Peter Hoffmann, *Behind Valkyrie: German Resistance to Hitler, Documents* (Montreal: McGill-Queen's University Press, 2011).

34   **Kharkiv, 'medieval barbarians'**: Greg Dawson, *Judgment before Nuremberg: The Holocaust in the Ukraine and the First Nazi War Crimes Trial* (New York: Pegasus, 2012).

34   **Ehrenburg**: Michael J. Bazyler and Frank M. Tuerkheimer, *Forgotten Trials of the Holocaust* (New York: New York University Press, 2014).

34–5   **'looking forward to the verdict'**: Andrey Kurkov, 'I have run out of words for the horror of Putin's crimes in Ukraine', *Guardian*, 13 March 2022; also in Kurkov, *Diary of an Invasion* (London: Mountain Leopard, 2022).

35   'ill-starred enterprise': Bass, *Stay the Hand of Vengeance*.

35   **murdered and beheaded:** The comedy-satire *Woe from Wit* by
       playwright-ambassador Alexander Griboyedov (1795–1829) remains
       popular in Russian theatres to this day; it is said to be the most quoted
       play in the Russian language. Laurence Kelly's *Diplomacy and Murder in
       Tehran: Alexander Griboyedov and Imperial Russia's Mission to the Shah of
       Persia* (London: I.B. Tauris, 2002) tells the story.

35–6   **Stalin proposed a toast, 'bumping off', Guy Liddell:** Bass, *Stay
       the Hand of Vengeance*. Ian Cobain: 'Britain favoured executions over
       Nuremberg trials for Nazi leaders', *Guardian*, 26 October 2012;
       'Churchill proposed "three for one" bombing of German villages in
       retaliation for massacre of Czech civilians', 2 January 2006.

36–7   **'really a joke':** Tom Hofmann, *Benjamin Ferencz: Nuremberg Prosecutor
       and Peace Advocate* (Jefferson, NC: McFarland, 2014).

38   **'bloodlands':** Timothy Snyder, *Bloodlands: Europe between Hitler and
       Stalin* (New York: Basic Books, 2010).

38   **London Conference, Claridge's, Trainin:** Francine Hirsch, *Soviet
       Judgment at Nuremberg: A New History of the International Military Tribunal
       after World War II* (New York: Oxford University Press, 2020) is packed
       with stories about the trial and the lead-up. Taylor, *The Anatomy of the
       Nuremberg Trials*.

39   **'may prefer death to life':** Elihu Lauterpacht, *The Life of Hersch
       Lauterpacht* (Cambridge: Cambridge University Press, 2012) includes
       Lauterpacht's letters. Sands, *East West Street* contains details on
       Lauterpacht and Jackson.

40   **Jackson's copy of *Axis Rule*:** Irvin-Erickson, *Raphaël Lemkin and the
       Concept of Genocide*.

41   **crumpled and torn by defeat:** John Dos Passos, 'Report from
       Nürnberg', *LIFE* magazine, 10 December 1945.

42   **'bench of shame':** Vasily Grossman, trans. Robert Chandler, *The
       People Immortal* (London: MacLehose, 2022). Grossman's masterpiece
       novel *Life and Fate* includes a final letter from a mother to her son, a
       powerful re-imagining of the last days of Grossman's own mother in the
       Berdychev ghetto in Ukraine in 1941.

42   **'preternaturally deep wrinkles', 'naughty-boy expression':** Rebecca
       West, 'Extraordinary Exile', *New Yorker*, 30 August 1946. John Dos Passos:
       'Report from Nürnberg'; *Tour of Duty* (Boston: Houghton Mifflin, 1946).

42   **'We can do it with incendiaries':** W. G. Sebald, trans. Anthea Bell, *On
       the Natural History of Destruction* (London: Hamish Hamilton, 2003).

42   **'as in the case of the bombardment at Rotterdam':** 'Tentative list of
       war crimes' (1942), in Elihu Lauterpacht (ed.), *International Law: Collected
       Papers of Hersch Lauterpacht* (Cambridge: Cambridge University Press,
       1977), vol. 5.

43   **'phosphorus flames', 'like a giant', 'the moon':** Sebald, *On the
       Natural History of Destruction*. Steve Crawshaw, 'Rubble-rousing stuff',
       Independent, 13 February 1995. Kurt Vonnegut, *Slaughter-House Five. Or,
       the Children's Crusade, a Duty-Dance with Death* (New York: Delacorte,
       1969).

43   **'bones of one British Grenadier':** Sinclair McKay, *Dresden: The Fire and
       the Darkness* (London: Penguin, 2020).

43–4   'appalling climate', 'cowed from the air': Frederick Taylor, *Dresden: Tuesday, 13 February 1945* (London: Bloomsbury, 2004). A. J. P. Taylor, *English History 1914–1945* (Oxford: Clarendon Press, 1965), quoted in Marek Pruszewicz, '1920s British air bombing campaign in Iraq', BBC, 7 October 2014.

44   'the silence of Nuremberg': Telford Taylor, *Nuremberg and Vietnam: An American Tragedy* (Chicago: Quadrangle, 1970).

44   'an army of rapists', 'act of blasphemy', books banned: Antony Beevor, '"The Russian soldiers raped every German female from eight to 80"', *Guardian*, 1 May 2002, on the occasion of the publication of *Berlin: The Downfall 1945* (London: Penguin, 2002). Antony Beevor, 'By banning my book, Russia is deluding itself about its past', *Guardian*, 5 August 2015.

45   'ugly offspring': Ilya Milshtein, 'The Lessons of Colonel Kovalyov', Radio Free Europe-Radio Liberty, 8 June 2009. *Russia and the War: Molotov's speech to the Supreme Soviet of the Soviet Union, October 31st 1939* (London: Modern Books, 1939). In his speech, Molotov said Hitler was 'striving for the earliest termination of the war and for peace', and described the idea of Poland's independence ever being restored as 'absurd'.

45   Katyn, Stalin approved the executions, 'unclear': Jane Rogoyska, *Surviving Katyń: Stalin's Polish Massacres and the Search for Truth* (London: Oneworld, 2021). Javier Cuesta, 'Russia rewrites the history of 22,000 Poles murdered by Soviet forces during World War II', *El País*, 28 April 2023.

46   'potentially risky move': Hirsch, *Soviet Judgment at Nuremberg*.

46   'quixotic undertaking': Robert Jackson, 'Nuremberg in retrospect: Legal answer to international lawlessness', *American Bar Association Journal*, 35:10 (October 1949).

46   nineteen guilty verdicts and three acquittals: Martin Bormann (who, unknown to the prosecutors, was already dead) was tried *in absentia*. There were originally twenty-four defendants (the maximum that the court could accommodate). Armaments magnate Gustav Krupp was not in court because of illness; Robert Ley committed suicide in prison before the trial began.

47   empty, stunned feeling: Martha Gellhorn, 'The Paths of Glory', in *The Face of War* (London: Granta, 1993; first published 1946).

47   'usually insubordinate': Hofmann, *Benjamin Ferencz*. Benjamin Ferencz and Michael P. Scharf, 'Last living Nuremberg trial prosecutor recalls his work on the Einsatzgruppen trial', *Judicature*, 105:3 (2021).

47   'lost and bedraggled fellow': Benjamin B. Ferencz, 'Mass murderers seek to justify genocide', benferencz.org.

48   'It cannot be said': *The Exhibition: Memorium Nuremberg Trials* (Nuremberg: Museen der Stadt Nürnberg, 2023), quoting Alfred Döblin (pseudonym Hans Fiedeler), *Der Nürnberger Lehrprozess* (Baden-Baden: Neuer Bücherdienst, 1946)

48   'an ambiguous body': Marlies Glasius, *The International Criminal Court: A Global Civil Society Achievement* (Abingdon: Routledge, 2006), quoting 'Jean-Paul Sartre's Inaugural Statement to the Tribunal', in John Duffett (ed.), *Against the Crime of Silence: Proceedings of the Russell International War Crimes Tribunal* (New York: Simon and Schuster, 1968).

49   'against the will, 'sham employment', 'worst hypocrisy': Gary J. Bass, *Judgement at Tokyo: World War II on Trial and the Making of Modern Asia* (London: Pan Macmillan, 2023). Ian Buruma, 'What the Tokyo trial reveals about empire, memory and judgment', *New Yorker*, 16 October 2023.

49   'Murayama apology': Statement by Prime Minister Tomiichi Murayama, Japanese Ministry of Foreign Affairs, 15 August 1995.

50   'Nuremberg will remain the fount', 'half accomplished': *New York Times*, 26 August 1946, quoted in Sands, *East West Street*. Hirsch, *Soviet Judgment at Nuremberg*.

50   'Nuremberg is enough!': Frieze (ed.), *Totally Unofficial*.

51   'tilting his lance in solitary grandeur': Quoted in William Korey, *An Epitaph for Raphael Lemkin*, Jacob Blaustein Institute, 2001.

51   'a Jew recently come': Lauterpacht, *The Life of Hersch Lauterpacht*.

52   'generations to come', seven people at funeral: Cooper, *Raphael Lemkin and the Struggle for the Genocide Convention*, quoting letter from Catherine Bradshaw Boyd. A. M. Rosenthal, 'On my mind: A man called Lemkin', *New York Times*, 18 October 1988.

Chapter Two: 'We Must Sin Quietly'

54   'sufficiently civilised': Robert Jackson, 'Nuremberg in retrospect: Legal answer to international lawlessness', 1 September 1949, via Robert H. Jackson Center.

55   Hitler a 'fine fellow': Anthony Read and David Fisher, *The Deadly Embrace: Hitler, Stalin and the Nazi-Soviet Pact 1939–1941* (New York: Norton, 1988).

55   'in line with international and state law': Vladimir Putin, '75th anniversary of the great victory: shared responsibility to history and our future', Kremlin, 19 June 2020.

56   Sarah Obama and torture: Ben Macintyre and Paul Orengoh, 'Beatings and abuse made Barack Obama's grandfather loathe the British,', *The Times*, 3 December 2008.

56   'Labour and freedom': This and other details come from Caroline Elkins's *Britain's Gulag: The Brutal End of Empire in Kenya* (London: Pimlico, 2005).

57   'sin quietly': Ian Cobain and Richard Norton-Taylor, 'Sins of colonialists lay concealed for decades in secret archive', *Guardian*, 18 April 2012. Ian Cobain, *Cruel Britannia: A Secret History of Torture* (London: Harvill Secker, 2012).

57   'all the hatreds': Elkins, *Britain's Gulag*.

57   'sincere regret': 'The UK regrets torture and compensates Kenyan victims after more than 50 years', REDRESS, 6 June 2013. 'The Mau Mau claims', Leigh Day Solicitors.

58–9   'All day, through the floorboards': This and other details come from Alistair Horne, *A Savage War of Peace: Algeria 1954–1962* (New York: New York Review Books 2006; first published 1977). Adam Shatz made powerful comparisons between Philippeville and Gaza in 'Vengeful pathologies', *London Review of Books*, 2 November 2023.

59   Sidi-Hamed: Steve Crawshaw, 'Algeria rejects UN help as stunned survivors tell of massacre horror', *Independent*, 21 January 1998.

60   'because it was unpunished', 'tortured then murdered': 'Déclaration sur du Président de la République sur la mort de Maurice Audin', Elysée, 13 September 2018. Angelique Chrisafis, 'France admits systematic torture during Algeria war for first time', *Guardian*, 13 September 2018. 'Reconnaissance par la France de l'assassinat d'Ali Boumendjel', Elysée, 2 March 2021. 'Macron admits French forces "tortured and murdered" Algerian freedom fighter', France 24, 3 March 2021.

60   'We are not prepared': International Conference on Military Trials, London, 1945: Minutes of Conference Session of July 23, 1945, via the Avalon Project.

60   'a fine dramatic statement': Bosley Crowther, 'The Screen: Judgment at Nuremberg', *New York Times*, 20 December 1961.

61   'massive, systematic and deliberate': Quoted in Geoffrey Nice, *Justice for All and How to Achieve It* (London: Scala, 2017).

61–3   'are we supposed to kill', just mowed 'em down, suddenly heard the crack, 'operation, not an aberration': Michael Bilton and Kevin Sim, *Four Hours in My Lai: A War Crime and its Aftermath* (London: Viking, 1992). Nick Turse, *Kill Anything That Moves: The Real American War in Vietnam* (New York: Metropolitan, 2013).

62   'US troops surround Reds': *Stars and Stripes*, Pacific edition, 18 March 1968, quoted in Bilton and Sim, *Four Hours in My Lai*.

63–4   today's tragedy, 'sheerest hypocrisy': Taylor, *Nuremberg and Vietnam*.

64   'ability to forget': Sebald, *On the Natural History of Destruction*.

64   'No one is a Nazi': Martha Gellhorn, 'Das deutsche Volk' in *The Face of War*; originally in *Collier's* magazine, 'We were never Nazis!', 26 May 1945.

65   'some Germans blame Hitler': Nicholas Doman, 'Political consequences of the Nuremberg trial', *Annals of the American Academy of Political and Social Science*, 246 (July 1946).

65   'death chambers etc', 'terrible suffering': Steve Crawshaw, 'Germans open the pages to reveal a censored past', *Independent*, 18 April 1995. Hans Ebeling, *Deutsche Geschichte* (Braunschweig: Westermann, 1952). Hans Thierbach, *Europa und die Welt* (Paderborn: Schöningh, 1956). Steve Crawshaw, *Easier Fatherland: Germany and the Twenty-First Century* (London: Continuum, 2004).

66   more than three thousand convicted: Frank Trentmann, *Out of the Darkness: The Germans 1942–2022* (London: Allen Lane, 2023).

66   Giordano: Andreas Mix, 'Als Westdeutschland aufwachte' ['When West Germany awoke'], *Der Spiegel*, 27 April 2008

67   'easy access by rail': Testimony of Rudolf Höss, Commandant of Auschwitz, 15 April 1946, via Famous Trials.

67   'more than ordinarily' compromising: Hannah Arendt, *Eichmann in Jerusalem: A Report on the Banality of Evil* (New York: Viking, 1963).

67   'It is the be-all and end-all': Fritz Bauer, 'Zu den Naziverbrecher-Prozessen', in *Stimme der Gemeinde zum Kirchlichen Leben, zur Politik, Wirtschaft und Kultur* 18 (September 1963), originally a radio interview (NDR, 25 August 1963), quoted in Rebecca Wittmann, *Beyond Justice: The Auschwitz Trial* (Cambridge, MA: Harvard University Press, 2005) and Ronen Steinke, trans. Sinéad Crowe, *Fritz Bauer: The Jewish*

Prosecutor who Brought Eichmann and Auschwitz to Trial (Bloomington: Indiana University Press, 2020).

68   **'The more horrible'**: Martin Walser, 'Unser Auschwitz', in *Heimatkunde: Aufsätze und Reden* (Frankfurt am Main: Suhrkamp 1968), quoted in Wittmann, *Beyond Justice*.

68   **get rid of our exalted attitude**: Peter Weiss, *The Investigation* (London: Calder and Boyars, 1966).

69   **'condoned obedience'**: Mary Fulbrook, *Reckonings: Legacies of Nazi Persecution and the Quest for Justice* (Oxford: Oxford University Press, 2018). In more recent years, the theme of earlier German leniency for Nazi war criminals provided the hidden twist of Ferdinand von Schirach's bestselling novel, *The Collini Case* (London: Penguin, 2012; published in Germany in 2011). The 'what other options were left to me?' storyline contains clear echoes of the testimony of Soghomon Tehlirian at his murder trial in 1921, which originally influenced Raphael Lemkin. Von Schirach's own grandfather, Baldur von Schirach, had been head of the Hitler Youth and was convicted at Nuremberg for crimes against humanity. (Ferdinand von Schirach, 'Why I cannot answer questions about my grandfather', *Der Spiegel*, 23 September 2011.)

By contrast, Tobias Buck's *Final Verdict: A Holocaust Trial in the Twenty-First Century* (London: Weidenfeld & Nicolson, 2024) quotes the judge's summary at the trial of a former SS guard in Hamburg in 2020. Anne Meier-Göring described the ninety-two-year-old defendant – a teenager at the time of his complicity in thousands of murders in Stutthof concentration camp – as 'one of the helpers of this man-made hell'. Indirectly echoing Fritz Bauer from half a century earlier, the judge concluded: 'The decisive questions raised by this trial were: what crimes against humanity are humans capable of, and what brings people to commit cruelties like those at Stutthof concentration camp, or to take part in them? Because it is only from the answers to these questions that we as humans can learn for the future.'

70   **'destroy the rebellious tribes'**: Quoted by Ezer Weizman in 'Three genocides', *London Review of Books*, 25 April 2024 and by David Olusoga and Casper W. Erichsen in *The Kaiser's Holocaust: Germany's Forgotten Genocide* (London: Faber and Faber, 2010).

70   **'In both cases'**: Weizman, 'Three Genocides'.

70   **'From the Herero'**: Amos Goldberg, 'Yes it is genocide', originally published in Hebrew-language *Local Call*, translated by Palestine Project (thepalestineproject.medium.com), 18 April 2024; includes links to *Local Call* original and to *Haaretz* Hebrew-language article from 2011.

71   **'abominable atrocities'**: German government and Namibian government joint declaration, 15 May 2021, Dialogue on Namibia's Past. The dialogue between the two governments remains controversial, with complaints that communities most affected have been excluded. See e.g. 'The "reconciliation agreement" – A lost opportunity', European Center on Constitutional and Human Rights, June 2021.

71   **Court-martial? What are you talking about!, 'acted correctly'**: David Van Reybrouck, *Revolusi: Indonesia and the Birth of the Modern World* (London: Bodley Head, 2024). Manfred Gerstenfeld, 'How the

Netherlands hid its war crimes for decades', Begin-Sadat Centre for Strategic Studies, 31 August 2020.

72   'systematic and widespread': Daniel Boffey, 'Dutch PM apologises for state's role in abuses in 1940s Indonesian war', *Guardian*, 17 February 2022.

73   Operation MENU: Nick Turse, 'Blood on his hands: Survivors of Kissinger's secret war in Cambodia reveal unreported mass killings', *The Intercept*, 23 May 2023.

73   'They are murderous thugs': Meeting with Thai foreign minister Chatichai Chunhuwan, 26 November 1975, transcript at National Security Archive, George Washington University.

74   'an abomination': Elizabeth Becker, *When the War was Over: Cambodia and the Khmer Rouge Revolution* (New York: PublicAffairs, 1998; first published 1986).

74   geopolitics trumped human rights: The philosophy was explicit. In 1948, George Kennan, the influential policy planning director at the US State Department (who became famous for his views on 'containment' of the Soviet Union), argued: 'We should cease to talk about vague and ... unreal objectives such as human rights ... The less we are hampered by idealistic slogans, the better.' In Kennan's view: 'We should not hesitate before police repression by the local government ... It is better to have a strong regime in power than a liberal government if it is indulgent and penetrated by Communists.' The lethal consequences of that policy would become clear, not least in Chile a quarter of a century later. (Quoted in Lawrence Weschler, *A Miracle, a Universe: Settling Accounts with Torturers* (Chicago: University of Chicago Press, 1998).)

74   'Much sooner than later': Quoted in Andrew Hsiao and Andrea Lim, *The Verso Book of Dissent: From Spartacus to the Shoe-Thrower of Baghdad* (London: Verso, 2010).

75   instead of celebrating: Nixon-Kissinger State Department transcript, 16 September 1973, in Peter Kornbluh, *The Pinochet File: A Declassified Dossier on Atrocity and Accountability* (New York: New Press, 2013), and National Security Archive online.

75   'nothing but human rights', 'did a great service': Kornbluh, *The Pinochet File* and National Security Archive.

75   'pretty gentlemanly uniforms': Televisión Nacional de Chile, 27 March 1991.

75–6   Everywhere I turned: Ariel Dorfman, 'A vicious circle', *Guardian*, 17 January 2008.

76   'All houses have been burned': Steve Crawshaw, 'Election offers no hope of an end to killings', *Sunday Times*, 20 October 1985. *South American Handbook 1985* (Bath: Trade and Travel, 1984)

76–7   'Give it to them!': Robert Nickelsberg, 'Witnessing dignity amid death in Guatemala's civil war', *New York Times*, 29 November 2017.

77   'like little ants': Ed Stocker, 'Victims of "death flights": Drugged, dumped by aircraft – but not forgotten', *Independent*, 27 November 2012.

78   'executed in accordance', 'most savage tragedy': Sam Ferguson, *The Disappeared: Remnants of a Dirty War* (Lincoln, NE: University of Nebraska Press, 2023).

78   'hell or heaven': Jorge Luis Borges, 'Lunes 22 de julio de 1985', *Clarin*, 23 July 1985. *El País*, 9 August 1985.

79   **'I will kill them all'**: Joost Hiltermann, *A Poisonous Affair: America, Iraq, and the Gassing of Halabja* (Cambridge: Cambridge University Press, 2007).

79   **'strongly in favour'**: Winston Churchill, War Office Memorandum, 12 May 1919, America's National Churchill Museum. Geoff Simons, *Iraq: From Sumer to Saddam* (London: St Martin's Press, 1994).

80   **'killed all natural life', 'last embrace', 'day of judgment'**: Hiltermann, *A Poisonous Affair*. David Hirst, 'The Kurdish victims caught unaware by cyanide', *Guardian*, 22 March 1988. *Genocide in Iraq: The Anfal Campaign against the Kurds*, Human Rights Watch, 1993. Andrew Cockburn, 'An inconvenient truth', *The Nation*, 23 August 2007.

81   **golden cowboy spurs, 'We already knew'**: Hiltermann, *A Poisonous Affair*. Shane Harris and Matthew M. Aid, 'CIA files prove America helped Saddam as he gassed Iran', *Foreign Policy*, 26 August 2013.

81   **'give pause to tyrannical regimes'**: *Genocide in Iraq*, Human Rights Watch.

81   **'using weapons of mass destruction'**: David E. Sanger and Thom Shanker, 'War planners begin to speak of war's risks', *New York Times*, 18 February 2003.

82   **'human cost of Saddam's polices'**: *Saddam Hussein: Crimes and Human Rights Abuses*, Foreign and Commonwealth Office, December 2002.

82   **'In 1988 they closed their eyes'**: Agence France Presse, 22 October 2002, quoted in Hiltermann, *A Poisonous Affair*.

Chapter Three: 'Everything is Going to Plan'

85   **'respect for the highest standards'**: London Conference, Statement of Principles, 26 August 1992, Peace Agreements Database.

85   **'peace with justice'**: Steve Crawshaw, 'Search for the peace principle', *Independent on Sunday*, 23 August 1992.

85–6   **'The community of nations'**: Statement delivered by Klaus Kinkel, London Conference, 26 August 1992, Special Collections and Archives, University of Liverpool.

86   **'we have a policy for peace'**: Steve Crawshaw and Tony Barber, 'Peace? What peace?', *Independent on Sunday*, 30 August 1992.

87   **'taxi drivers for the Serbs'**: Steve Crawshaw, 'Where hope is dying', *Independent Magazine*, 1 August 1992.

87   **'declarations', 'resolutions'**: *Oslobodjenje*, 17 July 1992.

87   **'true compassion'**: Zbigniew Herbert, trans. Czesław Miłosz, 'Report from a Besieged City', *New York Review of Books*, 18 August 1983.

88   **'he'll come tomorrow'**: Samuel Beckett, *Waiting for Godot* (London: Faber, 2010; first performed 1953).

88   **'age-old feuds and hatreds'**: John Major, Comments on the Balkans, 31 December 1992, John Major Archive. Brendan Simms, *Unfinest Hour: Britain and the Destruction of Bosnia* (London: Allen Lane, 2001), powerfully dissects the diplomatic failures at that time.

88   **'shockwaves through the entire federation'**: Steve Crawshaw, 'Violence simmers in Kosovo', *Financial Times* syndication service, 2 July 1982.

89   **'nice idea', 'hundreds, probably thousands', 'Serbs will gain victory'**: Steve Crawshaw: 'Slovene referendum could define the future shape of

Yugoslavia: Tomorrow's vote may mark the beginning of the end for the country', *Independent*, 22 December 1990; 'A town just waiting to trigger a civil war', 10 April 1991; 'A nation at boiling point', 15 April 1991; 'Worst "yet to come" in Yugoslavia', 8 May 1991.

89   **made to sit in the dock:** Mirko Klarin, 'Nuremberg now', *Borba*, 16 May 1991. Included in *The Path to The Hague: Selected Documents on the Origins of the ICTY* (The Hague: UN – International Criminal Tribunal for the Former Yugoslavia, 1996).

90   **'Jackson Pollock':** Steve Crawshaw, 'Bosnian leader insists on co-existence', *Independent*, 29 August 1992.

90   *etničko čišćenje:* Like *'Endlösung der Judenfrage'* ('final solution of the Jewish question') half a century earlier, the phrase 'ethnic cleansing' began as a euphemism, then became a familiar shorthand for the crime itself. The Rome Statute of the International Criminal Court does not mention ethnic cleansing in those words, talking instead of 'deportation or forcible transfer of population'. But the once-euphemistic phrase that Bosnian Serb leaders themselves used is now usually accepted as a clear description of the crime itself.

90–3 **Bijeljina, Arkan, Sarajevo:** Steve Crawshaw: 'Serbian Tigers take over Bosnian towns', *Independent*, 11 April 1992; 'The war crimes secrets of Milošević that meant the death sentence for Arkan', 22 January 2000; 'Bosnian Serbs deaf to peace calls', 12 April 1992; 'Ten a day killed in a city of snipers', 17 July 1992; '"But tomorrow I may be shot"', 19 July 1992; 'Where hope is dying', 1 August 1992.

92–3 **Čelinac decree:** 'Decision on the status of the non-Serbian population of Čelinac municipality', Unified Court Records Database, 23 July 1992. Steve Crawshaw, 'Bosnia doubts London pledges', *Independent*, 29 August 1992

94   **'With their luggage, and everything':** Steve Crawshaw, 'A strange world in which Bosnian Serbs can do no wrong', *Independent*, 31 July 1992.

95   **'We know what "Never again!" mean's:** David Rieff, *Slaughterhouse: Bosnia and the Failure of the West* (New York: Simon and Schuster, 1995).

95   **'fig leaf':** Crawshaw, 'Unfinished business'.

95   **'no budget':** Quoted in Bass: *Stay the Hand of Vengeance*.

96   **'Like being born a second time':** Steve Crawshaw, 'Srebrenica 20 years after the genocide: why the survivors need closure', *Independent*, 7 July 2015.

96   **'We give this town':** 'Ratko Mladić trial told of Srebrenica chaos', BBC, 17 May 2012.

97   **'doing a little filming now', 'Come down, Nermin!', 'More than any other UN official':** 'Scorpions unit footage, unknown date after 12 July 1995', srebrenica.sensecentar.org. The Osmanović video is included in 'The Trial of Ratko Mladić', *Frontline*, PBS, 2019. David Rohde, *Endgame: The Betrayal and Fall of Srebrenica, Europe's Worst Massacre since World War II* (London: Penguin, 2012).

98   **'They took them to the meadow':** International Criminal Tribunal for the Former Yugoslavia, Case IT-96-22-T.

98   **'no apprehension under any circumstances':** Crawshaw, 'Unfinished business'.

99   'must have good relations': 'In Plain Sight', *Public Eye*, CBS, 8
            October 1997.
100   Kill them all in turn: 'Srebrenica trial: a chilling radio interception
            puts Krstić on the spot', Institute for War and Peace Reporting, 4
            November 2000. Crawshaw, 'Unfinished business'. Julian Borger, *The
            Butcher's Trail: How the Search for Balkan War Criminals Became the World's
            Most Successful Manhunt* (New York: Other Press, 2016).
100   'We live like dead people': Steve Crawshaw, 'Serb leader stokes fires of
            war in Kosovo', *Independent*, 26 March 1998.
101   'He just destroyed our country': Steve Crawshaw, 'Milošević faces
            rally of 20,000', *Independent*, 18 July 1999.
101   'just received': Steve Crawshaw and Marcus Tanner, 'Milošević told:
            your time is up', *Independent*, 7 October 2000.
102–3   'This is an abduction!', gorilla suit, Are your superiors aware?,
            'Who are you?': Borger, *The Butcher's Trail*.
104   'moral dignity of our country': Nenad Pejić, 'Mladić's arrest. Serbia's
            gain', Radio Free Europe/Radio Liberty, 26 May 2011.
104   Balkan Investigative Reporting Network: As a journalist covering
            the Balkans, I worked closely with Gordana Igrić; I am on the board
            of BIRN.
105   '*Peux ce que veux*': Roméo Dallaire, *Shake Hands with the Devil: The
            Failure of Humanity in Rwanda* (Toronto: Random House, 2003)
105   'carnage which is to come', 'bad patriot', 'my children': Alison Des
            Forges: 'The method in Rwanda's madness', *Washington Post*, 17 April
            1994; '"Take care of my children"', 8 April 1994.
105   'not my struggle': Quoted in Prudence Bushnell, 'Leadership and
            policy-making: Lessons from the US government', *Brown Journal of World
            Affairs*, 25:2 (spring/summer 2019).
106   'sweetly sickening odor': Alison Des Forges, *Leave None to Tell the
            Story: Genocide in Rwanda*, Human Rights Watch, 1999
106   'ceasefire with the Jews', 'a laughing stock': Linda Melvern, *A People
            Betrayed: The Role of the West in Rwanda's Genocide* (London: Zed Books,
            2000).
107–8   'actually "do something"', 'every reason to believe', 'radios don't
            kill people': Power, *A Problem from Hell*.
108   'didn't fully appreciate', 'people that were bringing these decisions
            to me': *Ghosts of Rwanda*, PBS, 2004, quoting Clinton visit to Kigali in
            1998 and meeting with students in Arkansas in 2003.
108   'horrors of the Holocaust': Clifford Krauss, 'US backs away from
            charge of atrocities in Bosnia camps', *New York Times*, 5 August 1992,
            quoted in Power, *A Problem from Hell*.
109   'spoils of war': Bill Berkeley, 'Judgement Day', *Washington Post*, 11
            October 1998.
110   'screamed', 'diatribe': John Hooper, 'I was sacked as Rwanda genocide
            prosecutor for challenging president, says Del Ponte', *Guardian*, 15
            September 2003. Carla del Ponte with Chuck Sudetic, *Madame Prosecutor:
            Confrontations with Humanity's Worst Criminals and the Culture of Impunity*
            (New York: Other Press, 2009).
111   'soil on the volcano': Steve Crawshaw, '"They made us wait in a line to
            be killed, then put the bodies in a hole"', *Independent*, 27 January 2001.

111   'overwhelming' responsibilities: Barbara Wojazer and Melissa Bell,
        'Macron seeks forgiveness for France's role in Rwanda genocide, but
        stops short of apology', CNN, 27 May 2021.
111   'waiting a long time': Julian Borger, 'Rwandan war criminal tracked to
        South Africa', *Guardian*, 25 May 2023.

Chapter Four: 'An Idea Whose Time has Come'

113   'The goalposts are on the move': Steve Crawshaw, 'A region where
        goalposts are on the move', *Independent*, 26 January 1989.
114   'What I saw after my release': Adam Michnik, 'Letter from the
        Gdansk prison', *New York Review of Books*, 18 July 1985. Included in
        Michnik, *Letters from Prison and Other Essays*.
114   'We finished off': Steve Crawshaw, 'A Pole apart', *Independent on Sunday*
        magazine, 14 February 1999.
115   'tanks can solve nothing': 'Baltic Independence' (dir. Ian Taylor),
        The World This Week, Channel 4 Television, 19 August 1989.
        Steve Crawshaw, 'Estonia looks ahead to secession', *Independent*, 13
        March 1989.
115   'weapons in the hand': 'Staatsfeindlichkeit nicht länger dulden'
        ['Hostility to the state can no longer be tolerated'], *Leipziger Volkszeitung*,
        6 October 1989. Steve Crawshaw: 'Militias submit to the power of the
        flower', *Independent*, 11 October 1989; 'Another crack in the Wall', 12
        September 1989; 'In search of a King Canute', 18 October 1989; 'The
        redundant symbol of the Berlin Wall', 8 November 1989; 'Havel asks for
        change before it is too late', 4 November 1989.
116   'zigzag to the precipice', Herodotus: Ryszard Kapuściński: *Shah
        of Shahs* (New York: Houghton Mifflin Harcourt, 1985); *Travels with
        Herodotus* (New York: Vintage, 2007). Herodotus, trans. Tom Holland,
        The Histories (London: Penguin, 2013). I was honoured that Kapuściński
        described my *Goodbye to the USSR*, published shortly before his own
        Imperium, as a book that 'should be read by everyone interested in the
        most important world event of the late twentieth century'.
117   'an absolute zero': Steve Crawshaw, 'Czech PM backs reform
        movement', *Independent*, 27 November 1989.
117   'We are at the beginning': 'Bush-Gorbachev news conference in
        Malta', *New York Times*, 4 December 1989.
117   'absurdly hopeful': Timothy Garton Ash, *The Magic Lantern: The
        Revolution of 1989 Witnessed in Warsaw, Budapest, Berlin and Prague*
        (London: Polonia, 1990).
117   hope and history rhymed: Seamus Heaney, *The Cure at Troy: A Version
        of Sophocles' Philoctetes* (New York: Farrar, Straus and Giroux, 1990).
118   'let us have hope': Haidar Abdel Shafi, quoted in Donald Macintyre,
        Gaza: Preparing for Dawn (London: Oneworld, 2017).
119   Wingspread, 'walking in space': Robert K. Woetzel (preface), A. N. R.
        Robinson (foreword), *A Report on the First and Second International Criminal
        Law Conferences* (Racine: Johnson Foundation, 1973). A. N. R. Robinson,
        *In the Midst of It: The Autobiography of Former President and Former Prime
        Minister of the Republic of Trinidad and Tobago* (Hertford: Hansib, 2012).
119   'like a piece of unripened fruit': Benjamin Ferencz, *An International
        Criminal Court: A Step Toward World Peace* (New York: Oceana, 1980).

120 **'unassailable windmills'**: Václav Havel, foreword to Steve Crawshaw and John Jackson, *Small Acts of Resistance: How Courage, Tenacity and Ingenuity Can Change the World* (New York: Union Square Press, 2010).

120 **'live with the mockery'**: Exhibition video, Memorium Nuremberg Trials.

120–1 **'genocide, racial discrimination', 'architects of the world of tomorrow', 'leery of supranational law'**: A. N. R. Robinson (foreword), *Report on the First and Second International Criminal Law Conferences*. Cherif Bassiouni, 'Chronology of efforts to establish an International Criminal Court', *Revue internationale de droit pénal*, 86 (2015, originally published 1992). M. C. Bassiouni, 'International law and the Holocaust', *California Western International Law Journal*, 9:2 (1979).

122–3 **NGO coalition and Rome:** Claude E. Welch Jr and Ashley Watkins, 'Extending enforcement: The coalition for the International Criminal Court', *Human Rights Quarterly*, 33 (2011) includes an account of the negotiations. Glasius, *The International Criminal Court*. Thanks to Bill Pace and Richard Dicker for additional details.

123 **'unfettered'**: Statement by A. N. R. Robinson, 18 May 1998, via ICC Legal Tools.

124 **'stubborn and losing propositions', 'rogues' gallery'**: These and other quotations come from David Scheffer, *All the Missing Souls: A Personal History of the War Crimes Tribunals* (Princeton: Princeton University Press, 2012).

124 **'agreement was not possible'**: Silvia Fernández de Gurmendi, 'A Path to Global Justice', Inamori Ethics Prize speech 2020.

125 **'humanity's finest hour'**: 'UN diplomatic conference concludes in Rome with decision to establish permanent international criminal court', UN, 20 July 1998.

125 **'gift of hope'**: 'Secretary-General says establishment of international criminal court is gift of hope to future generations', UN, 20 July 1998.

125 **'Nuremberg took tangible form'**: '75th anniversary of the start of the Nuremberg trials', Der Bundespräsident, 20 November 2020.

125 **'America's inspiring role'**: Robert S. McNamara and Benjamin B. Ferencz, 'For Clinton's last act', *New York Times*, 12 December 2000.

126 **'no legal obligations', 'happiest moment'**: Letter to UN Secretary-General Kofi Annan, US Department of State, 6 May 2002. Olivia Gazis, 'In first major address, John Bolton attacks old foe', CBS News, 10 September 2018.

127 **'most satisfying moment'**: Robinson, *In the Midst of It*.

127 **'shabby pretext'**: Benjamin B. Ferencz, 'Misguided fears about an International Criminal Court', benferencz.org.

128 **'shooting ourselves in the foot'**: Condoleezza Rice, 'Trip Briefing en route to Chile, March 10 2006', US Department of State Archive.

128 **'prolonged and divisive debate'**: Richard Boucher, daily press briefing, US Department of State, 23 June 2004.

128 **'prevent and punish'**: Frieze (ed.), *Totally Unofficial*.

128 **'resisted acknowledging'**: Power, *A Problem from Hell*.

128–9 **'vicious, invisible war', 'potential horror story', crimes against humanity:** 'Darfur: "Too many people killed for no reason"', Amnesty International, February 2004. 'Darfur rising: Sudan's new crisis',

International Crisis Group, March 2004. *Darfur in Flames: Atrocities in Western Sudan*, Human Rights Watch, 2 April 2004.

129   **'frighteningly real'**: '"Risk of genocide remains frighteningly real"', Secretary-General tells Human Rights Commission', UN, 7 April 2004.

129   **'International reflexes'**: 'Rwanda's lessons: international reflexes are still too slow', *Financial Times*, 7 April 2004.

129   **'deafening silence'**: Gill Lusk of *Africa Confidential* and others, 'Another Rwanda is happening now', *Guardian*, 8 April 2004.

130   **'struggle for a hundred years'**: Steve Crawshaw, 'Peace in the wasteland', *Independent*, 13 March 1999.

130   **'reign of terror'**: 'Violations in Darfur may constitute war crimes, crimes against humanity, says UN rights office report', OHCHR, 7 May 2004. The chronology of the leaking to media of the UN report ahead of publication was described in Human Rights Watch's second report, *Darfur Destroyed*, published in May 2004.

131   **'Rape, torture'**: Declan Walsh, 'Rape, torture and one million forced to flee as Sudan's crisis unfolds. Will we move to stop it?', *Independent*, 23 April 2004.

131   **'genocide and other crimes'**: President's statement on violence in Darfur, Sudan, White House, 9 September 2004, georgewbush-whitehouse.archives.org.

131   **'make more noise'**: Des Forges, *Leave None to Tell the Story*. George Packer, 'Alison Des Forges', *New Yorker*, 13 February 2009.

132   **'if politicians and officials don't see'**: Steve Crawshaw, 'Genocide, what genocide?', *Financial Times Magazine*, 21 August 2004. Steve Crawshaw, Select Committee on International Development: Written Evidence, 'Darfur: Crisis, Response and Lessons', House of Commons: International Development – Written Evidence, November 2004.

132   **'advises against other measures'**: Report on the International Commission of Inquiry on Darfur to the UN Secretary-General, OHCHR, 25 January 2005.

133   **'one permanent member moves not an inch'**, **'don't want to be a party'**: Steve Crawshaw, 'Justice for Darfur needs more than "consensus"', *Independent*, 7 February 2005.

134   **'much strong dissent'**: Condoleezza Rice, *No Higher Honor: A Memoir of My Years in Washington* (New York: Crown, 2012).

134   **'long-term stability'**: 'Security Council refers situation in Darfur, Sudan to prosecutor of the International Criminal Court', UN, 31 March 2005.

134   **'the vilest scramble'**: Joseph Conrad, 'Geography and Some Explorers', in *Last Essays* (London: J. M. Dent, 1926).

135   **'regrets'**: Nosmot Gbadamosi, 'Belgium offers regret – but no reparations – to Congo', *Foreign Policy*, 15 June 2022.

135   **gold and massacres**: *The Curse of Gold*, Human Rights Watch, 1 June 2005. Adam Hochschild, *King Leopold's Ghost: A Story of Greed, Terror and Heroism in Colonial Africa* (Boston: Houghton Mifflin, 1998) is a powerful account of the colonial history.

136   **'should be judged'**, **stood impassive**: Steve Crawshaw: 'Bringing justice to the heart of darkness', *Independent*, 6 February 2006; 'Guilty of war crimes, the brutal warlord who terrorised the Democratic Republic of Congo', 7 March 2014.

136 'slow awakening': Benjamin B. Ferencz, 'Ferencz closes Lubanga case for ICC prosecution', benferencz.org, August 2011.

137 'bring the culprit to The Hague': Savious Kwinika, 'Sudan President Bashir, accused of war crimes, would be arrested in South Africa, says ANC', *Christian Science Monitor*, 28 July 2010.

138 'stability of Kenya is in jeopardy': Statement issued by the African Union Panel of Eminent African Personalities, Nairobi, 12 November 2009.

138 'slaying the dragon of impunity': Quoted in James Verini, 'The prosecutor and the president', *New York Times Magazine*, 22 June 2016.

138 biased court: Geoff Dancy and others, 'What determines perceptions of bias toward the International Criminal Court? Evidence from Kenya', *Journal of Conflict Resolution*, 64:7–8 (August–September 2020).

138 witness intimidation, 'dark day for international criminal justice': Statement of ICC Prosecutor Fatou Bensouda on withdrawal of charges against Uhuru Kenyatta, 5 December 2014.

139 'colonial court': 'Sudan President Bashir hails "victory" over ICC charges', BBC, 13 December 2014.

139 Bashir's escape: Angela Mudukuti, 'Judicial integrity and independence: The South African Omar al-Bashir matter', Southern Africa Litigation Centre. Supreme Court of Appeal of South Africa, Case 867/15, 15 March 2016. 'South African court rules failure to detain Omar al-Bashir was "disgraceful"', *Guardian*, 16 March 2016.

140–1 'Do these leaders', 'less need': 'Annan defends international court', Kofi Annan Foundation, 5 August 2009.

140 'a political tool': Hannah Ellis-Petersen, 'Rodrigo Duterte to pull Philippines out of international criminal court', *Guardian*, 13 March 2018.

142 'omertà': Frédéric Mégret, 'International criminal justice as a peace project', *European Journal of International Law*, 29:3 (August 2018).

142–3 Goldsmith memo, 'amounts to the crime of aggression': Philippe Sands, *Lawless World: Making and Breaking Global Rules* (London: Penguin, 2005, updated edn 2006). 'Full text: Iraq legal advice', *Guardian*, 28 April 2005. 'Wilmshurst resignation letter', BBC, 24 March 2005,

143 God told him: Ewan MacAskill, 'God told me to end the tyranny in Iraq', *Guardian*, 7 October 2005.

145–6 Pinochet, Napoleon, 'loved his fatherland', 'bewildered': Andy Beckett, *Pinochet in Piccadilly: Britain and Chile's Hidden History* (London: Faber, 2002). Jon Lee Anderson, 'The dictator', *New Yorker*, 11 October 1998. '"Bewildered" Pinochet vows to fight on', *New York Times*, 9 November 1998. Madeleine Davis, *The Pinochet Case: Origins, Progress and Implications* (London: Institute of Latin American Studies, 2003).

146 'would mock us forever': Ariel Dorfman: 'The general's handiwork', *Washington Post*, 12 May 2001; *Exorcising Terror: The Incredible Unending Trial of Augusto Pinochet* (New York: Seven Stories, 2002).

147 'no immunity whatever': 'Nail-biter in the Lords', BBC, 25 November 1998.

147 'only political prisoner': Christina Lamb, 'Tea with Pinochet', *New Statesman*, 26 July 1999.

147   'as offensive, if not more offensive': Philippe Sands (ed.), *From Nuremberg to The Hague: The Future of International Criminal Justice* (Cambridge: Cambridge University Press, 2003).

148   'giant bomb': Sebastian Rotella, 'Pinochet arrest forces Chile to revisit past', *Los Angeles Times*, 25 October 1998.

148   'disturbingly uncertain': 'The Pinochet effect', *The Times*, 1 December 1998.

148   'disgusting': Jonathan Franklin, 'Chilean calls grow for Pinochet trial', *Guardian*, 6 March 2000.

148   'subtle displacement': Dorfman, *Exorcising Terror*.

149   'always acted in a democratic way': 'Pinochet: I was a democrat', *Guardian*, 23 November 2003.

149   gun battle with Almog's bodyguards: 'UK court issues warrant against Israeli general', Hickman & Rose, 15 September 2016. Vikram Dodd, 'Terror police feared gun battle with Israeli general', *Guardian*, 19 February 2008.

149–50 'going wild': Kim Sengupta and Donald Macintyre, 'Israeli cabinet divided over fresh Gaza surge', *Independent*, 13 January 2009.

150   'appalling situation': Owen Bowcott, 'Tzipi Livni spared war crime arrest threat', *Guardian*, 6 October 2011.

150   'He bothers no one': Mort Rosenblum, 'In southern France, exiled Duvalier is just part of the posh landscape', Associated Press/*Los Angeles Times*, 28 January 1990.

151   'Mama, what was your role': The story of Women of Liberia Mass Action for Peace is told in the award-winning *Pray the Devil Back to Hell* (dir. Gini Reticker, 2008) and in Leymah Gbowee, *Mighty be Our Powers: How Sisterhood, Prayer and Sex Changed a Nation at War* (New York: Beast, 2011).

151   'History will be kind to me': 'Liberian president Taylor steps down', *Guardian*, 11 August 2003.

151   'in a class of his own': Kevin Jon Heller, 'Taylor sentenced to 50 years imprisonment', OpinioJuris, 30 May 2012.

151–5   Hissène Habré: Many details come from Reed Brody, *To Catch a Dictator: The Pursuit and Trial of Hissène Habré* (New York: Columbia University Press, 2022). Also Celeste Hicks, *The Trial of Hissène Habré: How the People of Chad Brought a Tyrant to Justice* (London: Zed, 2018). 'Ex-Chad dictator enjoyed luxury in Senegal', Associated Press, 6 July 2013. Ruth Maclean, 'Chad's Hissène Habré found guilty of crimes against humanity', *Guardian*, 30 May 2016. 'Catching Dictators with Reed Brody', *Asymmetrical Haircuts* podcast, 15 December 2022.

154   'We regret': Marlise Simons, 'Senegal told to prosecute ex-president of Chad', *New York Times*, 20 July 2012.

Chapter Five: 'The Rules of the Game are Changing'

157   'copying the brutal manner': Jane Mayer, *The Dark Side: The Inside Story of How the War on Terror Turned into a War on American Ideals* (New York: Doubleday, 2008).

158   'horrific': President Khatami at UN General Assembly, 9 November 2001, A/56/PV.42-EN.

158–9   'sort of the dark side', 'authority to order torture': Mayer, *The Dark Side*. Mark Fallon, *Unjustifiable Means: The Inside Story of How the CIA, Pentagon, and US Government Conspired to Torture* (New York: Regan Arts, 2017). 'Globalising Torture: CIA Secret Detention and Extraordinary Rendition', Open Society Justice Initiative, 2013. Dick Cheney on *Meet the Press*, NBC, 16 September 2001.

160   *Battle of Algiers*, 'lose the war of ideas': David Ignatius, 'Think strategy, not numbers', *Washington Post*, 26 August 2003.

161   'Carlotta's story', 'hard to get their mind around': Eric Umansky, 'Failures of imagination: American journalists and the coverage of American torture', *Columbia Journalism Review*, September 2006 (republished online, 8 August 2014).

162   'leading this fight by example': Statement by the President, UN International Day in Support of Victims of Torture, White House, 26 June 2003, georgewbush-whitehouse.archives.org. 'Bush administration rules out using cruel treatment to fight terrorism: a joint statement concerning UN Torture Victims Recognition Day by human rights organizations and torture victim treatment centers', Human Rights Watch, 26 June 2023.

162   'advice of a mob lawyer to a mafia don': Anthony Lewis, 'Making torture legal', *New York Review of Books*, 15 July 2004.

163   'enhanced interrogation techniques': The phrasing echoed Nazi attempts to cloak their use of torture in pseudo-legal language. 'Enhanced interrogation' implied the need for an improved outcome by bringing an unclear image into sharper focus. So, too, sixty years earlier the Gestapo had authorised *verschärfte Vernehmung* – enhanced or 'sharpened' interrogation. *Verschärfte Vernehmung* was to be used only in specific circumstances, including against saboteurs, terrorists and 'asocial persons'; it became the subject of war crimes prosecutions after 1945. See e.g. Andrew Sullivan, '"Verschärfte Vernehmung"', *Atlantic*, 29 May 2007.

163   'You'll have My Lais': Mayer, *The Dark Side*.

163   'blindsided': 'Rumsfeld tells Congress of his "failure"', CNN, 10 May 2004.

164   'our inspiring, abstract notions': Quoted in Mark Danner, 'The logic of torture', *New York Review of Books*, 24 June 2004.

164   'treat the prisoners like dogs': Janis Karpinski interview, 'The Torture Question', *Frontline*, PBS, posted 18 October 2005.

164   'our future terrorists': Philip Gourevitch and Errol Morris, 'Exposure', *New Yorker*, 17 March 2008.

164   'protect our values': Jane Mayer, 'The memo', *New Yorker*, 19 February 2006.

165   'Not only did I let down': John McChesney, 'Abu Ghraib guard sentenced to six months', NBC News, 17 May 2005.

165   tip of the iceberg: See e.g. *Command's Responsibility*, Human Rights First, 2006; *No Blood, No Foul*, Human Rights Watch, 2006.

165   'pouring water up his nostrils', 'Damn right': Glen Kessler, 'Cheney's claim that the US did not prosecute Japanese soldiers for waterboarding', *Washington Post*, 16 December 2014. George W. Bush, *Decision Points* (New York: Crown, 2010), quoted in *Getting Away with Torture: The*

Bush Administration and Mistreatment of Detainees, Human Rights Watch, 12 July 2011.

164 **'In authoritarian states'**: Conor Gearty, *Homeland Insecurity: The Rise and Rise of Anti-Terrorism Law* (Cambridge: Polity Press, 2024).

164 **'rules of the game'**: 'Rights laws to be overhauled as Blair says "the game has changed"', *Independent*, 6 August 2005. Steve Crawshaw, 'Not worth the paper they're written on. Despite what the Prime Minister says, the rules of the game have not changed', *Independent*, 13 August 2005.

166–7 **'risk losing their legitimacy'**: Human Rights Annual Report, Foreign & Commonwealth Office, 2005.

167 **Downing Street and torture**: Kenneth Roth and Minky Worden (eds), *Torture: Does It Make Us Safer? Is It Ever OK?* (New York: New Press, 2006). Cherie Booth, 'Rules prohibiting torture are vital', *Financial Times*, 2 March 2006. Mark Oliver, 'Booth: Government must be "responsive" on torture', *Guardian*, 2 March 2006. 'Cherie Booth calls for West to stand up for human rights', *Independent*, 2 March 2006. 'Torture: Bending the Rules', Channel 4 debate, 7 March 2006.

168 **'inexcusable'**: 'UK "knew US mistreated rendition detainees"', BBC, 28 June 2018. Intelligence and Security Committee, 'Detainee mistreatment and rendition, 2001–2010' (HC1113, HC 1114)

168 **'least we could do for you'**: 'Documents reveal Libya rendition details', Human Rights Watch, 9 September 2011. Ian Cobain, 'Special report: Rendition ordeal that raises new questions about secret trials', *Guardian*, 8 April 2012. 'The Tripoli documents', *Al Jazeera*, 18 December 2013. 'PM apologises for UK role in abduction, torture, and rendition of Abdul-Hakim Belhaj and Fatima Boudchar', Reprieve, 10 May 2018.

169 **'law-abiding nations'**: Statement by the President, UN International Day in Support of Victims of Torture

170 **'dark halls'**: Security Address on Counter-Terrorism by the Honorable Barack Obama, US Senator from Illinois, Wilson Center, 1 August 2007.

170 **mamboed their way**: Connie Bruck, 'Why Obama has failed to close Guantánamo', *New Yorker*, 25 July 2016.

170 **'willingness to openly confront'**: Statement by the President, Report of the Senate Select Committee on Intelligence, 9 December 2014.

170 **'We treated detainees'**: Fallon, *Unjustifiable Means*.

170 **'we tortured some folks'**: President Obama: 'We tortured some folks', C-SPAN, 1 August 2014

170 **'absolutely' works**: James Risen and Sheri Fink, 'Trump said "torture works". An echo is feared worldwide', *New York Times*, 5 January 2017. 'President Trump tells ABC News' David Muir he "absolutely" thinks waterboarding works', ABC News, 25 January 2017.

171 **Haspel**: Carol Rosenberg and Julian E. Barnes, 'Gina Haspel observed waterboarding at CIA black site, psychologist testifies', *New York Times*, 3 June 2022. 'Haspel personally observed CIA waterboarding, witness testifies', National Security Archive, 23 June 2022. 'CIA nominee supervised detainee torture at Thailand black site, drafted cable to destroy evidence,' National Security Archive, 26 April 2018. Hina Shamsi, 'What Gina Haspel got wrong about the torture tapes she helped destroy', American Civil Liberties Union, 9 May 2018.

171   **love of impunity:** Richard Spencer, 'I was fired as Navy secretary. Here's what I've learned because of it', *Washington Post*, 27 November 2019.

172   **Overseas Operations Bill:** Kim Sengupta, 'Government to introduce 5-year limit on prosecuting armed forces for human rights abuses', *Independent*, 13 March 2020. Lucy Fisher, 'Law to protect soldiers "would harm reputation of UK armed forces"', *The Times*, 18 September 2020. 'Torturing UK values', *Daily Mail*, 13 April 2021. Imy Harper, 'A U-turn on torture', interview with Steve Crawshaw, Tortoise Media, 19 May 2022. Signatories of the letter to the prime minister, coordinated by Freedom from Torture, were: Dominic Grieve, former attorney-general; Lord Guthrie, former head of the armed forces; Bruce Houlder, former director of military prosecutions; General Sir Nicholas Parker, former commander of land forces; Malcolm Rifkind, former defence and foreign secretary.

172   **'garbage':** Rt Hon Johnny Mercer, Twitter, 8 September 2020.

172–3   **'Implying troops are untouchable':** 'Torturing UK values', *Daily Mail*, 13 April 2021.

173–6   **'You couldn't MAKE IT UP!', 'played right into the hands':** 'War Crimes Scandal Exposed', *Panorama*, BBC, 18 November 2019. Hannah O'Grady and Joel Gunter, 'SAS unit repeatedly killed Afghan detainees, BBC finds', BBC, 12 July 2022. 'Bereaved families welcome unprecedented statutory inquiry into allegations of extrajudicial killings by UK Special Forces in Afghanistan', Leigh Day Solicitors, 15 December 2022. Larisa Brown, 'Johnny Mercer "would go to jail before giving up SAS whistleblowers"', *The Times*, 2 May 2024. INSIGHT team, 'The SAS murders: How a senior officer exposed a war crime cover-up', *Sunday Times*, 5 May 2024.

175   **'disgraceful and a profound betrayal':** Nick McKenzie, Anthony Galloway and Chris Masters, 'Australian special forces soldiers committed up to 39 murders: ADF report', *The Age*, 19 November 2020.

176   **'We're a nation':** 'Remarks by the President on the way forward in Afghanistan', White House, 22 June 2011, obamawhitehouse.archives.gov.

176   **Drone attacks, 'disastrous ways':** Azmat Khan and Anand Gopal, 'The uncounted', *New York Times Magazine*, 16 November 2017. Azmat Khan, 'Hidden Pentagon records reveal patterns of failure in deadly airstrikes', *New York Times*, 18 December 2021.

176–7   **zero civilian casualty figures:** Emma Graham-Harrison and Joe Dyke, 'Lives torn apart by British airstrikes in Mosul give lie to UK's "perfect" precision war', *Guardian*, 21 March 2023. Emma Graham-Harrison, 'Ministry of Defence lacks "effective oversight" of civilian casualties, tribunal hears', *Guardian*, 30 November 2023.

178–9   **'Am I going to die?', 'propaganda war', 'superior fieldcraft', 'Many young people':** Don Mullan, *Bloody Sunday: Massacre in Northern Ireland. The Eyewitness Accounts* (New York: Roberts Rinehart, 1997). 'Widgery memo damns British', Museum of Free Derry. David McKittrick and David McVea, *Making Sense of the Troubles: A History of the Northern Ireland Conflict* (Belfast: Blackstaff, 2000).

180 **'no innocent people':** David McKittrick and others, *Lost Lives: The Stories of the Men, Women and Children who Died as a Result of the Northern Ireland Troubles* (Edinburgh: Mainstream, 1999).

180 **'eat that pillar', 'good to have peace':** Steve Crawshaw: 'Easter 1998: Is the agony really over?', *Independent on Sunday*, 12 April 1998; 'The ANC approves: They met Sinn Fein and spoke of the time to sit with the enemy, but in Ulster many remain pessimistic', 3 May 1998; 'Hope wins over pessimism', 24 May 1998.

181 **'building a secure future':** Hansard, 29 January 1998.

181 **'There is no doubt':** 'PM: Statement on Saville Inquiry', Prime Minister's Office, 15 June 2010.

182 **'scarcely believe', 'no triumphalism':** Simon Winchester, 'Amid the tears and cheers, a full stop of Britain's colonial experience in Northern Ireland', *Guardian*, 15 June 2010. Edward Daly, 'A new dawn for Derry after Saville', *Guardian*, 18 June 2010.

182 **'rapidly deteriorating situation', 'fulsome apology', 'serious mistakes':** Steve Crawshaw and Kim Sengupta, 'Kosovo general acknowledges role in Bloody Sunday', *Independent*, 27 March 2000. 'Bloody Sunday killings "unjustified and unjustifiable"', BBC, 15 June 2010. (The scoop about Jackson's involvement in Bloody Sunday belonged to Kim Sengupta, who with typical generosity invited me to join him for the interview. Kim was one of the most talented and bravest correspondents of his generation. He died, much too early, in 2024.)

183–4 **Ballymurphy, 'tied into the war effort', '"bad apples"', 'wiped out IRA hardcore':** *The Ballymurphy Precedent* (dir. Callum Macrae), Channel 4 Television, 2018. Frank Kitson, *Low Intensity Operations: Subversion, Insurgency, Peacekeeping* (London: Faber, 1971). Callum Macrae, '"You can remember the truth, but you can't remember the lies": The lessons of the Ballymurphy massacre', Pulitzer Center, 23 June 2021.

184 **'should have said "alleged"', 'entirely innocent', 'ability to understand':** Rebecca Black, 'Ballymurphy inquest hears from General Sir Mike Jackson', BelfastLive, 30 May 2019. 'In the matter of a series of deaths that occurred in August 1971 at Ballymurphy, west Belfast', Judiciary NI, 11 May 2021. 'Ballymurphy inquest findings', Hansard, 13 May 2021.

184 **'We weren't looking':** 'Aidan McAnespie killing: Ex-soldier Holden avoids jails over Troubles shooting', BBC, 2 February 2023.

185 **zero security deaths:** 'No security-related deaths in Northern Ireland for first time since records began', BBC, 5 January 2024.

Chapter Six: 'I am Glad to be Deceived'

186 **'change them like gloves':** Andrei Zolotov, 'President draws criticism from all political camps', *Moscow Times*, 10 August 1999.

187 **'We will pursue the terrorists':** Robyn Dixon, 'Chechen war propels Putin to front ranks', *Los Angeles Times*, 1 January 2000.

187 **'How can they think of an action like this?':** Steve Crawshaw, 'Killing casts light on Moscow's dirty war in Chechnya', *Independent*, 24 August 1995.

187 **'intelligent, strong, energetic':** Statement by Boris Yeltsin, Kremlin, 31 December 1999.

188   **Novye Aldy:** *February 5: A Day of Slaughter in Novye Aldy*, Human
       Rights Watch, 2000.
188   **'long-suffering territory':** David Hoffman, 'Russia celebrates conquest
       of Chechnya', *Washington Post*, 21 February 2000.
188   **'cherish the traditions':** 'Acting President Vladimir Putin addressed
       the people of Ingushetia and Chechnya on the occasion of the 56th
       anniversary of their deportation', Kremlin, 23 February 2000.
189   **'difficult to understand':** 'Mr Putin does not deserve praise unless he is
       a catalyst for change', *Independent*, 28 March 2000.
189–91 **Ryazan bombing:** Alexander Litvinenko and Yuri Felshtinsky, *Blowing
       up Russia* (London: Gibson Square, 2007) was first published in Russian
       in 2002 (the book was banned in Russia); Litvinenko was murdered in
       2006. John B. Dunlop, *The Moscow Bombings of September 1999* (Stuttgart:
       Ibidem Press, 2012), includes additional detail. Russia's NTV channel
       showed a film on 'Ryazan Sugar' in March 2000; the authorities said the
       programme 'crossed a line' and later took NTV over by force ('Ten years
       ago, Russia's Independent NTV, the talk of the nation, fell silent', Radio
       Free Europe/Radio Liberty, 14 April 2011).
191   **'nonsense', 'insane':** Quoted by Amy Knight in 'Finally, we
       know about the Moscow bombings', *New York Review of Books*, 22
       November 2012.
191   **'burning of the Reichstag':** Anna Politkovskaya, trans. John Crowfoot,
       A Dirty War: A Russian Reporter in Chechnya (London: Harvill Press,
       2001), quoted in book review: Steve Crawshaw, 'Russians might ignore
       this war, but we must not', *Independent*, 20 July 2001.
191–2 **fireworks, 'Our president!':** Steve Crawshaw, 'Putin plays the emperor
       at the White Nights ball', *Independent*, 30 June 2001.
192   **'tremendous hope':** 'Blair and Putin in show of unity', *Daily Telegraph*,
       26 June 2003. 'Blair urged to speak out on Chechnya', Human Rights
       Watch, 20 June 2003.
192   **'my job . . . to like Mr Putin', 'it led to tragedy':** Anna Politkovskaya:
       Is Journalism Worth Dying For?: Final Dispatches (Brooklyn: Melville
       House, 2011); *Putin's Russia* (London: Harvill, 2004).
193   **'glad to be deceived':** Anna Neistat, 'What Mr Blair should say to the
       Russian President', *Independent*, 26 June 2003.
193   **'a sense of his soul', 'flawless democrat':** Press Conference by
       President Bush and Russian President Putin (Slovenia), Office of the
       Press Secretary, 16 June 2001. 'Moscow mon amour: Gerhard Schröder's
       dangerous liaison', *Der Spiegel*, 1 December 2004.
194   **meeting with NGOs, 'different traditions':** Arkady Ostrovsky,
       'Glimpse of the real Russia behind the polished façade', *Financial Times*,
       17 July 2006. Nick Paton Walsh, 'PM's wife risks Kremlin wrath to
       meet NGOs', *Guardian*, 18 July 2006. 'Cherie Booth QC offers support
       to Russian NGOs', Human Rights Watch, July 2006. 'Press conference
       following talks with US President George W. Bush', Kremlin, 15
       July 2006.
195   **'extremely insignificant':** 'Russia: Where's Putin?', Radio Free
       Europe/Radio Liberty, 10 October 2006. 'Putin's comments on
       Politkovskaya anger activists', Radio Free Europe/Radio Liberty, 11
       October 2006

195   **'unstoppable force':** Steve Crawshaw, 'An elephant tries to repaint itself with zebra stripes', *Independent*, 28 July 1989.

195   **'within its internationally recognised borders', 'save lives':** UN Security Council Resolution 1808, 15 April 2008. Statement by President of Russia Dmitry Medvedev, Kremlin, 26 August 2008. Russia accused Georgia of 'opting for genocide' – as it would do with Ukraine, fourteen years later.

196   **South Ossetia warrants:** 'Situation in Georgia: ICC pre-trial chamber delivers three arrest warrants', ICC, 30 June 2022.

Other former Soviet republics have also turned to the International Criminal Court for protection. Armenia ratified the court's Rome Statute in November 2023. That was too late to be applicable to crimes committed during what Armenia describes as a second 'genocide' – Azerbaijan's expulsion a few weeks earlier of a hundred thousand Armenians from the enclave of Nagorno-Karabakh (known by the Armenians as Artsakh) at the end of a nine-month starvation blockade. But the ratification angered Russia, whose president was by now an ICC-arrestable indictee; Moscow said ratification was 'unacceptable' and warned of 'serious consequences'. Armenians argued that Moscow had deliberately allowed Azerbaijan's ethnic cleansing to go ahead as punishment for Armenia's close ties to the West.

As so often, governments were eager to move on. At the COP29 climate summit hosted by Azerbaijan in 2024 – 'COP of peace', as Azerbaijan itself described it – the crimes committed a year earlier went mostly unmentioned, as did the increased repression in Azerbaijan. ('Armenia joins the ICC Rome Statute', ICC, 17 November 2023. Caolán Magee, '"We are starving to death": Residents of Nagorno-Karabakh fear for future under blockade', CNN, 7 September 2023. David Scheffer, 'Ethnic cleansing is happening in Nagorno-Karabakh. How can the world respond?', Council on Foreign Relations, 4 October 2023. Arshaluys Barseghyan, 'Armenian official accuses Russia of "returning" Nagorno-Karabakh to Azerbaijan', Open Caucasus Media, 27 June 2024. Michelle Langrand, 'Behind Baku's "COP of peace" façade, a conflict is simmering', Geneva Solutions, 11 November 2024. *'We Try to Stay Invisible': Azerbaijan's Escalating Crackdown on Critics and Civil Society*, Human Rights Watch, 8 October 2024.)

196   **'reset' button:** Clinton's button in fact used the wrong Russian word, showing 'overload' (*peregruzka*) instead of 'reset' (*perezagruzka*). But neither side wanted to dwell on that. In search of friendly relations, Clinton and Lavrov laughed off the mistranslation.

196   **decisions still made in Moscow:** Another former Soviet republic which has come under pressure from Moscow because of its pro-European choices is Moldova, tucked between south-west Ukraine and Romania. Like the Baltic states, Moldova was annexed by Moscow (officially: 'liberated from the Romanian yoke') as part of the Hitler–Stalin pact of 1939. Like Georgia and Ukraine, Moldova has long tried to assert a separate identity from Moscow. When I was in still-Soviet Moldavia in 1989, protesters were demanding the use of the Latin script instead of Cyrillic, imposed for the past fifty years. They waved home-made flags, too in the forbidden colours of blue, yellow and red; Moscow ordered

materials in those colours to be withdrawn from sale, in an attempt to block pressures for change.

Thirty-five years later, tensions remained unresolved. In 2024, the Moldovan government organised a referendum which was expected to show strong pro-European sentiment; talks to join the European Union had already begun. But the vote ended up being in favour of Europe by only the slimmest of margins, apparently after Russian-backed interference. President Maia Sandu talked of an 'unprecedented assault on democracy'. Russia denied any involvement. (Steve Crawshaw, 'Moldavians want more rights from Moscow', *Independent*, 21 July 1989. Sarah Rainsford: 'Moldova says "Yes" to pro-EU constitutional changes by tiny margin', BBC, 20 October 2024; 'Russian cash-for-votes flows into Moldova as nation heads to polls', BBC, 20 October 2024.)

197 **'Crimea has always been':** 'Address by President of the Russian Federation', Kremlin, 18 March 2014.

198 **'explosion will be greater than in Yugoslavia':** Steve Crawshaw, 'Ukrainians' new navy sails into a sea of troubles', *Independent*, 1 April 1993.

198 **'joy of this entire region':** James Coomarasamy, 'Crimea: Yuri revels in reversal of fortune', BBC, 23 March 2014.

199 **'changing Moscow's calculus':** Ulrich Speck, *The West's Response to Ukraine Conflict: A Transatlantic Success Story* (Washington DC: Transatlantic Academy/German Marshall Fund of the United States, 2016).

199 **'eighteen golden days':** Ahdaf Soueif, 'The Arab spring: one year on', *Guardian*, 13 January 2012.

199 **'unless it's led by a crazy person':** 'Defiant Assad denies ordering bloody Syrian crackdown', Barbara Walters interview, ABC News, 7 December 2011.

199–200 **'We waved olive branches':** Anna Neistat, 'No excuse for failing Syria', Amnesty International, 14 March 2015.

200 **'an alibi' for inaction:** Patrick Wintour, 'UN Syria investigator quits over concern about Russian obstruction', *Guardian*, 7 August 2017.

200 **'more quiet and stable and secure':** John Kifner, 'Syrian troops are said to battle rebels encircled in central city', *New York Times*, 12 February 1982.

201 **'nothing is true', mannequin, Russian television:** Peter Pomerantsev, *Nothing is True and Everything is Possible: Adventures in Modern Russia* (London: Faber, 2015). Guy Faulconbridge, 'Kremlin says Bucha is "monstrous forgery" aimed at smearing Russia', Reuters, 5 April 2022. Factchecks by *Newsweek*, Agence France Presse and others.

201–2 **'staged a bloody mass murder', 'staged provocation':** 'Foreign ministry spokeswoman Maria Zakharova on the second anniversary of the staged Bucha massacre', Ministry of Foreign Affairs, 2 April 2024. 'Russian troops don't hit hospital in Mariupol, it's Kyiv's information provocation – Russian defense ministry', Interfax, 10 March 2022.

202–3 **'Don't bother us now', *Killing Fields*:** Steve Crawshaw, 'An urgent need for UN action on Sri Lanka', *Huffington Post*, 6 June 2009. I was happy to play a small role in making *Sri Lanka's Killing Fields* happen. Like other human rights advocates, I felt frustration and guilt at our collective failure to create more pressure on Sri Lanka at the time of the killings of so many civilians in 2009. For months on end, I badgered a friend who was head of news and current affairs at Channel 4 to commission a full-length documentary, building on previous reports by Jonathan Miller, Asia correspondent of Channel 4 News. She argued back, before becoming a key champion of the themes. Although I always believed a high-profile programme might make a difference, I could never have imagined how much impact Callum Macrae's three award-winning films (*Sri Lanka's Killing Fields*, *War Crimes Unpunished* and *No Fire Zone*, 2011–13) would eventually make.

203   **post-war victory lap:** Steve Crawshaw, 'Sri Lanka's misguided attempt to win the world', Amnesty International, 15 November 2013.

203   **'assault on the entire framework':** 'Report of the Secretary-General's Panel of Experts on Accountability in Sri Lanka', UN, 31 March 2011.

203   **digital possibilities began to come of age:** Another early harbinger of change was the 'green revolution' in Iran in June 2009, which also became known as the 'Twitter revolution'. Haunting phone video of the last moments of twenty-six-year-old protester Neda Agha-Soltan after she was fatally shot by government forces, for example, went viral in Iran and around the world. Samantha Shapiro wrote a perceptive early piece from Cairo in 2009 – 'Revolution, Facebook-style' – in which she interviewed Egyptian activists about their use of social media and their belief in change (*New York Times* magazine, 25 January 2009). Others, however, continued to insist the new digital possibilities would never make any real difference. Even after the 'We are all Khaled Said' Facebook page gained momentum in Egypt in 2010, Malcolm Gladwell wrote a four-thousand-word piece explaining why this was all a fuss about nothing ('Small change: why the revolution will not be tweeted', *New Yorker*, 4 October 2010). Mubarak fell four months later, after a revolution that was kickstarted by a YouTube video watched by millions. (Steve Crawshaw [foreword by Ai Weiwei], *Street Spirit: The Power and Protest of Mischief* (London: Michael O'Mara, 2017).

204   **'insults common sense':** Assad interview with *Izvestia* newspaper. Khaled Yacoub Oweis, 'Dogged rebels the target of Syria gas attacks – activists', Reuters, 26 August 2013.

204–6   **'UK-based armchair observer', MH17, 'dived into the haystack', 'Group of bloggers':** Eliot Higgins, *We are Bellingcat: An Intelligence Agency for the People* (London: Bloomsbury, 2021). 'MH17: The Open Source Evidence', Bellingcat. 'The group of bloggers unearthing MH17 intel quicker than US spies', Mashable, 23 July 2014.

207–8   **Cameroon:** 'Credible evidence that army personnel responsible for shocking extrajudicial executions caught on video', Amnesty International, 12 July 2018. 'Anatomy of a Killing', *Africa Eye*, BBC, 24 September 2018. Mathew Ingram, 'A master class in how to verify a video using digital tools', *Columbia Journalism Review*, 24 September 2018. Sam Dubberley, Alexa Koenig and Daragh Murray (eds), *Digital Witness: Using Open Source Information for Human Rights Investigation, Documentation, and Accountability* (Oxford: Oxford University Press, 2020).

208   **Libya and ICC:** Prosecutor vs Mahmoud Mustafa Busayf al-Werfalli,

ICC, 2017–2018 (al-Werfalli was never arrested; he was assassinated in Benghazi in 2021).

208 **Berkeley Protocol:** *Berkeley Protocol on Digital Open Source Investigations: A Practical Guide on the Effective Use of Digital Open Source Information in Investigating Violations of International Criminal, Human Rights and Humanitarian Law*, Human Rights Center, Berkeley and UN Office of the High Commissioner for Human Rights (OHCHR), 2022.

208 **'dawning realisation':** Shakiba Mashayekhi, 'The Berkeley Protocol on Open Source Investigations', interview with Alexa Koenig, pantheon. berkeley.edu, 28 January 2020.

209 **'complete meltdown of humanity', 'whining':** Kareem Shaheen, 'Children trapped in building under attack in Aleppo, doctor tells UN', *Guardian*, 13 December 2016. 'Russia says it's tired of US "whining" over Aleppo', *Independent*, 13 December 2016.

209 **pre-printed forms:** Examples at Auschwitz.org, Historical Pictures and Documents, 'Report on removal of gold teeth'.

210–13 **Caesar:** Adam Ciralsky, 'Documenting evil: Inside Assad's hospitals of horror', *Vanity Fair*, June 2015. 'If the dead could speak: Mass deaths and torture in Syria's detention facilities', Human Rights Watch, December 2015. Garance le Caisne, *Operation Caesar: At the Heart of the Syrian Death Machine* (Cambridge: Polity Press, 2018). Exchanges between Caesar and author.

211 **'Who took these pictures?':** Jonathan Tepperman, 'Syria's president speaks: A conversation with Bashar al-Assad', *Foreign Affairs*, March–April 2015.

212 **Raslan trial, 'landmark leap':** 'Torture in Syria on trial in Koblenz: A documentation of the Al-Khatib proceedings', European Center for Constitutional and Human Rights. *Branch 251*, podcast series. 'German court's historic crimes against humanity finding in Syria case must spur momentum for international justice', OHCHR, 13 January 2022.

213 **ICJ judgment, 'tag on their forehead':** 'Syria accused of "pervasive" torture in first global case over civil war', *Guardian*, 10 October 2023.

213 **Caesar Act, sanctions:** The courage and determination of a single individual has led to sanctions in other contexts, too. US-born British financier Bill Browder has faced repeated death threats for his campaign in connection with his friend and lawyer, Sergei Magnitsky, tortured and killed in a Moscow prison cell in 2009 after investigating a $200 million tax fraud implicating high-level allies of Putin. In Browder's words: 'Magnitsky died because he believed in the rule of law.' As a result of Browder's persistent advocacy over many years, 'Magnitsky Acts' and 'Magnitsky sanctions' in the United States and other countries make it possible to impose travel bans or asset-freezes on those responsible for serious human rights violations. (Bill Browder, *Freezing Order: A True Story of Russian Money Laundering, Murder and Surviving Vladimir Putin's Wrath* (London: Simon and Schuster, 2022). Edward Lucas, 'Bill Browder: The unlikely human rights hero', *The Times*, 18 November 2024.)

214 **'The Syrian army':** 'Marie Colvin's final CNN interview', CNN, 22 February 2012.

214 **'targeted murder':** Laurel Wamsley, 'US court orders Syria to pay $300

million for killing of journalist Marie Colvin', National Public Radio, 31 January 2019.

214   **Mamlouk investigations:** Katie Benner and Adam Goldman, 'After American's killing in Syria, FBI builds war crimes case against top officials', *New York Times*, 17 April 2023. Christophe Ayad, 'Torture in Syria: Paris court sentences three senior officials from Assad's regime to life imprisonment', *Le Monde*, 25 May 2024.

216–19 **Halabi and Austrian intelligence:** 'How the highest-ranking Syrian regime suspect tracked by CIJA evaded arrest', Commission for International Justice and Accountability, 11 January 2021. 'Syria: Visit reveals torture chambers', Human Rights Watch, 17 May 2013. 'If the dead could speak'. Ben Taub, 'How a Syrian war criminal and double agent disappeared in Europe', *New Yorker*, 13 September 2021. Fidelius Schmid and Wolf Wiedmann-Schmidt, 'How Austrian intelligence hid a suspected Syrian war criminal from the law', *Der Spiegel*, 13 September 2021. 'The Disappearing General', *The Syria Trials* via 75podcasts.org. Earlier investigations include: Dominik Schreiber and Kid Möchel, 'So versteckte das BVT einen mutmasslichen Kriegsverbrecher in Österreich', *Der Kurier*, 14 November 2020 and Fabian Schmid, 'Syrischer "Foltergeneral" in Wien: Wie ein Mossad-Deal zum Fiasko wurde', *Der Standard*, 10 September 2021.

219   **'Is there a need for a serious opponent?':** Interview with Steve Rosenberg, BBC News, 20 March 2024.

Chapter Seven: 'If Not Now, When?'

219   **only women testify:** Victoria Amelina, trans. Valzhyne Mort, 'Testimonies', *New Yorker*, 7 August 2023.

222   **'there's no return':** Steve Crawshaw, 'Patchwork history led Lvov to rebel', *Independent*, 5 September 1991.

222   **'only in partnership with Russia':** Vladimir Putin, 'On the historical unity of Russians and Ukrainians', Kremlin, 12 July 2021.

222   **'genocidal tactics':** 'New torture chamber evidence uncovered from liberated Kherson', Global Rights Compliance, March 2023.

222   **'joyful shouts':** Raphael Lemkin, *Axis Rule in Occupied Europe: Laws of Occupation, Analysis of Government, Proposals for Redress* (Washington DC: Carnegie Endowment for International Peace, 1944), quoting *Frankfurter Zeitung*, 28 March 1941. Remarkably (and impossible for Lemkin to have guessed at), the Germans may in fact have invented this particular example of Nazi crimes, presumably for propaganda reasons. Barbara Finkelstein, 'The mystery behind the lost books of a cherished Lublin Yeshiva', *The Forward*, 31 August 2017.

223   **'librocide', 'ashes and blood':** Richard Ovenden, 'Putin's war on Ukrainian memory', *Atlantic*, 23 April 2023. Ed Vulliamy, '"My mum's books survived Putin's missiles": defiance after blast destroys Kherson children's library', *Observer*, 3 December 2023. Porter Anderson, 'Europe's publishers: Anger, solidarity after Kharkiv attack', Publishing Perspectives, 24 May 2024. Luke Harding, '"They burned books, like the Nazis did 80 years ago"', *Observer*, 30 June 2024.

224   **'pleading to you for forgiveness':** 'Russian soldier on trial asks victim's widow to forgive him', Associated Press, 19 May 2022.

224 **gradually became murderers:** Christopher Browning, *Ordinary Men: Reserve Battalion 101 and the Final Solution in Poland* (New York: HarperCollins, 1992/1998).

225 **'First question ... then shoot them', 'his ears were cut off', 'doesn't matter whether they're civilians':** Melanie Amann, Matthias Gebauer and Fidelius Schmid, 'German intelligence intercepts radio traffic discussing the murder of civilians', *Der Spiegel*, 7 April 2022. Erika Kinetz: '"Never saw such hell": Russian soldiers in Ukraine call home', Associated Press, 24 February 2023; '"Kill everyone": Russian violence in Ukraine was strategic', 27 October 2022 (in association with 'Putin's Attack on Ukraine: Documenting War Crimes', *Frontline*, PBS, 25 October 2022).

225 **'in case he drops a bomb', office in a schoolroom:** Sarah Rainsford, 'The children's camp that became an execution ground', BBC, 16 May 2022. *When Spring Came to Bucha* (dir. Mila Teshaieva and Marcus Lenz, 2022).

226–8 **protests and reactions:** Shira Li Bartov, 'Russian protestor arrested, fined for sign showing only asterisks', *Newsweek*, 22 March 2022. Steve Rosenberg, 'Russian human rights campaigner Oleg Orlov sentenced to jail', BBC, 27 February 2024. Ilya Yashin, '"People are running from you, Mr President. Can't you see?"', *Moscow Times*, 9 December 2022. Vladimir Kara-Murza, 'Vladimir Kara-Murza's last statement to Russian court: A reckoning will come', *Washington Post*, 10 April 2023. Sarah Rainsford, 'Russian dissident tells BBC he thought he would die in "Putin's prison"', BBC, 5 August 2024.

228 **'embers of dead empires':** Bill Chappell, 'Kenyan UN ambassador compares Ukraine's plight to colonial legacy in Africa', National Public Radio, 22 February 2022.

229 **'cooperate with the court':** 'Ukraine accepts ICC jurisdiction over alleged crimes committed since 20 February 2014', ICC, 8 September 2015.

229 **'crime scene', 'intrinsic buckle':** Rory Sullivan, 'ICC prosecutor declares Ukraine a "crime scene" after visiting Bucha to investigate Russia's war', *Independent*, 14 April 2022. 'Statement of Karim Khan at Arria formula meeting of UN Security Council', ICC, 27 April 2022.

230 **'remain responsible':** 'Summary of the judgment' (Ukraine vs Russian Federation), ICJ, 2 February 2024.

230 **re-examining carve-outs:** 'Statement on Russia's invasion of Ukraine: A Crime of Aggression. The need to amend the crime of aggression's jurisdictional regime', Global Institute for the Prevention of Aggression, 24 March 2022.

231–2 **tribunal proposal, Chatham House event:** Philippe Sands, 'Putin's use of military force is a crime of aggression', *Financial Times*, 28 February 2022. 'A criminal tribunal for aggression in Ukraine', Chatham House, 4 March 2022.

232 **'doesn't threaten anyone', denials continued:** Vladimir Isachenkov, 'Kremlin denies plans to invade Ukraine, alleges Nato threats', Associated Press, 12 November 2021. 'Defence secretary meets Russian counterpart in Moscow', Ministry of Defence, 11 February 2022.

233–4 **'on the conscience of Ukraine's ruling regime', 'not our plan to occupy':** Address by President of Russian Federation, Kremlin, 21 February 2022 and 24 February 2022.

234 **'persecuted with bloody terror', 'not wage war against women and children', 'shall give a propagandist cause':** Proclamation by Adolf Hitler to the German army, 1 September 1939. Address by Adolf Hitler before the Reichstag, 1 September 1939. Adolf Hitler, 22 August 1939, quoted in 'Judgment: The Aggression against Poland'. All via the Avalon Project, Yale Law School.

234–5 **Putin–Carlson:** 'Interview to Tucker Carlson: Vladimir Putin answered questions from Tucker Carlson, a journalist and founder of Tucker Carlson Network', Kremlin, 9 February 2024.

235–6 **'truly a historic moment', 'first prosecutions … in the modern era':** Ambassador van Schaack's remarks at United for Justice conference, Lviv, 3 March 2023. Ambassador van Schaack's testimony for Senate Judiciary Committee, Washington, 19 April 2023.

236–7 **Putin indictment:** 'ICC judges issue arrest warrants against Vladimir Putin and Maria Lvova-Belova', ICC, 17 March 2023. Steve Crawshaw, 'Milošević finally stood trial at The Hague – and Vladimir Putin isn't above the law either', *Guardian*, 22 March 2023.

238 **'some negativity', we will manage:** Elena Romanova, 'Who is Maria Lvova-Belova, the children's rights advocate accused of war crimes alongside Putin?', Novaya Gazeta. Europe, 6 April 2023. Alex Leff, Michele Kelemen and Charles Maynes, 'The International Criminal Court issues an arrest warrant for Putin', National Public Radio, 17 March 2023. 'Vstrecha z Upolnomochennym po pravam rebyonka Mariei L'vovoi-Belovoi' ('Meeting with children's commissioner Maria L'vova-Belova'), Kremlin, 16 February 2023.

238–9 **'sweeping the cobblestones', 'squeeze and pressure', 'Eight minutes later':** Julia Davis, 'Putin cronies resort to begging on live TV over war failures', *Daily Beast*, 4 December 2022. Brendan Cole, 'Russian state TV figures react to Putin's arrest warrant', *Newsweek*, 18 March 2023. 'ICC concerned by Russia's "threats" over Putin warrant', *Al Jazeera*, 23 March 2023.

239 **warrant for Khan:** 'Russia indicts ICC prosecutor and judge that issued Putin arrest warrant', JURIST, 22 May 2023.

239 **'I'm a mother':** Isobel Yeung, Maya Rostowska and Ana Archen, 'We interviewed the Russian woman accused of "stealing" 20,000 children', *Vice*, 1 May 2023.

240 **'Africa will come to Russia':** Nicolas Camut, 'Russian state media spins Putin pulling out of South Africa summit', Politico, 20 July 2023.

240 **'contribute to the prevention':** ICC judges issue arrest warrants against Sergei Kobylash and Viktor Sokolov, ICC, 5 March 2024.

241 **'committed by [Ukraine's] citizens':** Tom Dannenbaum, 'Unforced error: Article 124 and the regrettable caveat to Ukraine's proposed ratification of the ICC statute', Just Security, 20 August 2024. 'Ratifying the Rome Statute a welcome step, but limitations must be addressed', Amnesty International, 22 August 2024.

242 **'until the end of my life':** '5 AM: "I woke to the sounds of bombs in Kyiv"', Netherlands Helsinki Committee, 14 March 2023.

242   **'afraid that the idea of freedom will prevail'**: Oleksandra Matviichuk, 'Time to take responsibility', Nobel Prize lecture, 10 December 2022.

244   **'ecocide'**: Isabella Kaminski, 'EU criminalises environmental damage "comparable to ecocide"', *Guardian*, 17 November 2023.

245   **Mariupol documentation:** *Our City was Gone: Russia's Devastation of Mariupol (report), Beneath the Rubble: Documenting Devastation and Loss in Mariupol*, Human Rights Watch/SITU Research/Truth Hounds, February 2024.

246–8   **'That made me stop', 'found ourselves in hell', 'very chic', 'plague of impunity'**: Joanna Kakissis, 'She saved the diary of a Ukrainian writer killed by Russia. Then she was killed, too', National Public Radio, 15 July 2023. Luis de Vega, 'Writer Héctor Abad survives Ukraine bombing: "We were having a laugh and suddenly found ourselves in hell"', *El País*, 29 June 2023. Nataliya Gumenyuk, 'My friend was out for pizza when the missile hit. Putin's targeting of civilians must be punished', *Guardian*, 3 July 2023. Richard Spencer, 'Ukrainian writer killed in Russian strike had nearly finished book on war', *The Times*, 6 July 2023. Alexander Motyl, 'Russian elites flaunt their inhumanity', *The Hill*, 7 July 2023.

247   **'how Russia kills', 'new Executed Renaissance'**: Andrey Kurkov, *Our Daily War* (London: Open Borders Press, 2024). Sasha Dovzhyk, 'How the light gets in. Remembering Victoria Amelina', London Ukrainian Review, 24 August 2023, quoting foreword by Victoria Amelina in Volodymyr Vakulenko, *I am Transforming . . . Occupation Diary. Selected Poems* (Kyiv: Vivat, 2023). Victoria Amelina, *Looking at Women, Looking at War: A War and Justice Diary* (London: William Collins, 2025).

248   **Kramatorsk 'hoax'**: Brendan Cole, 'Pro-Kremlin media U-turns over Kramatorsk station attack in Ukraine', *Newsweek*, 8 April 2022.

249   **notebooks disorganised:** Janine di Giovanni, 'Holding Russia to account for war crimes in Ukraine', *Vanity Fair*, 24 August 2022.

250–2   **Aleppo–Kharkiv–Mariupol:** Nima Elbagir and others, 'Russian general who oversaw atrocities in Syria led cluster bomb attacks on civilians in Ukraine', CNN, 14 May 2022. Pjotr Sauer, 'Sergei Surovikin: The "General Armageddon" now in charge of Russia's war', *Guardian*, 10 October 2022. Mary Ilyushina, 'Russia's new commander in Ukraine was decorated after brutality in Syria', *Washington Post*, 12 October 2022.

253   **'freaking goldmine'**: *The Cranes Call* (dir. Laura Warner), Channel 4 Television, 2024.

253   **hope for indictments:** 'CFJ files cases in Germany against Russian commanders for crimes committed in Ukraine', Clooney Foundation for Justice, 26 October 2023.

254–5   **'lesson from 1938', 'put it to good use'**: Patrick Wintour, 'We're in 1938 now: Putin's war in Ukraine and lessons from history', *Guardian*, 8 June 2024.

257   **'distorted picture'**: Robert Chandler in Vasily Grossman, *The Road: Short Fiction and Essays* (London: MacLehose Press, 2011).

258   **'does not target civilians'**: 'Attack on funeral reception in Hroza, 5 October 2023', UN Human Rights Monitoring Mission in Ukraine, October 2023.

260   **Moscow, as always, denied it:** Anthony Borden, 'Hospital attack

continues Russia's war on children', Institute of War and Peace Reporting, 11 July 2024.

Chapter Eight: 'Remember Amalek'

263 **denials were themselves the lie, 'like seeing a horror film':** Documentation of the events of 7 October includes: 'Report of the Independent International Commission of Inquiry on the Occupied Palestinian Territory', A/HRC/56/26, UN, 27 May 2024, and the 230-page '"I can't erase all the blood from my mind": Palestinian armed groups' October 7 assault on Israel', Human Rights Watch, 17 July 2024. *We Will Dance Again* (dir. Yariv Moser, 2024). Disinformation and denial of well-documented crimes on both sides has been rife.

263 **Philippeville:** See also Chapter Two, including Shatz, 'Vengeful pathologies'.

264 **'prevent the establishment of a Palestinian state':** Tal Schneider, 'For years, Netanyahu propped up Hamas. Now it's blown up in our faces', *Times of Israel*, 8 October 2023.

264 **apparent criminality:** It was not just in the context of international war crimes that Netanyahu's behaviour was questioned. His trial on charges of bribery, fraud and breach of trust began in Jerusalem District Court in 2020; despite delays, the trial continues at the time of writing. Some argued that the Gaza conflict helped Netanyahu by distracting the focus from those accusations. Netanyahu says the gifts he received were legitimate. Before the attacks of 7 October, there were huge protests in Israel against his proposals for judicial overhaul, which would have included the government's ability to overrule the Israeli Supreme Court. Chen Maanit, 'Israeli court rejects Netanyahu's request to delay testifying in his corruption cases', *Haaretz*, 13 November 2024. Yossi Verter, 'Netanyahu sounds like he's busy prepping a defense. The panic in his office is palpable', *Haaretz*, 13 November 2024.

264 **accuracy vs damage:** Bethan McKernan and Quique Kierszenbaum, '"We're focused on maximum damage": Ground offensive into Gaza seems imminent', *Guardian*, 10 October 2023. (Israel took issue with a common paraphrase, which summarised the statement as: 'The emphasis is on damage and not on accuracy.' The IDF claimed that this paraphrase was 'blatantly false' and that the IDF always took 'extensive measures to mitigate harm to the civilian population in Gaza'. IDF press release clarification, 25 December 2023.)

264 **no longer functioning:** Noon briefing, UN Secretary-General's spokesperson, quoting World Health Organization, 27 March 2024.

264 **'no food, no fuel ... human animals':** Emanuel Fabian, 'Defense minister announces "complete siege" of Gaza: No power, food or fuel', *Times of Israel*, 9 October 2023.

265 **'I painted a beautiful future':** Beth McKernan, 'The Gaza physiotherapist: My house was bombed – and my baby son and beloved husband died', *Guardian*, 25 July 2024.

265 **'I wish for death':** Orla Guerin, 'Gazan girl begs rescuers to save brother first as entire family killed', BBC, 22 March 2024.

265 **'human pinballs':** 'People of Gaza "being told to move like human

pinballs", but nowhere is safe, Secretary-General tells Security Council',
UN, 8 December 2023.

265   **'last thing I would be able to do'**: 'Palestinians mourn poet Refaat
Alareer killed in Israeli air strike', *Al Jazeera*, 8 December 2023 (with
link to *Electronic Intifada* podcast interview, 9 October 2023). Sinan
Antoon, '"If I must die", A Poem by Refaat Alareer', *In These Times*, 27
December 2023.

266   **'They are shooting at us'**: 'The killing of Hind Rajab', Forensic
Architecture, in collaboration with Earshot and *Al Jazeera*'s 'Fault Lines',
21 June 2024.

266   **children's deaths**: Kanishka Singh, 'UNICEF says over 13,000 children
killed in Gaza in Israel offensive', Reuters, 18 March 2024.

266   **WCNSF**: 'Gaza coins a new acronym: WCNSF – Wounded Child No
Surviving Family', *Middle East Monitor*, 7 November 2023.

266   **'grim milestone'**: 'Turk pleads for end to fighting as death toll passes
40,000', OHCHR, 15 August 2024.

266   **'concerted effort'**: 'UN Commission finds war crimes and crimes
against humanity in Israeli attacks on Gaza health facilities and treatment
of detainees, hostages', OHCHR, 10 October 2024.

266–7 **'as if it were a human decision'**: Yuval Abraham: '"Lavender": The
AI machine directing Israel's bombing spree in Gaza', *+972 Magazine*,
3 April 2024; '"A mass assassination factory": Inside Israel's calculated
bombing of Gaza', *+972 Magazine/Local Call*, 30 November 2023.

267   'Indiscriminate attacks', 'Constant care': Protocol additional to the Geneva
Conventions of 12 August 1949 (Protocol 1), of 8 June 1977. A UN report
found the largest single category of those killed to be infants and young
children. Seventy per cent of deaths in Gaza were reported to be women
and children, in what the UN described as 'a systematic violation of the
fundamental principles of international humanitarian law, including
distinction and proportionality'. The UN human rights commissioner
called for 'due reckoning' through 'credible and impartial judicial bodies'.
('There must be "due reckoning" for horrific violations, possible atrocity
crimes in Gaza', OHCHR, 8 November 2024.)

267   **'the highest number', reasons for hunger, 'intentional starvation'**:
Secretary-General's press encounter on Gaza, UN, 18 March 2024. 'UN
human rights chief: Israel's "extensive restrictions" on Gaza aid may be
war crime', *Times of Israel*, 19 March 2024. 'Manufacturing famine: Israel
is committing the war crime of starvation in the Gaza Strip', B'Tselem,
April 2024.

268   **'entire nation'**: 'One-on-one with President Herzog', CNN transcript,
15 October 2023. Herzog said later he was 'disgusted' by the way his
words were quoted, including by the International Court of Justice
('"A blood libel": Herzog says ICJ "twisted my words" to support
"unfounded" contention', *Times of Israel*, 29 January 2024). Herzog
noted that in addition to the quoted words, he had also told a media
briefing (12 October): 'Israel abides by international law, operates by
international law.' He appeared to believe that that 'trumped' his other
statements, even where those were in contradiction with the assurances.

268   **'What is wrong with you?'**: Sky Television interview, 12
October 2023.

268   **'Burn Gaza', 'no innocents'**: 'Deputy Knesset speaker calls for burning Gaza', *Times of Israel*, 17 November 2023. 'Ahead of Hague hearing, Likud MK doubles down on call to "burn Gaza"', *Times of Israel*, 10 January 2024.

268   **'especially serious war crime'**: Hans-Peter Kaul, judge and vice-president of ICC, 'Peace through justice? The International Criminal Court in The Hague', ICC, 2 November 2009.

268   **'Was it worth it?'**: Tzipi Hotovely, interview with Piers Morgan, Talk TV, 16 October 2023.

269   **'most moral'**: Ben Farmer, 'IDF is most moral army in the world, says Netanyahu', *Daily Telegraph*, 28 December 2023 (and other occasions).

269   **great-uncle**: Isaac Herzog's maternal grandmother was Leah Ambache *née* Steinberg, sister of Rachel Lauterpacht. Leah's daughter Aura married Chaim Herzog, sixth president of Israel; their son Isaac is eleventh president of Israel.

269   **'legal duty to respect'**: 'Sovereignty and human rights', in Lauterpacht (ed.), *Collected Papers of Hersch Lauterpacht*, vol. 3.

269   **'cannot justify', 'justifying terrorism'**: 'Secretary-General's remarks to the Security Council on the Middle East', UN, 24 October 2023. 'Israel accuses UN chief of justifying terrorism for saying Hamas attack "didn't happen in a vacuum"', Associated Press, 26 October 2023.

269   **Israeli letter**: Emma Graham-Harrison and Quique Kierszenbaum, 'Israeli public figures accuse judiciary of ignoring incitement to genocide in Gaza', *Guardian*, 3 January 2024.

270   **'no guilt, not even a tiny bit'**: Gideon Levy, 'In Israel, 20,000 Gazans are responsible for their own deaths. I've never been so ashamed', *Haaretz*, 17 December 2023.

270   **detained for displaying posters**: Standing Together, X, 18 October 2023.

271   **too little force**: Peace Index – January 2024, Tel Aviv University. Other polls showed similar results.

271   **'world sees something completely different', 'claim it's fake news', no Hamas atrocities**: Anat Saragusti, 'Israelis don't see images from Gaza because our journalists are not doing their job', *Haaretz* podcast, 13 December 2023. Yuval Noah Harari, 'From Gaza to Iran, Netanyahu is endangering Israel's survival', *Haaretz*, 18 April 2024. It is not just today's crimes that Israeli audiences do not see. History is sometimes treated as off-limits, too, including the mass ethnic cleansing of 1948 known as the *nakba* or 'catastrophe', when three quarters of a million Palestinians lost their homes. As *Haaretz* noted on the seventy-fifth anniversary of the *nakba* in 2023: 'For Palestinians, the Nakba is not the past. It is the present. The process that began in 1948 has essentially never ended.' In 2024, blocked films included *1948 – Remember, Remember Not*, based on diaries and letters from Jews and Arabs, by the Israeli documentary-maker Neta Shoshani. Those who were eager to deny the possibility of Israeli crimes had earlier accused Shoshani of 'blood libel' in connection with her film on the notorious Deir Yassin massacre of April 1948. (Doltan Halevy et al., 'Six basic facts about the nakba everyone should know', *Haaretz*, 18 May 2023. 'Ben-Gvir's police thwart screenings of films presenting the Palestinian narrative', *Haaretz*, 14 October 2024. Nrit Anderman,

'Another film ban in Israel: Film Review Council forbids screenings of documentary on 1948 war', *Haaretz*, 6 November 2024. Ofer Aderet, 'Testimonies from the censored Deir Yassin massacre: "They piled bodies and burned them"', *Haaretz*, 16 July 2017.)

271   **mirrored by attitudes on the other side:** Public opinion poll no. 92, Palestinian Center for Policy and Survey Research, 10 July 2024.

271–2   **suicide bombings:** Joe Stork, 'Erased in a Moment: Suicide Bombing Attacks against Israeli Civilians', Human Rights Watch, November 2002. Chris McGreal, 'Suicide attacks "are war crimes"', *Guardian*, 1 November 2002.

272   **'does not depend on reciprocity', 'the enemy's fault':** 'People of Gaza "being told to move like human pinballs"'. Omer Bartov, 'As a former IDF soldier and historian of genocide, I was deeply disturbed by my recent visit to Israel', *Guardian*, 13 August 2024.

272   **'Goliath is kicking David's ass':** Liza Rozovsky, '"We are the Gazans of yesterday and tomorrow. We are they and they are us"', *Haaretz*, 20 April 2024.

272–3   **'mowing the grass', 'periodic slaughter', 'Dahiya doctrine', 'landlord has gone crazy':** Zehava Galon, 'Israelis are concerned with tactics, not morality', *Haaretz*, 7 June 2022. 'Israel warns Hezbollah war would invite destruction', Reuters, 3 October 2008. Akiva Eldar, 'The landlord's craziness', *Haaretz*, 3 July 2006.

273   **'tribalised pain':** Zeid Ra'ad al-Hussein, 'Building Peace: Israel-Palestine and the importance of moral consistency', International Peace Institute, 31 October 2023.

274   **'a new heat':** Bronwen Maddox, 'The Director's Annual Lecture 2024', Chatham House, 23 January 2024.

274   **'war crimes', 'pure terror':** 'Russian attacks on Ukraine infrastructure are war crimes – EU's von der Leyen', Reuters, 19 October 2022.

274   **'disastrous message':** Virginie Malingre, 'Von der Leyen fuels EU discontent after closely-watched Israel visit', *Le Monde*, 24 October 2023.

274–5   **indictments, 'changed circumstances':** 'Statement of ICC Prosecutor Karim Khan: Applications for arrest warrants in the situation in the state of Palestine', ICC, 20 May 2024. 'Prosecution's withdrawal of the Prosecutor's application under article 58 of a warrant of arrest against Ismail Haniyeh', ICC, 2 August 2024.

276   **'blood libels':** Statement by PM Netanyahu, Prime Minister's Office, 20 May 2024.

277   **'outrageous', 'deeply unhelpful', 'Let me be clear':** Statement from President Joe Biden on the warrant applications by the International Criminal Court, White House, 20 May 2024. Fiona Hamilton, 'Rishi Sunak slams "deeply unhelpful" ICC for Israel war crimes inquiry', *The Times*, 21 May 2024.

277   **'equates the victim':** 'Reactions to ICC prosecutor's request for arrest warrants for Israeli, Hamas leaders', Reuters, 20 May 2024.

278   **'shies away from politicisation':** 'UK's Karim Khan elected next ICC prosecutor, will replace controversial Bensouda', *Times of Israel*, 3 February 2021.

279   **'birth certificate':** 'Abbas calls for Palestinian unity after "birth certificate" for Palestinian state', CNN, 3 December 2012.

279   **'reasonable basis'**: 'Statement of the prosecutor, Fatou Bensouda, on the conclusion of the preliminary examination in Ukraine', ICC, 11 December 2020. In 2024, Finland arrested Yan Petrovsky (who had changed his name to Voislav Torden), a former commander of the Russian neo-Nazi 'Rusich' unit, in connection with alleged war crimes in Ukraine in 2014. ('Finnish prosecutor charges Russian ultranationalist leader with war crimes,' Radio Free Europe/Radio Liberty, 31 October 2024.)

279–80 **'reason and balance', 'not a panacea'**: 'Statement of ICC Prosecutor Fatou Bensouda respecting an investigation of the situation in Palestine', ICC, 3 March 2021.

279–80 **'scandalous', 'moral and legal bankruptcy', 'under attack', 'height of hypocrisy'**: 'Foreign Minister Ashkenazi: ICC probe decision "an act of moral and legal bankruptcy"', *Times of Israel*, 3 March 2021. 'President Rivlin comments on the International Criminal Court decision', Ministry of Foreign Affairs, 3 March 2021. Peter Beaumont, 'ICC opens investigation into war crimes in Palestinian territories', *Guardian*, 3 March 2021.

280   **'strategic threat'**: Raphael Ahren, 'Netanyahu: Fighting ICC war crimes probe among government's key objectives', *Times of Israel*, 17 May 2020.

280   **'political body and not a judicial institution'**: 'Netanyahu: An ICC investigation of Israel would be "pure anti-Semitism"', *Times of Israel*, 6 February 2021.

280–1 **attack on al-Haq**: Shawan Jabarin, 'We document human rights violations. Israel wants to silence us', *New York Times*, 23 September 2022.

281   **spied, smear campaign**: Yuval Abraham and Meron Rapoport, 'Surveillance and interference: Israel's covert war on the ICC exposed', *+972 Magazine*, 28 May 2024. Harry Davies, 'Revealed: Israeli spy chief "threatened" ICC prosecutor over war crimes inquiry', *Guardian*, 28 May 2024. Harry Davies, Bethan McKernan, Yuval Abraham and Meron Rapoport, 'Spying, hacking and intimidation: Israel's nine-year "war" on the ICC exposed', *Guardian*, 28 May 2024.

282   **'there in black and white'**: 'Statement of ICC prosecutor Karim Khan from Cairo on the situation in the state of Palestine and Israel', ICC, 30 October 2023.

282   **'under no misapprehension', 'any discernible change'**: 'Statement of ICC prosecutor Karim Khan from Ramallah on the situation in the state of Palestine and Israel', ICC, 6 December 2023. Karim Khan, X, 12 February 2024.

282   **new lawyers**: Yoav Zitun, 'IDF readies for legal onslaught following war in Gaza', Ynetnews, 20 March 2024.

282   **'unparalleled and unprecedented', 'nothing like the siege in Gaza'**: 'Secretary-General's press conference', UN, 20 November 2023. Jan Egeland and others, 'We are no strangers to human suffering, but we've seen nothing like the siege of Gaza', *New York Times*, 11 December 2023.

283   **'outrage of historic proportions', 'antisemitic hate crime'**: 'Statement by Prime Minister Benjamin Netanyahu', Ministry of Foreign Affairs, 30 April 2024.

283   **'inconvenient, inopportune or politically embarrassing':** Lauterpacht
       (ed.), *Collected Papers of Hersch Lauterpacht*, vol. 5.

283   **'impede, intimidate or improperly influence':** International Criminal
       Court, X, 3 May 2024. Tovah Lazaroff, 'ICC in veiled warning to
       Netanyahu: Stop intimidation tactics', *Jerusalem Post*, 3 May 2024.

284   **'we will target you':** Matt Berg, '"You have been warned": GOP
       Senators caution ICC over Israeli arrest warrants', Politico, 6 May 2024.

286   **French reaction:** 'Prosecutor applies to ICC for arrest warrants', Foreign
       Ministry, 20 May 2024. 'France backs ICC after it seeks arrest warrants
       for Israel's Netanyahu, Hamas leaders', Reuters, 21 May 2024.

286   **belligerent response:** 'Netanyahu said to ask AG to probe him and Gallant
       in bid to avert ICC arrest warrant', *Times of Israel*, 12 September 2024.

286   **Palestine recognition, 'severe consequences':** Kathryn Armstrong,
       'Ireland, Norway and Spain to recognise Palestinian state', BBC, 22
       May 2024.

287   **'Jewish history teaches us':** Lord Neuberger and others, 'The laws of
       war must guide Israel's response to Hamas's atrocity', *Financial Times*, 17
       October 2023.

287   **new judge responded:** 'Annex to the notification of Judge Hohler's
       provision of information', ICC, 20 November 2024. The eight-page
       response of Beti Hohler to Israel's challenge was published one day
       before the arrest warrants were confirmed. Judge Hohler, who is from
       Slovenia, said she 'appreciate[d] the opportunity' to provide factual
       information in response to Israel's list of questions about her prior
       employment with the Office of the Prosecutor which Israel had implied
       should disqualify her. In her response, she emphasised the importance of
       impartiality being approached from the perspective of 'the fair-minded
       and informed observer, founded firmly on facts'.

287   **allegations of sexual misconduct, 'utmost urgency':** 'Prosecution's
       withdrawal of the "Prosecution's application under article 58 for a
       warrant of arrest against Ismail Haniyeh"', 2 August 2024', published in
       redacted form, ICC, 9 September 2024. 'ICC pre-trial chamber I rejects
       the State of Israel's challenges to jurisdiction and issues warrants of arrest
       for Benjamin Netanyahu and Yoav Gallant', ICC, 21 November 2024.
       As this book was going to press, Khan's requests for arrest warrants – at
       that point, not yet confirmed – became further complicated when it
       emerged that the prosecutor faced accusations that he had tried to force
       a female co-worker into a relationship and had groped her against her
       will. The *Wall Street Journal* argued that the requested warrants had been
       an attempt to distract from those allegations (although preparations for
       the May 2024 announcement were well advanced by the time that the
       allegations were made). The Associated Press reported that court officials
       had said the allegations could be part of 'an Israeli intelligence smear
       campaign to discredit the court'. Khan himself insisted that there was
       'no truth' to the allegations, and said: 'This is a moment in which myself
       and the International Criminal Court are subject to a wide range of
       attacks and threats.' The ICC's governing body, the Assembly of States
       Parties, called for an external inquiry 'to ensure a fully independent,
       impartial and fair process'. Following reports that he had been asked to
       temporarily step aside, Khan said he would remain in post.

Theoretically, there should be no connection between the arrest warrants, on the one hand, and the truth or untruth of allegations against the prosecutor, on the other. If the prosecutor committed abuse, that does not mean that his request for arrest warrants was unjustified. Conversely, if he was wrongly accused, that does not automatically mean that arrest warrants deserved to be approved. Inevitably, however, the allegations muddied conversations around the warrants themselves. ('A mess at the International Criminal Court', *Wall Street Journal*, 23 October 2024. Janet Anderson, 'Pressure mounts on the ICC', Justiceinfo, 24 October 2024. Joshua Goodman and Molly Quell, 'International court prosecutor who charged Netanyahu faces sexual misconduct accusation', Associated Press, 25 October 2024. Karim Khan, X, 24 October 2024. Harry Davies and Robert Flummerfelt, 'ICC prosecutor allegedly tried to suppress sexual misconduct claims against him', *Guardian*, 27 October 2024. Joshua Goodman and Molly Quell, 'International prosecutor who charged Netanyahu vows to cooperate with sexual misconduct investigation', Associated Press, 28 October 2024. Stephanie van den Berg and Anthony Deutsch, 'Exclusive: ICC to investigate alleged misconduct by war crimes prosecutor, sources say', Reuters, 9 November 2024. 'Statement by the President of the Assembly of States Parties on investigation into alleged misconduct by an ICC elected official', ICC, 11 November 2024. Molly Quell, 'International Criminal Court prosecutor won't step down during new probe into misconduct accusations', Associated Press, 11 November 2024.)

287 **'rush to seek arrest warrants', 'strong response':** 'US rejects ICC arrest warrants for Israeli officials, White House spokesperson says', Reuters, 21 November 2024. 'How US politicians responded to Netanyahu's ICC arrest warrant', *Al Jazeera*, 21 November 2024.

288 **'blood libel', 'preposterous':** 'Government spokesman Eylon Levy says Israel will challenge South Africa's "blood libel" at The Hague', *Times of Israel*, 2 January 2024. Tovah Lazaroff, 'Genocide claim to ICJ is "preposterous", Herzog tells Blinken', *Jerusalem Post*, 9 January 2024.

288 **'deranged ideas':** 'Genocide charge against Israel must serve as a wake-up call', *Haaretz*, 3 January 2024.

288 **'greatest shows of hypocrisy':** Hearing of the South African petition at the ICJ, Ministry of Foreign Affairs, 11 January 2024.

288 **'hopelessly flawed':** Stephanie van den Berg, 'Russia calls on World Court to throw out Ukraine genocide challenge', Reuters, 18 September 2023.

289 **'meritless':** Press briefing by press secretary Karine Jean-Pierre and NSC coordinator for strategic communications John Kirby, White House, 3 January 2024.

289 **'horrific irony', 'friend and ally':** David Rose, '"I'll always stand by Israel" Sunak tells CFI event', *Jewish Chronicle*, 22 January 2024. 'Prime Minister Boris Johnson confirms UK opposition to ICC investigation in Israel', Conservative Friends of Israel, 13 April 2021.

290 **'real and imminent risk':** Order of 26 January 2024, ICJ.

291 **'Hague schmague':** 'Minister dismisses world court after it says Israel must take measures to prevent genocide in Gaza', Sky News, 26

January 2024. 'Ben Gvir, an irresponsible provocateur', *Haaretz*, 14 February 2023.

291   **firm handshakes:** Raoul Wootliff, 'Netanyahu touts friendship with Putin in new billboard', *Times of Israel*, 28 July 2019.

292   **rolled out the red carpet:** Greg Mills and Ray Hartley, 'What explains South Africa's tortured like-and-loathe path to hypocrisy?', *Daily Maverick*, 24 January 2024.

292   **'famine is already setting in', 'disastrous':** Orders of 28 March 2024 and 24 May 2024, ICJ.

293   **compulsory rulings:** 'Joint stakeout by Estonia, Belgium, France, Germany and Poland on Myanmar', Estonian Mission to the UN, 4 February 2020. 'UN fails to take action on order against Myanmar on Rohingya', *Al Jazeera*, 5 February 2020.

293   **'come with a heavy price':** Barak Ravid, 'Israel asks Congress to press South Africa to drop ICJ genocide case', Axios, 9 September 2024.

293   **'one place for Germany: on Israel's side':** 'In deep solidarity and friendship with Israel', Statement by Chancellor Olaf Scholz to the Bundestag, 12 October 2023.

294   **Gaza 'ghetto':** Masha Gessen, 'In the shadow of the Holocaust', *New Yorker*, 9 December 2023. Calder McHugh, 'Masha Gessen kicks the hornet's nest on Israel and the Holocaust', Politico interview, 16 December 2023.

294   **'facilitating' genocide:** Republic of Nicaragua institutes proceedings against the Federal Republic of Germany and requests the Court to indicate provisional measures, ICJ, 1 March 2024.

294   **'tantamount to crimes against humanity':** Nicaragua's grim reality: Investigation by UN experts reveals crimes against humanity targeting civilians, including children and students, for political ends, OHCHR, 29 February 2024.

294–5   **'accusations have been swirling':** Marina Kormbaki and Christoph Schult, 'Berlin's support for Israel is damaging its international standing', *Der Spiegel*, 5 April 2024.

295   **'particularly important' on arms transfers:** Order of 30 April 2024, ICJ.

295   **60 per cent are orphans, 'will seek revenge':** 'A tale of two spies', *The Rest is Politics* podcast with Alastair Campbell and Rory Stewart, 1 April 2024. Yagil Levy, 'The Israeli army has dropped the restraint in Gaza, and the data shows unprecedented killing', *Haaretz*, 9 December 2023.

296   **'right to defend themselves':** 'Taoiseach says Israeli actions in Gaza "not acceptable"', RTÉ, 13 October 2023.

296   **antisemitic and Islamophobic attacks:** Aamna Mohdin and Neha Gohil, 'British Jews adjusting to "new reality" after year-long surge in antisemitism', *Guardian*, 2 October 2024. Neha Gohil, 'Record amount of anti-Muslim abuse reported in UK since 7 October attack', *Guardian*, 4 October 2024. 'Joint statement of special envoys and coordinators combating antisemitism', European Commission, 6 November 2023. 'Joint statement of the coordinators, special representatives, envoy and ambassadors on combating anti-Muslim hatred and discrimination', European Commission, 30 November 2023.

297   **'possible without the global south? Definitely not':** 'Justice must

become the new global rule supported by global unity', speech by President Volodymyr Zelenskyy at the 3rd summit for democracy, President's Office, 20 March 2024.

297   'bad for the goose': Saket Gokhale, 'Bear hugs double standards', *The Economist* (letter), 25 July 2024.

298   'stand united against impunity': 'International Criminal Court members speak out', Human Rights Watch, 17 June 2024.

298   'no worries': 'Kremlin says it has "no worries" about Putin visit to Mongolia despite an ICC warrant for his arrest', Associated Press, 30 September 2024.

298–9 **West Bank deaths, 'Pogroms', 'to the point where it has disappeared', seizure of land:** 'Israel kills more than 500 Palestinians in the West Bank since October 7', *Al Jazeera*, 16 May 2024. Oren Ziv, '"The soldiers opened the way for the settlers": Pogroms surge across the West Bank', +972 *Magazine*, 18 April 2024. Ronen Bergman and Mark Mazzetti, 'The unpunished: How extremist settlers took over Israel', *New York Times*, 16 May 2024. Lorenzo Tondo and Peter Beaumont, 'Israel has approved "largest West Bank land grab in 30 years", watchdog says', *Guardian*, 4 July 2024. 'The government declares 12,000 dunams in the Jordan Valley as State Lands', Peace Now, 3 July 2024.

299   **jail violence, torture:** Josh Breiner, 'Palestinian, Arab prisoners report surge in violence by guards in Israeli prison since October 7', *Haaretz*, 2 January 2024. Aaron Boxerman, 'UN report describes physical abuse and dire condition in Israeli detention', *New York Times*, 17 April 2024. 'Strapped down, blindfolded, held in diapers: Israeli whistleblowers detail abuse of Palestinians in shadowy detention center', CNN, 11 May 2024. 'Palestinian detainees held arbitrarily and secretly, subjected to torture and mistreatment', OHCHR, 31 July 2024. *Welcome to Hell: The Israeli Prison System as a Network of Torture Camps*, B'Tselem, 5 August 2024. 'Israel: Palestinian healthcare workers tortured', Human Rights Watch, 26 August 2024.

300   **'established process':** 'Legal consequences arising from the policies and practices of Israel in the Occupied Palestinian Territory', Written statement from UK, ICJ, 20 July 2023.

300   **'sustained abuse', 'tantamount to the crime of apartheid':** 'Advisory Opinion, Legal consequences arising from the policies and practices of Israel in the Occupied Palestinian Territory, including East Jerusalem', ICJ, 19 July 2024.

300   **'absurd', 'antisemitic', 'ill-judged':** Benjamin Netanyahu, X, 19 July 2024. 'Israeli leaders slam ICJ's call for end to "illegal" activities in Palestinian territories', *Jerusalem Post*, 19 July 2024. 'Herzog on ICJ ruling: one-sided and ill-judged', *Israel National News*, 19 July 2024.

301   **'a virtual invitation', 'broad consensus', 'pariah status':** Kenneth Roth, 'The ICJ has demolished Israel's claims that it is not occupying Palestinian territories', *Guardian*, 22 July 2024. Alon Pinkas: 'ICJ's decision on the occupation goes beyond Israel's worst fears', *Haaretz*, 19 July 2024; 'For Israel, pariah status now beckons', 29 July 2024.

301   **US, EU, UK sanctions, 'red line':** Simon Lewis, 'US sanctions ally of Israeli minister, fundraisers over settlers', Reuters, 19 April 2024. 'UK sanctions extremist groups and individuals for settler violence in

the West Bank', Foreign Commonwealth & Development Office, 3
May 2024. Jacob Magid, 'UK joins European Union in sanctioning
supremacist Lehava group and extremist settlers', *Times of Israel*, 3 May
2024. Amir Tibon and Ben Samuels, 'US set to sanction ultra-Orthodox
Israeli army battalion based in the West Bank', *Haaretz*, 20 April 2024.
'Israeli officials lash out over potential US sanctions on military unit',
New York Times, 21 April 2024.

301–2   **'utmost severity', export pressures, 'clear risk':** Kevin Liptak, 'Biden
says he will stop sending bombs and artillery shells to Israel if it launches
major invasion of Rafah', CNN, 9 May 2024. Kevin Liptak and Samantha
Waldenberg, 'White House says attack at Rafah camp did not cross Biden's
red line over supporting Israel', CNN, 28 May 2024. Stephanie van
den Berg, 'Dutch court orders halt to export of F-35 jet parts to Israel',
Reuters, 12 February 2024. 'UK suspends around 30 arms export licences
to Israel for use in Gaza over International Humanitarian Law concerns',
Foreign, Commonwealth and Development Office, 2 September 2024.
Ben Samuels, 'Will the US sanction Ben-Gvir and Smotrich for trying
to set the Mid-East on fire?', *Haaretz*, 28 August 2024. Julian Borger and
Quique Kierszenbaum, 'US imposes sanctions on extremist Israeli settlers
in West Bank', *Guardian*, 28 August 2024.

302   **al-Shifa hospital:** Aya Batrawy and Omar El Qattaa, 'Here's what we
found after Israel's raid on al-Shifa', National Public Radio, 6 April
2024. David Gritten, 'UN rights chief "horrified" by mass grave reports
at Gaza hospitals', BBC, 24 April 2024. Solcyré Burga, 'Mass graves
of hundreds uncovered in Gaza sound alarm', *Time*, 26 April 2024.
Stephanie van den Berg, 'Gaza hospital staff questioned by ICC war
crimes prosecutors', Reuters, 30 April 2024. Yolande Knell, 'Mass graves
and body bags: al-Shifa hospital after Israel withdrew its forces', BBC,
5 June 2024. William Booth and Lorenzo Tugnoli, 'Inside the ruins of
Gaza's al-Shifa hospital,' *Washington Post*, 1 April 2024.

302   **'We want answers':** Press briefing by National Security Advisor Jake
Sullivan, White House, 24 April 2024.

302   **ban on quoting statistics:** Nick Robertson, 'House votes to ban State
Department from citing Gaza Health Ministry death toll statistics', The
Hill, 27 June 2024. Lauren Leatherby, 'Gaza's death toll was largely
accurate in early days of war, study finds,' *New York Times*, 25 July 2024.

302–3   **arms exports, 'arbitrary denial', 'currently assess':** Brett Murphy,
'Israel deliberately blocked humanitarian aid to Gaza, two government
bodies concluded. Antony Blinken rejected them', ProPublica, 24
September 2024. 'US approves $20 billion in weapons sales to Israel
amid threat of wider Middle East war', Associated Press, 14 August
2024. Brian Finucane, 'Section 6201: No military assistance to states
restricting US humanitarian assistance', Just Security, 19 March 2024.

303   **gunshots to the head:** Feroze Sidhwa, '65 doctors, nurses and
paramedics: What we saw in Gaza', *New York Times*, 9 October 2024.
In an unusual rebuttal of the widespread denials, the *New York Times*
detailed the factchecking process and concluded: 'Any implication that
[the article's] images are fabricated is simply false.' (Kathleen Kingsbury,
'Response to recent criticisms on *New York Times* opinion essay', *New
York Times*, 15 October 2024.)

303 **human shields:** Yaniv Kubovich and Michael Hauser, 'Israeli army uses Palestinian civilians to inspect potentially booby-trapped tunnels in Gaza', *Haaretz*, 13 August 2024. Malak A. Tantesh, Julian Boger and Sufian Taha, 'Palestinians described being used as "human shields" by Israeli troops in Gaza', *Guardian*, 21 October 2024.

304 **'Be optimistic', 'watched in horror':** Bilal Shbair and Erika Solomon, 'He dreamed of escaping Gaza. The world watched him burned alive', *New York Times*, 20 October 2024. 'Remarks by Ambassador Linda Thomas-Greenfield at a UN Security Council briefing on the situation in the Middle East', United States Mission to the UN, 16 October 2024.

304 **'invisible firewall':** Noa Landau, 'A voluntary, invisible firewall cuts Israelis off from what's happening in Gaza', *Haaretz*, 16 October 2024.

304 **'village should be burned down':** Eden Solomon, 'Arab Israeli girl, 12, suspended from school after empathizing with Gazan children', *Haaretz*, 24 September 2024.

304 **'generals' plan':** The generals' plan suggested that after an evacuation order anybody remaining would become a military target. Ethnic cleansing ('deportation or forcible transfer of population', defined by the ICC Rome Statute as a crime against humanity) now became standard policy. Brigadier-General Itzik Cohen, commander of the 162nd Division in northern Gaza, said there was 'no intention' to allow residents to return to their homes: 'We received very clear orders. My task is to create a cleansed space.' There were echoes of events in Grozny twenty-five years earlier, when Putin's forces warned civilians that they would be treated as 'terrorists and bandits' unless they abandoned the Chechen capital; the UN would later describe Grozny as the most destroyed city on earth. Sam Sokol, 'Netanyahu tells lawmakers he's considering "Generals' Plan" to lay siege to northern Gaza', *Times of Israel*, 22 September 2024. 'Is Israel really implementing a plan of siege and starvation in Gaza?', *Haaretz*, 22 October 2024. 'Netanyahu's ethnic cleansing in Gaza is on display for all to see', *Haaretz*, 10 November 2024. Michael R. Gordon, 'Russians issue an ultimatum to rebel city', *New York Times*, 7 December 1999.

304 **Israel would face restrictions:** The messages were confused, at best. In October 2024, Blinken and Austin gave Israel a thirty-day deadline to allow access to humanitarian aid, or face suspension of weapons deliveries. (Barak Ravid, 'US demands Israel improve humanitarian conditions in Gaza or risk losing military aid', Axios, 15 October 2024. Tom Bateman, 'US top diplomat issues warning to Israel over Gaza aid', BBC, 23 October 2024.) Those demands were not met. As the deadline expired, the UN said the past month had marked 'a severe deterioration' in the 'already restrictive operating environment' for humanitarian operations in Gaza. A joint assessment by aid agencies found Israel had failed to comply and that the entire Palestinian population in north Gaza was now 'at imminent risk of dying from disease, famine and violence'. Human Rights Watch accused Israel of crimes against humanity for starvation and forced displacement, and called for a halt to arms sales. In the words of one Gaza resident: 'The scenes of the 1948 catastrophe are being repeated . . . Israel is carrying out ethnic cleansing under the sight and hearing of the impotent world.' But Washington, while

acknowledging the 'dire humanitarian situation', decided the threatened sanctions would not be appropriate, after all. ('Humanitarian access snapshot, Gaza Strip, October 2024', UN Office for the Co-ordination of Humanitarian Affairs, 11 November 2024. 'The Gaza Scorecard: Israel fails to comply with US humanitarian access demands in Gaza', Mercy Corps (with Oxfam, Save the Children and others), 13 November 2024. Peter Beaumont, 'Israel accused of crimes against humanity over forced displacement in Gaza', *Guardian*, 14 November 2024. *'Hopeless, Starving and Besieged': Israel's Forced Displacement of Palestinians in Gaza*, Human Rights Watch, 14 November 2024. 'Secretary Antony J. Blinken, remarks to the press', US Department of State, 13 November 2024.)

304 **'thimble for an inferno':** Dahlia Scheindlin, 'America's warning to Israel about Gaza aid came too late, for too many', *Haaretz*, 16 October 2024.

305 **'fancy silk robes':** 'PM Netanyahu's address to a joint meeting of the US Congress', Prime Minister's Office, 24 July 2024.

306 **Uzbekistan:** Steve Crawshaw, 'All talk', *Guardian*, 13 October 2008. *Bullets were Falling like Rain: The Andijan Massacre*, Human Rights Watch, June 2005.

306 **'treating Netanyahu like Putin':** Eran Yashiv, 'Autocrats of a feather: Israel's future rests on treating Netanyahu like Putin', *Haaretz*, 27 August 2024.

306–7 **US opinion, 'kissed babies':** Jeffrey M. Jones, 'Majority in US now disapprove of Israeli action in Gaza', Gallup News, 27 March 2004. Laura Silver, 'Younger Americans stand out in their views of the Israel-Hamas war', Pew Research, 2 April 2024. Mark Mazower, 'The week that shook Columbia', *Financial Times*, 27 April 2024. Youssef Munayyer, 'US support for Israel is collapsing. And Aipac knows it', *Guardian*, 7 August 2024.

307–8 **'in total denial', 'stick a finger in the eye', vote crumbled:** Andrew Marantz, 'Among the Gaza protest voters', *New Yorker*, 23 September 2024. Ben Samuels, 'Could Harris's approach to Arab-American voters cost her the White House?', *Haaretz*, 31 October 2024. Madeline Halpert, 'Trump courts divided Arab-American voters in must-win Michigan', BBC, 1 November 2024. Hafiz Rashid, 'Here's how badly Kamala Harris has lost Arab American voters', *New Republic*, 6 November 2024. Trevor Hunnicutt, Nandita Bose and Stephanie Kelly, 'Kamala Harris made a historic dash for the White House. Here's why she fell short', Reuters, 6 November 2024. Michael C. Bender, 'Why was there a broad drop-off in Democratic turnout in 2024?', *New York Times*, 11 November 2024.

308 **determining genocide:** Francesca Albanese, 'Anatomy of a genocide', Report of UN special rapporteur on human rights in the occupied Palestinian territories, UN, 24 March 2024. Amos Goldberg, 'Yes, it is genocide', The Palestine Project, 18 April 2024. Aryeh Neier, 'Is Israel committing genocide?', *New York Review of Books*, 6 June 2024. On 'special intent' ('*dolus specialis*'), see e.g. William A. Schabas, *An Introduction to the International Criminal Court* (Cambridge: Cambridge University Press, 2004).

309 'sterile debate', 'contribution to the law', 'disquieting incongruity':
William A. Schabas, 'Convention for the Prevention and Punishment
of the Crime of Genocide', UN Audiovisual Library of International
Law (2008) and *An Introduction to the International Criminal Court.*
Hersch Lauterpacht, review of Lemkin: *Axis Rule in Occupied Europe*, in
Cambridge Law Journal, 9 (1945). Hersch Lauterpacht (ed.), *International
Law: A Treatise*, vol 1: 'Peace' (London: Longman, Green and Co., 1955).

311 **only 15 per cent:** 'Only 15% of Israelis want Netanyahu to keep job
after Gaza war, poll finds', *Times of Israel*, 2 January 2024.

311 **future might seem bleak:** Raja Shehadeh, *What Does Israel Fear from
Palestine?* (London: Profile, 2024).

311 **'head of the snake':** Elia Ayoub, 'Killing Hezbollah leaders failed 30
years ago. It won't work now', *+972 Magazine*, 4 October 2024. Includes
links to Dimi Reider, X, 28 September 2024, with commentaries after
the assassination of Hizbollah leader Abbas al-Musawi in 1992.

311–12 **Lebanon:** Willem Marx and Jane Arraf, 'Lebanon counts nearly 500
killed in a day of Israeli strikes, with over 1,600 wounded', NPR, 23
September 2024. David Brennan, 'Israel's offensive in Lebanon has
displaced 1.2 million, prime minister says', ABC News, 4 October 2024.

312 **Germany found its voice:** 'Statement by the foreign ministers of France,
Germany, Italy and the United Kingdom on attacks against UNIFIL
bases', German Foreign Ministry, 14 October 2024. Netanyahu called the
accusations 'completely false': 'Netanyahu denies targeting UNIFIL, calls
for withdrawal. UNIFIL says we're staying', Reuters, 14 October 2024.

312 **'crushing response', 'abyss', 'spiral of doom':** Jon Gambrell, 'Iran's
supreme leader threatens Israel and US with a "crushing response" over
Israeli attack', Associated Press, 2 November 2024. 'In Beirut, Jordanian
FM says Israel's war with Hezbollah pushing region into abyss', *Times of
Israel*, 7 October 2024. Emma Farge, 'UN said workers fear same "spiral
of doom" in Lebanon as Gaza', Reuters, 8 October 2024.

Chapter Nine: 'I am Smelling Justice'

313 **'era of impunity is over':** Ban Ki-moon, 'Secretary-General's "An
Age of Accountability" address to the ICC review conference', UN, 31
May 2010.

313 **'justice cascade':** Kathryn Sikkink, *The Justice Cascade: How Human
Rights Prosecutions are Changing World Politics* (New York: W. W. Norton,
2011).

314 **125 states:** Ukraine officially joined the court in 2025, following the
process described in Chapter Seven. ('On January 1 2025, Ukraine will
become the 125th member state of the International Criminal Court',
President of Ukraine, 25 October 2024.)

314 **demand for universal jurisdiction, 'truly universal':** Universal
jurisdiction database and annual review, TRIAL International. 'Justice
beyond borders', Clooney Foundation for Justice. 'Building a universal
jurisdiction movement', *Asymmetrical Haircuts*, 3 May 2024.

315 **'judicial tyranny':** Henry Kissinger, 'The pitfalls of universal
jurisdiction', *Foreign Affairs*, 80:4 (July/August 2001), quoted in Chris
Stephen, *The Future of War Crimes Justice* (London: Melville House,
2024).

315   **collaboration in investigating war crimes:** 'Adoption of milestone treaty on international cooperation set to advance the fight against impunity', International Commission of Jurists, 31 May 2023.

315   **crimes against humanity, agreed to negotiations:** 'UN General Assembly must open formal negotiations on crimes against humanity convention', Amnesty International, 9 October 2024. 'Road to a new crimes against humanity treaty', *Asymmetrical Haircuts*, 4 October 2024. 'States must negotiate a robust treaty on crimes against humanity after breakthrough resolution', Amnesty International, 22 November 2024.

316   **'very dangerous':** Ilene R. Prusher, 'Battling warlords try civility: a grim human-rights report spurred Afghan warlords to stop targeting civilians', *Christian Science Monitor*, 9 May 2002. *Paying for the Taliban's Crimes*, Human Rights Watch, April 2002. Sara Darehshori, *Selling Justice Short: Why Accountability Matters for Peace*, Human Rights Watch, July 2009.

316   **jailed for life:** Christina Anderson and Farnaz Fassihi, 'Ex-Iranian official convicted by Swedish court for prison executions', *New York Times*, 14 July 2022.

316   **'smelling justice', 'hold them to account':** Emma Farge, 'Gambian ex-minister faces rape, torture charges in long-awaited Swiss trial', Reuters, 8 January 2024. 'Gambian government says it will prosecute exiled ex-ruler Jammeh', *Al Jazeera*, 25 May 2022. 'Gambian former minister of interior Ousman Sonko sentenced to 20 years in prison for crimes against humanity in historic Swiss trial', TRIAL International, 16 May 2024.

316   **Germany, Netherlands:** 'German court hands down second genocide conviction against ISIS member following enslavement and abuse of Yazidi women in Syria', Doughty Street Chambers, 28 July 2022. Margherita Capacci, 'Netherlands to open first trial on crimes against Yazidis', Justiceinfo, 22 May 2023.

317   **'no need to worry':** Christina Lamb, *Our Bodies Their Battlefield: What War Does to Women* (London: William Collins, 2020).

317   **'Every Yazidi', 'the voice of every Yazidi':** Nadia Murad (foreword by Amal Clooney), *The Last Girl: My Story of Captivity, and My Fight Against the Islamic State* (New York: Tim Duggan, 2017).

317   **'absence of trials':** 'Statement made by Mr Luis Moreno Ocampo at the ceremony for the solemn undertaking of the Chief Prosecutor of the ICC', ICC, 16 June 2003.

318   **'sense of pride':** Agustín Mango, 'Forget the Oscars, "Argentina, 1985" already won', *Buenos Aires Herald*, 13 March 2023.

319   **'impunity ... overwhelmed us':** Uki Goni, 'Argentina's junta trials to resume', *Guardian*, 15 June 2005.

319   **'as many people':** David Pion-Berlin, *The Ideology of State Terror: Economic Doctrine and Political Repression in Argentina and Peru* (Boulder: Lynne Reinner, 1989).

320   **'to defend his mother':** Sikkink, *The Justice Cascade*.

321   **'demonic forces':** Tom Phillips, 'Nicolás Maduro vows to "pulverise" challenge to his rule after disputed Venezuela election', *Guardian*, 5 August 2024.

321   **'unprecedented repression'**: 'Unprecedented Venezuela repression plunging nation into acute human rights crisis', OHCHR, 17 September 2024.

321   **'Truth is the primary word'**: Aaron McCarroll Gallegos, 'Bishop Gerardi's truth', Sojourners, July–August 1998.

321   **'with the knowledge or by the authority'**: Priscilla B. Hayner, *Unspeakable Truths: Facing the Challenge of Truth Commissions* (New York: Routledge, 2002).

321   **'of great personal integrity'**: Remarks in San Pedro Sula, Honduras, following a meeting with President Jose Efrain Rios Montt of Guatemala, 4 December 1982, Ronald Reagan Library and Museum.

322   **'conscience was clear'**: Nate Thayer, 'Day of Reckoning', *Far Eastern Economic Review*, 30 October 1997. Seth Mydans, 'In an interview, Pol Pot declares his conscience is clear', *New York Times*, 23 October 1997.

323   **'evidence, not politics'**: 'Cambodia: Political pressure undermining tribunal', Human Rights Watch, 22 July 2009.

323   **'not possible for a country to recover'**: Jack Losh, 'The lonely prosecutor: one man's historic fight for justice in central Africa', *Prospect*, 8 June 2019.

323–4 **Congo trial**: 'Kavumu trial: High military court confirms all condemnations', TRIAL International, 26 July 2018.

324   **'Serbs are victims, too'**: Steve Crawshaw, 'Serbs are victims, too', *Independent*, 28 July 1999.

324   **messy and imperfect**: Messiest of all has been the Special Tribunal for Lebanon, mostly notable as a 'how-not-to' guide to achieving accountability. The tribunal was created in 2009 in connection with the car-bomb assassination of former prime minister Rafiq Hariri and twenty-one others in Beirut in 2005. In the words of Habib Nassar of Impunity Watch, many Lebanese saw the tribunal as 'the mountain that gave birth to a mouse'. The billion-dollar Hague-based tribunal combined, as Nassar put it, 'a costly process, heavy bureaucracy and disconnect from those it is meant to deliver justice to – with the most acute problems that so often characterize national criminal processes: strong suspicions of political interference and serious security risks for those involved'. (Habib Nassar, 'The mountain that gave birth to a mouse', Justiceinfo, 8 January 2021.)

324–5 **'Justice is not perfect'**: Hannah Ellis-Petersen, 'Khmer Rouge leaders found guilty of genocide in Cambodia's "Nuremberg" moment', *Guardian*, 16 November 2018.

325   **'more than can be expected', 'resonates very strongly', 'hits a nerve'**: Raphael Schäfer, 'The echo of quiet voices: Liechtenstein's veto initiative and the American Six Principles', EJIL: Talk!, 10 October 2022. Maria Luisa Gambale, 'The UN veto initiative "hits a nerve"', PassBlue, 12 September 2024.

325–6 **'Change will come'**: Steve Crawshaw, 'In fear of shadows', *Independent on Sunday* magazine, 22 November 1998.

326   **'iceberg of misinformation'**: Michael Safi, 'Aung San Suu Kyi says "terrorists" are misinforming world about Myanmar violence', *Guardian*, 6 September 2017.

326   **'destroy the Rohingya as such'**: 'Rohingyas could face further

violence if they return to Myanmar, UN adviser warns', UN News, 13 March 2018.

327   **'impunity will end':** 'Two more years of atrocities in Myanmar', statement by Nicholas Koumjian, Independent Investigative Mechanism for Myanmar, 1 February 2023.

327–8   **Myanmar, world court:** Application instituting proceedings and request for provisional measures, Gambia vs Myanmar, ICJ, 11 November 2019. 'Myanmar's Aung San Suu Kyi takes the stand', *Foreign Policy*, 12 December 2019. Application of the convention on the prevention and punishment of genocide, request for indication of provisional measures, ICJ, 23 January 2020. Owen Bowcott and Rebecca Ratcliffe, 'UN's top court orders Myanmar to protect Rohingya from genocide', *Guardian*, 23 January 2020.

328   **'vindicate their resilience':** Statement of ICC Prosecutor Karim A. A. Khan, KC: Application for an arrest warrant in the situation in Bangladesh/Myanmar, ICC, 27 November 2024. Judges had earlier ruled that an ICC investigation into Myanmar is possible because, although Myanmar is not a member of the Court, some of the crimes were also cross-border in nature, impacting Rohingya in Bangladesh. Bangladesh is a member of the court.

328–9   **Xinjiang:** Joel Gunter, 'China committed genocide against Uyghurs, independent tribunal rules', BBC, 9 December 2021. Ambassador Zheng Zeguang at online press conference on Xinjiang, Chinese Ministry of Foreign Affairs, 10 September 2021. 'China responsible for "serious human rights violations" in Xinjiang province: UN human rights report', UN News, 31 August 2022. 'Fight against terrorism and extremism in Xinjiang: truth and facts', Permanent Mission of China to UN Office at Geneva, OHCHR, 31 August 2022.

329–30   **'collective entrancement', 'likely to be repeated':** Tom Gardner, 'From Nobel Prize to civil war: how Ethiopia's leader beguiled the world', *Guardian*, 20 June 2024. Tom Gardner, *The Abiy Project: God, Power and Civil War in the New Ethiopia* (London: C. Hurst, 2024). Statement of Mohamed Chande Othman, Chairperson of the International Commission of Human Rights Experts on Ethiopia, at the 78th Session of the UN General Assembly, OHCHR, 25 October 2023.

330   **'doomed to see history repeat':** 'Protect civilians and respect international humanitarian law, says UN special adviser as she raises alarm on Sudan conflict', Alice Wairimu Nderitu, UN special adviser on prevention of genocide, UN, 13 June 2023. None of the lessons were learned. In 2004, as described in Chapter Four, it was difficult to get governments to pay attention to the slaughter. In 2024, it was not so much difficult as impossible, despite the incomparable horror. *The Economist* reported that as many as 150,000 might already have died, and that millions were likely to die in the years to come, in perhaps 'the biggest and most destructive [conflict] in the world today'. ('An intensifying calamity: Anarchy in Sudan has spawned the world's worst famine in 40 years', *The Economist*, 29 August 2024.)

331   **'waiting for this moment':** Ola Westerberg, 'Sudanese victim tells Swedish court of horror in oil execs' war crimes case', Organised Crime and Corruption Reporting Project, 28 May 2024.

331   **hold Western companies and their executives to account:** It is not just in connection with dictatorial governments and lawless terror groups that allegations of corporate complicity are now actively addressed for the first time. As described in Chapter Five, every US president for the past twenty years has sought to block accountability for American torture. In 2024, however, at the end of a lawsuit brought by the New York-based Center for Constitutional Rights, a US court ordered a Virginia-based military contractor to pay $42 million in compensation and punitive damages for torture and cruel, inhuman and degrading treatment at Abu Ghraib in Iraq twenty years earlier. One of those involved in the case was Salah al-Ejaili, detained in 2003 while working for the Al Jazeera news channel. As al-Ejaili stood naked, hooded and handcuffed, his captors sang 'Happy birthday, Al Jazeera.' After the verdict, al-Ejaili said: 'This is a big day, even for America. Finally, we reach some justice for some of the Abu Ghraib detainees.' (Salah Al-Ejaili, Center for Constitutional Rights, 22 September 2017. 'US jury awards $42 million to Iraqi men abused at Abu Ghraib', *New York Times*, 12 November 2024. 'Iraqi torture survivors win landmark case as jury holds private contractor CACI liable', Center for Constitutional Rights, 12 November 2024.)

Chapter 10: Balancing the Scales

333   **'victims for six hundred years', 'defending the country':** Steve Crawshaw: 'Serb opposition leader predicts "hot summer" of unrest as Albanians bury the slaughtered', *Independent*, 6 July 1999; 'Srebrenica 20 years after the genocide. Why the survivors need closure', *Independent*, 7 July 2015.

335   **'Do what you have to do':** Isaac Arnsdorf, John Hudson and Michael Birnbaum, 'Trump signals support in call with Netanyahu', *Washington Post*, 25 October 2024.

335   **'moral deterioration':** Avner Gvaryahu, 'Occupation has corrupted the humanity of Israel's military', *New York Times*, 20 May 2024.

335   **'adhere permanently . . . to international instruments':** Eliav Lieblich and Yoram Shachar, 'Cosmopolitanism at a crossroads: Hersch Lauterpacht and the Israeli Declaration of Independence', *British Yearbook of International Law*, December 2014.

Acknowledgements

I owe a particular debt to Richard Dicker, Wilder Tayler and Reed Brody, who first encouraged a colleague with zero legal training to become engaged on the themes of international justice. Their wisdoms and experience have all in different ways influenced my thinking and are reflected throughout this book.

I am grateful to those who gave me the opportunities to become involved in such interesting and fulfilling work for the past twenty years: Carroll Bogert, Peggy Hicks and Ken Roth at Human Rights Watch, Widney Brown and Salil Shetty at Amnesty International and Sonya Sceats at Freedom from Torture. I am grateful, too, to Stephen Glover and Andreas Whittam Smith, founding foreign editor and founding editor of the *Independent*, who gave an untested journalist the opportunity to report on historic changes in the world; those experiences all paved the way for what I did next.

The list of those who have offered advice or rescued me from errors is long. That includes the legal and other wisdoms of Dapo Akande, Clive Baldwin, Conor Gearty, Tessa Gregory, Richard Hermer, Daniel Leader, Daniel Machover, Juan Méndez, James Ross, Andreas Schüller, Jennifer Trahan and Elizabeth Wilmshurst. Special mentions go to Patrick

O'Connor and Philip Grant, who made valuable suggestions and corrections on a dizzying range of themes.

On and in Ukraine, many people were generous with their time and knowledge, including Roman Avramenko, Tony Borden, Rachel Denber, Janine di Giovanni, Nataliya Gumenyuk, Wayne Jordash, Angelina Kariakina, Oleksandra Matviichuk, Olha Opalenko, Tetyana Pechonchyk, Oksana Pokalchuk, Olha Reshetylova, Roman Romanov, Oleksandra Romantsova, Maryna Slobodianiuk, Solomiia Stasiv and Nadya Volkova. Thanks as always to Anya Neistat and her talented human rights clan, in Paris and then Kyiv. Thanks also to Yuri Belousov (and his colleagues from the prosecutorial teams in Kherson and Kharkiv), Anton Korynevych and Igor Zhovkva for insights and engagement.

In and on Israel/Palestine, thanks among others to Sahar Francis, Tania Hary, Harold Immanuel, Shawan Jabarin, Tony Lerman, Haggai Matar, Michael Sfard, Yuval Shany, Raja Shehadeh and Yaël Stein. Thanks and admiration to Yonatan Zeigen for finding time to talk to me and for his grace and humanity in impossible circumstances.

On the Balkans, thanks to Marija Ristić and Gordana Igrić, as well as to Nerma Jelačić on Bosnia, Syria and other themes.

On Syria, thanks to Anwar al-Bunni, Caesar, Nadim Houry and Ibrahim Olabi.

For a mixture of suggestions, improvements and corrections on a variety of other themes, thanks to Brad Adams, Bob Bierman, Dorothy Byrne, Robert Chandler, Emma Daly, Sara Darehshori, Sam Dubberley, Mark Fallon, Emma Graham-Harrison, Joost Hiltermann, Leslie Lefkow, Kathy Lerman, Richard Lloyd Parry, Callum Macrae, Angela Mudukuti, Bill Pace, Elaine Pearson, Peter Pomerantsev, Nicola Reindorp, Sonya Sceats, John Sifton, Carina

Tertsakian, Anneke Van Woudenberg and Sam Zarifi.

In Nuremberg, thanks to Evelyn Müller and Axel Fischer of the International Nuremberg Principles Academy and the Memorium Nuremberg Trials. Thanks to the staff at the London Library, the Institute of Advanced Legal Studies and the British Library for help in tracking down materials both obvious and obscure.

Thanks to Karim Khan for making time to meet with me at an impossibly busy time and to Fatou Bensouda, with admiration for her calmness in response to the extraordinary pressures she faced because of her work.

Thank you to my agent Bill Hamilton whose advice I have relied on for so many years and who persuaded me to believe, even when I had only a chaotic ragbag of ideas to share, that there could be an interesting book on these themes.

I feel blessed to have had Sameer Rahim as an editor. He believed in this book from the start and helped shape it at every stage. *Prosecuting the Powerful* would not be what it is without Sameer. Many thanks also to Zoe Gullen for improving the text throughout, as well as to the team at The Bridge Street Press more broadly. No author could wish for more.

Last but not least, love and thanks as always to Eva and Ania, tolerant readers of confused and messy first thoughts, who have encouraged and helped nudge the project into shape in the past two turbulent years.

Index